# WASHINGTON STATE PARKS

A Complete Recreation Guide

# WASHINGTON STATE PARKS

## A Complete Recreation Guide

## MARGE & TED MUELLER

**THE**
**MOUNTAINEERS**

Published by The Mountaineers
1011 SW Klickitat Way, Suite 107
Seattle, Washington 98134

Published simultaneously in Canada by Douglas & McIntyre, Ltd., 1615 Venables Street, Vancouver, B.C. V5L 2H1

Published simultaneously in Great Britain by Cordee, 3a DeMontfort Street, Leicester, England, LE1 7HD

Manufactured in the United States of America

Edited by Meredith Waring
Maps by Marge Mueller
All photographs by the authors unless otherwise noted
Cover design by Watson Graphics
Book design and layout by Marge Mueller

Cover photographs: *top left*, Palouse Falls; *top right*, Admiralty Head Lighthouse in Fort Casey State Park; *bottom left*, Pearrygin Lake State Park; *bottom right*, the beach at West-haven State Park.
Frontispiece: The footbridge over the Chehalis River provides views of the falls at Rainbow Falls State Park.

Library of Congress Cataloging in Publication Data
Mueller, Marge.
    Washington state parks: a complete recreation guide / Marge & Ted Mueller.
      p.     cm.
    Includes index.
    ISBN 1-898863-324-4
      1. Outdoor recreation--Washington (State)--Directories. 2. Parks-
-Washington (State)--Directories.   3. Washington (State)-
-Guidebooks.  I. Mueller, Ted.  II. Title.
GV191.42.W2M85   1993
796.5'02573--dc20               92-39612
                                CIP

# TABLE OF CONTENTS

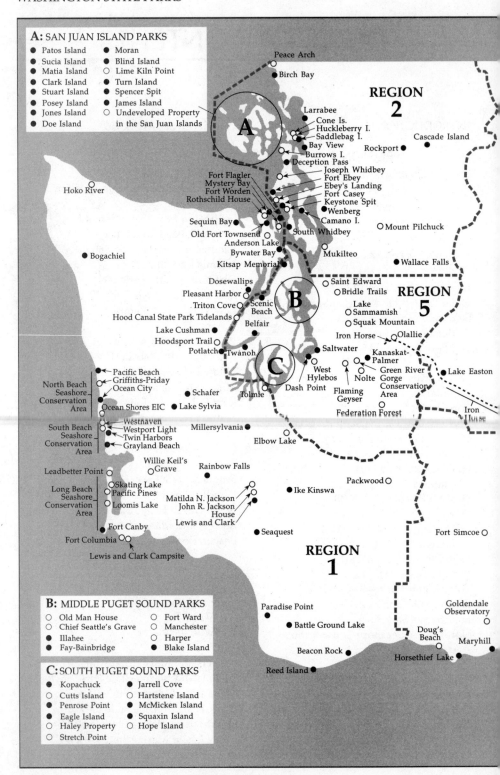

**A:** SAN JUAN ISLAND PARKS

- ● Patos Island
- ● Sucia Island
- ● Matia Island
- ● Clark Island
- ● Stuart Island
- ● Posey Island
- ● Jones Island
- ● Doe Island
- ● Moran
- ● Blind Island
- ○ Lime Kiln Point
- ● Turn Island
- ● Spencer Spit
- ● James Island
- ○ Undeveloped Property in the San Juan Islands

Peace Arch

● Birch Bay

REGION 2

A

● Larrabee
Cone Is.
Huckleberry I.
Saddlebag I.
Bay View
Burrows I.
Deception Pass
Joseph Whidbey
Fort Ebey
Ebey's Landing
Fort Casey
Keystone Spit
● Wenberg
Camano I.

Cascade Island

Rockport ●

Fort Flagler
Mystery Bay
Fort Worden
Rothschild House

Sequim Bay ●
Old Fort Townsend
Anderson Lake
Bywater Bay
Kitsap Memorial

○ Mount Pilchuck

South Whidbey

Mukilteo

Hoko River

● Bogachiel

● Wallace Falls

Dosewallips
Pleasant Harbor
Triton Cove
Hood Canal State Park Tidelands
Lake Cushman ●
Hoodsport Trail
Potlatch
Twanoh

Scenic Beach

Belfair

B

○ Saint Edward
○ Bridle Trails
Lake Sammamish
○ Squak Mountain

REGION 5

Iron Horse
Saltwater
West Hylebos
Dash Point
Flaming Geyser

Olallie
Kanaskat-Palmer
Green River Gorge Conservation Area

● Lake Easton

Iron Horse

C

Nolte

Federation Forest

Pacific Beach
Griffiths-Priday
Ocean City

North Beach Seashore Conservation Area

● Schafer

● Lake Sylvia

Ocean Shores EIC

Tolmie

Millersylvania ●

South Beach Seashore Conservation Area

Westhaven
Westport Light
Twin Harbors
Grayland Beach

Elbow Lake

Willie Keil's Grave

Rainbow Falls

Leadbetter Point

Long Beach Seashore Conservation Area

○ Skating Lake
○ Pacific Pines
○ Loomis Lake

Matilda N. Jackson
John R. Jackson House
Lewis and Clark

● Ike Kinswa

Packwood ○

Fort Canby
Fort Columbia
Lewis and Clark Campsite

● Seaquest

Fort Simcoe ○

REGION 1

**B:** MIDDLE PUGET SOUND PARKS

- ○ Old Man House
- ○ Chief Seattle's Grave
- ● Illahee
- ● Fay-Bainbridge
- ○ Fort Ward
- ○ Manchester
- ○ Harper
- ● Blake Island

Paradise Point

● Battle Ground Lake

Beacon Rock ●

Reed Island ●

Goldendale Observatory

Doug's Beach

Maryhill

Horsethief Lake ●

**C:** SOUTH PUGET SOUND PARKS

- ● Kopachuck
- ○ Cutts Island
- ● Penrose Point
- ○ Eagle Island
- ○ Haley Property
- ○ Stretch Point
- ● Jarrell Cove
- ○ Hartstene Island
- ● McMicken Island
- ● Squaxin Island
- ○ Hope Island

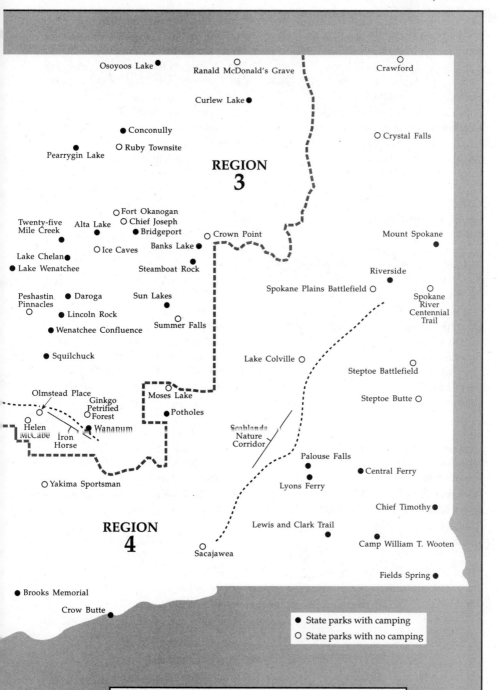

Osoyoos Lake ●
Ranald McDonald's Grave ○
Crawford ○

Curlew Lake ●

● Conconully
○ Ruby Townsite
Pearrygin Lake ●

○ Crystal Falls

**REGION 3**

○ Fort Okanogan
○ Chief Joseph
Twenty-five Mile Creek
Alta Lake ●
● Bridgeport
○ Crown Point
Mount Spokane ●

Lake Chelan ●
○ Ice Caves
Banks Lake ●
● Lake Wenatchee
Steamboat Rock ●

Riverside ●

Spokane Plains Battlefield ○

Peshastin Pinnacles ○
● Daroga
Sun Lakes
Spokane River Centennial Trail ○

● Lincoln Rock
Summer Falls ○
Wenatchee Confluence ●

Lake Colville ○
Steptoe Battlefield ○

● Squilchuck

Olmstead Place
Ginkgo Petrified Forest ○
Moses Lake ●
Steptoe Butte ○

Helen McCabe ○
Iron Horse
● Wanapum
● Potholes
Scablands Nature Corridor

Palouse Falls ●
● Central Ferry

○ Yakima Sportsman
Lyons Ferry ●

Chief Timothy ●

**REGION 4**

Lewis and Clark Trail ●
Camp William T. Wooten ●

○ Sacajawea
Fields Spring ●

● Brooks Memorial
Crow Butte ●

● State parks with camping
○ State parks with no camping

# WASHINGTON STATE PARKS

## REGION 3

- Okanogan
- Methow
- Chelan
- Wenatchee
- Ellensburg
- Upper Yakima River

## REGION 4

- Colville
- Spokane
- The Palouse
- Snake River
- Scablands
- Columbia River

**Note**: Since publication of this book, State Parks has restructured and renamed its regions. Region 1, less those parks in Clallam County, is now the Southwest Region. Region 2, plus the Clallam County parks, is the Northwest Region. Regions 3 and 4 have been combined into the Eastern Region, and Region 5 has been renamed the Puget Sound Region.

*The bridge that soars over Deception Pass is one of many remarkable sights at Deception Pass State Park.*

# INTRODUCTION

Washington residents can be justifiably proud of their superb state park system. The quantity of parks, and their diversity in features and recreational activities, are second to none in the nation. Where else does the state parks system include such gems as:

- A 1,100-foot-long limestone cave
- An astronomical observatory open to public use
- Two abandoned railroad beds, one 103 miles long and the other 131 miles long
- More than 70 miles of ocean beach
- Two dozen good-sized islands
- Historic relics of a dozen army or Coast Artillery forts
- A petrified forest
- A group of sandstone pinnacles that challenge every level of rock climber
- An oceanfront site dedicated to whale watching

Recreation is similarly unlimited. In addition to the usual camping and picnicking, state parks provide a wondrous list of summer and winter activities, ranging from the sedate to the thrilling, that includes birdwatching, windsurfing, kite flying, kayaking, horseback riding, fishing, mushrooming, hang gliding, cross-country skiing, rock climbing . . . and the list goes on.

Although they are most heavily concentrated around Puget Sound population centers and the vacation centers of the coast and San Juan Islands, the parks are scattered to every corner of the state, providing a full inventory of the state's geographical and natural features, from the crashing waves of the coast to the blue-hazed hills of the Palouse.

## BUT HOW DID THESE TREASURES COME TO BE?

When, in 1913, Washington embarked on its state parks program, it was among the first few states to set aside land for public recreation. Unfortunately, the Parks Board was not given guidance from the legislature as to its mission and received no funding for park acquisitions. Two years later the Parks Board accepted donation of its first two properties: the John R. Jackson House and Larrabee State Park. The pattern of acquiring property by donation continued through the early years. Park properties were also transferred from other state agencies (such as Lewis and Clark State Park from the Lands Commission), or from federal sources (such as Deception Pass from the U.S. Congress).

In 1921 the legislature finally codified the activities of the State Parks Committee and authorized them to contract with concessionaires and charge fees for camping. Still, no funds were provided for park acquisition. In the following year's report, the committee listed seven major parks and eleven small parcels of land within the system. Citizens began to expect more parks distributed throughout the state for both outdoor recreation and historical preservation. The parks system continued to grow rapidly, as did park usage, and Washington's parks were already receiving national recognition and visitors from across the country.

With the growth of the state highway system, the Parks Committee added "auto campgrounds" to its holdings; by 1928 these included Twanoh, Bay View, Sequim Bay, and Dry Falls (now Sun Lakes). That same year brought a major crisis to the system, when a conflict between the governor and the legislature over the purpose of the parks (preservation vs. development) led to a veto of all funds for park operation and maintenance. No additional operating funds were provided until 1932, when a new governor was elected. In the interim, many of the existing parks were vandalized and deteriorated badly.

*This rustic restroom at Riverside State Park is typical of those built throughout the state by the Depression-era Civilian Conservation Corps.*

## The Civilian Conservation Corps and the post-Depression years

In 1933, in order to combat the Depression, the new administration of Franklin D. Roosevelt created the Civilian Conservation Corps (CCC), which put unemployed men between the ages of eighteen and twenty-five to work on public construction projects. Washington State was quick to take advantage of the CCC, and it appropriated funds for a parallel program. The CCC refurbished existing park facilities and added campgrounds, picnic and kitchen shelters, bathhouses, restrooms, water and septic systems, and trail networks. Even today this work is evident in the older state parks, where the sturdy rock and log structures of the CCC are easily recognized.

With logging beginning to deplete forests, the Parks Committee focused on preserving forests along the state's scenic highways and lobbied timber companies to leave roadside forests intact. With substantial assistance from the Washington State Federation of Women's Clubs, in 1929 the state parks were able to acquire an old-growth Federation Forest tract near Snoqualmie Pass. When heavy winds caused severe damage to the trees, the property was sold and in 1940 another timbered site was purchased near the northeast approach to Mount Rainier.

The few parks acquired in the 1930s expanded the parks' scope, with the addition of Ginkgo Petrified Forest and its stone encapsulation of geological history, and Bridle Trails, dedicated primarily to equestrian use. Over a million people annually made the trek to Washington's state parks by 1936.

## The post-World War II era

Although the Great Depression of the 1930s and the war years of the early 1940s dramatically slowed park acquisition activities, by the late 1940s prosperity had returned to the state and nation, and the growing availability of money and free time put an explosive demand on recreational facilities. In addition, the state began to realize the economic value of tourism— and it certainly had the natural attractions to capitalize on it!

In 1947 the legislature revamped the old State Parks Committee and created the present-day independent State Parks and Recreation Commission, an active citizen board to make policy and set direction for the state parks. The old bugaboo of park funding was stabilized in 1949 when a portion of an increase in driver's license fees was set aside for state parks. Acquisitions increased almost overnight, and by 1950 there were 41 developed parks and 15 undeveloped properties.

By 1960 the system had grown to a total of 130 parks and undeveloped sites, and saw over 7 million visits annually. Many of the additions were the result of cooperation with other governmental agencies: the Bureau of Reclamation for Banks Lake; the Yakima Indian Tribe for Fort Simcoe; the General Services Administration for the surplused Forts Casey, Worden, Ward, Ebey, Canby, and Columbia; and other sites in conjunction with the state Wildlife Department, the state Department of Natural Resources, the U.S. Forest Service, and the U.S. Army Corps of Engineers.

With the explosion of boating in the Puget Sound region, the need for marine parks became evident, and the commission began acquiring island property in the San Juan Islands and shorefront property elsewhere in Puget Sound. In a grand move to benefit the recreational public and to prevent beaches from being pillaged, in 1967 the state declared as public all seashores bounding the Pacific Ocean, from the high-tide level to extreme low tide, with the exception of Indian reservations. Jurisdiction for these beaches was placed with the Parks Commission.

Although funding had been stabilized and assured, the demand for growth in the parks system outstripped available money,

and the citizens of the state supported additional growth with a 1963 referendum to provide $10 million for additional park acquisitions. More referenda and bond issues were passed to tap matching federal dollars from the Land and Water Conservation Fund. Other state funding sources were created, but by the 1980s the commission had to refocus from acquisition and development to acquisition of critical property of unique historical or natural significance and maintenance and renovation of existing parks. By 1988 the parks system included 105 developed parks with full-time staff, additional satellite properties, and more than twenty properties held in their natural state or reserved for future development. Total park areas exceeded 232,000 acres.

All of this would not be possible were it not for the foresight and astute management of the Parks and Recreation Commission and the dedication, courtesy, and pride in their parks of the hundreds of park managers, rangers, aides, and interpreters.

## Into the future

As the state parks system approaches the twenty-first century, all is not serene, as the parks, like any other state agency, are locked in a continual battle for funding, and their very popularity stretches maintenance dollars to the limit. Less-used trails are not maintained as often as needed, portions of parks and park hours are reduced in off-peak periods, informational brochures are reduced in size and consolidated with others, and many properties that have been deeded to the parks over the years lie undeveloped and unknown.

The park system was especially hard hit in 1992 when severe budget cutbacks due to the economic recession eliminated all lifeguards at swimming beaches and may close all park interpretive centers until the state's financial condition improves. If even a small proportion of the millions of recreationists who visit the state parks each year make their pleasure and support known to the managers, the Parks Commission, their legislators, and elected state officials, Washington will continue to have the most outstanding parks in the nation now, and when their grandchildren and great-grandchildren start to enjoy them.

# ABOUT WASHINGTON'S STATE PARKS

This book describes the state's developed or reserved park properties as of 1993. Those undeveloped properties with no available public access were omitted, and other undeveloped park-owned properties with little recreational potential in their present state, and some park-owned properties that are developed and maintained by respective cities or counties have also been omitted.

The state classifies all park property into the following categories (some parks may fall into more than one of these designations):

*Recreation Areas:* Sites that are suited for and developed for high-density outdoor recreational use.

*Natural Areas:* Sites dedicated to conserving a natural environment in a nearly undeveloped state for passive, low-density outdoor recreation activities.

*Heritage Sites:* Sites that preserve and interpret unique or unusual geological, paleontological, archeological, historical, scientific, and cultural features of the state that transcend local interest and are of statewide or national significance.

*Launch Areas:* Sites devoted solely to launching or retrieving boats.

*Conservation Areas:* An aggregation of recreationally developed and undeveloped open spaces legally dedicated to sustained recreational use.

*Ocean Beach Accesses:* Sites of limited acreage along the Washington coastline that provide public access to water and shore for recreational opportunities.

*Environmental Learning Centers (ELCs):* Resident camping facilities made available to interested groups to provide their members the opportunity to live, work, study, and play in an outdoor environment.

*Natural Forest Areas:* Forest sites that are natural ecosystems, including old-growth forests of more than 150 years of age that have large old-growth trees, large snags, or large fallen logs; mature forests that have developed between 90 and 150 years; or unusual forest communities.

*Natural Area Preserves:* Sites considered important for preserving vanishing flora, fauna, geological, natural historical, or similar features of educational value.

## Using the state parks

Today over 40 million people visit Washington's state parks annually. Park managers or rangers are charged with seeing that the parks are maintained for the safety and enjoyment of the public. Along with their staff, they may be found doing everything from conducting evening fireside programs to fixing the plumbing.

A volunteer program has been established to aid rangers and provide service to the visiting public. Volunteers may become campground hosts at a particular park for a minimum period of time, ranging from a week to thirty days, and serve as greeters, provide information to visitors, and do some nominal work such as picking up litter. In return, the volunteers receive a free campsite (with hookups, in most cases), and all the fresh air and relaxation they can soak in—what a way to spend a vacation or retirement! For information about this program, contact the volunteer coordinator at the state parks address listed in Appendix A on pages 270–273.

## Park hours and seasons

The information block at the beginning of each park description indicates the hours the park is open. "Standard park hours," which are applicable in most parks, are 6:30 A.M. to 10:00 P.M. from April 1 through October 15, and 8:00 A.M. to 5:00 P.M. from October 16 through March 31. A few parks have unique hours, which are indicated.

Parks that have overnight camping usually observe standard hours and are gated at night. Late-arriving campers or those who leave the premises in the evening may find themselves locked out. If planning an early departure, check the gate hours before rolling out of the sack for naught.

Some parks close during winter months due to lack of use, while other parks cut back on their hours between Labor Day and Memorial Day or close some facilities, such as swimming beaches, interpretive centers, and sections of campground, in order to reduce operating expenses when park usage is low. In off-season, avoid disappointment by confirming that a park is open before planning a visit.

## Park fees

There is no charge for entering state parks or for day-use of any of the facilities, with the exception of areas that are reserved for groups, and there is no admission charge for any of the interpretive centers. All park campgrounds charge a fee for overnight stays, which is collected either by rangers at a contact station or at self-registration sites within the campground. Hookup camp sites have an additional fee for the additional facilities.

Camping is limited to ten consecutive days at any one park and, with the exception of reservation campgrounds, is on a first-come, first-served basis. Staking out campsites with personal property, signs, or camping equipment to reserve them for friends is prohibited, as well as blatantly discourteous.

The state parks have a pass program, with reduced camping fees for senior citizens (sixty-two or older), senior citizens off-season, disabled persons, and a lifetime free-camping pass for disabled veterans. Regional park headquarters or the Olympia park headquarters office can provide more details on the pass program.

Only a single group at a time may use a group camp or Environmental Learning Center; the fees vary with the facilities available. For group camps, advance reservations must be made with the park in question and must be accompanied by a reservation fee (nonrefundable). For ELC information and reservations, contact the ELC Reservation Office at state park headquarters in Olympia.

Overnight moorage fees are charged for use of any park docks, floats, and buoys. Fees vary by boat length; in some remote parks collection is on a self-registration basis. Annual moorage permits are available; again, rates vary by boat size. Continuous moorage at any one facility is limited to three consecutive nights. There is no fee or time limit for anchoring.

Fees may change annually, but as a general reference, park fees as of 1994 were:
Standard campsite: $10.00
Campsite with utilities: $14.00
Primitive site, motorized access: $7.00
Primitive site, no motorized access: $5.00
Popular destination camping surcharge: $1.00
Limited Income and Disability: No charge
ELCs: Variable, depending on facilities
Reservation application fee: $5.00
Trailer dump fee, per use: $3.00
Extra vehicle fee: $4.00
Mooring buoys: $5.00
Docks and floats: Boats under 26 feet, $8.00; 26 feet and over, $11.00
Annual moorage passes: Boats under 26 feet, $50.00; 26 feet and over, $80.00

## Reservations

Campgrounds that accept reservations between Memorial Day and Labor Day are:

| | |
|---|---|
| Belfair | Birch Bay |
| Fort Flagler | Ike Kinswa |
| Steamboat Rock | Fort Worden |
| Lincoln Rock | Lake Chelan |
| Pearrygin Lake | Moran |

Reservations are accepted April 1–September 30 at Fort Canby; May 1–September 30 at Twin Harbors and Grayland Beach.

Campsite reservations, postmarked at least fourteen days in advance of the first requested camping date, are made by mailing a Campground Reservation Application, reservation fee, and first night's standard campsite fee to the individual park, regional offices, or headquarters in Olympia. No reservations may be made by telephone. Reservation fees are nonrefundable, but rainchecks may be available for persons who call in to cancel.

At reservation parks, any unreserved campsites are available on a first-come, first-served basis, but chances of finding these are slim during summer months. Campsites are available to the parties who reserved them after 3:00 P.M. on the desired start date; check-in at the campground must be made prior to 9:00 P.M., or the site will be made available to others. If you know you will be arriving late, you can make specific arrangements by calling the park.

Some parks have day-use facilities, such as kitchen shelters and playfields, that can be reserved for group use. In metropolitan parks such as Lake Sammamish most available dates are usually claimed as soon as reservations are accepted in early January. Contact the park ranger for specific facilities and fees for a particular park.

## Facilities and regulations

The information blocks at the beginning of each park description attempt, as briefly as possible, to give information on park facilities.

**Handicap facilities.** The newest state parks have handicap access to restrooms, and concrete ramps leading to picnic sites and other areas. Unfortunately, because many of the state parks date back to the 1930s, easy handicap access is not common. However, in many parks the paths are wide and gentle enough that they can be maneuvered by a wheelchair.

**Restrooms, showers, and dump stations.** All the larger state parks that have overnight camping have restrooms with showers. Others may have restrooms in the main camping areas, but have only vault toilets in outlying camp areas or in group camps. Some of the more remote and lesser used parks and ocean beach accesses may have only vault toilets or sani-cans. Similarly, larger state parks have dump stations for trailers, and several state parks that have saltwater boating facilities have marine pumpout stations. Day-use parks with swimming beaches often provide bathhouses with changing rooms and showers.

**Garbage.** Most public areas of state parks have solid waste–disposal containers. The exceptions are undeveloped or natural areas and several marine state parks that do not have garbage pickup. In these locations you are expected to pack your garbage out with you. Even in parks with garbage pickup you are urged to take cans and bottles home with you and recycle them. Boaters should not toss their trash overboard, as it can pollute the water, create hazards for marine life, or eventually end up on the beach.

Several of the parks in forested regions have problems with raccoons, bears, or other wildlife. These parks usually have ani-

mal-resistant containers; garbage should be placed in these containers as soon as possible to prevent raids.

**Fires.** Fireplaces (low concrete enclosures topped with a metal grate) or braziers (metal enclosures on a waist-high metal stand) are provided in all areas where fires are permitted, and some parks have beach firerings. In a few places wood may be available in a pile, or pressed-wood logs may be purchased from the ranger or concessionaire. Cutting or damaging living trees is prohibited, as is removing dead or downed wood, as this disturbs the natural ecosystem, which relies on decaying wood for nutrients. Similarly, driftwood helps stabilize beaches, and its use for firewood is prohibited. The best method is to bring wood or charcoal briquettes with you—it may not be the pioneer way, but it is the most ecological one.

All fires must be confined to provided fireplaces. Picnic tables, docks, and other wooden structures must be adequately protected from portable barbecues to prevent any damage to them.

**Concession-operated services.** At some larger parks, where necessary goods and services are not nearby, private concession aires provide goods and services ranging from snacks, food, groceries, restaurants, fishing supplies, boat rentals, and horse rentals to cabins, swimming pools, golf courses, and ski lifts. Concessions, with the exception of ski lifts, are typically open only during heavy-use summer months, even though the park may be open longer.

**Picnic sites.** Picnic areas usually have piped drinking water and solid waste containers (except for some marine state parks), and either restrooms or vault toilets. Individual picnic sites have picnic tables and braziers or fireplaces. Typically, there are also a few picnic shelters or kitchen shelters for groups or for when inclement weather calls for some protection. On the ocean beaches or in open areas of eastern Washington many picnic sites are provided with windscreens.

**Campsites.** Over half the state parks offer some type of camping facilities. A "standard site" consists of a vehicle pulloff, a picnic table, a fireplace, and a moderately level space for pitching a tent. Standard sites are grouped in campground loops that have water, sink waste drains, solid waste–disposal containers, and a restroom.

The term "RV sites" used in this book indicates that these campsites have additional features for RVs and trailers, such as power and water hookups and holding tank sewer connections. Depending on the campsite, some or all of these features may be provided.

Facilities at "primitive sites" may vary, but usually they have a picnic table, fire grate, and tent space, but only vault or pit toilets. They have no vehicle access, and may or may not have water. Marine state parks with onshore camping have only primitive sites, and several do not have potable water.

Primitive sites often appeal to bicyclists, as they usually have space available, and they offer accommodations at lower rates. Large groups of cyclists should contact the park in advance to be assured of space.

**Playfields.** Many parks have places for organized sports such as softball diamonds, volleyball courts, tennis courts, horseshoe pits, and even golf courses. In all cases visitors must bring their sports equipment with them. Use of these facilities is on a first-come, first-served basis, unless prior arrangements for group use has been made with the park. Park users are urged to not monopolize play areas and to exercise courtesy toward those who have games underway.

**Group-use areas.** Some state parks have day-use facilities that accommodate groups of twenty or more people for picnics and activities such as church services or reunions. Typically, these include picnic or kitchen shelters, which may be reserved for the group. Many state parks that offer camping also have one or more areas set aside for group camping. These areas often include open fields for play activities, space for pitching tents, picnic tables, fire grates, vault toilets, one or more picnic shelters, and in a few cases adirondack shelters. Parks with

*Many parks such as Lyons Ferry, shown below, have spaces set aside for group sports.*

group day-use and camping facilities and their capacities are shown in Appendix B, the Quick Reference Table to Facilities and Recreation, as well as the information blocks.

**Environmental Learning Centers (ELCs).** The most comprehensive group overnight facilities are at Environmental Learning Centers. These most closely resemble the summer camps fondly (or not) remembered from our youth, and they were originally established to provide youth a place to enjoy, experience, and learn from camping.

Today ELCs may be reserved by any organized group, young or not-so-young, such as scout troops, church groups, school classes, or family reunions. Although ELCs vary in their facilities, most include a kitchen/mess hall, rustic sleeping cabins, playfields, campfire circles, and classroom space. In addition, others have tennis courts, swimming pools, adirondack shelters, canoes, cook cabins, and infirmaries. Your group must provide supervisory personnel, food, bedding, and other supplies, and you must plan your own activities, although sometimes park personnel will, on request, provide interpretive talks or hikes.

**Conference center.** The most elaborate group facilities are found at Fort Worden, where, in addition to all of the amenities found in group camps or ELCs, the park has facilities that can accommodate from 12 to 400 people, including conference rooms, three dormitories, a dining hall, a restaurant, and twenty-four refurbished officers' quarters with kitchens.

**Hostels.** Three parks, Fort Worden, Fort Flagler, and Fort Columbia, have hostels operated by American Youth Hostels, Inc. They offer inexpensive dormitory-style lodging for bicyclists and travelers. It is not necessary to be a member of the organization to enjoy use of the hostel facilities.

**Heritage sites.** Nearly forty Heritage Sites are administered by the State Parks Commission, some in conjunction with other state parks and others as stand-alone parks. These sites are of unique historical, geological, archeological, scientific, or cultural significance to the state or nation. All have plaques or exhibits telling of their significance. Approximately a third of these sites have park-staffed interpretive centers with artifacts, exhibits, and audiovisual programs. Many of the others offer guided tours or interpretive campfire programs.

**Marine facilities.** Nearly all parks with water frontage have launch ramps for trailered boats, most with adjacent floats for loading and unloading boats. Moorage at these floats is restricted to 30 minutes or less. Space at the ramp itself is generally tight, and boaters should launch or recover boats as rapidly as possible and move cars and boat trailers to separate parking areas. A few parks also have launch areas dedicated to hand-carried boats. Lakes within parks are often restricted to hand-powered boats; check individual park rules before using motors on boats.

Most marine state parks, and several others with water frontage, have either docks, floats, or mooring buoys available for overnight use by visiting boaters. Rafting on docks and floats is not required, but is encouraged (with permission of inboard boaters). Rafting on buoys is subject to the following limits: for boats up to 24 feet, four boats maximum on a buoy; for boats between 25 and 36 feet, three boats, for boats between 37 and 45 feet, two boats; for boats over 45 feet, one boat.

Use of mooring facilities is on a first-come, first-served basis, and neither buoys nor dock space may be reserved by tying dinghies or personal property on them (and may result in that property being cut loose). Boaters who anchor off state parks should make sure that hooks are solidly set and ample swing room is left to avoid bumping into other boaters, especially at low tide.

**Water sports.** Windsurfing, surfboarding, waterskiing, and jet skiing are popular at various parks. When engaged in any of these sports, it is your responsibility to use care in regard to your safety and the safety and enjoyment of others using the park. Wear proper safety equipment, and be aware of natural conditions and your own limitations.

**Swimming beaches.** Many parks with freshwater frontage have roped-off swimming beaches during summer months. Beaches are usually divided into shallow wading areas and deeper swimming areas, with the latter sometimes provided with swim floats. A few parks also moor additional floats farther offshore for use by water skiers. Buoys offshore from swimming beaches mark the limits where boats must operate at no-wake speeds. Budget cuts in 1992 eliminated all lifeguards, so safe swimming is the responsibility of the park visitors and their companions. Rules with respect to safety and courtesy are posted at all swimming beaches.

**Ocean beaches.** The state park maintains over twenty Ocean Beach Access Points, in addition to developed ocean beach state parks, along the Pacific Ocean. Most of these access points have hard-packed roads through the dunes and across the soft sand to the drivable beach.

Within Washington, drivable public beaches on the Pacific Ocean are legally considered part of the highway system. "Drivable" here means only that portion of hard-packed wet sand above the courtesy poles designating razor clam beds; driving is not permitted in the soft sand higher on the beach or on the dunes. Because this area is legally a highway, vehicles must be street legal and licensed, drivers must be licensed, and traffic laws are strictly enforced. The beach speed limit is 25 mph, and pedestrians always have the right-of-way. All regulations that apply to four-wheel vehicles apply also to mopeds.

There are some restrictions on beach driving, however, and at a few areas of high pedestrian concentration or unique wildlife habitats, driving is prohibited year-round. At some areas driving is prohibited from April 15 to the day after Labor Day, except during razor clam season, because of heavy pedestrian use; other areas do not have the razor clam–season exception. The text describing the individual Seashore Conservation Areas defines these limits and where they are applicable.

**Fishing, scuba diving, and beach foraging.** Within state parks the only living beach life that may be taken are those forms that are edible and under regulation by the Department of Wildlife. Valid state licenses

are required to take shrimp, razor clams, or fresh- or saltwater fish within state parks. Department of Wildlife catch and possession limits apply.

A number of artificial underwater reefs have been built near state parks to encourage growth of marine life. Most of these are open to scuba diving, but many are classified as underwater sanctuaries, and taking of living creatures is prohibited. Check with park regulations before using underwater spearfishing gear.

Bivalve shellfish, such as clams, oysters, mussels, and scallops, which feed by filtering seawater, concentrate toxic substances in the water in their bodies. In certain areas toxic chemical wastes, effluents, bird and mammal feces, or poisonous algae blooms ("red tide," which causes paralytic shellfish poisoning [PSP] ) may be concentrated at levels that make shellfish unsafe for human consumption. The Department of Health regularly monitors all shellfish areas in the state, and when contaminants near unsafe levels, beaches are closed to taking of shellfish. Closure notices are publicized in newspapers, on a Department of Health "hot line," and on bulletin boards at individual parks.

Razor clams, once the greatest trophy of ocean beaches, have unfortunately suffered some serious setbacks in recent years. In 1984 and 1985 the season was closed due to a parasite that, although harmless to humans, attacked the clams and caused devastation to their population. In 1991 and 1992 the high levels of domoic acid, which causes nausea in people who consume the clams, caused a closure of the digging season. With careful management, future years should see this important resource return once more to its glory.

**Walking and hiking.** Although hiking is listed as an attraction at most state parks, hiking trails vary dramatically from park to park. Hikes range from short (0.25-mile or less) paved walks in smaller parks to many miles of hiking trails at such places as Moran, Beacon Rock, Mount Spokane, Iron Horse, and Scablands Nature Corridor. Unfortunately, in the parks with the most trail mileage, always-austere park budgets are concentrated in the areas of highest visitor usage, and back-country trail maintenance tends to suffer as a result. Before hiking on a remote park trail, check with local rangers about its condition. Longer hikes within state parks require the same attention to clothing, footgear, backpacks, food, and emergency supplies as on other remote forest trails.

Many parks that have unique or diverse ecosystems within their boundaries have established interpretive nature walks, most of which are less than a mile in length. Sometimes these walks have accompanying park brochures that are keyed to numbered stations describing the flora, fauna, geology, history, or ecology found near that station. Some parks simply route trails

*The smile says it all. Even very young hikers love the trails of the state parks.*

through the same type of forest system and leave it to the visitor to identify the flora found there. These walks are enjoyable, but not as informative as those with some type of interpretation. Groups can often arrange for ranger-guided nature walks by advance request to the park manager.

**Equestrian use of the parks.** Ten state parks have designated trails open to equestrian use, and many of these have unloading facilities for horse trailers. No extra fees are charged for riding horses. Lake Wenatchee, Sun Lakes, and Riverside state parks have concessionaire-operated horse rentals within the parks; at Ocean Shores and a few other state parks, privately operated horse rentals are nearby. Horses are not permitted in swimming, campground, or picnic areas, and must never be left unattended or insecurely tied. Riders are responsible for keeping their mounts under control.

Horseback riding is allowed year-round on all Pacific Ocean beaches in the Seashore Conservation Areas (essentially from Moclips to Ilwaco). Horses are permitted only on the hard-sand area above the clam beds; riders must yield to pedestrians and must walk their mounts through areas of heavy pedestrian concentration.

Walkers should remember that on equestrian trails horses have the right-of-way; move to the side of the trail and stand quietly. Use special care that dogs are on a leash and under control around horses.

**Bicycling.** Bicycling is becoming increasingly popular in Washington state parks, as both transportation and recreation. All roads within parks are open for bicycle use, but bicyclists should follow common rules of courtesy and safety, such as obeying all traffic laws, riding single file on the shoulder in the direction of traffic flow, and using adequate lighting after dark.

Restrictions on trail use by bicycles varies by park. Hikers have first priority for trail use, and when there is a possible safety problem with joint use, bicycles will be prohibited. Check with local park rangers to find out which trails are open to bicycles. Bicycles can only be used on roads and designated trails, and should not be ridden cross-country or on lawns or natural vegetation.

**Winter recreation.** Although some state parks close and many reduce services during the winter, a number of the parks in the higher elevations that receive substantial snowfall are as heavily used in winter as in summer. Cross-country skiing and snowshoeing are the most common forms of winter fun at those state parks, but at Mount Spokane and Squilchuck concessionaires operate ski lifts or tows for alpine skiing, and a sledding hill is maintained at Fields Spring. A few other parks have roads that are open to snowmobiling.

At these parks the State Parks Commission, in cooperation with the Department of Natural Resources and the U.S. Forest Service, provides cleared parking areas. A Sno-park permit must be displayed on the vehicle at these parking areas. Fees generated by the Sno-park program go to maintaining trails. The parks headquarters in Olympia sells a pocket guide to Sno-park ski trails; Sno-park permits may be purchased there or at any of 125 retail sporting goods stores throughout the state.

**Metal detectors.** Use of metal detectors is permitted but regulated in nearly 100 of the state parks. Persons planning to metal detect must register with the park office and must follow state park regulations. From the Friday before Memorial Day through Labor Day, use of metal detectors is permitted in the day-use areas of those parks only in the morning, from park opening time to 10:00 A.M. During the rest of the year, metal detecting is allowed all hours that those parks are open to the public.

## General regulations

**Pets.** Dogs rampaging unleashed through a campground or incessantly barking when their owners are away are not only annoying to other campers, but unlawful as well. Seriously consider leaving pets at home— where they are probably more comfortable anyway. If brought into a park, pets must be on a leash under 8 feet long and must be under control at all times. With the exception of dogs assisting handicapped persons, pets are not allowed on any swimming beach or in any public building. Pets may not be permitted to molest, annoy, or disturb the peace of other visitors. Owners are responsible for cleaning up pet feces by putting it in a paper or plastic bag and depositing it in a solid waste container.

**The natural environment.** It is unlawful to hunt or harrass wildlife in a state park, and discharge of firearms or fireworks is prohibited. Trees, bushes, and other vegetation within the park, including flowers, may not be picked or damaged. Gathering edible berries and mushrooms for personal consumption is permitted. State Department of Fisheries regulations govern the taking of fish and shellfish from saltwater areas; freshwater areas are under regulations of the Department of Wildlife. It is unlawful to remove any living animals, such as starfish, sand dollars, or sea anemones, from beaches, except for those animals defined as edible and regulated by the Department of Fisheries.

**Alcoholic beverages.** Alcoholic beverages may be consumed only in designated areas (typically individual campsites). Kegs of beer are prohibited.

**Noise.** Tastes in music may differ, but at a certain decibel level it's all noise. Try not to inflict your choice on neighboring campers. Park campers are requested to observe quiet hours from 11:00 P.M. to 6:30 A.M. Generators may only be operated between the hours of 8:00 A.M. and 9:00 P.M.

**Vandalism.** Destruction or defacing of park property is senseless, as well as illegal, since it prevents others from enjoying the very things that you and they have come to the park to experience, and costs state residents scarce tax dollars to repair. Sometimes acts of vandalism result from ignorance or thoughtlessness—early visitors to Gardner Cave in Crawford Park probably didn't realize that touching the delicate limestone formations left subtle traces of human body oils that killed further growth of the formations. But deliberate vandalism—initials carved into picnic tables, spray-painted graffiti on old fort bunkers, pornography scratched into rest-room walls—is inexcusable, and offenders should be reported promptly to state park rangers.

## SAFETY CONSIDERATIONS

Visitor safety is a primary concern in the design and maintenance of park facilities, but mishaps can occur. Not all the areas described in this book are suitable at all times, or for all people: dangerous undertows can occur on ocean beaches, trails can be treacherously slippery in bad weather, old army bunkers can be dangerous to the unwary, and storms can make beach approach by boat hazardous. Children should not be allowed to roam unsupervised. At all times independent judgement and common sense must be used to ensure that your visit is a safe and enjoyable one.

### Emergencies

It is hoped that no emergency will mar your stay at a state park. But if one should, the park manager will render assistance. If there is no resident manager at the park you are visiting, the county sheriff has legal authority in all unincorporated areas. There are usually telephones within the park or nearby.

For boaters at the marine state parks, the U.S. Coast Guard has primary responsibility for safety and law enforcement on Washington waters. The Coast Guard continuously monitors marine VHF channel 16, and that should be the most reliable means of contact for emergencies on the water. The Coast Guard also monitors Citizen's Band channel 9 at some locations and times, but it has no commitment to a full-time radio watch on this channel. Several volunteer groups do an excellent job of monitoring the CB emergency frequency and will assist as best they can with relaying an emergency request to the proper authorities. Cellular telephone companies in the Puget Sound area provide a quick-dial number, *CG, that will immediately connect a cellular telephone to the Coast Guard Vessel Traffic Center in Seattle. This center coordinates all marine safety and rescue activities for the region.

# MAP SYMBOLS

Picnicking

Standard campsite

RV site with hookups

Primitive campsite

Trailer dump station

Ranger station or park manager's office

Lighthouse

Concession stand

Scenic attraction

Nature trail

Handicap access

Hiking

Rock climbing

Horseback riding

Bicycling

ORV riding

Alpine skiing

Cross-country skiing

Snowmobiling

Sledding

Birdwatching

Bird blind

Wildlife may be seen

Swimming

Shellfish (clams, oysters)

Crabs

Tide pools, marine life

Fishing

Mooring buoys

Anchorage

Boat launch

Boat put-in (hand carry)   (HC)

Marine pumpout station

Sailing

Power boating

Paddling or rafting

Scuba diving

Artificial reef

Water skiing

Golf

Tennis

Buildings

Cemetery

Mine

Trail (hiking or equestrian)

Gated road (walkable but not open to vehicles)

Unpaved road

Paved road

Highway

Railroad

Bridge

Park boundary

River/stream

Waterfall

Intermittent stream

Body of water

Dock or pier

Sand

Marsh

Bluff

Mountain peak

# REGION 1

- *The Olympic Peninsula*
- *West Shore of Hood Canal*
- *Chehalis River*
- *Pacific Ocean*
- *Cowlitz River*
- *Columbia River Gorge*

## BOGACHIEL STATE PARK

**Hours/Season:** Overnight; standard hours; year-round

**Area:** 123.1 acres; 2,800 feet of freshwater shoreline on the Bogachiel River

**Facilities:** 34 standard campsites, 6 RV sites, 2 primitive campsites, 2 picnic shelters, adirondack shelter, 6 picnic sites, kitchen shelter, restrooms, trailer dump station, 100 yards of trail

**Attractions:** Camping, picnicking, hiking, fishing, rafting

**Access:** On US 101, 4.4 miles south of Forks.

While the Olympic Peninsula certainly doesn't lack for recreational lands, most of its mountainous heart and wave-torn ocean shore is national park. Bogachiel is the only developed state park in the entire northwest peninsula area. Although modest in size, the park is nonetheless impressive in its beauty. The entrance road drops down through a striking stand of hemlock, a reminder of the ancient forest that once blanketed the region.

A campground loop with restrooms and a picnic shelter sits amid tall stands of spruce above the meandering Bogachiel. The road beyond this campground loop swings downhill past more campsites to a turn-around loop and an adirondack shelter. The uphill side of the loop has primitive walk-in/bicycle campsites. A large, rustic kitchen shelter anchors the heart of this area. Short paths from the campground lead through the forest to the riverbank.

In all but high-water season, the river bed is an expanse of smooth water-worn rocks, with intermittent pools where trout lurk. A state steelhead rearing area that lies 8 miles downstream contributes to the excellent runs of winter steelhead. The state park is a put-in site for paddling trips down the passive river to its confluence with the Soleduck, some 15.5 river miles away. Here the merged waterways become the Quillayute River and flow on for 5 more miles to the Pacific Ocean.

## HOKO RIVER STATE PARK (UNDEVELOPED)

**Area:** 580.3 acres; 1,520 feet of saltwater shoreline on the Strait of Juan de Fuca; 18,480 feet of freshwater shoreline on the Hoko and Little Hoko rivers

**Facilities:** None

*Opposite: The stump of an ancient tree fascinates youngsters.*

**Attractions:** Beachcombing, shellfish, hiking, fishing

**Access:** Only the portions of the park property lying on the Strait of Juan de Fuca are presently open to public access. Take Highway 112 4.2 miles west from Sekiu to reach the east end of the beach property, which runs from here west to about 0.25 mile from the Sekiu River. Another section of beach property that lies between Sekiu and Kydaka Point is inaccessible by land.

⊥ East of the mouth of the Sekiu River, State Highway 112 parallels the beach. The land north of the highway as well as a small inland segment is a portion of undeveloped Hoko River State Park. This Strait of Juan de Fuca beach is flat and exposed, except for a narrow forested strip at either end. The beach is composed mostly of loose sand and gravel. A second, isolated strip of park beach property is located about 2 miles farther east, on the east side of Eagle Point. The beach, which is sand above and hardpan below midtide levels, holds primarily piddock clams and mussels. The property can be reached only by boat.

A third section of park property, the Cowan Ranch, lies inland astride the junction of the Hoko and Little Hoko rivers. Use of this property is retained by its former owners for their lifetime, and it is not open for public access.

## SEQUIM BAY
## STATE PARK

**Hours/Season:** Overnight; standard hours; year-round; launch floats removed during the winter

**Area:** 91.5 acres; 4,909 feet of saltwater shoreline on Sequim Bay

**Facilities:** 60 standard campsites, 3 primitive campsites, 26 RV sites, 78 picnic sites, 3 kitchen shelters, restrooms, trailer dump station, boat launch ramp, dock and float, 6 mooring buoys, 2.5 miles of hiking trail; Environmental Learning Center with kitchen, dining hall, and 8 adirondack shelters

**Attractions:** Camping, picnicking, hiking, tennis, birdwatching, fishing, boating, paddling, clamming, scuba diving, beach walking

**Access:** *By land,* on US 101, 4 miles southwest of Sequim. *By boat,* follow the marked channel between the two parallel sandspits at the entrance to Sequim Bay. The park is on the southwest side of the bay. Nearest launch ramp is at John Wayne Marina at the north end of Sequim Bay.

⊥ The two parallel sandbars that guard the entrance to Sequim Bay hid it from the first three expeditions to visit the area. Neither Quimper in 1790, Eliza in 1791, nor Vancouver in 1792 recorded the inlet. It was not until 1841 that it was finally discovered by the Wilkes Expedition, which named it Washington Harbor. It was later renamed to the Clallam Indian word meaning "quiet water." The same sandbars that frustrated the discovery of the bay challenge boaters today. The channel between them is marked by navigation aids, but it is unforgivingly narrow and shallow. Once in the bay, however, the placid waters live up to their Indian name.

The park is on the southwest end of the harbor on a terraced bluff. A dock extends well out over the shallow water to a float

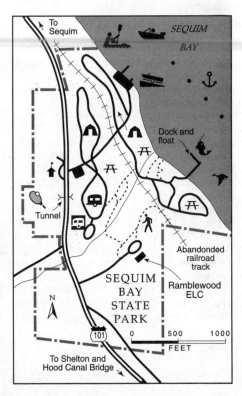

*A bluff-top trail overlooks the dock and float on Sequim Bay.*

that is available for both fishing and moorage. Buoys with more water under them than the float are set offshore. At the north end of the park, a paved road drops down the bluff to a two-lane launch ramp.

The upland portions of the park are divided by the bed of an abandoned railroad track. The campground loop below the railbed has a few sites with water views, but most are tucked into the wooded hillside. All the sites in the loop above the track are in open timber with no views of the bay, and they are close enough to the highway to pick up traffic noise.

A hookup campground loop, with a group picnic site and swingsets, lies in conifer-shaded grass south of the entrance near the road. A path leads through a concrete underpass beneath the highway to an open grass field with a baseball diamond and tennis courts near the ranger's residence. The lower picnic area is isolated by both the railroad bed and a deep stream-carved ravine. A canopy of western red cedar with a

few Douglas and grand fir shades the picnic sites and play area, which are more rustic than those above.

Ramblewood, the park's Environmental Learning Center, is also located south of the ravine. Open year-round, the ELC has a playfield, restrooms, and a picnic area with a campfire circle. The lodge and eight adirondack shelters can accommodate up to seventy-five overnight guests or 100 for day-use. Trails lead through the forest to other park areas.

## ANDERSON LAKE STATE PARK

**Hours/Season:** Day-use; standard hours; closed from the end of October to the middle of April

**Area:** 410 acres; 8,250 feet of freshwater shoreline on Anderson Lake

**Facilities:** Picnic site, vault toilets, boat

launch ramp, 4.4 miles of trail

**Attractions:** Hiking, fishing (*only electric motors permitted*)

**Access:** Take Highway 20 south from Port Townsend for 6.7 miles, or north 3.8 miles from US 101, then turn east on Anderson Lake Road to reach the park in another 1.1 miles.

⚲The mirrored surface of Anderson Lake reflects the surrounding forested hillsides and shoreside marshes, hiding the cutthroat and rainbow trout that lure anglers to its waters. Park facilities are minimal: a pair of vault toilets, a single-lane launch ramp, a water faucet, and a solitary picnic table beneath a towering Douglas fir at the water's edge.

The 59-acre lake, which is only 25 feet deep at its deepest spot, was once choked by algae, threatening the fish; however, an aeration system installed through the cooperative effort of the park, the Department of Game and Wildlife, and a local sportsman's club has restored the oxygen balance and thus the viability of the lake's aquatic population. A primitive trail that circles the lake helps fishermen reach shoreside accesses.

# OLD FORT TOWNSEND STATE PARK

**Hours/Season:** Overnight; standard hours; closed September 16 to April 30 except for group reservations

**Area:** 376.7 acres; 3,960 feet of saltwater shoreline on Port Townsend Bay

**Facilities:** 40 standard campsites, 3 primitive campsites, 75-person group camp, picnic tables, fire rings, 4 kitchen shelters, 100-person group day-use area, children's play equipment, restrooms, vault toilets, trailer dump station, 4 mooring buoys, 6.5 miles of hiking trail, 0.25-mile historical interpretive trail, 0.25-mile nature trail

**Attractions:** Camping, picnicking, hiking, fishing, boating, clamming, crabbing, nature interpretation

**Access:** *By land*, from Highway 20, 4 miles south of Port Townsend, turn east on Old Fort Townsend Road, and reach the park in 0.5 mile. *By boat*, buoys are located 1 mile south of Glen Cove on the west side

of Port Townsend Bay. Nearest launch ramps are at Port Townsend, Fort Flagler, and Hadlock.

⚲Although most of the well-known forts on Puget Sound are of World War I vintage, this one harkens back to the short-lived Indian War of 1855–56. That uprising struck sufficient fear into the hearts of the local settlers that a company of the Fourth Infantry was sent to Puget Sound. Construction on their garrison, Fort Townsend, began in 1856. Local military commanders felt the fort a poor defensive position and tried (unsuccessfully) to shut it down. After 20 years an accident accomplished what military channels could not when, in 1895, a lamp exploded and burned down the barracks. The post was permanently abandoned a few months later. The fort retained its "never say die" character, however, when it was used during World War II as an enemy munition defusing station.

Today a row of campsites line up with military precision above the fort's old parade field. The remainder of the campground is located along a loop road heavily

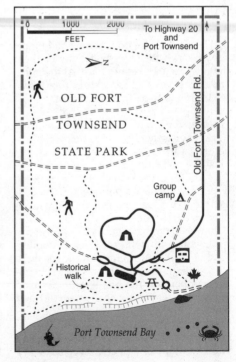

*Mount Baker is framed by pilings on the beach at Old Fort Townsend State Park.*

wooded with cedar and Douglas fir, with a thick ground cover of salal, ferns, thimbleberry, and rhododendron. Picnic sites, ballfields, and a children's play area are all found on the grassy terrace below the campsites.

A gated service road drops steeply down the bluff to the beach, where a line of pilings that once supported the fort's wharf march out into the bay. The gently tapering rock and cobble beach lies beneath the high bluff fronting the park; mooring buoys for boating visitors are offshore. A self-guided nature trail that parallels the service road passes stations identifying local flora: red alder, Douglas fir, wild rose, ocean spray, tall mahonia, bitter cherry, Oregon grape, salal, sword fern, and other species.

The munition defusing station has now been transformed into a group camp, and more than 6 miles of trails and fire roads thread the woods between here and the main area of the park.

## ROTHSCHILD HOUSE HERITAGE AREA

**Hours/Season:** Day-use; open 11:00 A.M. to 4:00 P.M. from April 1 through September 30; weekends only, from October 1 to March 31; *$1 donation*
**Area:** 0.5 acre
**Facilities:** Restored historic house
**Attractions:** Historical interpretation
**Access:** From Highway 20, entering Port Townsend from the south, bear uphill to the left on Washington Street. In 10 blocks turn left on Taylor Street. The Rothschild House is located 1 block north, at the intersection of Taylor and Franklin.

This historic home is not quite as elaborate as some of the showcase Victorian-era homes in Port Townsend, but it is an excellent example of typical architecture and decor of the period. The wood frame

29

house, which is listed on both the state and national Register of Historic Places, was built in 1868 by D. C. H. Rothschild, a German immigrant who became a prominent Port Townsend merchant.

The original carpets, wallpaper, and woodwork of the home have been carefully restored and maintained. Many of the furnishings are those of the original owners, and over 2,500 antiques are incorporated into the decor. Outside, the gardens are representative of those in the late 1800s, including herbs, roses, peonies, and lilacs.

# FORT WORDEN STATE PARK AND CONFERENCE CENTER

**Hours/Season:** Overnight; standard hours; year-round; dormitories closed in December and January, launch floats removed in winter; *248th Coast Artillery Museum,* seasonal adjustments—inquire at park office; *Port Townsend Marine Science Center,* Saturday and Sunday noon to 4:00 P.M. from March 1 through June 14; Tuesday through Sunday noon to 6:00 P.M. from June 15 through Labor Day; Saturday and Sunday noon to 4:00 P.M. from Labor Day through October 31; other times by appointment

**Area:** 433.6 acres; 11,020 feet of saltwater shoreline on Admiralty Inlet and the Strait of Juan de Fuca

**Facilities:** 80 RV sites, 25 units of vacation housing with kitchens, 3 primitive campsites, 43 picnic sites, 8 miles of hiking trail, youth hostel, restrooms, bathhouse, vault toilets, 2 boat launch ramps with floats, mooring float, 8 mooring buoys, underwater marine park, snack bar/grocery (concession), laundromat, abandoned Coast Artillery fortifications, marine interpretive center, Coast Artillery Museum, pavilion, tennis courts, ballfield, conference center with theater, dormitories, chapel, gymnasium, cafeteria, trailer dump station.

**Attractions:** Camping, picnicking, fishing, boating, scuba diving, hiking, bicycling, historic sites, military museum, marine science study, conferences, hosteling, cultural arts, beachcombing

**Access:** *By land,* from Port Townsend follow the well-signed route north to the park. *By boat,* moorage buoys and docks are on Admiralty Inlet, 1 mile north of Point Hudson or 1 mile south of Point Wilson.

▲ Fort Worden, which was once an imposing fortification, has improbably become a major center for recreation and performing arts. This was one of three major Coast Artillery forts built in the early 1900s to protect Puget Sound. Its design incorporated the defensive technology of the period—massive concrete emplacements with huge guns mounted on exposed, fixed carriages, groups of mortars in concrete-rimmed pits protected from direct naval fire, and smaller batteries intended to prevent naval landing attacks. The fort was activated in 1902, during a period of transition in naval technology. Over the next 10 years, the fortifications were supplemented by newer batteries with guns on disappearing carriages (which could be raised out of their protective emplacements so that the guns were exposed only long enough to fire) and more advanced rapid-fire gun batteries were added. As battleships were designed with increasingly bigger and more accurate guns, the fort's batteries became obsolete almost as soon as they were placed.

Changes in naval operating strategies, improved shipboard fire control systems, and the advent of military aircraft finally tolled a death knell for these large Coast Artillery dinosaurs. Most of the guns and mortars were removed from the fort and sent to Europe during World War I, where they were mounted on railcars to serve as mobile heavy artillery. In 1920 antiaircraft guns were mounted in some of the old emplacements in tacit recognition of the latest change in military technology. During World War II the fort was headquarters of the Harbor Defense of Puget Sound, which monitored new underwater sonar and sensing devices and radar sites, and coordinated Canadian and U.S. defensive activities in the Strait of Juan de Fuca and Puget Sound. The last of the fort's big guns were scrapped in the early 1940s, and in 1953 the Harbor Defense Command was deactivated, ending forever the fort's coastal defense role. No shots were ever fired in actual defense of Puget Sound from any of the forts.

Although the guns themselves are gone,

the massive concrete emplacements remain—silent witnesses to half a century of change in defensive strategies and technology. The fort is now on the National Register of Historic Places and is designated as a National Historic Landmark.

Because the road to upper hill emplacements is gated, many visitors see only those few batteries found near the road to the beach. To gain a better appreciation of the history of the fort, pick up one of the park brochures describing the gun batteries and walk the road to the top of the hill, or follow the trail uphill from the campground. It is here that a major portion of the original emplacements remain.

A less strenuous historical walk, for which a brochure is also available, loops through the "people" portion of the old fort, passing the post headquarters, barracks, hospital, powerhouse, PX, gymnasium, warehouses, guardhouse, theater, balloon hangar,

officers' row, and parade ground. The 248th Coast Artillery Museum occupies a portion of one of the barracks buildings along the north side of the parade ground. Photos of the old gun batteries and of the various Coast Artillery companies stationed at the fort decorate the walls. Display cases are filled with uniforms, small arms, and military memorabilia; examples of the huge shells fired by the batteries stand about. An interpreter is available to answer questions on the history of Fort Worden and other coastal fortifications.

The commanding officer's house is one of the fort's finest buildings—a fully refurbished example of Victorian architecture and decor. The house, which was completed in 1904, housed 33 different military families during the period that the fort was active. Each of the twelve rooms has been decorated in a different style representative of the period. A brochure that guides

*The massive concrete emplacement of Battery Quarles fascinates young visitors.*

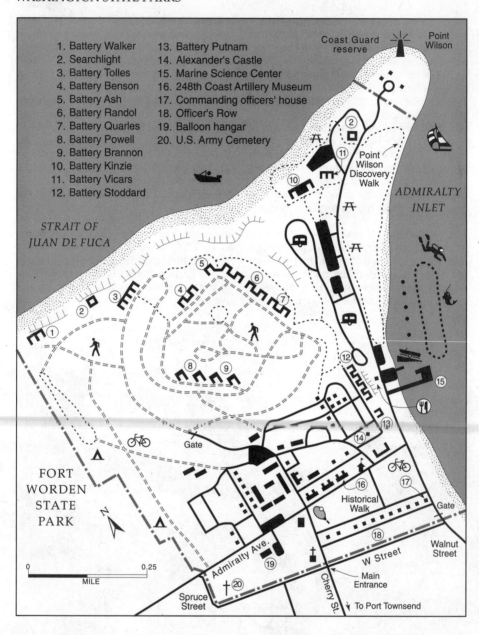

1. Battery Walker
2. Searchlight
3. Battery Tolles
4. Battery Benson
5. Battery Ash
6. Battery Randol
7. Battery Quarles
8. Battery Powell
9. Battery Brannon
10. Battery Kinzie
11. Battery Vicars
12. Battery Stoddard
13. Battery Putnam
14. Alexander's Castle
15. Marine Science Center
16. 248th Coast Artillery Museum
17. Commanding officers' house
18. Officer's Row
19. Balloon hangar
20. U.S. Army Cemetery

Coast Guard reserve

Point Wilson

Point Wilson Discovery Walk

ADMIRALTY INLET

STRAIT OF JUAN DE FUCA

FORT WORDEN STATE PARK

N

0        0.25
MILE

Gate

Historical Walk

Gate

Walnut Street

Admiralty Ave.

W Street

Main Entrance

Cherry St.

To Port Townsend

Spruce Street

you through the house provides information about the furnishings.

The unique vacation housing at the park consists of twenty-three houses that were originally residences for officers and non-commissioned officers, which are no longer military white, but have been painted a rainbow of pastels. Larger groups can be accommodated in barracks converted to

dormitories, complete with a cafeteria. Contact the park for reservations.

The park has conference facilities available in some of the old fort buildings. Additionally, the Centrum Foundation leases buildings for numerous cultural and educational events, including workshops, seminars, writers' conferences, readings by authors, and classes in various arts and crafts. The old balloon hangar, which has been converted into a performing arts pavilion, hosts symphony concerts, music festivals ranging from chamber to jazz to bluegrass, folk dance festivals, and plays. Most performances are open to the public.

The park's campsites are located in an open, windy flat between the beach and the bluff at the east side of the park. Here also are picnic sites, the park's boating facilities, and the wharf holding the Port Towsend Marine Science Center. Of the two wharfs that once served the fort, the only remaining is the one that was used by the Corps of Engineers at the time the Coast Artillery batteries were being built to bring in supplies, locomotives, construction materials, and guns. Today the sturdy wharf protects a small float for the use of visiting boaters.

A building at the end of the wharf houses the Port Townsend Marine Science Center, which is operated by the Port Townsend Marine Science Society as a resource for teachers and school marine programs. It also conducts classes in marine ecology and offers beach walks, slide shows, workshops, and fish printing sessions. The center contains glass tanks and open "wet tables" with live marine life and intertidal creatures. The center is open to the public.

The waters inside Point Wilson are designated as a Marine Underwater Park opear fishing is not permitted. Scuba divers explore rocky pinnacles that rise from the bottom on the north side of the point. The sandy bottom of the east shore and pilings of the old wharfs provide more varied opportunities to view marine life. The swift current is a hazard.

The beach can be walked from the wharf all the way around Point Wilson to the spot on the north shore where steepening shores dictate a turn inland. From here join the path near Battery Kinzie to return to the starting point. The Point Wilson Lighthouse, at the northeast end of the beach, is not open to the public. An alternate route, the Point Wilson Discovery Walk, which omits the beach by the lighthouse, heads east across a meadow near the park boundary, passes the searchlight tower, and circles Battery Kinzie. A keyed park brochure describes features along the way. At low tide the beach can be walked west to North Beach County Park or south to Chetzemoka City Park.

# FORT FLAGLER
# STATE PARK

**Hours/Season:** Overnight; standard hours; year-round, mooring floats removed during the winter

**Area:** 783.3 acres; 19,100 feet of saltwater shoreline on Admiralty Inlet, Port Townsend Bay, and Kilisut Harbor

**Facilities:** 102 standard campsites, 14 RV sites, 40- and 80-person group camps, 4 primitive campsites, 59 picnic sites, 100-person group day-use area, restrooms, trailer dump station, interpretive displays, abandoned Coast Artillery fortifications, 3 Environmental Learning Center camps, youth hostel, snacks and groceries (concession), 2 boat launch ramps, moorage dock and floats, 7 mooring buoys, fishing pier, nature trail, 4 miles of hiking trail, Fish and Wildlife Service marine lab, underwater park

**Attractions:** Camping, picnicking, hiking, historical interpretation, beachcombing, fishing, boating, clamming, crabbing, scuba diving, windsurfing, bicycling

**Access:** *By land*, from Oak Bay Road, 1 mile south of Hadlock on Oak Bay Road, turn east on Flagler Road, cross onto Marrowstone Island, and follow the road 6.7 miles north to the park entrance. *By boat*, enter the west end of the marked channel behind the sandspit at the head of Kilisut Harbor. Moorage facilities are at the east end of the first leg of the channel.

Fort Flagler, the first of the three major Coast Artillery forts at Admiralty Inlet to be activated, served for a time as the headquarters for the Harbor Defense of Puget Sound. However, in 1899 the remote tip of Marrowstone Island was a long haul from civilization, and civic and political pressures led to the relocation of the headquarters to Fort Worden in 1904, although the fort itself remained active. The commanding officer and his staff were then closer to the swinging social life at Port Townsend, and the town gained the musical talents of the Artillery Band.

Because the main gun batteries at Fort Flagler were installed during a period of transition in the technology of artillery, they were of the older style, on fixed barbette mounts, and thus were always exposed to potential enemy fire, even though they were set in massive emplacements. Concrete pits that held mortar batteries were protected from direct fire by a small hill at the center of the fort. Smaller guns designed to hold off landing parties were later added to the fortifications; two more batteries incorporating newer-design guns on disappearing carriages were added in 1907.

In World War I the fort served as a training center for troops, and most of its guns and mortars were removed and sent to Europe. After the war the fort was used only for National Guard and ROTC training camps. During World War II inductees were again trained here; it was home to a few engineering support units until it was permanently deactivated in 1953.

Emplacements for 3- and 6-inch batteries can be seen along the road on the east side of the park; a similar pair are found above the north shore at the end of a gated service road. These batteries, along with mortar emplacements on the north side of the road that leads to the campgrounds, are open to the public. For safety reasons access to the fort's main gun batteries is restricted; this is unfortunate for military history buffs, as their construction differs somewhat from

that of the newer batteries here and at the other Admiralty Inlet forts.

What remains of the fort's barracks, houses, and other buildings now comprise the Environmental Learning Center. Guesthouses, dormitories, mess hall, auditorium, classrooms, and athletic fields are available for use by organized groups. This area surrounds the old parade ground on the open bluff above the east side of the point. A group camp with picnic shelter and campfire circle lies to the west.

The Marrowstone Point Lighthouse, on the northeast tip of the beach, is not open to the public; however, the adjacent Bureau of Sports Fisheries and Wildlife Research Lab will provide tours of its facility, on advanced request. The old engineering wharf, used by the Army Corps of Engineers to bring in construction materials and supplies when the fort was built, juts far out into Admiralty Inlet just south of the ELC area. An underwater park on either side of the wharf attracts scuba divers, and the wharf itself is used for fishing. At low tide beachcombers can walk the shoreline between here and the lighthouse.

The park's camping is divided between two areas. Sites at the upper campground line a loop on a heavily wooded bluff at the

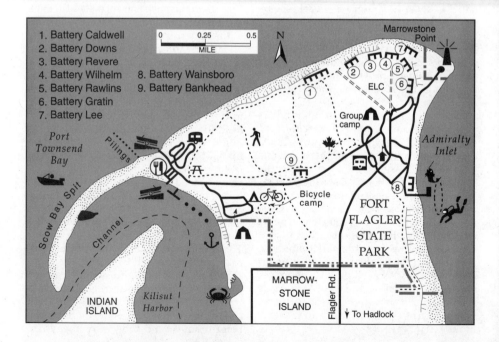

1. Battery Caldwell
2. Battery Downs
3. Battery Revere
4. Battery Wilhelm
5. Battery Rawlins
6. Battery Gratin
7. Battery Lee
8. Battery Wainsboro
9. Battery Bankhead

0   0.25   0.5
MILE

N

Marrowstone Point

ELC

Port Townsend Bay

Pilings

Scow Bay Spit

Channel

Group camp

Admiralty Inlet

Bicycle camp

FORT FLAGLER STATE PARK

INDIAN ISLAND

Kilisut Harbor

MARROW-STONE ISLAND

Flagler Rd.

To Hadlock

*Digging for clams on Scow Bay Spit; Indian Island in the distance*

southwest corner of the park. Walk-in bicycle campsites are available at the east end. The lower campground loops are in flat, open grass just above the beach at the northwest tip of the island. Here also are picnic sites, a concessionaire-run store, and two boat launch ramps. One ramp drops north into Port Townsend Bay, and the second drops west into Kilisut Harbor. A dock with a mooring float and a string of mooring buoys are also located at this bend in the channel into Kilisut Harbor.

The north end of the harbor is blocked by the 0.75-mile-long finger of Scow Bay Spit; the channel into the harbor runs along its south side. The spit is partially submerged at high tide, but not enough so for safe boat passage over it. At low tide, park visitors can search the soft sandy spit for clams and probe seaweed for elusive crab. A mouldering set of pilings running north from the spit toward Port Townsend is all that remains of the anchorage of an antisubmarine net that stretched across this span of water during World War II.

Trails lead from the upper camp area and the mortar battery south through the woods, and then east along the southern park boundary. A second loop trail follows the north side of the road to the lower campground, then heads east through the thick woods along the north bluff of the park before joining the service road at the north bluff gun batteries. Three other north–south spurs truncate the perimeter loop trail along the way. Just west of the group camp is the self-guided "Roots of the Forest" interpretive trail, with fourteen stations keyed to a park brochure describing the forest ecology.

## MYSTERY BAY MARINE STATE PARK

**Hours/Season:** Day-use; standard hours; year-round

**Area:** 10 acres; 685 feet of saltwater shoreline on Kilisut Harbor

**Facilities:** 4 picnic sites, picnic shelter, boat launch ramp, dock with floats, 7 mooring buoys, marine pumpout station, vault toilet

**Attractions:** Picnicking, boating, clamming, crabbing

**Access:** *By land,* from Oak Bay Road, 1 mile south of Hadlock, turn east on Flagler Road, cross the bridge to Marrowstone Island, and follow the road for 4 miles to Nordland and the park entrance. *By boat,* follow the marked channel behind the sandspit at the head of Kilisut Harbor. *Caution: The narrow, shallow channel makes an S-curve at the entrance; any deviation from the center of the channel can lead to grounding.* Mystery Bay is on the east side, 2 miles south of the entrance.

Back in Prohibition days, smuggling booze from Canada was a profitable and somewhat honored occupation in the remote waters of northwest Washington. Sequestered between Marrowstone and Indian islands, Kilisut Harbor was one refuge used by smugglers to evade Coast Guard vessels. The smugglers' shallow-draft boats were readily hidden in the overhanging trees at a small bay near the end of the harbor, and their disappearance here was categorized by the Coast Guard as "mysterious," hence the name for the bay. In more recent years the Navy had repair shops here to service a mothballed World War II–era fleet that was anchored in the harbor.

The park is considered a marine recreation area, as its facilities are primarily of interest to boaters. A pier leads out to a long float that is available for overnight moorage for boats, or for fishing by land-bound visitors. Several buoys offshore provide additional moorage. A single-lane launch ramp drops down the gently tapering beach west of the float. Onshore amenities in the tiny park are limited to a few picnic tables and a shelter. Clams can be found on the beach at low tide, and crabbing is good in the water offshore.

# BYWATER BAY STATE PARK (WOLFE PROPERTY)

**Hours/Season:** Day-use; standard hours; year-round

**Area:** 134.6 acres; 16,092 feet of saltwater shoreline on Hood Canal.

**Facilities:** 20 primitive campsites, vault toilets, interpretive sign

**Attractions:** Camping, hiking, clamming, crabbing, fishing, boating, beach walking, scuba diving, windsurfing

**Access:** At the west end of the Hood Canal Bridge, turn northeast onto Paradise Bay Road, then immediately southeast onto Termination Point Road. At the bottom of the hill, a dirt road heads northeast to the camping area. Beach access is also available by continuing northeast on Paradise Road for 0.5 mile, then turning north on Seven Sisters Road, a narrow dirt road. In another 0.5 mile reach a parking lot and access to Bywater Bay tidelands.

A narrow sandspit, built by wave action, attaches Hood Head to the mainland and encloses Bywater Bay. The shores of the shallow bay, the end of which becomes a mudflat at a minus tide, are prime areas for clamming and for searching out crab

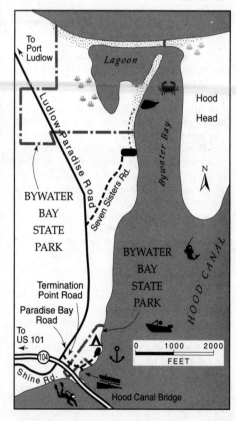

*Low tide at Bywater Bay reveals an orange-colored morning sun sea star.*

that hide in seaweed in shallow water. Public tidelands run from the west end of the Hood Canal Bridge to the head of the bay. On the northwest side of the bay, a densely wooded section of property enclosing a saltwater lagoon has also been acquired for the park, although this section is totally undeveloped.

Such park development as there is lies at the south end of the tidelands, where a single-lane dirt road leads to a number of primitive campsites along the beach. Garbage cans, vault toilets, and a self-administered pay station are the sole amenities. This is rough camping, but despite that the sites are almost always full during minus tides when clamming and crabbing are best. Saltwater anglers also use the campsites and the launch ramp just north of the bridge; however, the beach tapers so gently that unless boats can be beached they must be anchored well offshore and the shore reached by dinghy or wading.

## HOOD CANAL STATE PARK TIDELANDS (UNDEVELOPED)

**Facilities:** None
**Attractions:** Beachcombing, clamming, oystering, scuba diving

▲ Four stretches of saltwater tidelands on Hood Canal are under the State Park Commission's administration. The beaches are open to public usage below mean-high-tide level; only one has land access. Harvesting clams and oysters is subject to usual Department of Fisheries regulations, with possible additional closures during red tide warnings.

**Toandos Tidelands.** 10,455 feet of tidelands on the south end of the Toandos Peninsula between Tskutsko Point and Oak Head, and east of Fisherman Harbor. *Boat access only.*

**H. J. Carroll Property.** 560 feet of tidelands and 2.8 acres of undeveloped uplands 0.2 mile north of Pulali Point on the west side of Dabob Bay. *Boat access only.*

**Right Smart Cove.** 200 feet of tidelands 5 miles north of Brinnon and 0.3 mile west of Wawa Point on the west side of a creek draining a saltwater estuary. *Boat access only.*

**Lilliwaup Tidelands.** 4,122 feet long, lying below the bluff at a gravel pulloff alongside US 101, 0.5 mile north of Lilliwaup. Crude access trails lead down the bluff at either end of the beach. The property line is marked with state park boundary signs.

# DOSEWALLIPS STATE PARK

**Hours/Season:** Overnight; standard hours; year-round
**Area:** 424.5 acres; 5,500 feet of saltwater shoreline on Hood Canal; 5,400 feet of freshwater shoreline on the Dosewallips River
**Facilities:** 88 standard campsites, 40 RV campsites, 2 primitive campsites, 135-person group camp, 35 picnic sites, 2 picnic shelters, restrooms, vault toilets, trailer dump station, 6 miles of hiking trail
**Attractions:** Camping, picnicking, hiking, fishing, shrimping, wildlife watching, mushrooming (*clamming and oyster picking are closed indefinitely due to poor water quality*)
**Access:** The park is 1 mile south of Brinnon or 40 miles north of Shelton on US 101.

From its headwaters in the heart of the Olympics, the Dosewallips River tumbles down the glacier-scooped valley, past the precipitous south ridge of Mount Constance, to deliver its icy waters to Hood Canal. Sediments clawed from the upper course of the river settle at the mouth of the river, forming a broad, sandy fan that extends into Hood Canal. Dosewallips State Park occupies the south bank of the river, straddling the river mouth and the alluvial plain of Brinnon Flats.

The major portion of the campground lies in an open grass flat west of the highway, where hookup sites radiate in wagon wheel–fashion around a series of circular loops. Evergreen landscaping divides the area into smaller segments. An older section of campground is situated in open woods along the riverbank east of the highway. Low clearance under the end of the

38

*Harbor seals frequent the beach and offshore waters of Dosewallips State Park.*

bridge precludes use of this area by RVs or trailers. At any rate, none of these sites have hookups.

The picnic area is also east of the highway, at the south end of the park. Here an open meadow is scattered with picnic tables. Although this area theoretically fronts on the beach, a morass of marshes, saltwa-ter channels, and dense brush prevents any beach access at this point; however, a trail leads from here through the older section of the campground to the bridge and connects to the beach trail.

To reach the beach area, cross the bridge to the north side of the river. Here a trail that starts along the bank travels through the

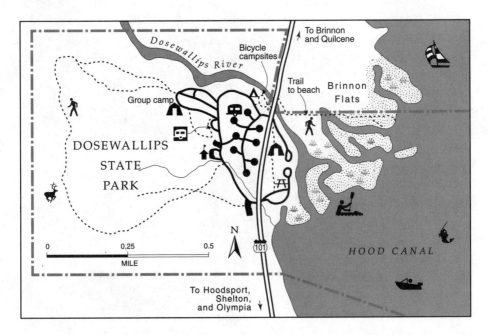

alder and cedar woodland, then passes dense patches of blackberries that taper to sow thistles and beach grass. Near high-tide level the trail picks its way around slick, grass-covered mud hummocks, then vanishes onto the broad, flat cobble beach. At minus tides the beach is bared out for another 0.25 mile.

This transition zone from fresh to salt water, which nurtures a wide variety of plants, birds, waterfowl, fish, and intertidal creatures, is a fascinating place to explore. The beach was once a prime area for harvesting clams and oysters; however, in recent years a dramatic increase in the number of seals in the vicinity, who have contaminated the beach with their feces, has led to a ban on gathering shellfish here. Fences around the creek areas and an offshore haul-out float for seals have allowed the reopening of 400 feet of beach to shellfish harvesting.

A loop trail that pierces the forested in-land portion of the park starts at the park administration area and meanders along the west boundary of the park before returning to its starting point. In winter a quiet hiker may see some of the elk herd that retreats to the park from snow at higher elevations. In August look for delicious chanterelles. If you don't enjoy eating mushrooms, please don't destroy them—leave them for those who love them.

## PLEASANT HARBOR STATE PARK

**Hours/Season:** Overnight; standard hours; year-round
**Area:** 0.8 acre; 100 feet of saltwater shoreline on Hood Canal
**Facilities:** Dock with float, vault toilet
**Attractions:** Boating, scuba diving
**Access:** *By land,* follow US 101 along the

*Hood Canal provides a bonanza of low-tide exploration.*

west side of Hood Canal to 1.25 miles south of Brinnon. The dock is at the end of a narrow paved road that leaves the highway at a deserted grocery store. *By boat*, Pleasant Harbor lies behind Black Point on the west side of Hood Canal. The second dock inside the harbor entrance belongs to the park. Nearest launch ramps are at Triton Cove on the west shore of the canal and Misery Point on the east.

▲ The Hood Canal shoreline has few coves or indentations, and the beaches drop off steeply in rock walls, except at the alluvial fans of the large rivers that drain the Olympics. As a result, safe, bombproof refuges for boaters are scarce and coveted when storm winds whistle up and down the canal. A good place to wait out bad weather or enjoy beautiful calm evenings is secluded behind the small peninsula of Black Point on the west shore of the canal, due west of Seabeck.

The entrance to Pleasant Harbor is through a narrow channel on the northwest side of the point, which leads into a cove surrounded by steep forested hillsides—a moorage as enticing as its name implies. Two private marinas are in the bay. The good-sized marina at the head of the harbor has fuel, water, and transient moorage. The state park, however, is rather small and spartan. It consists of just a dock and float and a few feet of shorefront, with no facilities except a vault toilet and a trash can at the head of the dock. The park is located on the west side of the harbor, just inside the entrance. Look for the park sign on the dock, as all other docks nearby are private.

## TRITON COVE STATE PARK

**Hours/Season:** Day-use; standard hours; year-round
**Area:** 28.5 acres; 592.7 feet of saltwater shoreline on Hood Canal
**Facilities:** 6 RV campsites, restrooms, boat launch ramp, dock
**Attractions:** Picnicking, boating, camping
**Access:** *By land*, Triton Cove is on US 101, 6 miles south of Brinnon or 7 miles north of Eldon. *By boat*, Triton Cove is on the west

side of Hood Canal, 4 miles north of the mouth of the Hamma Hamma River and 2.5 miles south of the mouth of the Dosewallips River.

▲ Triton Cove is the site of what was once a privately owned trailer park and boat launch.

The State Parks Commission acquired the property in 1990, and in 1994 will replace the existing launch ramp, float, and on-shore facilities with a new and easier access road to the ramp, a new ramp and dock, parking, and six RV campsites. The park may be closed until construction is finished in late 1994.

## HOODSPORT TRAIL STATE PARK

**Hours/Season:** Day-use; standard hours; closed from the middle of November to the end of March
**Area:** 80 acres
**Facilities:** 3 picnic sites, vault toilet, 2 miles of hiking trail
**Attractions:** Picnicking, hiking, mushrooming
**Access:** At Hoodsport, on US 101, turn west on Lake Cushman Road to reach the park in 3.1 miles.

▲ Here is a chance for an easy sampling of the wealth of flora to be found in second-growth Olympic forests. A parking area just off Lake Cushman Road holds a few picnic tables, a vault toilet, and the start of the park's trails. Although it is small, an amazing amount of trail mileage has been squeezed into the park's compact area. Signs at the trailhead indicate two loops: the lower 0.5 mile long, and the upper 1 mile long (although, in fact, a third trail segment cutting diagonally across the upper loop offers yet another option).

The trail first passes through second-growth fir and cedar at the top of a bank along the south side of Dow Creek. Near the north park boundary, a rustic wooden bridge crosses the creek, and the trail swings back, parallel to the north side of the creek, continuing to a Y-intersection. Here the north leg heads uphill to the upper loop

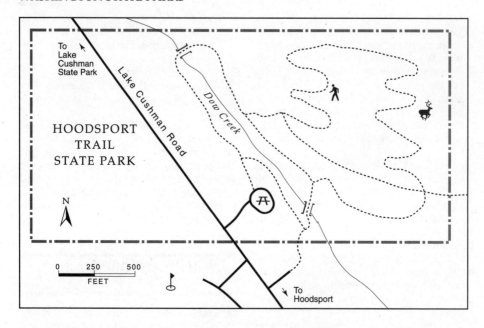

and the south leg continues along the creek drainage. An expansive grove of mature alder straddles the creek.

Shortly, another Y-intersection is reached; the south leg leads through brush to a second bridge, then up the bank to the return route of the lower loop. From the other leg of the Y, the upper loop soon pulls away from the creek, heading past huge stumps of the logged old-growth cedar, some as much as 8 feet in diameter.

At the eastern park boundary, the trail starts gently uphill in a series of lazy switchbacks. After skirting the park's northern boundary, near the top of a gentle hill, the trail switchbacks down to the initial Y-intersection. The diagonal trail across the upper loop, and the spur heading southeast out of the park at the return leg of the lower loop make routefinding more complicated.

## LAKE CUSHMAN STATE PARK

**Hours/Season:** Overnight; standard hours; weekends and holidays only, from December 1 to the end of March; winter camping in the day-use area only

**Area:** 602.9 acres; 41,500 feet of freshwater shoreline on Lake Cushman

**Facilities:** 50 standard campsites, 30 RV sites, 2 primitive campsites, 60-person group camp, picnic tables, picnic shelter, restrooms, trailer dump station, boat launch ramp, 4 miles of hiking trail

**Attractions:** Camping, picnicking, hiking, boating, fishing, waterskiing, swimming, mushrooming

**Access:** At Hoodsport, on US 101, turn west on Lake Cushman Road to reach the park in 7.4 miles.

Even in the early 1900s little Lake Cushman was popular with hunters and anglers, and two rustic resorts flourished on its shores. In 1926 Tacoma City Light constructed a hydroelectric dam at its outflow, flooding the resorts and increasing the surface of the lake a hundredfold. New resorts and lakeshore developments sprang up along the shoreline, and in time a section of land halfway up the east shore of the lake, surrounding a long, narrow inlet below Big Creek, was acquired for use as a state park. The deep, 0.75-mile-long inlet that penetrates the heart of the park gives it even more shoreline than would be expected for its size.

Big Creek Inlet divides the park in two. The main park facilities, consisting of the day-use area, boat launch, and one campground, all lie on the southeast side of the

*Enjoying the water at Lake Cushman State Park*

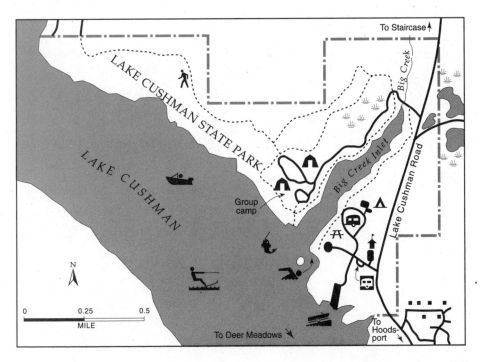

inlet. A second park entrance 0.7 mile farther north up the road leads to a second campground, a group camp, and much of the inland area of the park. At the south section of the park, a two-lane concrete launch ramp links the gently sloping beach with a large paved parking lot, capable of holding more than fifty vehicles with boat trailers—a testimony to the popularity of the park among boaters.

A forest of mixed conifers with a heavy undergrowth of salal surrounds the day-use area. A swimming beach fronts the picnic area, and a gravel island just offshore sits at the apex of a roped-off beach. A campground loop north of the picnic area has sites framed by stands of small conifers. A few primitive walk-in sites are found at the northeast corner of the loop. A second smaller campground loop and a group camp lie a scant 2,000 feet away on the north side of Big Creek Inlet. To reach them, unless a boat is at hand, it is necessary to drive or hike more than 1.5 miles around the narrow finger of the inlet.

In the north section of the park, over 4 miles of trails lead through the forest and along the Big Creek shoreline. Rhododendrons add their pink blush in spring. Chanterelles and other mushrooms begin to emerge in late July and linger until September, depending on the rainfall and the timing of the first hard frost.

For boaters, a hidden treasure exists at the south end of the lake, where a tiny segment of park property, Deer Meadows, surrounds a small spit west of the Lake Cushman Dam spillway. This small day-use area, accessible only by boat, is a quiet, relaxing nook with a few picnic tables, fire braziers, and a vault toilet.

## POTLATCH
## STATE PARK

**Hours/Season:** Overnight; standard hours; year-round
**Area:** 57 acres; 9,570 feet of saltwater shoreline on Hood Canal
**Facilities:** 17 standard campsites, 18 RV campsites, 2 primitive campsites, 81 picnic sites, picnic shelter, restrooms, bathhouse, showers, 5 mooring buoys, 0.5 mile of hiking trail
**Attractions:** Camping, picnicking, hiking, boating, paddling, clamming, fishing, scuba diving, birdwatching
**Access:** *By land,* the park is on US 101, 12 miles north of Shelton or 3 miles south of Hoodsport. *By boat,* the park is on the west side of Hood Canal on Annas Bay, 3 miles south of Hoodsport. Nearest boat launch ramps are at Union and Tacoma City Light's Potlatch Boat Launch.

The potlatch was an important ceremony common to Northwest Indians. At a potlatch a chief might designate an heir, family rights might be bestowed on children, a dead chief might be mourned and a new one recognized, or a social misadventure (such as the chief's "loss of face" by stumbling or falling in public) might be acknowledged and repaired. Protocol required that the guests—the witnesses who validated the claims—be given gifts by the host. The more esteemed the host and the more auspicious the occasion, the grander the gifts. Potlatch State Park is located at a site once used by local tribes for these festivities.

The park's campground lies on the west side of US 101, and the picnic and day-use area on the east, along the Hood Canal shoreline. The wooded campground loop is relatively small, so campsites are snugly packed together. A few primitive walk-in sites are maintained at the west end of the loop.

The picnic area is a spacious table-filled lawn. The large parking lot attests to the park's day-use popularity. The cobble-strewn mud beach tapers gently into Annas Bay, exposing a broad foreshore at a minus tide for digging clams and picking oysters. The waters of the bay are also a popular scuba diving site, with only nominal tidal currents to concern novices.

Mooring buoys, situated well offshore in deeper water, accommodate visiting boaters. Canoes or kayaks can be carried to the beach for paddle exploration of the Great Bend of Hood Canal or the nearby estuary of the Skokomish River. Seals often forage in these waters. Flocks of water birds seek shelter in the protected channels; watch for yellow-billed loons as well as more common birds.

*A bold raven greets the morning at Potlatch State Park.*

The park's upland has two short trail loops that weave through a predominately cedar forest. You have a chance of seeing squirrels, rabbits, deer, and a wide variety of birds that make the forest home.

## TOLMIE
## STATE PARK

**Hours/Season:** Day-use; standard hours; closed Mondays and Tuesdays from the end of September to the end of March
**Area:** 106.2 acres; 1,800 feet of saltwater shoreline on the Nisqually Reach of south Puget Sound
**Facilities:** 42 picnic sites, 2 kitchens, bathhouse, restrooms, outside shower, 5 mooring buoys, underwater park, 3.4 miles of hiking trail
**Attractions:** Picnicking, clamming, fishing, beachcombing, scuba diving, hiking, boating, nature displays, historical displays
**Access:** *By land,* take Exit 111 (Yelm, Marvin Road, Highway 510) from I-5. Follow Marvin Road north for 3.8 miles to 56th

NE, turn east on 56th, and in 0.5 mile turn north on Hill Road NE to reach the park entrance road in 0.3 mile. *By boat,* the nearest launch ramps are at Luhr Beach and Johnson Point.

At high tide the waters of south Puget Sound flood a small saltwater marsh hidden behind a beach-front gravel bar at Tolmie State Park. The freshwater flow from a creek and a twice-daily saline flux of the sound nurture plants such as eelgrass and pickleweed that thrive in this shallow, fragile habitat. Lugworms, ghost shrimp, and tiny, shrimplike amphipods burrow in the soft mud, feeding on detritus. Juvenile salmon hide from predators and bottom fish scavenge wastes that sink to the bottom. With the increasing press of urbanization in the Puget Sound area, unique saltwater marshes such as this are rapidly disappearing, much to the detriment of the region's ecology.

Interpretive displays at the beach describe the evolution and ecology of the shoreline. Another display at the upper picnic area tells the story of the park's namesake, pio-

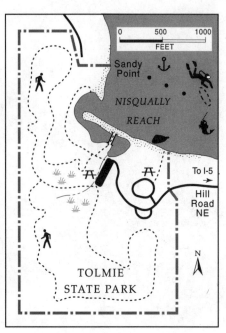

*A boardwalk covers marshy spots in the trail at Tolmie State Park.*

neer doctor William Tolmie, a medical officer for the Hudson's Bay Company who was assigned to Fort Nisqually in the 1830s.

Although the park has no campsites, the picnic facilities are pleasant and attractive.

One picnic area is situated around a circular road on the wooded bluff just inside the park entrance. A trail leads down a gully from here to the east end of the park beach. A second picnic area lies just above the beach. A scattering of trees offers shade.

A 2.5-mile-long loop trail that starts at the lower picnic area meanders through the forest along the perimeter of the park. The trail rises and falls, but it is well maintained; marshy sections are bridged or planked over. Several split-log benches beside the trail invite a moment's rest and encourage one to stop and listen to the conversation of the forest: squirrels chattering, jays scolding, and unseen creatures chirping and rustling. Halfway through the loop a short-cut trail permits a quick return to the beach parking lot.

The beach tapers gently into Nisqually Reach, and minus tides reveal an expanse of sand for digging clams. Offshore, three wooden barges have been sunk below the lowest tide levels to form an artificial reef, attracting a variety of marine life including rockfish and cabezon. This underwater park is a favorite of novice scuba divers because the tidal current is minimal. West of the reef are a series of mooring buoys to accommodate visiting boaters.

# SCHAFER
# STATE PARK

**Hours/Season:** Overnight; standard hours; year-round; from September 30 to March 31, camping in the day-use area only
**Area:** 119.1 acres; 4,200 feet of freshwater shoreline on the Satsop River
**Facilities:** 47 standard campsites, 6 RV sites, 2 primitive campsites, picnic sites, 2 kitchen shelters, 100- and 200-person group day-use areas, restrooms, children's play equipment
**Attractions:** Camping, picnicking, hiking, fishing, river floating, wading
**Access:** At Exit 104 (US 101 N, Aberdeen, Port Angeles) from I-5 at Olympia, take US 101 west for 6 miles, then take Highway 8 west for 26 miles to the exit signed to Brady and Schafer State Park. Drive north through Brady to the Monte–Elma

Road in 0.2 mile, and continue straight ahead (north) on West Satsop Road. At a Y-intersection in 3.5 miles bear east, and at 7.9 miles at a T-intersection turn east to reach the park in another 1.3 miles.

In the early 1900s the three Schafer brothers began an ox-team operation and developed it into one of the largest and most successful logging companies in this part of the Olympic Peninsula. The Schafers reserved one of the prettiest corners of their land as a site for company picnics. The hardy loggers and their families gathered here, by the meandering East Fork of the Satsop River, to picnic, hold log-rolling contests, dance, and enjoy serenades by a brass band. Today groups of all sizes still meet here on the banks of the river to picnic, camp, fish, and enjoy the softly murmuring river. In season, the park is heavily used by anglers; the river offers steelhead fishing in

*Summertime splashing in the river at Schafer State Park*

winter, while mid-July to October brings sea-run cutthroat, followed by salmon.

East Satsop Road divides the park; all campsites lie on the west side of the road, while the day-use areas are on the east. A couple of picnic tables in a patch of grass beside the river just inside the campground entrance are reserved for bicyclists and walk-in campers. Beyond here a loop road meanders through moss-covered maple past campsites, some on the river and some inland. A few hookup sites are lined up near the entrance, on the south side of the loop. Rustic restrooms have sturdy walls of river stones.

Picnic spots spread along the riverbank east of the road are rimmed with ancient oak, alder, and Douglas fir. The forest east of the picnic area is laced with a series of abandonded roads that once led to other picnic sites, evidenced by a few moss-encrusted tables. A quiet walk along these old roads offers the opportunity to observe the squirrels, rabbits, deer, and birds that inhabit the less frequented portions of the park; in fall, chanterelles and other forest-loving mushrooms may appear.

## LAKE SYLVIA STATE PARK

**Hours/Season:** Overnight; standard hours; from the end of September to the end of March, camping in the day-use area only
**Area:** 233 acres; 15,000 feet of freshwater shoreline on Lake Sylvia
**Facilities:** 35 standard campsites, 2 primitive campsites, 120-person group camp (tents only), 118 picnic sites, beach kitchen, 2 kitchen shelters, 200-person group day-use area, children's play equipment, bathhouse, snacks (concession), boat rentals, swimming beach, boat launch ramp, restrooms, trailer dump station, 5 miles of hiking trail
**Attractions:** Camping, picnicking, hiking, swimming, fishing, paddling, boating (*gasoline-powered boats prohibited*)
**Access:** From US 12 at its junction with Highway 107, turn north into Montesano. At the stop light, turn west from Main Street onto Pioneer Avenue, and in 0.2 mile, turn north on N 3rd Street. Follow

the road straight ahead from N 3rd as it winds uphill, then downhill, reaching the park entrance in 0.9 mile.

The slender thread of Lake Sylvia is actually a backwater pond behind a dam that was built in 1878 as a log pond for a sawmill; the dam was reconstructed in 1909 for a water reservoir and electric power plant for the city of Montesano. Because of the 31-acre lake's long shape, nearly every park campsite has a waterfront view. The camping area lies on a narrow peninsula; a narrow channel separates the southern tip of the peninsula from a tiny island that holds a single old fir surrounded by deciduous growth.

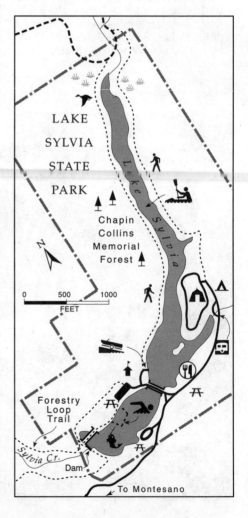

*Nearly every campsite at Lake Sylvia is on the water.*

Picnic sites shaded by cedar, hemlock, and alder line the east side of the lake between the entrance and the campground peninsula. The remainder of the day-use area is northwest of a bridge that spans the lower end of the lake. Here are more picnic sites, a children's play area, a swimming beach, and a boat launch ramp. A footbridge across a tiny cove serves as a fishing platform. Fishing lines and lures resplendent on the power lines above testify to a few rainbow trout that escaped an angler's hook. The trail continuing beyond the bridge leads to the dam. Here the Sylvia Creek Forestry Trail leaves the park and loops down one side of the stream and up the other, for a total distance of 2 miles. A brochure describes features along the way, such as logging sites, beaver dams, and pools where salmon spawn.

The park serves as a virtual museum to logging. One unique feature is a wooden ball, nearly 4 feet in diameter, hanging beneath a kiosk at the day-use area. A local logger, Purl Stone, carved this ball from the trunk of a Sitka spruce in 1925. The surefooted Stone regularly outdid other loggers, who had trouble even staying up on the ball, by standing atop it and spinning it from the bridge to the dam and back.

North of the day-use area is the start of an old railroad-bed trail that runs along the north lakeshore through the Chapin Collins Memorial Forest. The forest continues far beyond the park boundary. Hundreds of acres that have been logged over the years have been replanted with Douglas fir and western hemlock. Ever present are huge stumps from the original forest; many of these ancient stumps now nurse full-grown trees growing from their base.

The north end of the lake is filled with a series of marshy islands separated by narrow channels—a canoer's paradise. Silent paddlers or shore hikers will discover great blue heron, grebes, mergansers, and other waterfowl hiding in this aquatic maze. At the lake's end, a narrower trail heads back along the east shore, crossing side drainages on log bridges. The route is seldom far from the lake until it nears the entrance to the campground loop.

## NORTH BEACH SEASHORE CONSERVATION AREA

**Hours/Season:** Day-use; standard hours; year-round

**Beach Driving Restrictions:**

*Open all year:* Moclips Gap to Annelyde Gap, immediate vicinity of Roosevelt Gap, Copalis Head to the Copalis River, Benner Gap to Ocean City Access, Ocean City Beach access to Chance a la Mer access, Pacific Way access to Marine View Drive access

*Prohibited April 15 through the day after Labor Day, except during razor clam season:* Quinault Indian Reservation to Moclips Gap, Annelyde Gap to Roosevelt Gap, Roosevelt Gap to Copalis Head, Ocean City access to Ocean City Beach access, Chance a la Mer access to Pacific Way access, Marine View Drive access to North Jetty

*Prohibited all year, except during razor clam season:* Copalis River to Benner Gap

*Prohibited year-round:* Damon Point, Protection Island

**Area:** 22 miles of saltwater shoreline on the Pacific Ocean and Grays Harbor

**Attractions:** Picnicking, kayaking, kite flying, surf fishing, clamming, beach walking, birdwatching, horseback riding, windsurfing, sand-castle building, beachcombing

**Accesses:**

**Moclips.** At the end of 2nd Avenue on the north side of Moclips (vault toilet).

**Annelyde Gap.** At the north end of Pacific Beach, turn west on Homer Street, and in 0.1 mile turn north on a gravel road leading downhill to the beach access (vault toilet).

**Roosevelt.** At the end of an unidentified road spur west from Highway 109, 5 miles north of Copalis Beach on Highway 109 (vault toilet).

**Benner.** At the end of Benner Road on the north side of Copalis Beach (picnic sites and restrooms at the adjacent Griffiths-Priday State Park).

**Heath Gap.** At the end of Heath Road on the south side of Copalis Beach (vault toilet).

**Ocean City Beach.** At the end of 2nd Avenue in Ocean City, 2.1 miles north of the junction of Highways 109 and 115 (picnic sites and restrooms).

**Oyhut.** At the west end of Damon Road

*Trekking back from the beach*

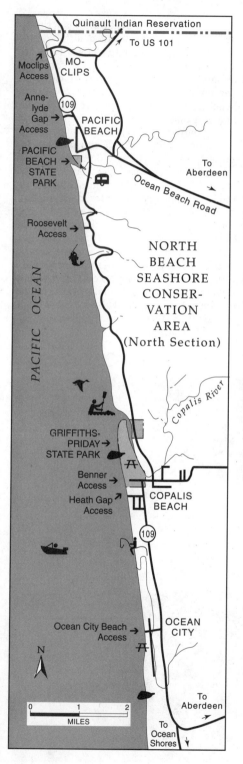

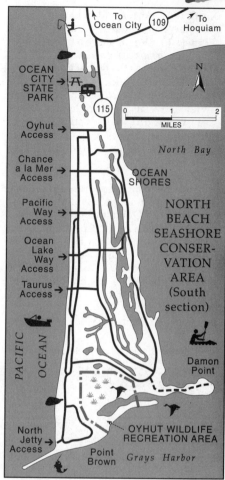

(Highway 115), 0.3 mile west of the entrance to Ocean Shores (picnic sites, restrooms).

**Chance a la Mer.** Turn west from Ocean Shores Boulevard onto Chance a la Mer 0.8 mile south of the entrance to Ocean Shores (parking).

**Pacific Way.** Turn west from Ocean Shores Boulevard onto Pacific Way 1.8 miles south of the entrance to Ocean Shores.

**Ocean Lake Way.** Turn west from Ocean Shores Boulevard onto Ocean Lake Way 2.5 miles south of the entrance to Ocean Shores.

**Taurus.** Turn west on Taurus Boulevard from Ocean Shores Boulevard 3.4 miles south of the entrance to Ocean Shores.

**North Jetty.** At the end of Ocean Shores Boulevard, 6.5 miles south of the entrance to Ocean Shores (interpretive signs). *No hard-pack access to the beach.*

**Damon Point.** At the end of Point Brown Road, 6 miles south of the entrance to Ocean Shores, turn south on Marine View Drive and in 0.4 mile turn southeast on the dirt access road that runs to the end of the point (parking, vault toilets, picnic tables). *No vehicle access to the beach.*

The true recreational shores of Washington State run south along the Pacific Ocean from the Quinault Indian Reservation to the mouth of the Columbia River. Grays Harbor and Willapa Bay divide the shore into three distinct sections: North Beach, South Beach, and Long Beach. This sectioning prevents a continuous north–south flow, although the beaches are quite similar in character.

North Beach begins at Moclips and runs south for 22 miles to Ocean Shores at the tip of Point Brown. A few steep cliffs extending from Pacific Beach to Copalis Rock are a last, faint echo of the rugged cliffs and offshore rocks of the northern coast. From here south the landscape flattens, and sandy beach reaches out to greet crashing surf. Beach grass-anchored dunes back the shores, while farther inland low spots hold bogs and shallow lakes. Salt marshes and protected estuaries provide nesting areas for several species of plovers. These are also favored stopovers for migratory birds along the Pacific Flyway; in winter many uncommon birds may be spotted here and in the dunes, as well as huge flocks of birds that normally range along the coast.

All the ocean beaches are open to the public; however, the uplands are private except for the accesses listed here and the developed state park lands. Vehicles can be driven onto the beach at all accesses, except as noted. The introduction to this book lists beach regulations.

*Semipalmated plovers play tag with ocean foam.*

# PACIFIC BEACH
# STATE PARK

**Hours/Season:** Overnight; standard hours; year-round
**Area:** 9 acres; 2,000 feet of saltwater shoreline on the Pacific Ocean
**Facilities:** 118 standard campsites, 20 RV sites, restrooms, trailer dump station
**Attractions:** Camping, picnicking, clamming, fishing, kite flying, beachcombing, birdwatching, paddling
**Access:** From Hoquiam drive Highway 109 west, then north along the coast for 29.1 miles to the park, on Joe Creek, at the south edge of the town of Pacific Beach. Alternatively, at a Y-intersection 8 miles west of Hoquiam, head north on Ocean Beach Road to reach Pacific Beach in 16 miles. *No vehicle beach access.*

▲ Pacific Beach State Park is a small, semicircular sand-and-gravel flat rimmed on the outside by a riprap wall between the park and the beach. The only shore vegetation is sparse beach grass and a row of low bushes along either side of a short row of campsites. The remainder of the sites are defined only by picnic tables and posts with power and water hookups. Sites are jammed together, but that suits most RVers, whose main interest is easy beach access to succulent razor clams. There's no shade here in sunny weather, and nothing to temper the winds whistling along the beachfront.

Beachcombing is great, and a good steady northerly makes for prime kite flying. At the south edge of the park, in the shallow flow near the mouth of Joe Creek, watch gulls and pelicans splash their wings against the water as they herd small schools of fingerlings into belly-filling concentrations.

# GRIFFITHS-PRIDAY
# STATE PARK

**Hours/Season:** Day-use; standard hours; year-round
**Area:** 358.7 acres; 7,776 feet of saltwater shoreline on the Pacific Ocean; 9,950 feet of freshwater shoreline on the Copalis River

**Facilities:** 10 picnic sites, picnic shelter, 200-person group day-use area, 2 windscreens with picnic tables, restrooms, boardwalk through the dunes to the beach
**Attractions:** Picnicking, fishing, horseback riding, hiking, paddling, kite flying, clamming, beachcombing, birdwatching
**Access:** From Hoquiam take Highway 109 west, then north along the coast for 19.6 miles to the park.

▲ Over the centuries the mouth of the Copalis River has been driven north by a narrow, accreted peninsula that is bordered on the west by the Pacific Ocean and on the east by the Copalis River. Today at the heart of this spit are grass-covered dunes surrounded by sandy beaches on both the ocean and the river sides. The entire spit comprises Griffiths-Priday State Park, named for its donor, Judge Griffiths, and the Pridays, his foster parents who brought him to this country from England as a child.

All of the park above the high-tide line is closed to public access from March 15 through the end of August. This is one of three nesting areas on Washington's Pacific beaches for the snowy plover, an endangered shorebird. Plovers lay their eggs in shallow depressions in the dry sand between the high-tide level and the dune grass. Any disturbance may cause the birds to leave their eggs or young unprotected, and the fragile eggs are easily broken by people walking on the sand in which the eggs are buried. A boardwalk beach trail leads past the environmentally sensitive dune area to the beach.

The remainder of the park's beach below the high-tide line is open to horseback riding, beachcombing, or razor clamming (in season); the mouth of the river is a good spot to try surf fishing for redtail surfperch. On the river side of the peninsula, paddling the smooth, protected waters of the Copalis River offers waterside views of birds and wildlife.

# OCEAN CITY
# STATE PARK

**Hours/Season:** Overnight; standard hours; year-round
**Area:** 111.8 acres; 2,100 feet of saltwater

shoreline on the Pacific Ocean

**Facilities:** 149 standard campsites, 29 RV sites, 3 primitive campsites, 40-person group camp, 6 picnic sites, 2 picnic shelters, restrooms with handicap access, vault toilet, trailer dump station

**Attractions:** Camping, picnicking, clamming, fishing, horseback riding, kite flying, surfboarding, scuba diving, beachcombing, birdwatching, mushrooming, paddling

**Access:** From Hoquiam take Highway 109 west for 15.5 miles to its intersection with Highway 115. Turn south and reach the park in 1.2 miles.

Although it is rather compact, Ocean City State Park has a remarkable variety of ocean beach habitat within its boundaries. The foredunes are separated from the beach by the trickle of a small creek, stained a rainbow of colors by the algae and shore plants that flourish in the merging of fresh and salt waters. Sandpipers and plover wade the creek and skitter about in search of snacks, while farther out on the beach clusters of gulls screech out the local gossip. Sharp beach grass cloaks the dunes, sprinkled with flashes of color from flowers such as the bright yellow northern dune tansy.

Dense thickets of shore pine and kinnikinnick hide the campground loops, protecting them from winds that sweep the beach, and offering seclusion for each site. A few hundred yards farther inland, deciduous trees mix with the pine, and freshwater marshes coalesce into a series of small ponds that parallel the beach. A variety of ducks, both resident and transient, feed along their reedy banks, and the chirps and twitters of a myriad of unseen birds are heard in the nearby brush.

Four campground loops penetrate the

*A secluded campsite at Ocean City State Park*

thick forest inland from the dunes. Lush grass carpets the floor of the campsites, and brush and trees snuggle around each. A wide green field, surrounded by trees and equipped with a campfire circle and picnic shelter, serves as a group camp. The day-use area consists mainly of a parking lot near the edge of the dunes with a path leading west for foot access to the beach. Picnic shelters and a few tables sit below the trees along one edge of the gravel lot.

Two of the small inland ponds have short trails leading from nearby parking to breaks in their marshy shoreline. Hand-carried boats can be launched for a paddle around the perimeter to observe birds and wildlife that inhabit this environment.

# OCEAN SHORES ENVIRONMENTAL INTERPRETIVE CENTER

**Hours/Season:** Wednesday through Sunday 11:00 A.M. to 6:00 P.M. from Memorial Day to Labor Day
**Facilities:** Interpretive center
**Attractions:** Historical and ecological interpretive displays
**Access:** From the intersection of Point Brown Avenue and Marine View Drive, drive 6 miles south of the entrance to Ocean Shores.

Although Point Brown, the 6-mile-long and 2-mile-wide peninsula that shelters the upper half of Grays Harbor, was used as a clamming and trading site by local Indian tribes long before the arrival of outsiders, it was first noted by white men when Captain Robert Gray sailed the *Columbia Rediviva* into present-day Grays Harbor in 1792.

Displays at the Ocean Shores Environmental Interpretive Center trace the natural and human history of the point. The center, which is open during summer months, has pictorial displays describing the process of accretion by which the peninsula was built, the ecology of the beach and dune life, and birds and animals that are found here.

Nearby Damon Point hosts over 200 species of bird and marine life. It marks the northernmost range of the snowy plover and the southernmost range of the semipalmated plover; it is the only place in the world where both species are known to breed. Except for the beach, the area south of the access road is closed from March to September to protect nesting birds.

# SOUTH BEACH SEASHORE CONSERVATION AREA

**Hours/Season:** Day-use; standard hours; year-round
**Beach Driving Restrictions:**
*Prohibited year-round:* Westhaven State Park beach.
*Prohibited April 15 through the day after Labor Day, except during razor clam season:* Westhaven State Park to Westport Light State Park, Westport State Park to Twin Harbors Access, North Cove Access south to Willapa Wildlife Refuge.
*Prohibited April 15 through the day after Labor Day, including razor clam season:* Westport Light State Park.
*Open all year:* Twin Harbors Access to Warrentown Cannery Road Access.
**Area:** 19 miles of saltwater shoreline on the Pacific Ocean
**Attractions:** Picnicking, kayaking, kite flying, fishing, clamming, beach walking, birdwatching, horseback riding, surfboarding, beachcombing
**Accesses:**
**Twin Harbors Gap Road.** At the intersection of Highway 105 E/W and 105 N/S, head west along the north side of Twin Harbors State Park to reach the beach in 0.2 mile (parking lot, restrooms with handicap access, windscreens, picnic tables). *No vehicle access to the beach.*
**Bonges Avenue.** From the intersection of Highway 105 E/W and 105 N/S, head south for 0.7 mile to Bonges Avenue, then turn west, and reach the beach in 0.4 mile (parking, vault toilets).
**Grayland Beach.** From the intersection of Highway 105 E/W and 105 N/S, head south for 3.6 miles to Grayland Beach Road (Cranberry Road is to the east of the intersection), then turn west,

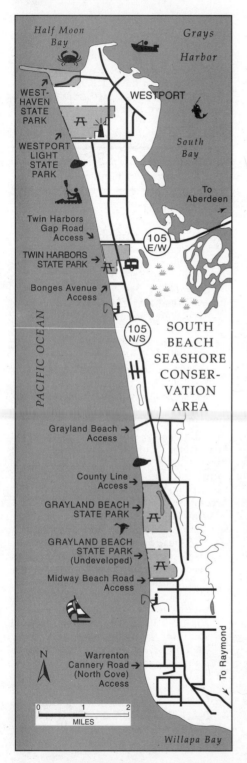

and reach the beach in 0.3 mile (parking lot, restrooms).

**County Line.** From the intersection of Highway 105 E/W and 105 N/S, head south for 4.9 miles to County Line Road, at the north side of Grayland Beach State Park. Turn west and reach the beach in 0.5 mile (parking lot, restrooms).

**Midway Beach Road.** From the intersection of Highway 105 E/W and 105 N/S, head south for 6.8 miles to Midway Beach Road, then turn west and reach the beach in 0.4 mile (vault toilet).

**Warrenton Cannery Road (North Cove Road).** From the intersection of Highway 105 E/W and 105 N/S, head south for 8.5 miles to Warrenton Cannery Road, then turn west and reach the beach in 0.9 mile (vault toilet).

South Beach runs for 19 unbroken miles between Grays Harbor and Willapa Bay. At its north end the town of Westport, which is totally oriented to sport fishing, boasts a fleet of charter boats. Boats aren't essential, however, as first-class fishing can be had from the jetties or shore. Surf-fishers can have success with even a light or medium spinning rod if the surf is not too rough. To many people Washington beaches mean razor clams, and South Beach is a prime spot for pursuing them. When digging seasons are officially opened in fall and spring, throngs descend in search of the Cadillac of clams. Buckets of succulent bivalves are soon carted away to a loving home where they are breaded, fried, and enshrined on a dinner plate.

## WESTHAVEN STATE PARK

**Hours/Season:** Day-use; standard hours; year-round

**Area:** 79.1 acres; 1,215 feet of saltwater shoreline on the Pacific Ocean

**Facilities:** 2 picnic sites, vault toilets

**Attractions:** Picnicking, fishing, clamming, horseback riding, kite flying, surfboarding, scuba diving, kayaking, beachcombing, crabbing (in Half Moon Bay)

**Access:** From US 101 on the south side of Aberdeen, take Highway 105 west for 18

miles, then north for 2 miles to its end in Westport at the intersection of W Ocean Avenue and Forrest Avenue. Continue north on Forrest, which becomes Wilson Avenue as it bends eastward and in 1.1 miles intersects Montesano Avenue. Turn northwest on Montesano, and in 0.2 mile the signed road to the park heads west. The park boundary is reached in 0.5 mile, and the beach in 1.2 miles. *No vehicle access to the beach.*

⚓ The long rock jetty built in the 1940s to reduce silting in the mouth of Grays Harbor led to the accretion of grass-covered dunes and the broad sandy shore that is now Westhaven State Park on South Beach. Rolling breakers from the Pacific Ocean make this the state's most popular surfing beach. Sea kayakers are also drawn here to test their skills maneuvering through the crashing waves.

The beach will hold a moderate swell

from almost any direction, but those from the north and northwest tend to be the cleanest (best for holding their shape and form). Since the bottom is all sand, it is difficult for storm surf or swells over 7 feet to hold their shape. Low and incoming tides usually produce the most ridable surf, no matter what the direction of the swell is, while high tide will ruin just about any swell, large or small.

Summer surf usually is slow and lazy, but very playful; fall and spring surf requires strong paddling muscles. When swells are large, there is usually a rip current along the jetty to help surfers paddle out. Wet suits are needed to survive the frigid ocean water, which doesn't warm above 60 degrees, even in summer. Warm summer days may require only a half wet suit, but in midwinter boots, gloves, and hood along with a full wet suit are the dress code.

In summer the wide beach attracts other

*Surf's up at Westhaven State Park!*

kinds of recreationists. Kids create sand castles while Mom and Dad comb the beach for sand-buffed agates or treasures brought in by the surf. Winter storms in 1993 ripped through the peninsula between the jetty and Half Moon Bay, slicing a 50-foot-wide channel through the park property into the bay, and cutting off access to fishing from the jetty. As of this writing, funding has not yet been found to close this breach, and it is uncertain when the necessary repairs will be made. Beach fishing and crabbing are popular activities in the placid waters along the shoreline of Half Moon Bay.

## WESTPORT LIGHT STATE PARK

**Hours/Season:** Day-use; standard hours; year-round
**Area:** 212.2 acres; 3,397 feet of saltwater shoreline on the Pacific Ocean
**Facilities:** 15 picnic sites, restroom
**Attractions:** Picnicking, fishing, clamming, horseback riding, kite flying, surfboarding, scuba diving, beachcombing
**Access:** From US 101 on the south side of Aberdeen, take Highway 105 west for 18 miles, then north for 2 miles to its end in Westport at the intersection of W Ocean Avenue and Forrest Avenue. At the intersection head west on W Ocean. In 0.3 mile a lighthouse viewing platform is on the north side of the road. Beach parking and access is another 0.5 mile west. *Motor vehicles prohibited on the beach from April 15 through the day after Labor Day.*

Westport Lighthouse is unique in several ways: at 107 feet, it is the tallest lighthouse on the West Coast of the U.S. and it is one of the few lighthouses where most of the original lighting system is still intact. The French-built Fresnel lens, originally assembled for it in 1895, and the vents in the tower walls, used to adjust the draft for the original oil lamps, are still in place, even though the present light source is a 1,000-watt lamp producing a beam of 1,520,000 candlepower, visible up to 25 nautical miles away. The lighthouse is on Coast Guard property immediately adjacent to its namesake state park. Just east of the park bound-

ary is a small viewing platform and a sign that tells the story of the light.

Rolling dunes covered with beach grass and shore pine form the inland portion of the park. All the facilities—a large paved parking lot, restrooms, and a number of windscreened picnic sites with one or more picnic tables and fire braziers—are found just above the beach at the southeast corner of the park. The road along the south edge of the park (W Ocean Avenue) continues through the foredunes to the beach. Beachcombing is especially popular during the winter, when storms may bring glass-ball fishnet floats and other treasures from the Pacific.

## TWIN HARBORS STATE PARK

**Hours/Season:** Overnight; standard hours; year-round
**Area:** 172 acres; 3,414 feet of saltwater shoreline on the Pacific Ocean
**Facilities:** 272 standard campsites, 49 RV sites, 5 primitive sites, 84-person group camp, 12 picnic sites, 100-person group day-use area, 3 fire rings, restrooms, kitchen shelter, clam cleaning shed, 1-mile nature trail, hiking
**Attractions:** Camping, picnicking, surf fishing, clamming, horseback riding, kite flying, beachcombing
**Access:** From US 101 on the south side of Aberdeen, take Highway 105 west for 17.8 miles. The main area of the park is on the south side of 105 E/W, 0.2 mile east of the intersection with Highway 105 N/S. Additional camping areas are found on the west side of the north–south leg of Highway 105 0.2 mile south of this intersection. Vehicle beach access is via the Bonges Avenue access, 0.5 mile south on Highway 105 N/S.

The largest of the two state park campgrounds in the South Beach area, Twin Harbors attracts capacity crowds in summer as well as during spring and fall razor clamming seasons. The extensive camping areas are on both sides of Highway 105. Hookup sites lie side by side in three paral-

*Westport Light has been operating since 1895.*

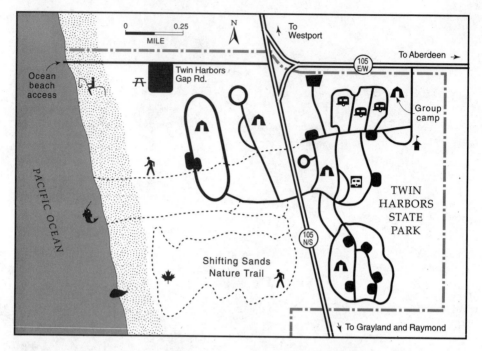

lel rows, just inside the entrance of the eastern section of the park. The remaining sites on this side of the highway line a series of loops, all shaded most of the day by dense brush and shore pines. A children's play area includes the hull of a boat for fanciful ocean voyages by young skippers.

Camping on the west side of the highway is along a road adjacent the highway, or around a large loop closer to the beach. These sites are more open than those to the east, but they are bordered with enough shore pine to provide a modicum of privacy and a little shade, as well as protection from the wind. Trails linking the camp areas and the individual sites eventually lead to the beach.

While the beach habitat may, on the surface, seem to be a simple one of sand, grass, and scrub, it is in reality complex, and includes a wealth of interdependent plant communities. A park brochure describes significant ecological features at twenty numbered stations along the Shifting Sands Nature Trail. The path begins on the west side of the highway about 50 feet beyond campsites 285–321 and loops counterclockwise through the dune area south of the campground. Some of the station posts on

the trail may be obscure or missing, and the starting and middle segments of the trail may be poorly marked.

Shore pine, wild strawberry, evergreen huckleberry, black twinberry, and kinnikinnick soon crowd the trail. In 0.25 mile the route breaks out in beach grass, then climbs to the top of the foredune overlooking the beach. Although unmarked and obscured by beach grass, the trail now heads south along the top of the dunes to the return leg; don't drop down to the beach, as you will have trouble finding the start of the return leg. On this final leg the transition in plant life is similar, except here the shore pine has grown taller and arches cathedral-like over the trail. Walk slowly and quietly and you may see brush rabbits, field mice, and possibly even deer.

## GRAYLAND BEACH STATE PARK

**Hours/Season:** Overnight; standard hours; year-round
**Area:** 411.2 acres; 7,449 feet of saltwater shoreline on the Pacific Ocean

**Facilities:** 60 RV sites, 3 primitive camp-sites, restroom, sani-cans, 0.25-mile interpretive trail to the beach, 1-mile interpretive trail around Borrow Lake

**Attractions:** Camping, picnicking, fishing, clamming, kite flying, horseback riding, beachcombing, hiking

**Access:** From US 101 on the south side of Aberdeen, take Highway 105 west for 18 miles and then south for 4.9 miles to County Line Road. Head west and reach the park entrance in 0.1 mile. Car beach access is via County Line Road, which runs along the north side of the park.

▲ Grayland Beach State Park is the second of the two parks on South Beach that have camping. Sites arranged around the perimeter of six paved circles, nine sites to a circle, are embraced by shore pine and kinnikinnick. A few primitive sites are hidden in the woods just inside the park entrance. There is no designated day-use area for picnickers; most will choose to pack their lunch to the shore.

The beach, of course, is the main reason for visiting the area. A short trail leaves the center of the campground and leads through dense growths of kinnikinnick to the fore-dune and the beach. On sunny summer days steady northwest winds lure kite fly-ers to the beach, and on blustery winter days flotsam at the high-tide line holds beachcombers' treasures. During razor clamming season the beach is a favorite spot for those pursuing this tasty bivalve. An 8-mile-long strip of beach north and south of the park is open to motorized vehicles.

Tiny Borrow Lake—actually more pond than lake—is sequestered in the shore pine south of the camping area; a self-guided nature trail runs around its perimeter.

A second, undeveloped portion of land that is part of the park lies 2 miles south, on the north side of the Midway Beach Road access. A primitive, rutted jeep road running north and south through the property may be walked but is not recommended for passenger cars or RVs.

*Horses and riders enjoy the beach and roaring surf of South Beach.*

# LONG BEACH SEASHORE CONSERVATION AREA

**Hours/Season:** Day-use; standard hours; year-round
**Beach Driving Restrictions:**
*Prohibited all year:* Fort Canby State Park
*Prohibited all year except during razor clam season:* Leadbetter Point State Park
*Prohibited April 15 through the day after Labor Day, except during razor clam season:* Leadbetter Point State Park to the Oysterville Access, Seaview Access to the Bolstad Access
*Open all year:* Oysterville Access to Bolstad Access, Seaview Access to Fort Canby State Park

**Attractions:** Picnicking, kayaking, kite flying, fishing, clamming, beach walking, birdwatching, horseback riding, beachcombing

**Accesses:**
**Oysterville.** From the intersection of US 101 and Highway 103 at Seaview, take Highway 103 (Pacific Highway) north for 11.5 miles to its end in Ocean Park. Turn west on Bay Avenue, and in 0.8

*A galaxy of kites fills the air at the Long Beach Kite Festival.*

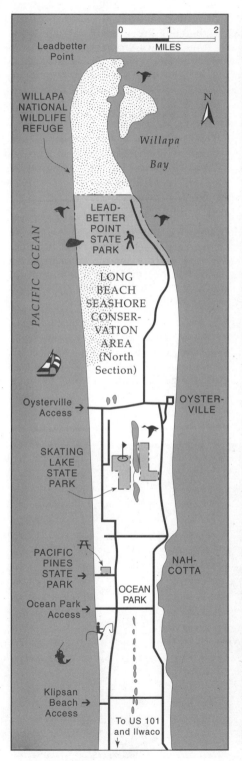

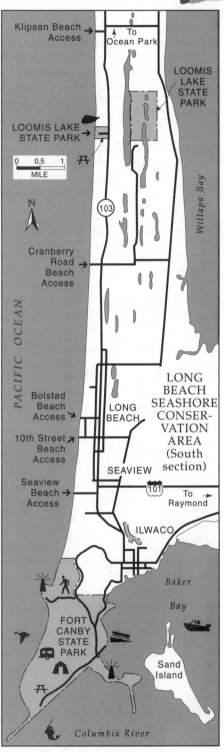

mile turn north on Sand Ridge Road (which becomes Peninsula Highway north of Nahcotta). In 4.2 miles, at a T-intersection, head west on Oysterville Gap Road and reach the beach in 1.5 miles (vault toilet).

**Ocean Park.** From the intersection of US 101 and Highway 103 (Pacific Highway) at Seaview, head north for 11.5 miles to the end of Highway 103 in Ocean Park. Turn west on Bay Avenue and reach the beach in 0.4 mile (vault toilet).

**Klipsan Beach.** From the intersection of US 101 and Highway 103 (Pacific Highway) at Seaview, head north for 9.6 miles to 225th Street, then west for 0.2 mile to the beach access (vault toilet).

**Cranberry Road.** From the intersection of US 101 and Highway 103 (Pacific Highway) at Seaview, head north for 4.6 miles to Cranberry Road, then west for 0.4 mile to the beach access (vault toilet).

**Bolstad.** From the intersection of US 101 and Highway 103 (Pacific Highway) at Seaview, head north for 1.5 miles to Bolstad Street, then west for 0.1 mile to the beach access and the north end of the Long Beach Boardwalk along the foredunes (restrooms).

**10th Street.** From the intersection of US 101 and Highway 103 (Pacific Highway) at Seaview, head north for 1.1 miles to 10th Street in Long Beach, then west for 0.3 mile to the beach access and the south end of the Long Beach Boardwalk along the foredunes (vault toilet).

**Seaview.** From the intersection of US 101 and Highway 103 (Pacific Highway) at Seaview, turn south, then in 0.1 mile head west on 38th Place to reach the beach in 0.5 mile (vault toilet).

Long Beach is the third and grandest of the state's recreational ocean beaches. Claimed to be the longest unbroken stretch of beach in the world, it sweeps southward for 29 miles from Willapa Bay to the mouth of the Columbia River.

Surf, sand, and dunes offer all the fun found on the two northern beaches; Fort Canby State Park, at the southern tip of the Long Beach peninsula, is the jewel in its recreational crown. The fare at other state parks ranges from birdwatching to camp-

*Tracks in the sand tell a tale of previous visitors.*

ing to golf. Ilwaco, which faces on Baker Bay on the Columbia River, is a commercial and sport fishing center, with numerous charter offices booking trips for salmon, tuna, sturgeon, and bottom fish. If time does not allow for one of these excursions, the jetty at Fort Canby offers good fishing, as well as views of the fishing fleet. Bird-watching groups can also charter boats for offshore observation of spectacular flocks of hundreds of thousands of migratory birds.

Unlike North Beach and South Beach, Long Beach is edged by water for most of its east side as well as its west; Leadbetter Point State Park has shoreline on both Willapa Bay and the Pacific Ocean. Tidelands on Willapa Bay are private, except for those in the state park or Willapa National Wildlife Refuge.

---

## LEADBETTER POINT STATE PARK

**Hours/Season:** Day-use; standard hours; year-round
**Area:** 807.3 acres; 15,840 feet of saltwater shoreline on the Pacific Ocean and Willapa Bay
**Facilities:** Vault toilets, 2.4 miles of hiking trail
**Attractions:** Hiking, picnicking, wildlife study, beachcombing, fishing, clamming
**Nearby:** Willapa National Wildlife Refuge
**Access:** From the intersection of US 101 and Highway 103 at Seaview, take Highway 103 (Pacific Highway) north for 11.5 miles to its end in Ocean Park. Turn east on Bay Avenue, and in 0.8 mile north on Sand Ridge Road (which becomes Peninsula Highway north of Nahcotta). In 4.2 miles, at a T-intersection, head west on Oysterville Road, then in 0.3 mile north on Stackpole Road. Reach the park entrance in another 3 miles, and road-end in 4.5 miles. *No vehicle access to the beach.*

Leadbetter Point State Park encompasses a band of land that stretches across the Long Beach peninsula, giving it beach frontage on both the ocean and Willapa Bay. The road runs in timber near the east shore; parking areas are midway at Stackpole Slough or at the far north end of the park, where the road ends. A 1.5-mile-long loop trail heads west from the north parking lot, then turns south before returning back through the forest to another parking area midway along the west side of the park. Branch paths lead to the beach.

A remarkable transition in ecology occurs in little over a mile, east to west. On Willapa Bay a grassy marshland reaches to the shoreline along the protected waters. East of here cedar, spruce, hemlock, and alder combine to make up the forest, which

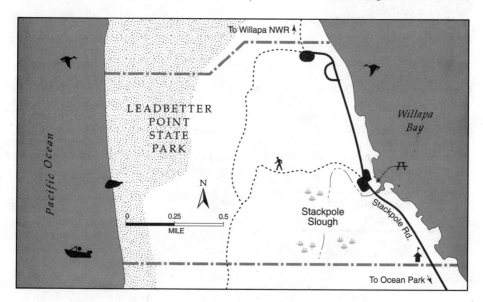

merges with a dense growth of kinnikin-nick, shore pine, blackberries, and huckle-berries, and becomes more sparse as the beach is neared. Saltwater marshes amid the dunes nourish arrowgrass and pick-leweed. Rolling dunes stabilized by hardy beach grass, wild strawberry, gorse, sand verbena, lupine, and beach pea finally give way to the wide, windswept sandy beach facing on the ocean.

The dunes running north from the park to the tip of the peninsula are one of three parts of the Willapa Bay National Wildlife Refuge; Long Island near the south end of Willapa Bay and shorelands at the end of the bay are its two other sections. A trail from the state park's northern parking lot leads into this section of the refuge.

Leadbetter Point is a "Holiday Inn" on the Pacific Flyway; among the migratory birds that stop here from fall through spring are sooty shearwaters, brant, Canada geese, white-fronted geese, canvasbacks, buffle-heads, pintails, and shovelers. Clouds of dunlins and sanderlings frequent the beaches, while dunes provide winter ref-uge for birds that nest in alpine meadows and on arctic tundra such as Lapland long-spurs, horned larks, and water pipits. From mid-July through October, you may see brown pelicans that have wandered north from their California breeding grounds. The north end of the wildlife refuge is closed to the public from April through August, when snowy plovers nest.

Aside from the bird population, the state park is home to raccoons, deer, berry-seeking black bears . . . and clouds of mos-quitos in summer.

A kiosk at Stackpole Slough describes the life cycle of oysters and tells the story of the growth and decline of the oyster industry on Willapa Bay. A short spur leads east to the shore of the bay and a lone picnic table. White stakes 100 yards offshore mark the inner boundary of private oyster beds.

## SKATING LAKE
## STATE PARK

**Hours/Season:** Day-use; standard hours; year-round
**Area:** 339 acres

**Facilities:** Golf course (concession)
**Attractions:** Golf, birdwatching, nature studies
**Access:** *East segment* access adjoins the west side of the Peninsula Highway 1 mile north of its intersection with Joe Johns Road. *West access (golf course),* follow the main roads north and west from Joe Johns Road for 1.5 miles to the golf course en-trance.

▲ Diversity is the norm in Washington's state parks, and Skating Lake State Park proves it. This recent addition to park lands consists of a nine-hole golf course, operated by a concessionaire. The state's prime inter-est, however, is preservation of the wet-lands that the golf course encompasses. The property includes the middle portion of Skating Lake, a slender, 1.5-mile-long combination marsh and pond that is a win-tering site for trumpeter swans and other waterfowl. Trails through the wetlands are planned for the future.

## PACIFIC PINES
## STATE PARK

**Hours/Season:** Day-use; standard hours, weekends and holidays only, September 30 to March 6
**Area:** 10.8 acres; 590 feet of saltwater shore-line on the Pacific Ocean
**Facilities:** 15 picnic sites, windscreens, rest-rooms with handicap access, trail to the beach
**Attractions:** Picnicking, clamming, beach-combing, hiking, surf fishing, kite flying
**Access:** From the intersection of US 101 and Highway 103 at Seaview, take Highway 103 north for 11.5 miles to its end in Ocean Park. Continue north on Vernon Avenue for 0.6 mile, then head west on 274th Place for 0.2 mile to reach the park. *No vehicle access to the beach.*

▲ A section of land north of Ocean Park that was once platted for a real estate development has, instead, become a small state park. Only the name given it by the realtor remains as an echo of its intended destiny. The park is little more than a glori-fied beach access, but its few amenities of restrooms and picnic tables with wind-screens are very nice, and they provide some sheltered spots for lunching when winds are too brisk on the beach.

The road here through the dunes to the beach is not a legal access point.

## LOOMIS LAKE STATE PARK

**Hours/Season:** Day-use; standard hours; weekends and holidays only, September 30 to March 27

**Area:** 295.5 acres; 425 feet of saltwater shore-line on the Pacific Ocean

**Facilities:** 24 picnic sites, 10 windscreens, restrooms with handicap access, trail to the beach

**Attractions:** Picnicking, clamming, beach-combing, hiking, fishing, kite flying, bird-watching.

**Access:** From the intersection of US 101 and Highway 103 at Seaview, take Highway 103 north for 10.9 miles. The eastern, un-developed portion of the park is on the east side of Loomis Lake, and includes Mallard Lake, Lost Lake, and the north end of Island Lake. The west portion of the park is at the end of the road to the west of the highway. *No vehicle access to the beach.*

▲ The developed portion of Loomis Lake State Park is a 13.5-acre strip of land that faces the ocean, but doesn't touch Loomis Lake itself. A king-sized parking lot pro-vides a spot for beachgoers to leave their cars when headed for clam digging or other

*Trumpeter swans frequent secluded inland lakes and ponds at Long Beach. (Photo by Bob and Ira Spring)*

enticing beach activities. Picnic tables with windscreens are handy for a sustenance stop before hiking the short distance to the shore.

The 280-acre section of park that lies on the west shore of the lake is undeveloped. The property and the small ponds that it encompasses are a wintering habitat for trumpeter swans. These magnificent birds were nearly hunted to extinction; in 1931 a mere 35 birds were counted. By virtue of conservation measures, they have made a remarkable comeback, and large flocks now range in the western U.S. and Canada. The park lands will remain undeveloped in order to preserve the wildlife habitat.

Loomis Lake is the largest lake on the Long Beach peninsula, and the only one that is planted for fishing. The 2.5-mile-long lake contains rainbow trout. A Game Department boat launch and public fishing site is on its west shore, across from the state park property.

# FORT CANBY STATE PARK

**Hours/Season:** Overnight; standard hours; year-round; *Lewis and Clark Interpretive Center*, open daily in summer, in winter weekends only or by appointment

**Area:** 1,881.9 acres; 42,600 feet of saltwater shoreline on the Pacific Ocean and the mouth of the Columbia River; 7,000 feet of freshwater shoreline on Lake O'Neil

**Facilities:** 190 standard campsites, 60 RV sites, 4 primitive campsites, 50 picnic sites, restrooms, vault toilets, trailer dump station, snacks (concession), boat launch ramp, interpretive center, 2 Coast Guard lighthouses, historic Coast Artillery gun emplacements, 1.5-mile nature trail, 4 miles of hiking trail

**Attractions:** Camping, picnicking, beachcombing, fishing, clamming, boating, hiking, birdwatching, historic sites

*Jetty fishing at Fort Canby*

**Access:** From Ilwaco, at the stoplight on US 101 at 1st Street and Spruce Street SE, head west on Spruce Street, which becomes Robert Gray Drive. Reach the park boundary in 2.1 miles, the road to North Head Lighthouse in 2.3 miles, and the park entrance in 3.5 miles.

This stretch of bluffs and beach at the southern tip of the Long Beach peninsula is one of the most historically significant in the state; in fact, the Cape Disappointment area has been declared a National Historic District. It was here, in November 1805, that the Lewis and Clark Expedition first touched the waters of the Pacific Ocean. William Clark carved his name on a nearby tree.

As the Oregon Territory was settled, the site became vital to commerce, maritime safety, and the military defense of the mouth of the Columbia River. Treacherous currents at the bar that lies at the mouth of the mighty river caused the area to become known as the "Graveyard of the Pacific." The Cape Disappointment Lighthouse, which marks the river and warns sailors of the bar, was to be the first on the West Coast, but due to construction delays it did not begin operation until 1856, a year later than several in California. It was, however, the first lighthouse in Washington. A second lighthouse was added at North Head in 1898 to assist mariners traveling from the north who were unable to spot the Cape Disappointment light.

The 584-acre military reservation that was created in 1852 was the first site north of San Francisco considered worthy of military defenses. Smooth-bore cannons placed here in 1862 to guard the river's entrance were the first generation of Coast Artillery. The site was initially named Fort Hancock, but when it was activated in 1875 it was renamed for Major General Edward Canby, who had died in the Modoc Indian War in northern California. During the early 1900s the fortifications were upgraded with new gun and mortar batteries and control centers for underwater mines that were laid beneath the entrance to the Columbia. World War II saw the addition of a modern armored long-range rapid-fire battery atop McKenzie Head. The fort was deactivated after World War II, and in 1957 the property became a state park.

The rich history of Fort Canby State Park is rivaled only by its varied recreational fun. A boat launch ramp facing on Baker Bay on the Columbia River is just east of the park entrance gate. Weekends during salmon fishing season see long lines of trailered boats waiting to be launched here. The Coastal Forest Trail, a 1.5-mile-long loop nature trail north of the boat launch circles through a forest of 300- to 500-year-old Sitka spruce and hemlock, which has been undisturbed by man from the time of the original explorers of the area.

Waikiki Beach, the day-use area, is immediately south of the road to the campgrounds. Picnic tables line a lawn above the beach of this tiny, secluded cove. A trail leads up the steep wooded hillside from here to the interpretive center. The road continues out to the 800-yard-long rock jetty, constructed to help control the wave action and erosion at the mouth of the Columbia. The rock jetty provides superb fishing sites for rockfish, perch, and even some salmon. Benson Beach north of the jetty is excellent for surf fishing. Birdwatchers on the jetty can sometimes spot stray birds such as albatross that would normally be farther offshore.

The main campground area contains numerous wagon-wheel circles nestled in the shore pine near the beach below North Head. Some of the sites are interspersed with 50-foot-high rock outcroppings that offer challenges for young rock scramblers. Trails from each of these loops lead through the dunes to the sandy 2-mile-long expanse of Benson Beach. Additional campsites lie around the marshy rim of Lake O'Neil, near the park entrance.

Near the northern park boundary a road leads west to the North Head Lighthouse. A short path at road's end leads through woods of Sitka spruce to the lighthouse, perched above precipitous cliffs overlooking the crashing waves of the Pacific. The lighthouse can also be reached by a 1.5-mile-long trail that starts from the north side of the road to the campgrounds, 0.2 mile west of Lake O'Neil. The route wends through marshlands before climbing a wooded bluff to reach North Head.

Just south of the Lake O'Neil trailhead, and on the opposite side of the road, is a small parking area and the unmarked trail

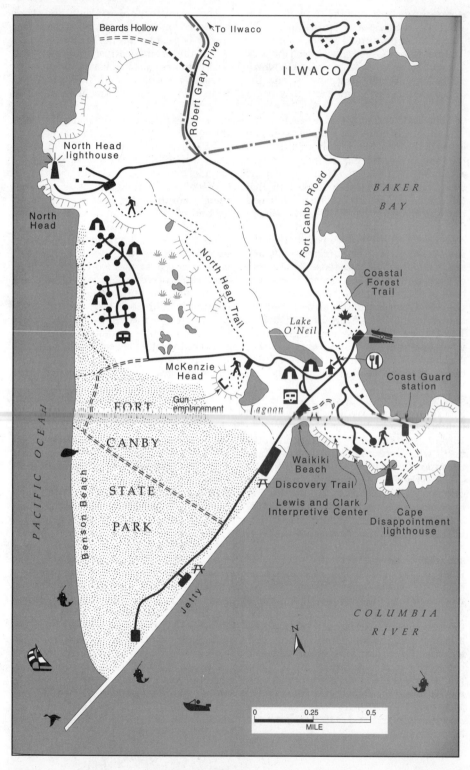

Beards Hollow

To Ilwaco

ILWACO

Robert Gray Drive

North Head lighthouse

North Head

BAKER BAY

Fort Canby Road

Coastal Forest Trail

North Head Trail

Lake O'Neil

McKenzie Head

Gun emplacement

FORT

Coast Guard station

CANBY

PACIFIC OCEAN

Benson Beach

STATE

PARK

Lagoon

Waikiki Beach

Discovery Trail

Lewis and Clark Interpretive Center

Cape Disappointment lighthouse

Jetty

COLUMBIA

N

RIVER

| 0 | 0.25 | 0.5 |

MILE

to McKenzie Head, a 150-foot-high wooded knob. This trail climbs steeply around the south side of the head before arriving at the remnants of the World War II gun battery. The two armored 6-inch guns are gone, but the bunker is open to exploration; a flashight is needed to poke into the dark rooms inside the tunnel between the two gun emplacements.

Behind the protective mass of Cape Disappointment is the only Coast Guard motor lifeboat station in the world that trains coxswains for heavy weather and heavy surf operations. The station is not open to the public. From the parking lot at the station, a gated road leads steeply uphill to the Cape Disappointment Lighthouse. A trail branching right midway uphill loops high above the head of a secluded cove to reach the parking lot at the interpretive center.

The Lewis and Clark Interpretive Center perches on a 200-foot-high cliff. A short path switchbacks uphill from the parking lot to the center; handicapped parking is available adjacent to the center. This cliff was originally the site of the turn-of-the-century Coast Artillery Battery Harvey Allen. The massive concrete emplacement that housed the battery is immediately behind the interpretive center.

By means of a "time line" that follows a ramp spiraling down the building and then back up, the interpretive center tells the story of the Lewis and Clark Corps of Discovery as it traveled from St. Louis to the Pacific Ocean. Diary quotes, photo montages, maps, and descriptive panels detail the expedition's history, including the reasons for the venture, President Thomas Jefferson's efforts to obtain funding for it, and finally, detailed descriptions of the long, incredible journey that changed the history of the Northwest. A multimedia theater on the lower level of the ramp offers short programs highlighting various aspects of the expedition. The ramp returns to the main floor, where an expanse of windows reveal breathtaking views of the Cape Disappointment Lighthouse, the Columbia River, the western reaches of the park, and the Pacific Ocean.

Other presentations in the interpretive center tell the history of shipwrecks at the Columbia bar, and of the Coast Guard lifesaving efforts here over the years. Displays and a videotape also describe the military history of Fort Canby and its fortifications and armaments.

The northern reaches of the park include an undeveloped access and beach at Beards Hollow, north of North Head. This was at one time an Indian campsite; archeologists discovered a large, well-preserved shell midden here.

# FORT COLUMBIA STATE PARK

**Hours/Season:** Day-use; standard hours; closed Mondays and Tuesdays, September 30 to March 27
**Area:** 592.6 acres; 6,400 feet of freshwater shoreline on the Columbia River
**Facilities:** 26 picnic sites, restrooms, youth hostel, 2 interpretive centers, historic fortifications
**Attractions:** Picnicking, hiking, historic sites, interpretive centers
**Access:** On US 101, drive 2.6 miles northwest of the junction of US 101 and Highway 401 at the north end of the Columbia River Bridge from Astoria

Fort Columbia was one of several Coast Artillery forts built on the West Coast between 1885 and 1905 during the period of frenzied construction of defensive fortifications. To destroy enemy ships that might attempt to enter the Columbia River, huge batteries, some on disappearing carriages, were mounted in massive concrete emplacements. Strings of underwater mines laid along the river bottom were to be detonated from a shore-based control center when enemy ships passed. A smaller rapid-fire battery protected the minefields from attempts to disarm them via small boats, and also prevented landing parties from attacking the fort. In World War II a new battery with long-range rapid-fire guns in armored turrets supplemented the older, outmoded batteries.

As with most of these early forts, the property is now a state park. The restored buildings and historical displays provide a glimpse into this military era. Recreational facilities are limited to a number of picnic tables scattered through the area below the upper gun battery emplacement. Although it fronts on the Columbia River, steep bluffs

71

prevent access to the water. It was these cliffs that made the site ideal for a fort.

The enlisted men's barracks at Fort Columbia serve as a historical interpretive center. The restored kitchen, mess hall, and squad room evoke memories of lines of uniformed artillery men, eagerly waiting to be served from huge steaming pots. In the kitchen, massive coal-fired ranges, an old oak refrigerator, and large sinks line the walls, while pots and utensils are hung about. A taped voice of an army cook explains what you see and describes his daily duties. In the adjoining room a mess table set with dishes is attended by a mannequin in a period Coast Artillery uniform. An upstairs squad room contains beds and lockers; posters remind soldiers of their duties and responsibilities.

Other rooms in the building are filled with displays detailing the post's fortifications, regional history from the time of the Lewis and Clark Expedition through pioneer times, marine traffic and trade on the Columbia, and the culture and way of life of the local Chinook Indians.

A historic walk starts at the interpretive center in the old enlisted men's barracks, then pauses at the Columbia House, the former commandant's home, which has been restored and decorated with period furnishings. From here the path passes the old powerhouse, with its display of generators that once powered the fort, then heads downhill through the various gun battery emplacements. A youth hostel, open from the first of June through the end of September, operates in the former post hospital. Uphill from the interpretive center, the quartermaster's storehouse has one room that shows the newspaper office of the *Chinook Observer* as it looked at the turn of the century. The paper is still published today.

## LEWIS AND CLARK CAMPSITE HERITAGE AREA

**Hours/Season:** Day-use; standard hours; year-round
**Area:** 0.8 acre

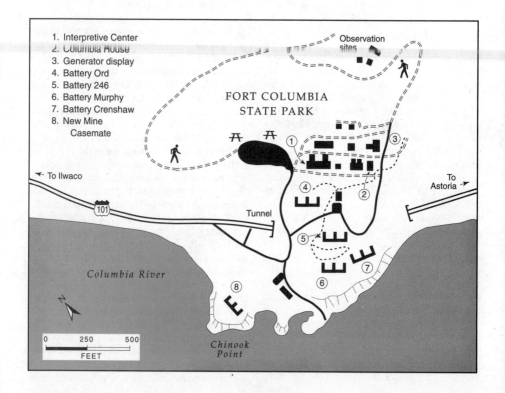

1. Interpretive Center
2. Columbia House
3. Generator display
4. Battery Ord
5. Battery 246
6. Battery Murphy
7. Battery Crenshaw
8. New Mine Casemate

FORT COLUMBIA STATE PARK

Observation sites

To Ilwaco

101

Tunnel

To Astoria

Columbia River

N

0   250   500
FEET

Chinook Point

*Camouflage nets are draped over the enlisted men's barracks at Fort Columbia.*

**Facilities:** Historical display, picnic tables
**Attractions:** Picnicking, historical interpretation
**Access:** On US 101, drive 1.9 miles west of the intersection of Highway 401 and US 101, at the north end of the Columbia River Bridge from Astoria

In mid-November of 1805 Lewis and Clark paused in their westward journey and camped at this spot. It was from this spot that they first saw the breakers of the Pacific Ocean and realized they had accomplished the mission set for them by President Thomas Jefferson.

This road wayside contains a pair of carved wooden statues depicting the explorers. A smally grassy meadow next to the memorial has a few picnic tables.

## WILLIE KEIL'S GRAVE HERITAGE AREA

**Hours/Season:** Day-use; standard hours; year-round

**Area:** 0.3 acre
**Facilities:** Historical display
**Attractions:** Historical interpretation
**Access:** Drive to the south side of Highway 6, 3.3 miles east of Raymond or 2.1 miles west of Menlo

A poignant, macabre, or hilarious tale, depending on your viewpoint: Willie Keil was a 19-year-old man designated to drive the lead wagon for a group of settlers headed west from Bethel, Missouri, along the Oregon Trail. In May of 1855, four days before the group's departure, he died. His overwhelming desire to go west with the colony led them to preserve his body in a metal-lined casket filled with alcohol (some accounts claim it was whiskey), converting the lead wagon to a makeshift hearse. Willie led the group west both in body and spirit(s). On November 26, 1855, he was finally laid to rest on a hillside above the tranquil Willapa River—his wish to reach the promised land fulfilled. A wayside stop along Highway 6 marks his grave site. The ornately carved sign depicts the long journey west.

# RAINBOW FALLS
# STATE PARK

**Hours/Season:** Overnight; standard hours; year-round

**Area:** 124.7 acres; 3,400 feet of freshwater shoreline on the Chehalis River

**Facilities:** 47 standard campsites, 3 primitive campsites, 60-person group camp, 65 picnic sites, 2 kitchen shelters, 150-person group day-use area, restrooms, trailer dump station, children's play equipment, ballfield, 0.5-mile interpretive trail, 6.5 miles of hiking trail

**Attractions:** Camping, picnicking, fishing, hiking, kayaking

**Access:** From I-5 take Exit 77 (Highway 6 W, Pe Ell, Raymond), and take Highway 6 west for 17.3 miles to the park entrance.

This venerable old state park remains as charming today as it was when it was established as a community park in the early 1900s. Due to its long history, some centuries-old trees remain, providing shade for the park and nurturing a unique forest habitat.

The CCC constructed most of the facilities, including the sturdy log residence of

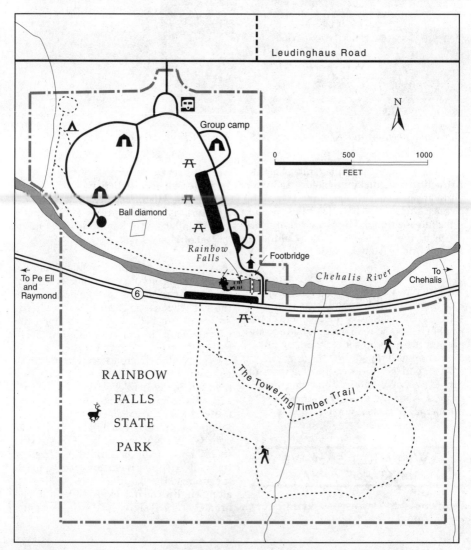

*The Chehalis River streams down rock slabs at Rainbow Falls.*

the ranger and the suspension bridge across the Chehalis River. The Rainbow Falls for which the park is named are low and relatively small, except during spring runoffs. However, most of the year the foaming water that surges through the narrow neck between two large rock outcroppings lifts a fine mist that, when hit by sunlight, creates a distinct rainbow. The falls and their rainbow namesake are best viewed from the vintage, springy suspension footbridge that crosses the river just downstream from them. Anglers try for cutthroat and rainbow trout that frequent pools above and below the falls.

The park's picnic area is a wide meadow shaded by immense old-growth Douglas fir and hemlock. Tables line the perimeter, and a ball diamond sits in one corner. Campsites along the loop road are in old fir, alder, and cedar, with an understory of salal and ferns. East of the entrance to the campground, a small group camp in a clearing has a picnic shelter and vault toilet.

Although its main facilities are to the north, a major portion of the park's acreage lies south of Highway 6. The wide shoulder along the north side of the highway provides parking for visitors using this part of the park. Aside from a picnic shelter and some playground equipment in a small clearing, this part of the park is devoted to hiking trails.

The shortest of these, "The Towering Timber," is a 0.5-mile-long interpretive trail. A park brochure identifies mosses, various species of ferns, and other plants along the trail. Douglas fir and western hemlock 175 to 200 feet tall give the trail its appropriate name. Other, longer trails that meander about this section of the park for several miles lead to additional grand views of spectacular trees.

## ELBOW LAKE STATE PARK (UNDEVELOPED)

**Area:** 320 acres; 13,000 feet of freshwater shoreline on Elbow, Beaver, and Bass lakes
**Facilities:** Primitive boat launch ramp, primitive campsites
**Attractions:** Boating, fishing, hiking

**Access:** At the intersection of Highways 507 and 510 on the east side of Yelm head southwest on Bald Hill Road SE. In 9 miles turn east on Elbow Lake Road SE, a deteriorating gravel road that reaches the park boundary in 1.3 miles. From here a jeep road continues another 1.4 miles around the south lobe of Elbow Lake to a primitive launch ramp.

⊥ This undeveloped state park consists of property around all but the extreme northern shoreline of Elbow Lake and extends east to include Beaver and Bass lakes. A rough, single-lane road, little more than a jeep path, leads to a tiny peninsula on the east shore at the "elbow" of the shallow, 36-acre lake. At the primitive dirt ramp here, visitors who want to fish or explore the shoreline can put in hand-carried boats.

De facto campsites have evolved on the peninsula and in the heavily wooded flat just above it, but there are no camping facilities here. A narrow road/path heads east just above this area to reach the strip of land separating tiny Bass and Beaver lakes. The lakes contain crappie, perch, catfish, and (appropriately) bass. This area is not serviced—pack it in, pack it out!

# MILLERSYLVANIA MEMORIAL STATE PARK

**Hours/Season:** Overnight; standard hours; year-round

**Area:** 841.7 acres; 3,300 feet of freshwater shoreline on Deep Lake

**Facilities:** 135 standard campsites, 52 RV sites, 4 primitive campsites, 20- and 40-person group camps, 216 picnic sites, 4 kitchen shelters, 300-person group day-use area, ballfield, restrooms, vault toilets, trailer dump station, 3 swimming beaches, bathhouse, boat launch ramp, 6.6 miles of hiking trail, 1.5-mile fitness trail; Environmental Learning Center with kitchen/dining hall, 16 squad huts, restrooms, 2 teaching shelters

**Attractions:** Camping, picnicking, hiking, fitness trail, swimming, boating, fishing

**Access:** At Exit 95 (Highway 121 S, Little Rock, Maytown) from I-90, take Maytown Road SW east for 2.6 miles, then turn north on Tilley Road SW, and reach the park in another 0.8 mile.

⊥ Millersylvania could actually be named "Mueller's Woods." This site was origi-

*A thick forest shades the campground at Millersylvania State Park.*

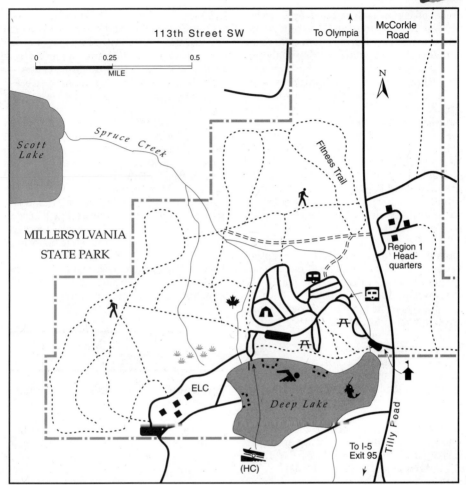

nally settled in 1881 by Johann Mueller (not known to be a relative of your authors). Mueller was a general in the Austrian army who married the daughter of Emperor Franz Josef I without benefit of official permission. For this transgression the couple was exiled to the U.S.; at some point their name was anglicized to Miller. Their homestead property was deeded to the state upon the death of the last remaining member of the family. During the the early 1930s the Depression-era Civilian Conservation Corps set up an area headquarters here, and most of the sturdy rock-and-log structures of the park reflect that time.

Northeast of the park's main road, numerous campground loops weave among enormous Douglas fir. The heavy shade of the forest canopy makes ground cover sparse, but the cathedral-like stand of cedar and fir provide privacy to the campsites. Tenting and hookup loops curve around a grassy playfield that is set up for baseball and volleyball. At the west end of the field, a massive stone fireplace is built into the outside wall of the park maintenance shops.

South of the road lies Deep Lake, ringed by pleasant woods. Parking loops lead to picnic areas and several massive log-and-stone picnic shelters and bathhouses. Picnic sites are scattered amid the trees along the shore; whatever grass was once here has long since been ground to dirt by the tread of thousands of visitors. The two swimming beaches are near-twins, although the one on the east is somewhat larger. Below the sandy beach, pilings topped by a chain link fence protect a shallow wading area, and a pier leads out to deeper roped-off water with a swim float at its outer edge. These beaches are the only spots where the shoreline is readily accessible; elsewhere the shore is held by trees and marsh growth.

A fishing pier and boat launch mark the west end of the main park area, next to a small private land holding within the park boundaries. "Boat launch" here means car-top or hand-carried boats only; a log barrier at water's edge prevents launching of trailered boats. The popular 66-acre lake, which is regularly planted with rainbow trout, provides good fishing from April through July. Motors are permitted; however, the speed limit is 5 mph. A commercial resort is on the east end of the lake.

The road continues west to the Environmental Learning Center. Here is another swimming beach, open playfields, picnic shelters, cabins, a kitchen/dining hall, and sheltered outdoor classrooms.

Trails weave through ferns, Scotch broom, an old orchard, and ancient timber. Watchful hikers may spot remnants of an old narrow-gauge railroad, several skid roads, and springboard notches in stumps, all evidence of logging activity dating to the early 1800s. Additional trails penetrate the wooded sections of the park north of the campground area. Some paths connect to a 1.5-mile fitness trail northeast from there. The State Parks Region 1 headquarters lies east of Tilley Road, across the road from the start of the fitness trail.

# JOHN R. JACKSON HOUSE STATE PARK

**Hours/Season:** Day-use; daily 2:00 P.M. to 4:00 P.M.; year-round
**Area:** 0.5 acre
**Facilities:** Historic log cabin
**Attractions:** Historical displays
**Access:** From Exit 68 (US 12 E, Morton, Yakima) from I-5, head east on US 12 for 2.6 miles to the intersection of US 12 and Jackson Highway. The state park is on the east side of the road just south of the intersection.

▲ This one-room log cabin was the first American pioneer home north of the Columbia River. It was built in 1848 by John R.

Jackson, an Illinois farmer who headed west to Oregon Territory and settled here on the fertile prairie land. Since Jackson's house was located on the north spur of the Oregon Trail, it was a favorite stop for travelers.

The house also served as a post office, as a voting place, and in 1850 as a courtroom for the U.S. district court. In later years the dwelling was enlarged and additional buildings were constructed to accommodate the increasing number of travelers visiting the Jacksons. Among these were Ulysses S. Grant and Isaac Stevens, Washington's first governor.

Age took its toll on the property, and all of the buildings except the original Jackson home were torn down. The house was saved and renovated by local and state historical societies. Most of the furniture and tools displayed in the cabin belonged to the Jackson family. It is open and staffed by a park interpreter for 2 hours each afternoon.

# MATILDA N. JACKSON STATE PARK

**Hours/Season:** Day-use; standard hours; year-round
**Area:** 5.2 acres
**Facilities:** Picnic tables, kitchen shelter, children's play equipment, vault toilets, historical monument
**Attractions:** Picnicking, historical display
**Access:** From Exit 68 (US 12 E, Morton, Yakima) from I-5, head east on US 12, and in 2.6 miles, at the intersection of US 12 and Jackson Highway, drive north for 0.3 mile; the park is located on the west side of the highway.

▲ John Jackson once had extensive property here on the banks of the south fork of the Newaukum River. Two small segments of his holdings have been donated to the State Parks and Recreation Commission. One is the site of the John R. Jackson house, described in the preceding section; the second is a small plot that is now a day-use park named for his wife, Matilda. The park is shaded by the only remaining Douglas fir in the immediate vicinity. A monument built by the Daughters of the American Revolution commemorates the fact that the Oregon Trail ran past the site.

# LEWIS AND CLARK STATE PARK

**Hours/Season:** Overnight; standard hours; year-round

**Area:** 528.3 acres

**Facilities:** 25 standard campsites, 80- and 120-person group camps, 62 picnic sites, 4 kitchen shelters, 100-person group day-use area, restrooms, horseshoe pits, children's play equipment, 3,500-square-foot building for rent to the public, vault toilets, interpretive trails, corral, horse loading ramps, 5 miles of hiking and equestrian trail

**Attractions:** Camping, picnicking, wading, playground activities, juvenile fishing, horseback riding, hiking

**Access:** From Exit 68 (US 12 E, Morton, Yakima), head east on US 12 for 2.6 miles, then drive south on the Jackson Highway to reach the main park entrance in 1.8 miles. The entrance to the equestrian area is east of Jackson Highway another 0.9 mile south of the main park entrance.

▲ Have you ever wondered what the forests in this area were like when the first pioneers saw them? Most of the forests we see today are second- or third-growth, and the predominate species are those that provide the most profitable timber harvests. At Lewis and Clark State Park one of the last major stands of old-growth forest remaining in the Puget Sound lowlands is preserved for our enjoyment and environmental education.

The 0.5-mile-long Old-Growth Forest Interpretive Trail loops through the the west side of the park, starting at a kiosk that tells the history of the old-growth forest and describes the habitat. Benches along the trail provide opportunities to stop and observe trees and plants and to consult the descriptive park brochure. Spectactular Douglas fir, grand fir, western hemlock, and western red cedar form a green canopy hundreds of feet overhead, and the faint whisper of wind through their upper branches is the only sound to be heard.

A second interpretive loop, the Trail of the Deer, leads past a series of stations, again described in a brochure, that depict the various life cycles in the forest ecosystem. The remainder of the park is laced with more hiking trails through equally spectacular timber. As magnificent as the forest is, not long ago it was even greater. The devastating Columbus Day windstorm of 1962 blew down over half of the park's trees; some 8.5 million board feet were lost.

The park's small campground has sites pressing back into timber and brush so dense that one feels like the only camper in the whole area. A small creek that runs through the day-use area near the entrance has been dammed to create a natural wading pool. The remainder of the picnic area and the adjoining playfield are grassy plots carved out of the thick surrounding woods. At a Y in the road to the Old-Growth Forest Trail, the left-hand spur leads to a small group camp at road's end. CCC construc-

*At Lewis and Clark State Park, several interpretive nature trails thread the forest.*

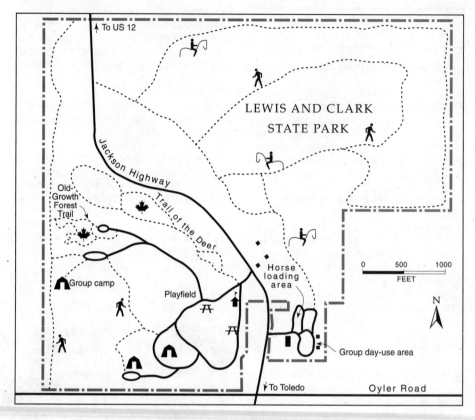

tion is evident throughout the park in the sturdy rock and log picnic shelters, restrooms, and ranger residences.

A second section of the park east of the Jackson Highway is devoted primarily to equestrian use. The entrance to this section is 0.1 mile south of the main park entrance, on the opposite (east) side of the road. A small corral, hitching posts, a loading ramp, and parking for horse trailers are along a pair of short loop roads. An equestrian trail leads northwest through the woods to the park boundary, then traces the north, east, and south perimeter of the park before returning to its starting point. Total loop distance is a little over 2 miles. A 1.75-mile-long hiking loop circles through the same area, inside the equestrian trail.

These modest facilities may soon be expanded. The Parks Commission, along with the Washington State Horse Council and the Department of Agriculture, is strongly backing a major equestrian center that is currently in the study and planning stage. When completed, the center will include both outdoor and covered arenas, judges' booth, bleachers, paddocks, and support facilities to make it suitable for hosting regional multiday championship events for both western and English riders. It is hoped that construction will begin in 1993.

This section of the park also has a day-use group camp located in a building that housed the Mount St. Helens Visitor Center for a time after the mountain's 1980 eruption. The center was later moved to a new facility at Seaquest State Park; the building is now available for daytime rental to organized groups for events such as classes or weddings.

## IKE KINSWA STATE PARK

**Hours/Season:** Overnight; standard hours; year-round

**Area:** 454 acres; 46,000 feet of freshwater shoreline on Mayfield Lake and the Tilton and Cowlitz rivers

**Facilities:** 60 standard campsites, 41 RV sites, 2 primitive sites, 51 picnic sites, restrooms, trailer dump station, children's play equipment, bathhouse, swimming beach, boat launch ramp, snacks (concession), 3.1 miles of hiking trail

**Attractions:** Camping, picnicking, boating, waterskiing, paddling, fishing, swimming, hiking, bicycling

**Access:** From Exit 68 (US 12 E, Morton, Yakima), head east on US 12 for 14 miles, then turn north on Silver Creek Road. At a Y-intersection in 1.9 miles, take Harmony Road east 1.6 miles to the park.

⚓ When electric companies construct dams for hydroelectric power, recreationists often benefit too, as they gain lakes for all sorts of water-oriented activities. This is the case with Ike Kinswa State Park, which was acquired from Tacoma City Light after the construction of the Mayfield Dam. The dam creates a 14-mile-long, 2,200-acre reservoir at the point where the Tilton River joins the Cowlitz; the state park stretches along the northeast corner of Mayfield Lake and extends 4 miles up the flooded arm of the Tilton. The spacious reservoir easily accommodates boating, paddling, fishing, waterskiing, and swimming without crowding. As a result, the state park is extremely popular during the summer, and its campgrounds are filled all season long.

The rivers were bountiful providers of fish for the Cowlitz Indians, who once had villages along the banks. With the construction of the dam, most of the ancient sites were flooded; a pair of graves within the park, marked for historic preservation, are the only vestige of this heritage. To acknowledge the history of the Cowlitz tribe in the area, the name of the park was changed in 1971 from Mayfield to Ike Kinswa, who was a member of the tribe that lived here in the 1880s and owned some of the land on which the park is located.

At the south end of the bridge over the mouth of the Tilton River, a single-lane boat launch ramp, with adjoining float, drops from a gravel parking lot to the water. The remainder of the park lies north of the bridge. Three camping loops are laid out on a triangular-shaped peninsula southeast of the road. The first loop, equipped with hookups, has some sites fronting on

the low-bank rocky beach of Mayfield Lake. The other two loops lie in woods, closer to the bank of the Cowlitz. At the beach between them a small grassy slope flows down to the water's edge, permitting easy beaching of boats. A trail circles the peninsula between the water and the campsites.

The day-use area is west of the highway. Here a small arm of the Tilton River loops around a wooded islet. The shallow channel behind the island is roped off at both ends for swimming and paddling. A broad swimming beach is roped off at the northwest end of the channel, and above it a grassy slope leads up to a bathhouse, concession stand, and playground equipment. A second side lawn tapers down to the west to the shore of the Tilton. Picnic tables are

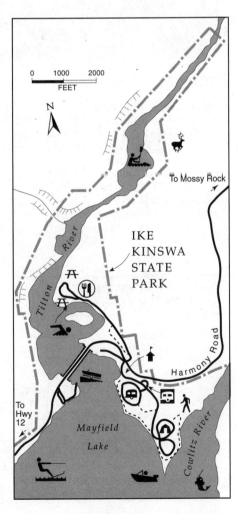

*The swimming beach at Ike Kinswa State Park is an attraction for all ages.*

scattered throughout both of these areas.

A segment of trail parallels the west side of the entrance road from the gate to the channel behind the island. With luck you might spot some of the deer, beavers, otters, and skunks that make the park home. From a boat, keep an eye out for tall, bare fir snags along the shoreline. Eagles nest here in winter months, and osprey "sublet" the sites when the eagles migrate during the summer.

## PACKWOOD STATE PARK (UNDEVELOPED)

**Area:** 174.6 acres; 1,000 feet of freshwater shoreline on Skate Creek and the Cowlitz River
**Facilities:** None
**Attractions:** Fishing, nature study, hiking
**Access:** From US 12 at Packwood, take Forest Road 52 northwest from town across the Cowlitz River. The park property lies west of this road, and south of Forest Road 47.

▲ This undeveloped state park property straddling Skate Creek is bounded on the west, north, and east by forest roads. Some of the property is covered by old-growth Douglas fir, and although there are no developed facilities at present, the property is accessible for short hikes or fishing in Skate Creek.

## SEAQUEST STATE PARK

**Hours/Season:** Overnight; standard hours; year-round
**Area:** 296 acres; 2,640 feet of freshwater shoreline on Silver Lake
**Facilities:** 76 standard campsites, 16 RV sites, 8 primitive campsites, 50-person group camp with 3 adirondack shelters and 2 kitchen shelters, 113 picnic sites, kitchen shelter, 100-person group day-use area, restrooms, horseshoe pits, children's play equipment, campfire ring, 8 miles of hiking trail
**Attractions:** Camping, picnicking, hiking, fishing, interpretive displays and programs at Mount St. Helens National Volcanic Monument Interpretive Center
**Nearby:** Mount St. Helens National Volcanic Monument Interpretive Center

**Access:** At Exit 49 (Highway 504 E, Toutle, Castle Rock) from I-5 head east on Highway 504, and in 5.6 miles arrive at the park entrance.

⏚ A splendid stand of timber near the shore of Silver Lake shelters Seaquest State Park. Gape in awe at the enormous old-growth trees, some over 7 feet in diameter, that have been preserved in the park.

The campground is split into three segments: the northwest pair of loops lie in a wooded area of tall fir and hemlock; in a second loop to the west, hookup sites line up side by side in an open field; the third loop, to the south near the highway, lies amid alder and maple, with thick brush undercover providing seclusion for the sites. A walk-in bicycle camping area is laid out west of the entrance to this loop.

The picnic area has picnic and kitchen shelters in a large meadow at the center, with individual sites placed in the woods along the edge. You can picnic in seclusion or communal conviviality, whichever you choose. A trail leads from the picnic area down through a huge conduit under the highway to the interpretive center. A road east of the picnic area ends at a long grassy ballfield and the entrance to the group camp. East of the picnic area, a short nature trail loops through the woods. A longer path wanders along service roads and then follows a trail through the forest at the north end of the park. You might see deer, squirrels, owls, or any of a variety of other birds that live here.

Although the park includes frontage on Silver Lake, the shoreline is a wide marsh, and no water access is available at the park. A public boat launch is 1 mile to the northeast. The 2,000-acre lake offers some of the best fishing in the state for bass, crappie, and other spiny rays.

The state park property is host to the U.S. Forest Service's Mount St. Helens National Volcanic Monument Interpretive Center—and quite some center it is! Telescopes outside the beautiful new building focus on the distant truncated rim of the volcano. Inside, displays trace the history of the mountain from the time of the Indians to its 1980 eruptions. A theater shows a short movie on the eruption of the mountain. Here also is a scale model of the region with various geographical features identified.

Most unique, however, is the 20-foot-diameter model of the mountain, with stairs descending into the interior. Walls along the staircase show the strata below the surface of the mountain; at its heart a red magma tube flows up from a hole crafted to create the illusion of looking deep into the molten core of the earth.

## PARADISE POINT STATE PARK

**Hours/Season:** Overnight; standard hours; weekends and holidays only, September 30 to March 27
**Area:** 88 acres; 6,180 feet of freshwater shoreline on the East Fork of the Lewis River
**Facilities:** 70 standard campsites, 9 primitive campsites, 29 picnic sites, restrooms, vault toilets, trailer dump station, primitive boat launch, 2.5 miles of hiking trail
**Attractions:** Camping, picnicking, hiking, boating, fishing
**Access:** At Exit 16 (NW 319th Street, La Center) from I-5, head east on NW 391th for 0.2 mile, then turn north on NW Paradise Park Road and reach the park entrance in 0.9 mile.

⏚ Paradise Point was perhaps aptly named when it was established some 35 years ago, before I-5 was built and thousands of cars daily roared along the thoroughfare. The campsites are immediately east of the northbound lanes of I-5, and the day-use area extends under it. As a consequence, traffic noise pervades all but the wooded hiking trails of the park. Although quiet and solitude are not one of its strong points today, the park does offer easy access to some fine boating and fishing on the East Fork of the Lewis River. The stream flows wide and smooth for a mile down to its junction with the main branch of the Lewis River, and then in 3 more miles meets the Columbia.

The campground is in a flat on top of a steep wooded bluff that drops down to the banks of the Lewis River. Some sites are shaded by timber; a few are in the meadow of an old orchard. At the west edge of the campground loops a gated service road leads into the woods to a series of primitive walk-in sites.

The road to the day-use area drops steeply downhill, ending just under the freeway. Here a single-lane gravel launch ramp enters the river, and picnic tables are scattered among the trees. A sandy beach below the freeway invites wading or swimming in the quiet water. Additional picnic sites are west of the freeway along the south shore. In late summer, dessert is provided from thick clusters of blackberry bushes.

A trail heads east along the bank of the river to the eastern end of the park. This trail is joined by two steep paths down the hillside from the camp area, one starting at the entrance to the campground loops, and the second descending a ravine at the east end of the string of primitive campsites. A short spur from this latter trail leads over to the creek that flows down the ravine, and to what, in the run-offs of spring and early summer, is a pretty 25-foot-high waterfall.

## BATTLE GROUND LAKE STATE PARK

**Hours/Season:** Overnight; standard hours; year-round

**Area:** 280 acres; 4,100 feet of freshwater shoreline on Battle Ground Lake

**Facilities:** 35 standard campsites, 15 primitive campsites, 32-person group camp with 4 adirondack shelters, 57 picnic sites, 3 kitchen shelters, 150-person group day-use area, restrooms, vault toilets, trailer dump station, children's play equipment, horseshoe pits, bathhouse, snacks (concession), launch ramp, swimming beach, 2 miles of hiking trail, primitive equestrian camping area, 5 miles of equestrian trail

**Attractions:** Camping, picnicking, swimming, boating, paddling, fishing, scuba

*Battle Ground Lake, with its deep, cold water, is a favorite with trout fishermen.*

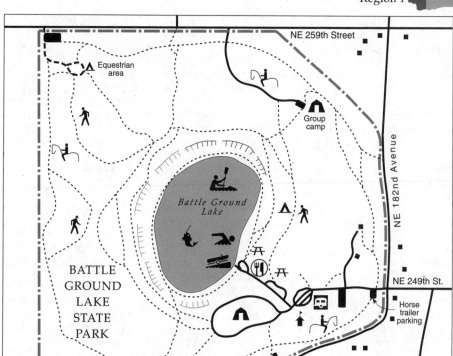

NE 259th Street

Equestrian area

Group camp

Battle Ground Lake

BATTLE GROUND LAKE STATE PARK

NE 182nd Avenue

NE 249th St.

Horse trailer parking

NE Palmer Road

0    500    1000
FEET

N

To Battle Ground

diving, nature study, hiking, horseback riding, organized sports

**Access:** From Main Street in the town of Battle Ground, turn north on Grace Avenue, and in 0.5 mile turn east on NE 229th Street. Continue east for 2.5 miles on this road, which at various corners successively becomes NE Hessien Road, NE 244th Street, and NE Palmer Road. The park entrance is at the intersection of NE Palmer Road and NE 249th Street. To reach the group camp and equestrian camp, continue north on NE 182nd Avenue (which NE Palmer becomes at the park entrance) for 0.5 mile, then turn west on NE 259th Street. The gated group camp entrance is on the south side of the road in 0.3 mile, and the equestrian camp entrance (unmarked) is another 0.4 mile.

What do Battle Ground Lake State Park and Crater Lake National Park have in common? Both lakes are believed to have been created by the collapse of a volcanic cone to form a caldera, which later filled with water. Dimensions are different, of course, because Battle Ground Lake is a modest 28 acres, while Crater Lake is 22 square miles in size, but the geological events that created the two are similar.

The park's main camping and day-use areas are found on the south side of the park. A campground loop through second-growth timber has gravel pulloffs and enough brush to provide some site isolation. A string of walk-in campsites runs around the south and east sides of the lake; a few towering Douglas firs shade the sites.

Douglas fir are also scattered around a large meadow just inside the park entrance; here are picnic shelters and tables, a snack stand, and children's playground equipment. Paths lead downhill to the lakeshore and a sandy beach above a roped-off swim-

85

ming area. At the south end of this beach is a single-lane boat launch ramp with an adjoining dock. Due to its volcanic origin, the spring-fed lake is exceptionally deep. The cold water contributes to excellent fishing: rainbow trout will eagerly strike at an angler's fly.

Trails trace the perimeter of the lake. One stays close to the water's edge, with periodic brush-free points that permit shoreside fishing; another path follows the forested rim of the crater above the lake. Rest stops at log benches along the way may once have offered scenic views of the lake, but forest growth now hides all but glimpses of the water. Occasional spurs link the trails. The upper trail becomes the access path to the primitive walk-in campsites.

Battle Ground is one of the few state parks that has facilities for equestrians. A primitive campground at the northwest corner of the park has been set aside exclusively for their use. Here a small meadow can be used for parking horse trailers and staking out horses; another similar meadow a short distance away has picnic tables, fire grates, and a vault toilet for riders who camp at the park. The several miles of service roads around the perimeter of the park are open to horses and riders. Equestrian trails may be used for hiking, but walkers should yield the right-of-way to horses and avoid spooking them.

## REED ISLAND MARINE STATE PARK

**Hours/Season:** Overnight; standard hours; year-round

**Area:** 508 acres; 6 miles of freshwater shoreline on the Columbia River

**Facilities:** 5 primitive campsites, 5 picnic sites, vault toilet, 0.5-mile hiking trail

**Attractions:** Camping, picnicking, fishing, hiking, boating, waterskiing, birdwatching, nature study

**Access:** *Boat access only.* Located in the Columbia River, 1 mile east of Washougal. Nearest boat launch ramp at the Port of Camas/Washougal.

It was on Reed Island that, in November of 1792, Lieutenant William Broughton, captain of the *Chatham*, claimed the Columbia River for Great Britain. Broughton was a member of the Vancouver Expedition, which was returning from its epic exploration of Puget Sound and the waters around Vancouver Island. Although both the *Chatham* and Captain Vancouver's *Discovery* had intended to explore the Columbia, only Broughton's ship was able to make it over the bar at its mouth. Earlier explorers had entered the mouth of the Columbia, but none had tried to travel up the river. Two of Broughton's small boats rowed 80 miles upstream before stopping at Reed Island, laying claim to the river, and also naming Mount Hood for the Lord of the Admiralty.

Today Reed Island is a marine state park, accessible only by boat, although the channel on its north side is nearly shallow enough to wade across during low water. Five primitive campsites, picnic sites, and a vault toilet are on the southeast side of the island; a sketchy trail leads from here through tall canary grass to the north shore. A heron rookery is on the west end of the island, and the Bridgefield Wildlife Refuge is to the north on the mainland. The park is an excellent place for spotting and photographing birds. The wooded interior of the island also hosts deer and other wildlife.

## BEACON ROCK STATE PARK

**Hours/Season:** Overnight; standard hours; main campground closed from the end of October to the end of March

**Area:** 4,482 acres; 9,500 feet of freshwater shoreline on the Columbia River

**Facilities:** 33 standard campsites, 2 primitive campsites, 200-person group camp, 71 picnic sites, 3 picnic shelters, restrooms, 50-person group day-use area, children's play equipment, 2 boat launch ramps, dock, 1.25-mile nature trail, 9.5 miles of hiking, bicycling, and equestrian trail, 13 miles of fire road

**Attractions:** Camping, picnicking, hiking, fishing, boating, paddling, rock climbing, horseback riding, mountain biking

**Nearby:** Bonneville Dam

**Access:** On Highway 14, drive 3 miles east of Skamania or 6.9 miles west of the Bridge of the Gods.

Beacon Rock is an andesite plug—the 848-foot-high basalt heart of a volcano that has long since eroded away. For local Indians the rock marked the lower end of the Columbia River rapids, below which the river flowed obstruction-free to the Pacific Ocean (dams have since flooded the rapids). The Lewis and Clark Expedition camped near the base of the rock and name it Beacon Rock, although for many years it was called Castle Rock until the original name was restored in 1916.

Legend has it that the rock was first climbed by an Indian princess, Wahatpolitan, in an attempt to save her son from the anger of her father, who disapproved of her marriage. She and her son died atop the rock, and the wailings of her spirit are said to be still heard when warm chinook winds whip over the summit.

The first recorded climb of Beacon Rock occurred in August of 1901, following closely the route used by the present-day trail. In 1915 Henry Biddle, who owned the rock at the time, started construction on the present 4,000-foot-long trail, which was completed in 1918. The trail begins at the northwest corner of the rock, adjacent the highway. From here it threads through fifty-three switchbacks up the south side of the rock before reaching the small, flat summit. Thousands of casual hikers reach the top each year, because the number of switchbacks makes the trail less steep and a railing protects its vertical outer edge. Leaving the trail at any point is dangerous, and hikers should be careful not to dislodge rocks or other debris that could be hazardous (or fatal) to rock climbers on the cliffs below. Views from the top are breathtaking in every direction. The vast Columbia River Gorge stretches east and west; to the north is the sheer 900-foot-high basalt face of Hamilton Mountain; to the south ribbons of delicate waterfalls plummet down the walls on the Oregon side of the river.

*Beacon Rock looms above the Columbia River.*

The vertical cliffs at the lower part of the south side of the rock provide some of the best and most challenging rock climbing routes in the Northwest. Only properly equipped rock climbers with advanced skills should attempt these routes; all must sign in and out at the park climbing register. Hazards here include poison oak below

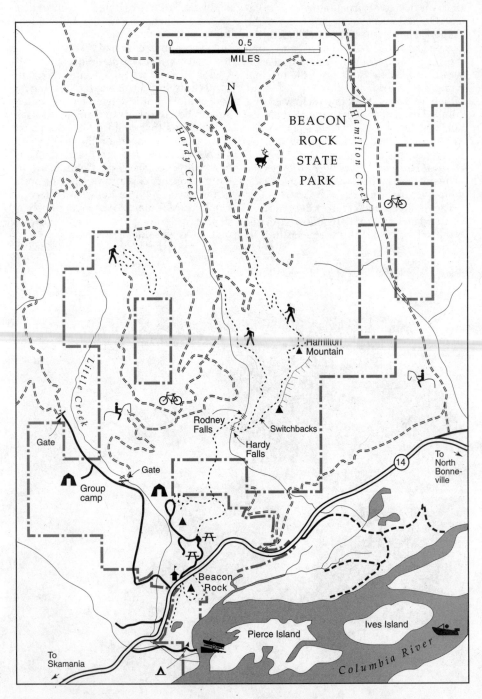

and rockfall from above.

Picnic and camping areas are located in the wooded uplands across the highway from Beacon Rock. Picnic areas lie on both sides of the road 100 yards uphill from the highway in a stand of Douglas fir and alder. The campground loop at the end of this road has sites in huge old-growth Douglas fir with dense ground cover. East of the rock, a paved road leads past the ranger station to a group camp in a meadow with picnic tables, vault toilets, and a pair of adirondack shelters.

The largest portion of the park lies inland and north of the highway, encompassing Hamilton Mountain and the Hardy Creek drainage. A gated service road 0.3 mile southeast of the group camp is the starting point for a string of more than 13 miles of narrow fire roads that climb through the forest to the steep ridgelines at the north and west sides of the park. These roads are open for equestrian and mountain bike use, as well as hiking.

From trailheads at both the campground and the east picnic area, foot trails join to climb uphill 1 mile to Hardy Creek, where short spurs lead to picturesque Rodney Falls above the trail and Hardy Falls below it. From here the trail continues uphill with a vengeance, gaining nearly 1,200 feet of elevation in a never-ending series of switchbacks to reach the summit of Hamilton Mountain. The route follows the ridgeline north before joining one of the fire roads that then loops back down, meeting the uphill trail about 0.5 mile above the Hardy Creek crossing.

West from the ranger station 0.3 mile, a road marked only by a Recreation Area sign leads east through commercial property, under the railroad track, and across a single-lane bridge to the park's marine facilities and yet another campground. Amid the wooded area around the road-end, the campsites are primitive and unstructured. Below, a launch ramp with adjoining boarding float drops into the Columbia River. A steep grass slope east of the

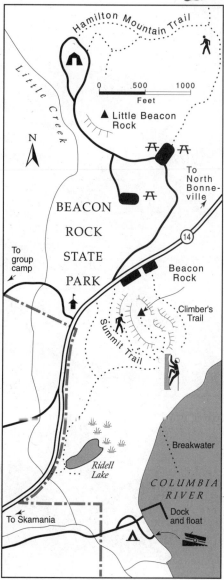

launch ramp has another narrow hand-carried boat ramp and a dock leading down to a 250-foot-long L-shaped float. From here enjoy wonderful views of the south and west faces of Beacon Rock.

# REGION 2

- *The San Juan Islands*
- *North Puget Sound*
- *Skagit River*
- *Skykomish River*

## PATOS ISLAND MARINE STATE PARK

**Hours/Season:** Overnight; year-round
**Area:** 207.4 acres; 20,000 feet of saltwater shoreline
**Facilities:** 4 primitive campsites, vault toilets, 2 mooring buoys, 1.2 miles of hiking trail, *no water, no garbage collection*
**Attractions:** Camping, picnicking, boating, paddling, fishing, hiking, beachcombing, tide pools, scuba diving
**Access:** *Boat access only.* Patos Island is 5.5 miles north of Orcas Island in the San Juan archipelago. Nearest launch facilities are at North Beach and West Beach on Orcas Island, or on the mainland at Bellingham, Larrabee State Park, Anacortes, or Hale Passage.

Patos Island, which sits near the Canadian border at Boundary Pass (the junction of Haro Strait and the Strait of Georgia) is the northernmost of all of the San Juan Islands. Its beacon on Alden Point marks the turning point for vessels headed to and from the Vancouver and Fraser River areas. Back in the days when lighthouses were manned, the entire island was a lighthouse reserve; now only the automated lighthouse and the boarded-up residences

are retained by the Coast Guard, and the remainder of the island is now a marine state park.

The only anchorage is Active Cove, at the west tip of the island. This narrow cove, with its wave-carved sandstone shore, is protected from the north by Alden Point, and the south by Little Patos Island. The cove has two mooring buoys and space for some additional anchorage, although dense eelgrass along the bottom makes setting a hook challenging. Boats of any draft must enter the cove from the west, as the narrow channel at the east end of Little Patos is very shallow and swept by tidal currents. The island's few primitive campsites lie on a low, grassy flat above the gravel beach at the east end of Active Cove.

A 1.75-mile-long loop trail that circles the wooded center rib of the island begins at the campground and proceeds along the rocky south-shore bluff before turning inland through the brushy woods. After starting its return leg on the wooded north flank of the island, the trail touches the north shore, offering beach access. The beach can be walked east to Toe Point.

The beach hike on the north shore of Patos Island is a delight, as each of the series of slight coves holds unique treasures to attract and fascinate the hiker. One cove may have kelp and seaweed creating

---

Opposite: *A quiet anchorage in Active Cove at Patos Island Marine State Park*

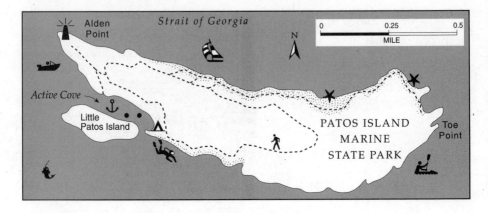

abstract patterns on boulders; the next rippled, flat sandstone coated with thousands of indigo mussels; another displays fanciful, wave-carved sandstone formations.

Toe Point is finally reached on the east end of the island, where sandstone headlands frame a tiny cove, and the icy cone of Mount Baker provides a backdrop. Although the hike is most enjoyable at minus tide, tide level should pose no hazard for the trip, as the low headlands between the beaches are easily crossed by short inland scrambles.

From the north beach access, the island loop trail cuts back inland, crossing the low backbone of the island near the old Coast Guard station. From here an overgrown service road leads back to the starting point of the trail at the campground.

## SUCIA ISLAND MARINE STATE PARK

**Hours/Season:** Overnight; year-round
**Area:** 564 acres; 77,700 feet of saltwater shoreline
**Facilities:** 55 primitive campsites, 16- and 25-person group camps, 3 picnic shelters, composting toilets, docks with floats, 50 mooring buoys, 6.2 miles of hiking trail, artificial reef
**Attractions:** Camping, picnicking, hiking, swimming, clamming, crabbing, fossil hunting, beachcombing, tide pools, boating, paddling, fishing, scuba diving, birdwatching
**Access:** *Boat access only.* Sucia Island is 2.5

miles north of Orcas Island. Nearest launch ramps are at North Beach and West Beach on Orcas Island, or on the mainland at Bellingham, Larrabee State Park, Anacortes, or Hale Passage.

This crown jewel of Washington's marine state parks benefits from startling geological formations. The island is formed from five layers of alternately hard and softer sandstone and shale that were deposited 65 million years ago in a great sea, and over time were severely folded and tilted. The horseshoe shape of the island is due to this folding, while the glaciers that covered the area, and the ocean waters that followed them, are responsible for the erosion patterns. Sandstone monoliths stand at water's edge, where waves have chiseled them from beach walls. Fossil seashells are found imbedded in the stratified wall on the southernmost finger of the island leading to Ev Henry Point.

The inland portions of the island are covered with dense brush and trees, broken only by service roads—formerly logging roads—that link the bays to the center of the island. Eleven clearings at the heads of the bays have designated campgrounds, with the most developed facilities at Fossil Bay; the park's administrative office is also located there. Snoring Bay and Ewing Cove have a few primitive sites. Camping is permitted only in designated areas—those who randomly pitch their tents may find themselves cited by a ranger.

The largest of the island's inlets is Echo Bay, which opens southeast toward Rosario Strait. More than a dozen mooring buoys line its head; anchorages here can be a bit bouncy when southeasterly winds from Rosario Strait push swells into the shallow head of the bay. Two long, wooded islands in Echo Bay, North Finger and South Finger, are the only privately owned islands of the Sucia Group. The small island off the inner tip of South Finger, tentatively named Justice Island, was confiscated from a drug-running operation and turned over to the state. Because it has nesting eagles and a seal rookery, it is closed to the public.

The arm of Sucia that forms the northern shore of Echo Bay ends at narrow Ewing Cove, framed on the south by a chain of rock islets—the Cluster Islands and Stoney Reef—and on the north by the long sandstone finger of Ewing Island. Hulls of three old vessels have been sunk just beyond the outer mooring buoy to form a fish habitat for an underwater park. Boaters should enter the cove cautiously from the east, keeping an eye out for the rocks of Stoney Reef. The small channel at the west end of Ewing Island is too shallow and raked by

tidal currents to provide a safe passage.

The end of Sucia's south arm is indented by two more bays, Snoring Bay and Fossil Bay. The smaller, Snoring Bay, is favored by kayakers who wish to avoid the crowds of the larger anchorages. Fossil Bay sees the most activity; in addition to a crowd of mooring buoys, it has two docks and the most developed camping facilities.

For those wishing to escape the bustle of Fossil Bay, yet not forego its shoreside amenities, just north of the narrow strip of land at its head is Fox Cove. This beautiful sandy-beached cove is protected on the south by a thin rock finger from the main island and on the west by Little Sucia Island. It is best to approach Fox Cove from the northwest, as the narrow channel on the south side of Little Sucia is bordered by unmarked submerging rocks. Little Sucia itself is open for day-use, but fires and overnight camping are prohibited.

Shallow Bay, which offers the best protection in heavy weather, lies on the west side of Sucia Island. Although rocks en-

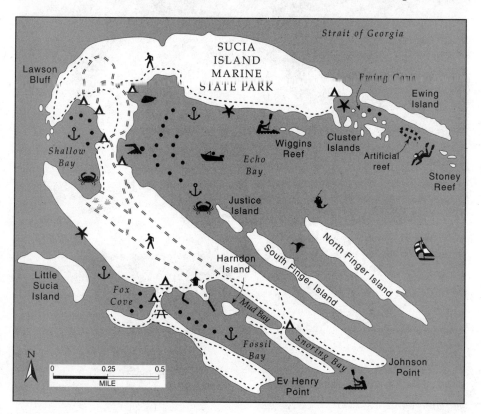

93

croach on the entrance on both sides, day marks clearly show a safe channel. When mooring or anchoring in the circular bay, be sure to check the depth and tide level, for its name was not chosen whimsically, and portions of the bay dry at minus tides. A particularly interesting sandstone formation is found at the edge of the trees at the northeast side of Shallow Bay: Chinaman Rock, a sandstone face pocked with worn hollows and body-sized caves which, legend has it, were used during the late 1800s as hiding places by smuggled Chinese aliens trying to avoid being spotted by immigration patrols.

A good long day can be spent exploring trails that probe the extended arms of land that make up the island. One trail runs out

*Caves in the sandstone bluffs of Sucia Island are said to have been used to hide smuggled Chinese aliens during the 1800s.*

the main south arm to Johnson Point, swinging near the beaches for views of South Finger Island and Snoring Bay. A second trail on this side of Fossil Bay crosses the narrow flat between Mud and Snoring bays, then runs down the center of the slim peninsula along their southern side. Trails head west from the head of Fossil Bay to the rocky point on the south side of Fox Cove and along the beach around the shale and sandstone promontory of Ev Henry Point.

Two trails leave the northernmost campground at Shallow Bay, one above the sheer rock face of Lawson Bluff, and one headed to the northeast end of the island and Ewing Cove. The Lawson Bluff trail runs mostly through dense forest, but occasional breaks provide gut-wrenching views down its cliffs and north to Patos Island. After a forested start, the Ewing Cove Trail swings back to the edge of the bench along the north side of Echo Bay. Here are impressive views of the bay and sandstone walls carved by waves in an endless variety of shapes and textures.

# MATIA ISLAND MARINE STATE PARK

**Hours/Season:** Overnight; year-round; floats removed in winter
**Area:** 145 acres; 20,676 feet of saltwater shoreline. *Public use restricted to 5 acres and 680 feet of saltwater shoreline*
**Facilities:** 6 primitive campsites, 7 picnic tables, composting toilet, dock and float, 2 mooring buoys, 1 mile of hiking trail, *no water, no garbage collection*
**Attractions:** Camping, picnicking, fishing, scuba diving, clamming, crabbing, tide pools, beachcombing, birdwatching, hiking, boating, paddling
**Access:** *Boat access only.* Matia Island is 2.5 miles north of Orcas Island and 1.5 miles east of Sucia Island. Nearest launch facilities are at North Beach and West Beach on Orcas Island, and on the mainland at Bellingham, Larrabee State Park, Anacortes, and Hale Passage.

Although it is a companion to popular Sucia Island State Park, scarcely more than 3 miles to the northwest, Matia sees far fewer visitors due to its limited anchorage

and camping space. Only 5 acres at the west end of Matia are developed for public use; the remainder of the island is a wildlife refuge under the jurisdiction of the U.S. Fish and Wildlife Service, with access permitted only as long as wildlife and seabirds remain undisturbed.

Tiny Rolfe Cove, where the state park lies, is enclosed by sandstone cliffs on the south side and by a small, steep-walled rock island on the north. A dock and float are located at the gravel beach at the head of the cove; two mooring buoys along the side of the cove provide the only other moorage. Anchorage here is chancy, as the gravel bottom is rather poor holding ground, and tidal currents swirling around the small island at the entrance to the cove tend to swing boats about their anchor point, pulling on the hook from undesired directions.

At one time a well existed at the campsite, but the water became unsafe to drink and the well was capped; bring in the water that you need, and carry garbage out with you. Six campsites lie in the trees above the beach, and an ingenious, high-tech marvel of a self-composting toilet rises at the base of a nearby hill.

A loop trail leads beyond the campground into the wildlife reserve, with one leg heading down the center of the island to emerge at the head of another long cove at the southeast side. The return loop of the trail runs along the south side of the island past faint traces of what were once the cabin and gardens of a recluse, Elvin Smith. Smith lived here for nearly 30 years, during which time he gained a reputation as a mystic and mail-order faith healer. He and a friend disappeared in 1921 in heavy weather while rowing back from Orcas Island with supplies.

The cove on the island's southeast side that is protected from the south by a long finger ridge would make a choice anchorage but for rocks near its entrance and a very shallow bottom. However, with caution it can still be used by keeping north of the entrance rocks and anchoring well out from the end of the cove.

A brushy, indistinct path follows above the steep, cliffy northern shoreline of this cove to the extreme east end of the island, where wave-cut sandstone walls rim a sandy beach that looks east to Puffin Island, just offshore. Puffin, which is also part of

*Tiny Rolfe Cove at Matia Island has space for several boats.*

the wildlife refuge, is a haul-out spot for seals and sea lions and a nesting area for colonies of murres, auklets, puffins, and pigeon guillemots. If you can follow the obscure trail, take binoculars and a camera to observe and photograph the activity from a distance—but please don't disturb the wildlife.

## CLARK ISLAND MARINE STATE PARK

**Hours/Season:** Overnight; year-round
**Area:** 55 acres; 11,292 feet of saltwater shoreline
**Facilities:** 8 primitive campsites, 2 picnic sites, 2 fire rings, vault toilets, 9 mooring buoys, *no water, no garbage collection*
**Attractions:** Camping, picnicking, hiking, beachcombing, tide pools, boating, paddling, fishing, birdwatching, clamming, mussels, scuba diving
**Access:** *Boat access only.* Clark Island is 1.75 miles north of Lawrence Point, the northeast tip of Orcas Island. Nearest launch

facilities are at North Beach and Obstruction Pass on Orcas Island, or on the mainland at Anacortes, Larrabee State Park, Bellingham, and Hale Passage.

Clark Island, Barnes Island, and The Sisters are a group of small islands off the northeast tip of Orcas Island. Barnes is privately owned, The Sisters are part of the San Juan Islands National Wildlife Refuge, and Clark Island is in its entirety a marine state park. The north half is covered with thick impenetrable brush and trees, which makes the narrow, steep, rocky shoreline in this part of the slender island accessible only by small boat or kayak. However, the undersea walls hold items of interest to scuba divers—starfish, urchins, anemones, and sea squirts. (All the seashores and seabed of the San Juan archipelago are a marine sanctuary. The taking or destruction of any marine specimen, except for food, is prohibited.)

The south end of the island has two broad beaches—rock and cobble on the east and sand on the west. The beaches are separated by a strip of brush and trees that

*Black oystercatchers frequent islands and rocks of the San Juan Islands National Wildlife Refuge. (Photo by Bob and Ira Spring)*

protects the island's eight primitive campsites. Trails that lace through the campsites join the two beaches. A longer path leads around the south end of the island along the edge of the bluff above the beach, dropping occasionally into small pocket coves with tide pools that harbor a wondrous array of marine creatures.

Mooring buoys are set on both sides of the island just off the south beaches. Those on the east side lie in a basin behind a baring rock reef; avoid the reef by approaching cautiously from the north near the shore. The island has no water, and no garbage collection—pack it in, pack it out.

## STUART ISLAND MARINE STATE PARK

**Hours/Season:** Overnight; year-round
**Area:** Prevost/Reid harbors, 85.3 acres, 33,030 feet of saltwater shoreline; Turn Point, 62.4 acres, 3,800 feet of saltwater shoreline on Haro Strait
**Facilities:** 19 primitive campsites, picnic

units, water, 22 mooring buoys, dock with float, marine pumpout station, hiking trails
**Attractions:** Camping, picnicking, hiking, clamming, crabbing, fishing, boating, paddling, sightseeing
**Access:** *Boat access only.* Stuart Island lies at the northeast side of Haro Strait, 5 miles northwest of San Juan Island. Nearest launch ramps are at West Beach on Orcas Island, and Roche Harbor, Mitchell Bay, or Jackson Beach on San Juan Island.

For diversity as well as beauty, few parks in the San Juan Islands can challenge Stuart Island. Reid Harbor, one of the two large bays that bracket the park land, is a miniature fjord with steep hillsides, while the second harbor, Prevost, is more shallow and open, with one side defined by a low, wooded islet. At the far end of Stuart Island, Turn Point offers stunning vistas to the rugged outlines of Canada's Gulf Islands. The beach at the end of Reid Harbor is one of the better clamming areas in the San Juans, and at minus tide little work is required to dig a limit of littleneck and

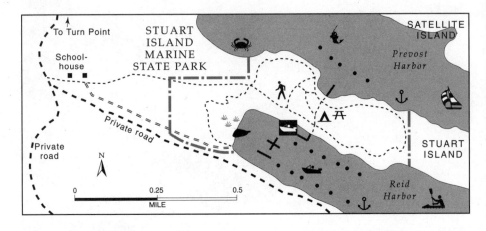

butter clams. Eelgrass in Prevost Harbor hides Dungeness crabs, and a crab pot over the side may result in an evening meal.

The state park laps over a high spine of timber-covered rock that separates its two anchorages. Campsites are found on this ridge and in the woods at the head of Reid Harbor. Both areas have water—a rarity in San Juan parks.

Satellite Island encloses the northeast side of Prevost Harbor; although there are channels around both ends of this island, the one on the south is laced with rocks and reefs. The only safe approach is at the north end of the harbor, between the north end of Satellite Island and Charles Point. Mooring buoys and a dock and float mark the site of the park. There is ample room for anchor-

*Morning comes to Stuart Island's Prevost Harbor.*

age in the harbor's uniform 6-fathom depth, but thick eelgrass on the bottom makes it a challenge to securely set a hook.

The entrance to Reid Harbor is partly blocked by tiny Cemetery and Gossip islands, both undeveloped public property administered by the Bureau of Land Management; the entrance channel passes to the west of both. Once inside, steep hillsides rise abruptly on either side of the long, narrow waterway, while the head of the harbor has a gently sloping beach. More than a dozen park mooring buoys ring the head of the harbor; two sets of floats and a marine head pumpout station have been built around pilings. On the north side of the harbor, a dock and float lead to a stairway that climbs up the ridge separating Reid and Prevost harbors.

Trails loop along the top of the headland and join the camping areas; one trail follows the ridgeline to the northwest, then descends in a series of switchbacks to the Reid Harbor beach. An extension of this trail continues another 0.5 mile along the ridgeline, past the park boundary, to a schoolyard with a classic one-room, white, clapboard schoolhouse. Across the yard is another school of more modern design—still one room, however.

A short distance beyond the schoolyard, a narrow dirt county road (which actually starts at the head of Reid Harbor) leads northwest for 2.5 miles to the old Turn Point Light Station. When the lighthouse was automated, the Coast Guard buildings were boarded up, and the remainder of the station property was turned over to the Bureau of Land Management, which leases a portion of the property to the state parks. It remains undeveloped. Here are expansive views of the Gulf Islands marine traffic on Haro Strait, and the boiling tide rips at the base of the cliffs where the waters of the strait twist around the point.

# POSEY ISLAND MARINE STATE PARK

**Hours/Season:** Overnight; year-round
**Area:** 1 acre; 1,000 feet of saltwater shoreline on Spieden Channel
**Facilities:** 2 picnic tables, vault toilet, *no water, no garbage collection*

**Attractions:** Primitive camping, picnicking, fishing, beachcombing, paddling, scuba diving, tide pools
**Access:** *Boat access only.* Posey Island is 0.25 mile north of Roche Harbor on San Juan Island. Nearest launch ramp is at Roche Harbor.

Miniscule Posey Island perches off the northwestern corner of Pearl Island, near the entrance from Spieden Channel into Roche Harbor. All of the surrounding waters are quite shallow, so visits must be made by dinghy, kayak, or canoe. The island is a short mile by water from the Roche Harbor Resort via the channel on the east side of Pearl Island. The spartan onshore facilities include a few weathered picnic tables and a vault toilet. Most of the flat island is covered with beach grass and brush; a few small picturesquely scrubby trees adorn its center.

Why come here at all? For at least two reasons: to enjoy the profusion of wildflowers that bloom here in late spring and early summer (look, but don't pick or stomp on, please), and to have a spectacular view of a local phenomena—afterglow. When the sun sets behind the western, rainy side of Vancouver Island, the blue-black island silhouettes are painted against a blazing golden sky, which slowly fades to orange, then crimson, then a lingering pastel glow of pink. The west beach of Posey has a ringside view of these gorgeous sunsets.

# JONES ISLAND MARINE STATE PARK

**Hours/Season:** Overnight; year-round
**Area:** 188 acres; 25,000 feet of saltwater shoreline
**Facilities:** 21 primitive camp/picnic sites, water, dock, floats, 7 mooring buoys, hiking trails
**Attractions:** Camping, picnicking, fishing, hiking, scuba diving, boating, beachcombing, clamming, crabbing, abalone
**Access:** *Boat access only.* Jones Island is 1 mile west of the southwest tip of Orcas Island. Nearest launch ramps are at West Beach on Orcas Island, and Roche Harbor and Jackson Beach on San Juan Island.

Lying just off the southwest tip of Orcas Island at the confluence of San Juan, Spieden, and President channels, Jones Island is a popular midway stop for boaters in the San Juan Islands. Park facilities are found at two small coves on the south side of the island and at a slightly larger, more protected one on its north shore.

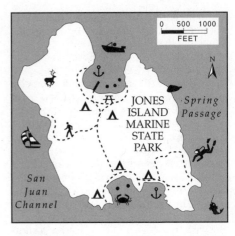

The north cove has mooring buoys and a dock with float, but the island's popularity generally attracts more boats than either can accommodate. Anchoring space is available; however, the rocky and steeply sloping bottom is a problem for securely anchoring. The small coves on the south side have only mooring buoys, and waves generated by traffic in Spieden Channel often make stays here rather rough.

Onshore, campsites are among the trees near the mooring areas. Drinking water is usually available, except in late summer. Campsites on the south side of the island are set on headlands that have more open and scenic views than those on the north. In the winter of 1990, a storm with 100-mph winds devastated Jones Island, toppling many of its old-growth trees. The park was

*A trail leads to a tiny cove that faces on Spring Passage on the east side of Jones Island.*

closed for over a year during clean-up efforts. Remaining downed timber still presents a potential fire hazard during dry months; please be careful with fires.

A trail leading across the island connects the anchorages, while a spur heads out to small coves on the west side of the island. Other paths have been etched by visitors along parts of the shoreline. In places, slippery scrambles down the low, rocky bank reach the beach.

Raccoons, weasels, martens, mink, eagles, a variety of seabirds, and a small herd of black-tailed deer inhabit the island. The deer have become so tame that they regularly mooch from campers—for their sake, resist their appeals, because people food is unhealthy for them and leads to dependence on humans.

## DOE ISLAND
## MARINE STATE PARK

**Hours/Season:** Overnight; year-round; moorage float removed in winter
**Area:** 6.1 acres; 2,049 feet of saltwater shoreline on Rosario Strait
**Facilities:** 5 primitive campsites, vault toilet, dock with float, hiking trail, *no water, no garbage collection*
**Attractions:** Camping, picnicking, fishing, scuba diving, hiking, beachcombing, boating, paddling
**Access:** *Boat access only.* Doe Island lies just off the southeast side of Orcas Island near Doe Bay. Nearest launch ramps are at North Beach and Obstruction Pass on Orcas Island, or at Bellingham, Larrabee State Park, or Anacortes.

▲ Tiny Doe Island, hidden away on the southeast side of Orcas Island, just south of Doe Bay, is a bit out of the way for most San Juan boaters, and is not as heavily used as the other marine state parks. A small anchorage behind its north side, protected from the winds and waves of Rosario Strait, holds a short dock. It is reserved for transient use between 8:00 A.M. and 3:00 P.M. Mooring buoys in the area are all private, so visitors should be prepared to anchor off the island unless their boats can be beached. At minus tides Doe Island is almost connected to Orcas by a tideflat off its north-

west tip. Kayakers frequently come ashore at small coves on the eastern tip and along the south side of the island.

A few primitive campsites with picnic tables and fire grates are set in the trees above the dock. Others with views of Cypress Island and Rosario Strait are found in grassy clearings above the south shoreline.

A trail around the perimeter of the island circles past the campsites, and short spurs drop down to wave-carved coves along the southern shore. Noisy flocks of gulls and seabirds rest on the rocky headland at the southern tip of the island. Spring and early summer bring a profusion of wildflowers, adding splashes of color along the trail.

## MORAN
## STATE PARK

**Hours/Season:** Overnight; standard hours; year-round
**Area:** 4,605.5 acres; 1,800 feet of saltwater shoreline on the Strait of Georgia; 45,300 feet of freshwater shoreline on Cascade, Mountain, Twin, and Summit lakes
**Facilities:** 151 standard campsites, 15 primitive campsites, 54 picnic sites, 5 kitchen shelters, restrooms, vault toilets, trailer dump station, 2 interpretive displays, 2 bathhouses, 2 boat launch ramps, 2 docks with boat rentals, swimming areas, children's play equipment, 31 miles of trail (plus 8.8 miles of unimproved road), nature trail, Environmental Learning Center, *campsite reservation required in summer*
**Attractions:** Camping, picnicking, swimming, paddling, hiking, nature trails, bicycling, fishing (*gasoline motors prohibited*), birdwatching, scenic views, interpretive displays
**Access:** From the ferry landing on Orcas Island, follow the Horseshoe Highway north to Eastsound, then continue east and south to the park entrance in 13 miles.

▲ Strangely, in the San Juan Islands, where the focus is salt water, boating, and all the accoutrements, one of the biggest visitor attractions is a state park that cannot be approached by boat and has no saltwater activities. True enough, a tiny portion of the park touches the Strait of Georgia, but the frontage is a steep rocky cliff of interest only to seabirds. Obviously, the park offers plenty to compensate for its lack of access to salt water, including two large trout-stocked lakes and three smaller ones; a mountain (the highest point in the San Juan Islands), from which can be seen all the archipelago, as well as a goodly part of the Gulf Islands; and several days' worth of trails along ridge, lake edge, and forest. The park is so popular that the campsites, available by reservation, are usually full all summer long, and would-be campers are often turned away.

Three of the park's four campgrounds, North End, Midway, and South End, are located at Cascade Lake. Additional sites are at Mountain Lake Landing, where there is a small campground west of the parking lot, and additional sites on a pretty little peninsula nearby. The large day-use area at Cascade Lake includes picnic areas, a swimming beach, and a dock. A short nature trail that explains the natural environment of

Orcas Island wanders in the trees west of the picnic area. Nearby, a display describes the forces of nature that are at work in the forest environment. Another day-use picnic area is found at Cold Springs, and picnic tables are at Little Summit and the top of Mount Constitution.

The Environmental Learning Center is located just off the south end of Cascade Lake. The facility, which is available for rental by large groups, has a fully equipped kitchen and mess hall, classroom, cook's cabin, infirmary, and nine sleeping cabins, as well as its own swimming beach and dock on the lake.

The clear, cold waters of the lakes make boating and fishing a favorite pastime at Moran. Paddle boats and rowboats can be rented at Cascade Lake, and a launch ramp for trailered boats is at Midway Campground. Mountain Lake also has rowboat rental and a launch ramp. Both of these large lakes provide excellent fishing for

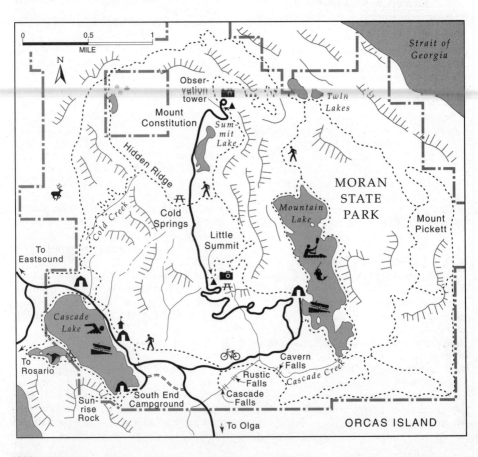

rainbow, eastern brook, and cutthroat trout, and kokanee salmon. Summit Lake is a marsh-rimmed, 0.5-mile-long pond, with only scramble access to launch a canoe and commune with the frogs. The park's two remaining lakes are Twin Lakes, which are reached via a steep, 1.5-mile-long trail from the summit. Although Twin Lakes are not stocked, they hold some trout. Outboard motors are prohibited on all park lakes.

Forest and shore provide habitat for nearly every animal found in the San Juans. Black-tailed deer are often seen in the campgrounds or along the trails and roads. Twilight lures out nocturnal animals such as raccoons, minks, otters, and muskrats.

Thousands of visitors come to the park for just a day to enjoy its scenic attractions. They usually begin at spectacular Cascade Falls, where crystalline water fans over a 100-foot-high cliff and plunges into a pool at its base. The falls is at its best from winter through early summer when the water flow is the greatest, but it is well worth the 0.25-mile walk to see it any time of year. Rustic Falls and Cavern Falls, two smaller cataracts that lie upstream, are anticlimactic after Cascade Falls, but are beautiful nonetheless.

The climax of Moran State Park is Mount Constitution and the views from its summit. The road that switchbacks to the top provides several pulloffs for enjoying the ever-expanding views of the islands. The road straightens out as it breaks out onto the south end of the summit plateau. Here at Little Summit, a path from a small parking area leads to picnic tables and dramatic views south over Entrance Mountain to the islands of Lopez Sound. On a clear day the ragged peaks of the Olympic Range and the distant ice cone of Mount Rainier pierce the sky.

The fascinating stone observation tower at the summit of Mount Constitution was patterned after a twelfth-century Caucasian mountain fortress. Plaques along the inside winding staircase tell the story of its construction. Other plaques at the top of the tower identify the jumble of islands lying below and the army of peaks stretched along the horizon.

From October through April the road is usually gated at 5:00 P.M. at its starting point just past Cascade Lake, but during fishing season it is left open as far as Mountain Lake. In the summer it remains open to the top until 10:00 P.M. to permit watching the stunning sunsets and to accommodate straggling hikers. The drive to the top of the mountain is not recommended for trailers, buses, or large mobile homes due to the many steep grades and sharp hairpin curves.

All roads within the park are open to bicyclists; the uphill pedal to the top of Mount Constitution is a strenuous haul, with over 2,000 feet of elevation gained in 6 miles (have brakes in good shape for the descent). Some of the park trails are closed to mountain bikes year-round, others are open to their use at any time, and still others are closed to bikes from mid-May to mid-September. The park brochure lists restrictions for each trail.

The more than 30 miles of hiking trails that interweave in the park provide countless options for long or short, level or steep hikes. Hikers with friends often start at the top of the mountain and arrange to be picked

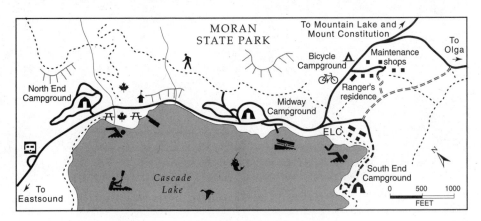

*The stone tower at the summit of Mount Constitution was patterned after a twelfth-century Caucasian mountain fortress.*

up at the bottom, avoiding the long haul back to the top. Distances can vary considerably, depending on which side trails or alternate routes are taken.

■ The Cascade Lake Loop is a 2.5-mile-long, mostly level circuit of the lake along road and trail. A 0.75-mile-long trail circles Rosario Lagoon, an arm of Cascade Lake.

■ A very steep, 0.5-mile-long trail begins at the South End Campground and climbs to the top of Sunrise Rock, overlooking Cascade Lake.

■ The most popular walk in the park is the one to spectacular Cascade Falls, which lies just 0.25 mile from the road. Smaller (although still pretty) falls can be reached by continuing upstream for another 0.25 mile.

■ A trail from Mountain Lake follows Cascade Creek past the falls all the way down to South End Campground at Cascade Lake. The total distance is 2.75 miles.

■ Another level hike is at Mountain Lake, where a 3.9-mile-long trail circles the lake.

■ A service road follows the long ridge of Mount Pickett above Mountain Lake. Begin the hike at Cascade Falls and end it at Twin Lakes. The distance is 4.4 miles.

■ For a challenge, an obscure, strenuous trail branches from the Mount Pickett trail, follows the southeast boundary, and ends up at the road that runs along the park's oaot boundary. Cpur trails provide other possibilities; the longest trail option is about 5 miles.

■ From the top of the mountain, a steep 1.5-mile trail drops to Twin Lakes. From here another trail continues down to the north end of Mountain Lake and joins the loop trail around the lake. The total distance from the summit to the parking lot at Mountain Lake is 3.7 miles.

■ A trail with loads of views starts at the top of the mountain and traverses the plateau down to Little Summit, 2.25 miles away. A branch trail continues to Mountain Lake in a little over 1 mile.

■ From the Cold Springs picnic area a trail follows Hidden Ridge and then switchbacks down Cold Creek to arrive at Cascade Lake in 2 miles. A 1-mile-long side path continues along Hidden Ridge to join the West Boundary Trail.

■ A 4.7-mile-long trail follows the west boundary of the park. It branches from the North Side Trail and drops down to the road near the northwest park entrance.

■ The North Side Trail branches from the Twin Lakes trail, swings along the north edge of the park, and in 2.2 miles reaches a junction with the Hidden Ridge Trail and the West Boundary Trail.

Severe winter storms periodically wreak havoc on the trails. Because trail maintenance resources are limited, some of the less frequently used trails may not be in the best of condition. Check with a ranger before striking out on the more remote trails.

# BLIND ISLAND MARINE STATE PARK

**Hours/Season:** Overnight; year-round
**Area:** 3 acres; 1,280 feet of saltwater shoreline on Harney Channel
**Facilities:** 4 primitive camp/picnic sites, vault toilet, 4 mooring buoys, *no water, no garbage collection*
**Attractions:** Camping, picnicking, bird-watching, fishing, boating
**Access:** *Boat access only.* Blind Island is immediately west of the Shaw Island ferry landing. Nearest launch ramps are at Obstruction Pass on Orcas Island, Jackson Beach on San Juan Island, or Odlin County Park on Lopez Island.

At the entrance to Blind Bay, on the north side of Shaw Island, is a 3-acre, grass-covered rock with a few struggling shrubs and trees: Blind Island Marine State Park. The island was once the home of a local hermit fisherman who built a cabin and shed here and scratched a tiny garden from shallow soil. The only remaining sign of his habitation is a concrete lining around a small spring (the water here is not potable).

Four mooring buoys are set off the south side of the island in Blind Bay. Because partially submerged rocks and reefs extend across the channel west of the island, the bay must be entered on its east side. Even here caution is required, as a baring rock rib protrudes into the channel from the east. The end of it has been marked with a pole by residents, but for safety's sake favor the west (Blind Island) side of the channel.

Because the island faces Harney Channel, immediately adjacent to the ferry landing at Shaw Island and directly across from the one at Orcas, ferry watching is a major attraction. After dusk the reflection in the channel of brightly lit decks doubles their visual size, making them appear like huge leviathans.

## LIME KILN POINT STATE PARK

**Hours/Season:** Day-use; standard hours; year-round
**Area:** 32.3 acres; 2,550 feet of saltwater shoreline on Haro Strait
**Facilities:** 10 picnic sites, 2 vault toilets, interpretive trail, *no water*
**Attractions:** Picnicking, hiking, whale watching, interpretive displays
**Access:** From the ferry terminal in Friday Harbor, drive west on Spring Street for 1.5 blocks, north on 2nd Street for 3 blocks, west on Guard for 1 block, then north on Tucker. At a Y-intersection in the road, bear left on Roche Harbor Road. In 9 miles head south on West Valley Road, and in 3.25 miles head west on Mitchell Bay Road. In 0.75 mile turn south on West Side Road and reach the park in another 6.5 miles.

Since 1914 the sequence of three flashes of white light from Lime Kiln Lighthouse has guided ships in Haro Strait on the west side of San Juan Island. Vessels are not the only things that utilize Haro Strait. Whales were here long before there was marine traffic, and they remain—although not in such great numbers as formerly. Whales cruise the nearby shoreline, feeding on rich offshore marine life and salmon runs headed for spawning grounds in the Fraser River.

The lighthouse still serves as a navigational beacon, although now, like most other lighthouses, it has been automated. All the former Coast Guard property except for that the lighthouse occupies is now a state park dedicated to whale watching. Trails reach overlooks where benches and picnic tables furnish spots to wait while watching for telltale riffles, a dorsal fin breaking the water's surface, or the exciting sight of their giant bodies leaping into the air as they breach.

Displays here tell of the various whales that patrol the area: pods of *Orcinis orca*, the toothed "killer whale" whose fierce reputation fades with more knowledge of the species; minke whales, a baleen whale that strains seawater through comblike struc-

*Watching for whales at Lime Kiln Point State Park*

*Pods, or family groups, of orca whales can be seen at times in the San Juan Islands.*

tures to collect the small anthropods that comprise its diet; pilot whales; harbor porpoises; and Dall's porpoises, smaller mammals with traits and markings similar to their larger relatives, the orca. Rangers are available during the late summer through fall season, when the whales are most likely to be present, to answer questions.

## TURN ISLAND MARINE STATE PARK

**Hours/Season:** Overnight; year-round
**Area:** 35.2 acres; 16,000 feet of saltwater shoreline on San Juan Channel
**Facilities:** 10 primitive campsites, vault toilets, 3 mooring buoys, 3 miles of trail, *no water, no garbage collection*

**Attractions:** Camping, picnicking, fishing, clamming, crabbing, tide pools, beachcombing, hiking, paddling, scuba-diving, birdwatching, boating
**Access:** *Boat access only.* Turn Island is off the northwest tip of San Juan Island, 1.75 miles from Friday Harbor. Nearest launch ramps are at Jackson Beach on San Juan Island and Odlin Park on Lopez Island.

⚓ Only a narrow waterway separates the south side of Turn Island from its large brother, San Juan Island. Although the channel looks as if it could almost be waded at low tide, with care it is deep enough for safe passage for boats even at low water. Because it lies so close to Friday Harbor, Turn Island is well within range for easy day trips by kayak or canoe.

A gravel beach at the west end of the

island has picnic sites in the timber. Three mooring buoys lie offshore. Wakes from boat traffic in San Juan Channel slosh the moorage, so boaters riding the buoys overnight are guaranteed to be rocked to sleep. Campsites are located in trees south of the moorage. Here a small spit that reaches toward San Juan Island becomes a tideflat with rocky tide pools on a minus tide. The pools harbor a veritable laboratory of multihued marine life. All the seashores and seabed of the San Juan archipelago are a marine sanctuary. The taking or destruction of any marine specimen, except for food, is prohibited.

The island is under the joint administration of the State Parks Commission and the U.S. Fish and Wildlife Service, and all but the south end where park facilities are located is a wildlife refuge. Public access is permitted, provided wildlife and birds remain undisturbed. A trail follows the high bluff around the perimeter of the island, with a shortcut crossing the center. Spur paths lead to a few secluded sandy coves below the steep headland on the southeast side, but for the most part the east and north sides of the island are high rocky cliffs with no accessible beach below.

A bald eagle nest once filled the top of one of Turn Island's stately trees, but a storm downed the tree. Although eagles are frequently seen, the nest has not been reestablished. Turn Rock, off the northeast tip of the island, which is capped by a navigation light, is usually crowded with pelagic cormorants and hundreds of noisy gulls.

# SPENCER SPIT STATE PARK

**Hours/Season:** Day-use; standard hours; year-round

**Area:** 129.6 acres; 7,840 feet of saltwater shoreline on Lopez Sound

**Facilities:** 34 standard campsites, 3 primitive campsites, 2 adirondack sites, 60-person group camp, 26 picnic sites, 3 picnic shelters, 50-person group day-use area, 16 mooring buoys, trailer dump station, restrooms, vault toilet

**Attractions:** Camping, picnicking, fishing, boating, paddling, clamming, crabbing, beachcombing, birdwatching, hiking

**Access:** *By land,* from the Lopez Island ferry landing, drive 1.2 miles to the first road junction and turn east on Port Stanley Road. In 3.8 miles turn east on Baker View Road, and reach the park in 1 mile. *By boat,* Spencer Spit lies on the east side of Lopez Island at the north end of Lopez Sound. Nearest mainland launch ramps are at Bellingham, Larrabee State Park, Anacortes, or Deception Pass State Park.

As one of the few state parks in the San Juan Islands accessible by land (with the help of a ferry), and as the only state park on

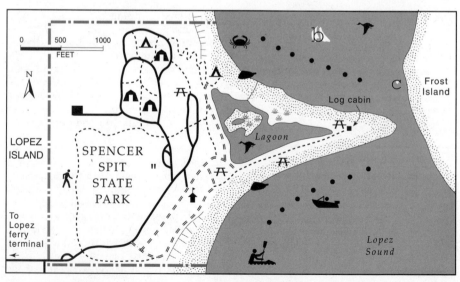

*Ambitious park visitors erected a driftwood shelter on the beach at Spencer Spit.*

Lopez Island, Spencer Spit is immensely popular with visitors. Campsites are usually filled every night in July and August. A sign at the Anacortes ferry terminal usually indicates when parks are filled so that visitors should make alternate plans. The park is equally popular with visitors who arrive via water, and the array of mooring buoys strung along both sides of the spit are usually claimed in summer. Boaters can also find good anchorages nearby in the muddy bottom.

Picnic tables are strung along the spit, and a rock-framed picnic shelter sits near the bank at the inland end of the spit. This is a remnant of the home built here by the Spencer family in the late 1800s. Another Spencer legacy is a one-room log cabin at the tip of the spit, which they built as a guest house. The original cabin collapsed, but was rebuilt and now serves as a picnic shelter.

Campsites are along a pair of loops in the wooded upland of the park, except for a string of walk-in campsites that are below the bluff at the head of the lagoon. Other walk-in sites are at the end of the camp-

ground loops. A tree-rimmed grassy field between the campground and the edge of the bluff serves as a group picnic area.

Paths lead through the woods between the campground and the park entrance and along the rim of the bluff at the south side of the park. Other wooded trails join the upland areas to the spit. Here a pair of long sandspits have joined over time to enclose a brackish saltchuck lagoon. The shallow lagoon is brightly painted with multihued algae and saltwater plants that flourish in this unique environment. Tiny sandpipers wade in the mud along its edge in search of tidbits, and in fall migratory waterfowl stop to rest. This unique ecosystem is very fragile; please stay out of the marsh and enjoy it from a distance.

When a minus tide exposes the wide, gently sloping beaches on either side of the spit, dimples in the sand that spurt water mark sites to dig for clams. Rabbits burrow in the hillside just above the beach. Campsites may be visited by black-tailed deer or stealthy raccoons.

To the north of Spencer Spit are the barren knob of little Flower Island and a chain

**109**

of rocks that ends in Leo Reef, which is marked by a navigation light. These are part of the San Juan Islands National Wildlife Refuge; clusters of seabirds rest here, and seals and sea lions are frequently seen hauled out on the rocks. After dusk in the channel just beyond, glowing lights reflect in the water as ferries pass by enroute to island stops.

## JAMES ISLAND MARINE STATE PARK

**Hours/Season:** Overnight; year-round; mooring float removed in the winter

**Area:** 113.65 acres; 12,335 feet of saltwater shoreline on Rosario Strait

**Facilities:** 13 primitive campsites, picnic shelter, dock with float, 5 mooring buoys, 1.5 miles of hiking trail, *no water, no garbage collection*

**Attractions:** Camping, picnicking, hiking, fishing, scuba diving, boating

**Access:** *Boat access only.* James Island is 0.25 mile east of Decatur Island, just south of Thatcher Pass. Nearest mainland launch ramps are at Bellingham, Larrabee State Park, Anacortes, or Deception Pass State Park.

The steep, cliffy headlands of this dog bone-shaped island are squeezed at the center by small coves on its east and west sides. The two tiny coves on the east have a pair of mooring buoys each, but the bulk of the island gives the moorages little protection from the wind and wave action from Rosario Strait, so mooring here can become exciting in foul weather.

The cove on the west side of the island, which is just across the channel from Decatur Head, has a dock with a float at the head of a rock-rimmed gravel beach. A single mooring buoy has been placed in this cove. Swirling tidal currents and a steeply sloping bottom often frustrate boaters' attempts to drop a secure anchor here.

Campsites are scattered among the trees on the saddle of land between the two coves. At night stow your food with you in your tent or on board your boat. Resident raccoons will remind you (in the dead of night!) if you don't.

A short marked trail leads through the thick woods of the south lobe of the island to a tiny beach. Several other ill-defined paths have been tramped out to other points along the the island's edge; many end atop rock faces that drop abruptly to the water.

## UNDEVELOPED STATE PARK PROPERTY IN THE SAN JUAN ISLANDS

Several tiny islands, some scarcely larger than rocks, as well as a few sections of tidelands in the San Juan Islands, are State Parks and Recreation Commission property. Although they are undeveloped (and probably will remain so), they are open to the public. Because they may be of interest to boaters, kayakers, or scuba divers, they are listed below in alphabetical order, along with their size and location. All are accessible from the water, with varying degrees of difficulty. If you visit, do not disturb nesting birds or the natural habitat. Fires and overnight camping are prohibited; take all garbage with you when you leave.

Be aware that eighty-four of the tiny rocks and islands in the San Juans are set aside as the San Juan Islands National Wildlife Refuge, providing sanctuary for pelagic birds and animals. Going ashore on any of these refuge islands is prohibited. If unsure whether you are approaching a refuge island or one of the state parks lands, err on the side of caution, and stay away!

**Castle Island.** 2 acres, 1,100 feet of saltwater shoreline; located off the southeast end of Lopez Island, 0.5 mile west of Point Colville.

**Dot Rock.** 0.5 acre, 500 feet of saltwater shoreline; located 0.2 mile southeast of White Cliff on the southeast side of Decatur Island.

**Freeman Island.** 1 acre, 720 feet of saltwater shoreline; located in President Channel, 0.3 mile off the northwest shore of Orcas Island between Point Doughty and West Beach.

**Iceberg Island.** 3.4 acres, 1,380 feet of saltwater shoreline; located on the south end of

*Many of the undeveloped state park islands in the San Juans serve as nesting or resting sites for birds such as these turnstones. (Photo by Bob and Ira Spring)*

Lopez Island in Outer Bay of Mackaye Harbor, between Johns Point and Iceberg Point.

**Lopez Island Tidelands.** 4,332 feet of saltwater shoreline; includes all of the tidelands in front of Odlin County Park on the north end of Lopez Island.

**Mud Bay Tidelands.** 11,360 feet of saltwater shoreline; located on Lopez Island's Mud Bay, at the south end of Lopez Sound. Includes all of the southwest end of the bay and the southeast shore of the bay up to Shoal Bight, with the exception of approximately 1,000 feet of private tidelands near the end of a road spur on the southeast side of the bay.

**Northwest McConnell Rock.** 2.5 acres, 2,000 feet of saltwater shoreline; located just off the northwest tip of McConnell Island and connected to the island with a sandspit at low tide.

**Olga.** 0.2 acre, 60 feet of saltwater shoreline; located on the south side of Orcas Island and the east side of East Sound at Olga. Consists of a public dock, float, and adjacent shoreline. Fresh water available at the head of the dock. Maintained by the Olga Community Club.

**Parks Bay Island.** 2.5 acres, 2,000 feet of saltwater shoreline; located on the southwest side of Shaw Island at the north side of the entrance to Parks Bay.

**Skull Island.** 1 acre, 750 feet of saltwater shoreline; located on the south side of Orcas Island, in West Sound at the north end of Massacre Bay.

**Twin Rocks.** 1 acre, 800 feet of saltwater shoreline; two rocks located on the south side of Orcas Island along the west shore of East Sound, due west of Olga.

**Victim Island.** 5 acres, 1,700 feet of saltwater shoreline; located on the south side of Orcas Island along the west side of West Sound, 0.3 mile north of Double Island.

**Unnamed Island #3.** 3 acres, 800 feet of saltwater shoreline; located on the east side of Lopez Sound at the north side of the bight at the south end of Decatur Island. Joins to Decatur by a sandbar at low tide.

**111**

**Unnamed Island #38.** 1 acre, 1,000 feet of saltwater shoreline; located on the southwest side of San Juan Island, just offshore from the center of Kanaka Bay.

**Unnamed Island #40.** 1 acre, 800 feet of saltwater shoreline; located on the southwest side of San Juan Island, 0.9 mile northwest of Pile Point.

**Unnamed Island #74.** 0.5 acre, 500 feet of saltwater shoreline; located in President Channel of the northwest side of Orcas Island. On the north side of the point between Beach Haven and West Beach.

**Unnamed Island #80.** 0.5 acre, 500 feet of saltwater shoreline; on the south side of Orcas Island on the west shore of West Sound, 0.2 mile west of Indian Point.

**Unnamed Island #81.** 0.5 acre, 500 feet of saltwater shoreline; located on the south side of Orcas Island, on the east side of West Sound, between Sheep Island and the West Sound marina.

**Unnamed Island #112.** 0.5 acre, 500 feet of saltwater shoreline; located just off the easternmost tip of McConnell Island.

**Unnamed Island #119.** 0.3 acre, 300 feet of saltwater shoreline; located on the west side of San Juan Island in Griffin Bay, just south of Dinner Island.

# PEACE ARCH
# STATE PARK

**Hours/Season:** Day-use; standard hours; year-round
**Area:** 20 acres
**Facilities:** 100 picnic sites, kitchen shelter, restrooms, 300-person group day-use area, 0.8-mile interpretive trail
**Attractions:** Picnicking, horticulture displays, interpretive signs, historic arch
**Access:** Take Exit 276 (Blaine City Center, Peace Arch Park) from I-5 just before reaching the U.S.–Canada border. Follow signs to 2nd Street, which ends at the park entrance immediately north of B Street.

▲ The two mottos CHILDREN OF A COMMON MOTHER and BRETHREN DWELLING TOGETHER IN UNITY emblazoned on either side of the magnificent white concrete arch that straddles the U.S.–Canada border at Blaine set the theme for Peace Arch State Park. The park and Canada's Provincial Park, its companion on the north side of the border, were developed in 1920 to commemorate 100 years of open, undefended boundary between the two countries, and to acknowledge the countries' shared origins. The parks flow together in wide lawns on the median and on both sides of the highway lanes between the two customs stations. A series of displays tells the history of the park and the significance of its construction. The columns of the 67-foot-high arch contain metal caskets that hold pieces of the Pilgrim ship *Mayflower,* and the Canadian steam vessel *Beaver,* brought to the Northwest by the British in 1837.

The park has become a meeting place for groups devoted to international peace and brotherhood; thousands of people gather here every year on the second Sunday in June for a celebration sponsored by the International Peace Arch Association. A large parking lot at the park is able to accommodate many of the horde of visitors. North of the lot is a long tree-bordered lawn with picnic tables, an enclosed kitchen shelter, and a group picnic area. Above the northbound lanes of the highway, more picnic tables are scattered about a tree-shaded lawn that is laced with flower gardens. From here a path leads down and across the highway to the Peace Arch.

The gardens themselves are enough reason for many visitors to pause at the park. Rhododendrons, azaleas, and heather blaze forth in shades of red, pink, and purple in spring; by summer, masses of annuals march in bright array along the borders of green lawns.

# BIRCH BAY
# STATE PARK

**Hours/Season:** Overnight; standard hours; year-round
**Area:** 193.2 acres; 12,940 feet of saltwater shoreline on Birch Bay; 14,933 feet of freshwater shoreline on Terrell Creek
**Facilities:** 147 standard campsites, 20 RV sites, 3 primitive sites, 194 picnic sites, 3 picnic shelters, 8 fire rings, 24- and 40-

CHILDREN · OF · A · COMMON · MOTHER

*The Peace Arch is a monument to friendly relations between the United States and Canada.*

person primitive group camps, bathhouse, restrooms, trailer dump station, 2.2 miles of hiking trail, nature trail, *campsite reservation recommended in summer*

**Attractions:** Camping, picnicking, fishing, hiking, crabbing, clamming, beachcombing, kite flying, birdwatching, boating, paddling, waterskiing, windsurfing, scuba diving, volleyball, guided interpretive walks

**Access:** At Exit 270 from I-5, 5 miles south of Blaine, head west on Birch Bay–Lynden Road, and in 3 miles turn south on Blaine Road. For beach access to the park, turn west in 1.5 miles on Anderson Road. In 0.8 mile reach the town of Birch Bay. The park gate is 1 mile south on Birch Bay Drive. Campers should use the east entrance, which is reached by continuing south on Blaine Road for 2 more miles, heading west on Bay Road for 1 mile, then south on Jackson Road. In 0.3 mile turn west on Helwig Road, and reach the park entrance in 0.5 mile.

Because of its nearness to the international border, the resort community of Birch Bay draws many visitors from British Columbia, and the state park on the south side of the town is as popular with Canadians as it is with state residents.

The campground loops are on a forested flat above the beach. A loop of sites with RV hookups and standard sites lies north of the main road through the park; three loops of standard campsites are south of the road near Terrell Creek. Short trails leading from the campground to the beach cross the stream on footbridges.

With more than 2 miles of superlative sandy beach, the majority of park activities are focused on the salt water. Beachside picnicking, waterskiing, windsurfing, volleyball, and kite flying are popular at any level of tide, but when minus tides expose large sections of the gently sloping beach, a host of intertidal creatures are on display for a brief time before the tidal waters return. Telltale dimples in the sand mark spots to dig for clams, and seaweed can be probed for red rock crab. Please treat all organisms kindly, even those destined for the dinner pot.

The beach is not the sole attraction, however. Along the south edge of the park, Terrell Creek trickles through a saltwater marsh before turning to flow northeast above the beachfront for the length of the park. A 0.5-mile self-guided interpretive trail weaves through the woodland northeast of the creek, reaching the edge of the marsh midroute. A park brochure identifies trailside flora such as black birch, western hemlock, Douglas fir, bigleaf maple,

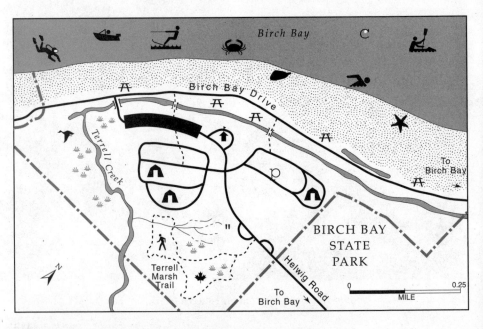

*Driftwood on the beach at Birch Bay provides comfortable spots to sun.*

alder, and western red cedar. Near the edge of the marsh, skunk cabbage blooms bright yellow in early spring. The marshland and beach grass are habitat for beavers, muskrats, opposums, and great blue heron. More than a hundred other species of birds live in or migrate through the area. Harlequin ducks, oldsquaws, and concentrations of loons may be seen on the bay in winter.

## LARRABEE STATE PARK

**Hours/Season:** Overnight; standard hours; year-round

**Area:** 2,501.2 acres; 8,100 feet of saltwater shoreline on Chuckanut and Samish bays; 6,700 feet of freshwater shoreline on Fragrance and Lost lakes

**Facilities:** 53 standard campsites, 26 RV sites, 8 walk-in sites, 3 primitive campsites, 40-person group camp, 67 picnic sites, 2 kitchen shelters, 50- and 100-person group day-use areas, restrooms, RV dump station, vault toilets, boat launch ramp, 10.4 miles of road, 9.2 miles of trail

**Attractions:** Camping, picnicking, boating, paddling, fresh- and saltwater fishing, clamming, crabbing, beachcombing, waterskiing, scuba diving, hiking, bicycling

**Access:** From I-5 in Bellingham, take Exit 205 to Highway 11 (Chuckanut Drive) and continue south for 7 miles to the park. Alternatively, take Highway 11 northwest from Exit 231 from I-5, 4 miles north of Mount Vernon, and reach the park in 17 miles. The launch ramp is located off Cove Road, 0.7 mile north of the park entrance.

Larrabee State Park holds many distinctions, its unique one being that it was Washington's first official state park. The initial 20 acres of land was donated to the state in 1915 by the Larrabee and Gates families; in 1923 it was dedicated as a park.

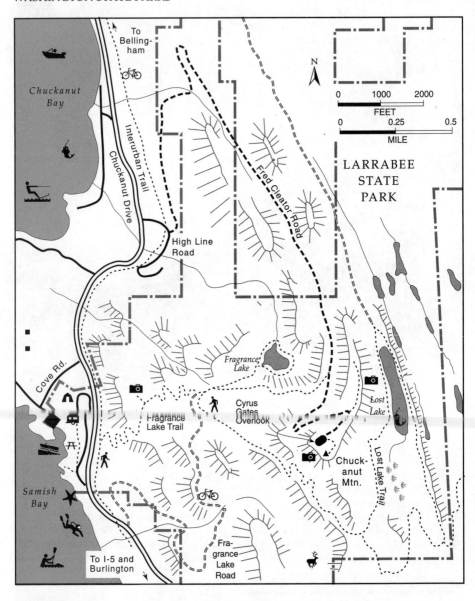

The popular beach and camping areas that lie on the west side of Chuckanut Drive comprise only a very small portion of the large present-day holdings. The bulk of the park reaches 3 miles inland to include several small lakes and the 1,941-foot-high lower summit of Chuckanut Mountain's long massif.

The park's campsites are packed along a pair of loops between Chuckanut Drive and the shore. Railroad tracks that run along the water add to the constriction of the area.

At the center of both camping loops, hookup sites are stacked side by side in cozy familiarity; standard campsites rim the outside of the loops, and walk-in sites line a path on the west side of the main campground loops. The picnic areas are also found in this strip of land.

Trails from the picnic area lead through a concrete underpass that runs under the railroad tracks and arrive at a series of small coves. At a narrow finger on the south side of Wildcat Cove, the trail descends to

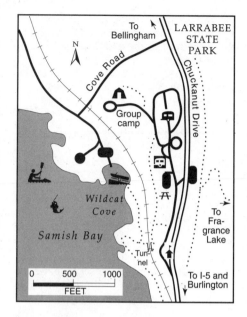

N

Cove Road

Chuckanut Drive

Group camp

Wildcat Cove

Samish Bay

Tunnel

To Fragrance Lake

To I-5 and Burlington

0   500   1000
FEET

water level, where low tide uncovers wave-worn hollows in the rock inhabited by limpets, mussels, crabs, shrimp, barnacles, tubeworms, and other intertidal creatures. At the middle of Wildcat Cove, a steep

concrete boat launch ramp leads down to water's edge. Parking and vault toilets are provided at the head of the ramp. Note that the ramp area cannot be reached by road from the main portion of the park; access is from Cove Road, north of the park entrance.

Just above the highway a wide, flat trail runs through the park and north to the Fairhaven District of Bellingham. This is the old roadbed of the Mount Vernon to Bellingham Interurban Railway, now converted into a hiking/bicycling/equestrian trail. Total trail distance to Bellingham is 5.5 miles.

The park has two nice-sized lakes, Fragrance and Lost, that offer good trout fishing and provide scenic destinations. The lakes, which snuggle in pockets below the bands of cliffs that form Chuckanut Mountain, can be reached by hiking directly from the campground. Fragrance Lake can also be reached by driving a gravel road up the mountainside and then catching a spur trail.

To drive to a viewpoint, a mile north of the park boundary turn east on High Line Road, which shortly becomes Fred Cleator Road, and winds up the steep sidehill of

*An aged madrona becomes a willing steed*

**117**

Chuckanut Mountain. At 2.5 miles a trail to the right heads to Fragrance Lake. The road reaches Cyrus Gates overlook at 3.5 miles, 100 feet below the nearby summit ridge. Here are expansive views north to Bellingham and west over Lummi Island to the northern San Juan Islands. A short spur trail from the last switchback to a lower viewpoint below Cyrus Gates provides glimpses down the steep timbered east face of the mountain into Lost Lake, beyond to Lookout Mountain, and to Mount Baker in the distance.

But why drive a gravel road when you can walk and enjoy the wildwood? The Fragrance Lake Trail begins across the road from the park campground and switchbacks steeply uphill, gaining some 800 feet of elevation in 1.5 miles. Don't miss the viewpoint at 0.9 mile with dizzying views down a cliff to Samish and Chuckanut bays or out to a tapestry of islands and mountains. As the path nears the lake, it is joined by a short side spur from the end of the Fragrance Lake Road, then descends gently for 0.25 mile through cedar and hemlock forest to the edge of the 6.5-acre lake.

Fragrance Lake Road, a gated gravel road that starts just outside the south park entrance, provides an alternate route up Chuckanut Mountain for hikers and mountain bikers. After intersecting the Lost Lake trailhead in 2.1 miles, the road ends at a cul de sac at 2.2 miles. A short spur trail from the road-end joins the Fragrance Lake Trail as it comes down from Fred Cleator Road. The lake itself is just 0.25 mile away. Primitive roads lace the backcountry beyond the park boundary; some are abandoned, others are gated logging roads.

The trail to 12-acre Lost Lake is a strenuous 2.5-mile-long route that leaves from near the end of the Fragrance Lake Road. It climbs a steep sidehill in a series of switchbacks through old-growth forest to a 1,600-foot-high saddle before crossing to the steep, timbered cliffs on the east side of the ridge. From here a long traverse across the face above the lake leads to the water's edge at the north end of the lake.

From this point a more obscure trail follows the top of the rib along the east side of the lake, and south of the lake joins a logging road spur that heads uphill toward the southwest. A trail continues from the upper end of this road over the top of a wooded knob and then drops back down to meet the main trail at the saddle southwest of Lost Lake.

Another spur trail 0.25 mile north of the saddle leads downhill through bogs at the south-end drainage of the lake.

# CONE ISLANDS STATE PARK (UNDEVELOPED)

**Area:** 9.85 acres; 2,500 feet of saltwater shoreline on Bellingham Channel
**Facilities:** None
**Attractions:** Kayaking, scuba diving
**Access:** *Boat access only.* The Cone Islands are between the east shore of Cypress Island and the north tip of Guemes Island. Nearest launch ramps are at Anacortes and Larrabee State Park.

▲ The Cone Islands are a grouping of three tiny, picturesque islands. The two southernmost islands are state park property. Steep, rocky slabs drop from their tree-tufted tops into the water without pausing to form a beach, making landing on the islands difficult. The underwater walls and nearby kelp beds are popular scuba diving spots. Eagles frequent the taller trees.

# HUCKLEBERRY ISLAND STATE PARK (UNDEVELOPED)

**Area:** 10 acres; 2,900 feet of saltwater shoreline on Padilla Bay
**Facilities:** None
**Attractions:** Kayaking, scuba diving
**Access:** *Boat access only.* Huckleberry Island lies at the north end of Padilla Bay, 0.3 mile east of Long Bay on the southeast end of Guemes Island. Nearest launch ramps are at Anacortes, Larrabee State Park, Bay View, and the north end of the Swinomish Channel.

▲ The north, east, and south sides of Huckleberry Island are sheer rock faces that dive sharply into the water, then continue underwater to depths of 60 feet or more. On the southwest side of the island, a white clay bluff drops to a reasonably wide gravel beach. This beach, which is a nice spot for a visit by kayak or a beachable boat, remains exposed except at extreme high tides. Although the water offshore from the beach is shallow enough for anchoring, it is unprotected from wind and waves, and several offshore rocks are potential hazards.

# SADDLEBAG ISLAND MARINE STATE PARK

**Hours/Season:** Overnight; year-round
**Area:** 23.7 acres; 6,750 feet of saltwater shoreline on Padilla Bay
**Facilities:** 5 primitive campsites, vault toilets, 1 mile of trail, *no water*
**Attractions:** Camping, picnicking, hiking, fishing, crabbing, scuba diving, boating
**Access:** *Boat access only.* Saddlebag Island is in the north end of Padilla Bay, 2 miles northeast of Anacortes. Nearest launch ramps are at Anacortes, Larrabee State Park, Bay View, and the north end of the Swinomish Channel.

▲ Saddlebag Island earns its name from its ⊥ configuration—a pair of rocky brush- and timber-covered headlands, linked by a narrow flat between coves that pinch the center of the island. The island sits at the north end of the shallow estuary of Padilla Bay, and at a minus tide a large portion of the bay for a mile to the east dries to a seaweed-covered mudflat. Since the city of Anacortes is only a little over 2 miles to the southwest, many visitors stop by for a day of fishing or to drop a crab pot in the hope of landing some of the island's renowned supply of Dungeness.

Park facilities are a few primitive campsites secluded in trees above the two coves. There are no mooring buoys, so boaters must either anchor in the island's two small coves or have a boat that can be beached on the gravel shoreline at the head of the coves. Holding ground for anchoring is solid in either cove; however, the one on the north side of the island is larger, has a softer bottom, and is generally more favored. Neither cove offers much protection in heavy weather, but with a safe haven less than 30 minutes away in Anacortes, few boaters

*Saddlebag Island provides quiet anchorages with good holding ground.*

would elect to ride out foul weather here.

A quick circuit of the island on impromptu trails that have been beaten along the top of the bluff of the two headlands offers views of its two neighbors, Dot and Hat islands immediately to the south, or across the channel to the west to Huckleberry and Guemes islands. Nearby Dot Island, which is a bird nesting area of the San Juan Islands Wilderness, usually teems with seabirds; occasionally visitors spot otters or harbor seals.

Dot, Hat, and Saddlebag all sit at the outer edge of a shallow underwater shelf that drops away steeply to the west. Approach by boat should therefore be made from the west to avoid possible grounding.

---

## BAY VIEW
## STATE PARK

---

**Hours/Season:** Overnight; standard hours; year-round

**Area:** 25 acres; 1,285 feet of saltwater shoreline on Padilla Bay

**Facilities:** 67 standard campsites, 9 RV sites, 3 primitive campsites, 59 picnic sites, 50-person group camp, kitchen shelter, 50-person group day-use area, restrooms, vault toilets

**Attractions:** Camping, picnicking, fishing, swimming, paddling, birdwatching

**Nearby:** Breazeale Padilla Bay Interpretive Center

**Access:** At I-5 Exit 231, 5 miles north of Mount Vernon, turn left, and in 300 yards head west on Josh Wilson Road. In 6.5 miles, at the town of Bay View, turn north on Bay View–Edison Road. Follow this north 0.3 mile to the park entrance.

Bay View State Park has a long history as a recreation spot. Even before the state acquired the land, a county agricultural association maintained a racetrack, a baseball diamond, and picnic sites here.

The park is split into two sections by Bay View–Edison Road. The upper region contains picnic sites and all of the park's camping. The lower section, reached by a tunnel under the highway, is a flat grassy day-use and picnic area with a low-bank beach fronting on Padilla Bay.

RV sites are on a small, open hillock just inside the park entrance. Beyond are wooded picnic sites, a kitchen shelter and restrooms, and a group camp. East from here, camping is available around the perimeter of a meadowy playfield. Additional secluded campsites are located along a wooded loop to the east of the playfield.

The beach is the heart of activity in the

*Black brant geese, which winter in Padilla Bay, are often seen at Bay View State Park.*

park, with ample opportunity for picnicking, sunbathing, kite flying, and wading (or just exploring the mud of Padilla Bay at low tide). Kayaks or small boats that can be carried the few feet from the parking lot to the water can be launched here for leisurely paddling on the bay. Most of the estuary is a mere 6 feet deep at high tide, so use care to avoid being stranded by an outgoing tide.

Over 11,000 acres of the marsh and tidelands of Padilla Bay are designated as a National Estuarine Sanctuary to protect its important ecological system. Breazeale Interpretive Center, 0.5 mile north of the state park, has fascinating displays describing the vegetation and wealth of creatures that live in the bay and along its shores. The protected estuary is an important migratory stop for waterfowl such as black brant and snow geese. Visitors often see hawks, eagles, owls, and herons along the shore.

## BURROWS ISLAND STATE PARK (UNDEVELOPED)

**Area:** 329.5 acres; 8,670 feet of saltwater shoreline on Rosario Strait
**Facilities:** None
**Attractions:** Beachcombing, boating
**Access:** *Boat access only.* Burrows Island is on the northwest side of Burrows Bay.

▲ State park property on Burrows Island adjoins the Coast Guard lighthouse property at the west tip of Burrows Island, and most of the park shoreline lies below steep cliffs along the northwest entrance to Allen Pass. In calm weather small boats can be beached in a cove on the north side of the lighthouse.

## DECEPTION PASS STATE PARK

**Hours/Season:** Overnight; standard hours; year-round
**Area:** (Including Heart Lake section) 3,599.3 acres; 77,000 feet of saltwater shoreline on the Strait of Juan de Fuca and Puget Sound; 28,200 feet of freshwater shore-

line on Cranberry, Pass, Campbell, and Heart lakes
**Facilities:** 246 standard campsites, 5 primitive bicycle/walk-in campsites, 60-person group camp, 306 picnic sites, 6 kitchens, 5 picnic shelters, restrooms, snacks (concession), swimming beach, bathhouse, 3 docks, 10 moorage floats, 11 mooring buoys, 7 boat launch ramps, 12 boarding floats, swim float, 5 fishing floats, Environmental Learning Center with amenities, 27.5 miles of hiking trail, interpretive trail, amphitheater, underwater park
**Attractions:** Camping, picnicking, swimming, scuba diving, paddling, boating, fishing (*gasoline motors prohibited on all freshwater lakes*), hiking, interpretive trails, CCC Interpretive Center, beachcombing, bicycling, sightseeing, birdwatching
**Access:** *By land from the north,* on Fidalgo Island, at a T-intersection 12 miles west of Mount Vernon, follow Highway 20 as it turns south. In 6.5 miles reach the north entrance. *By land from the south,* on Whidbey Island head north on Highway 525, which becomes Highway 20 midway up the island. In 45 miles reach the south park entrance. *To reach Heart Lake,* at the east end of Campbell Lake, stay right on Highway 20 as it splits and its northern leg first becomes Campbell Lake Road, and then Heart Lake Road as it passes the east side of Heart Lake. *By boat,* the park lies at the confluence of Rosario Strait and the Strait of Juan de Fuca. From the east side of Whidbey Island, it can be reached by following Saratoga Passage and Skagit Bay north.

▲ When making a list of Washington superlatives, Deception Pass State Park must certainly be included, so stunning is its scenery, so monumental is its bridge, and so diverse are the activities that it offers. The more than 3.5 million people who visit here annually make it the most used of all the state parks. The park is large enough that it can manage to accommodate the hordes of visitors, aside from those campers who must be turned away in summer due to full campgrounds.

The focal point of the park is the Deception Pass Bridge. Construction of the bridge was so difficult that it required two giant leaps to get from Fidalgo to Whidbey Is-

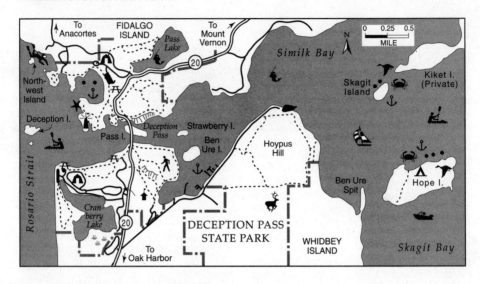

land, stopping midway on Pass Island between the watery channels of Canoe and Deception passes. The bridge elicits breathless admiration from visitors staring from the decking down the steep channel walls. Pulloffs at either end of the bridge and on Pass Island provide spots to leave cars and walk out onto the span.

The majority of the park's campsites are at Cranberry Lake on the south side of the pass, west of Highway 20. Here on a flat, densely wooded bluff above the beach are two camping areas, with a total of 246 campsites. Late-arriving bicyclists will usually find tent space at walk-in sites, even if the park is filled with car campers. A group camp that accommodates 60 is secluded in trees at North Beach, north of Cranberry Lake. Use of the group camp is by reservation. Another small campground in the north section of the park at Bowman Bay has sixteen car campsites in a wooded area. Day-use picnic areas are found throughout the park wherever there's a sunny spot within toting distance of an ice chest.

The park's Environmental Learning Center, which is available for use by organized groups of 25 or more (by reservation), is found on the shore of Cornet Bay. Facilities here include a kitchen/dining hall, 16 sleeping cabins, a cook's cabin, first aid cabin, recreation hall, heated swimming pool, campfire circle, and playing fields.

The extensive system of trails that thread through the park connects lakes, forests, cliff-rimmed beaches, and wide bays. Moderate to low tides offer added opportunities for long beach walks.

■ A short, self-guided nature trail circles through the woods just south of the ranger station at Cranberry Lake.

■ The Discovery Trail, which begins at the ELC and runs northeast to the highway, has a number of stations along the way that identify flora and geological and ecological points of interest. This route links with other paths that crisscross Goose Rock.

■ A trail from the Rosario Bay picnic area climbs to the top of Rosario Head and circles the top of the bluff; another branches east and follows the shores of Sharpe Cove and Bowman Bay.

■ Trails that begin at Bowman Bay branch out to Reservation Head, Lighthouse Point, and Lottie Bay.

■ North of Highway 20 on Fidalgo Island, unimproved trails that start at the launch ramp at Pass Lake allow shore access for anglers. Another set of unimproved trails on the east side of Highway 20 circle Bowman Hill; trailheads are at the pullout just north of the bridge.

■ From the highway pulloff on Pass Island, impromptu paths work down slabs that are sprinkled with sedges, wildflowers, and stubby, gnarled pine trees. The north, south, and west sides of the island end in cliffs; only at the eastern end is there any chance of getting near the shoreline, although the steep rocky bank should be

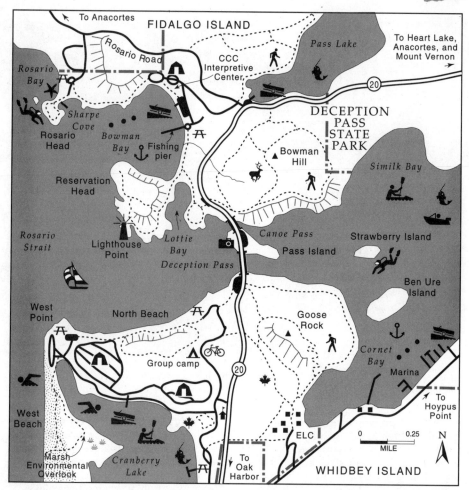

approached cautiously.

■ Cranberry Lake, a shallow freshwater lake that formed in a lagoon, provides an interesting contrast to the bordering forest. A path along the west side of the lake leads to a viewing platform over a marsh, then returns across the grass-covered dunes.

■ At North Beach, north of Cranberry Lake, a trail loop connects the campgrounds. Side routes lead down to a pair of beaches that have startling views upward at the Deception Pass Bridge. A trail spur continues under the bridge to Goose Rock.

■ East of Cornet Bay a trail circles through the dense lowland old-growth forest of Hoypus Hill. Trailheads are at a gated side road and a gravel pit.

On both the east and west sides of the park, kayakers will find waters ranging from protected to excitingly exposed. Bowman and Cornet bays are easiest, since they have only weak currents and are well protected in most weather. Both of the channels of Deception Pass require intermediate paddling skills; because capsizing is a distinct possibility, kayakers are advised to wear wet suits or dry suits and to travel in a group in case rescue is necessary. Tidal currents in the narrow, cliff-bound channels sometimes exceed 9 knots. Unless they are driving a very high-powered vessel, boaters must wait until slack tide to enter the channel, rather than challenge the maelstrom at maximum tidal currents.

The center of saltwater boating is Cornet Bay, on the southeast side of Deception Pass. Here there is a park dock, launch ramp, boarding floats, and offshore moor-

123

*Looking east from the Deception Pass bridge: Canoe Island lies in the foreground; Strawberry is the small island on the right.*

ing buoys. A private marina farther into the bay offers fuel, food, overnight moorage, and fishing and marine supplies. The bay is quite shallow, but safe passage into it from the east is marked by pilings and day marks.

Bowman Bay, on the west side of Deception Pass, has a gravel boat launch ramp and five mooring buoys. Sharpe Cove, a tiny inlet at the north side of the bay, contains a dock and float. The large pier near the heart of Bowman Bay that rests on tall pilings is too high above the water to be used by boaters. Both Coffin Rocks and Gull Rocks clutter the entrance to Bowman Bay; boaters need to be cautious and approach the bay along its southeast side.

With three large lakes within its boundaries, freshwater boating also gets ample attention at Deception Pass. At Cranberry Lake a launch ramp below the campground loops gives lake access for rowboats or canoes. The lake is a popular fishing spot that is regularly stocked with trout. At Pass Lake a parking lot at the south corner provides a launch spot. Pass Lake, which is

open only to fly fishing, provides catches of good-sized rainbow trout and Atlantic salmon. Down Highway 20 at Heart Lake, a parking lot just off the road on the east side of the lake offers shore access for fishing. Motors are prohibited on all park lakes.

Rosario Bay is headquarters for scuba divers headed to Northwest Island and nearby Urchin Rocks. During slack currents, experienced scuba divers sometimes explore the underwater cliffs of Pass Island. At minus tides the nearshore rocks at Rosario Bay hold tide pools for exploration. This is a protected marine sanctuary; taking of marine animals other than for food is prohibited.

Deception Pass State Park includes a number of small offshore islands. Some have anchorages, allowing approach by dinghy, while others are best reached by kayak. The nearer the pass, the more carefully the strength of the tide and the skill of the paddler should be considered.

■ Northwest Island is a flat, treeless rock, beloved of gulls and scuba divers, lying 0.5

*Scuba divers prepare to enter the water near Northwest Island.*

mile northwest of Rosario Beach.

■ Deception Island, the offshore guardian of the west entrance to Deception Pass, is a rocky outcropping with a few trees and a craggy shoreline. A shallow underwater shelf between the island and the pass is a favorite salmon fishing spot.

■ Strawberry and Pass islands lie at the east end of Deception Pass. Kayaks or small boats capable of being beached can find spots to go ashore on Strawberry, especially at the more gently sloping east end of the tiny island. Pass Island holds the midspan supports of the Deception Pass Bridge.

■ Skagit Island, which along with Hope Island lies at the head of Skagit Bay, is a 21-acre island covered with trees and brush. A primitive trail follows the top of the bluff around the island. Mooring buoys are placed offshore along its north side. Hope Island, whose 166 acres make it the largest of the park's islands, is an oversized twin of Skagit. It also has mooring buoys along its north side. A few primitive campsites are at Lang Bay on the north side. A trail crosses

from the campsites to cliff-top views to the south. Eagles and great blue herons frequently sit in tall snags on both islands.

■ Deadman and Little Deadman are two small islands lying southeast of Hope. Because the water around them is extremely shoal, they should only be approached at high tide, and even then with a shallow-draft boat and a whole lot of caution.

## JOSEPH WHIDBEY STATE PARK

**Hours/Season:** Day-use; standard hours; closed September 30 to March 30

**Area:** 112 acres; 3,100 feet of saltwater shoreline on the Strait of Juan de Fuca

**Facilities:** 20 picnic sites, picnic shelter, vault toilets, *no water*

**Attractions:** Picnicking, hiking, surf fishing, beachcombing

**Access:** *South of Oak Harbor,* from Highway 20 on Whidbey Island, turn northwest on

**125**

Swantown Road. The park is reached in 3 miles, at the intersection with West Beach Road. *North of Oak Harbor,* turn west from Highway 20 on Ault Field Road. In 2.2 miles turn south on West Beach Road, and reach the park in 2.3 miles.

⊥ Joseph Whidbey was a member of George Vancouver's 1792 Expedition. He explored Saratoga Passage, on the east side of Whidbey Island, up to Deception Pass, causing Vancouver to named the island for him. When the group sailed up the west shore of the island, Whidbey took a small boat through Deception Pass to the spot where he had been a few days before, thus becoming the first European to circumnavigate this 45-mile-long island (the longest in the U.S., by the way).

Despite its meager "amenities" (a few picnic tables, a shelter, and toilets), Joseph Whidbey State Park has one of the grandest beaches on Whidbey Island. Paths lead from the picnic area across a low rolling meadow, covered with beach grass to the broad sand and gravel beach facing on the Strait of Juan de Fuca. Logs and driftwood mark the high-tide line of the beach. The winds and waves rolling down the length of the strait toss beachcombing treasures along the high-tide margins, especially during winter storms. In the distance the low silhouettes of Smith and Minor islands can be spotted by the repeated solitary flash from the Smith Island Lighthouse.

A second access to the beach can be found next to the first residence on the south side of the park, where a path leads directly to the beach.

---

# FORT EBEY STATE PARK

**Hours/Season:** Overnight; standard hours; year-round
**Area:** 644.2 acres; 8,000 feet of saltwater shoreline on the Strait of Juan de Fuca; 1,000 feet of freshwater shoreline on Lake Pondilla
**Facilities:** 53 standard campsites, 3 primitive campsites, 24 picnic sites, restrooms, 3 miles of hiking trail
**Attractions:** Camping, picnicking, hiking,

fishing, bicycling, interpretive programs, beachcombing, historic display
**Access:** From Highway 20 on Whidbey Island, turn. west on Libby Road, 5.8 miles south of Oak Harbor. In 1 mile turn south on Hill Valley Drive, and reach the park entrance in 0.4 mile.

⊥ Although many Washington park-goers are familiar with the 1900s-vintage Coast Artillery defenses of forts Casey, Flagler, and Worden (all now state parks), far fewer people are aware of Fort Ebey. Small wonder, as it was a Johnny-come-lately in the coastal defense business. The big, obsolete guns at the other forts had been removed long before Fort Ebey was built.

The fortification at Point Partridge on Whidbey Island was one of three intended to protect Puget Sound from Japanese attacks during World War II; others were at

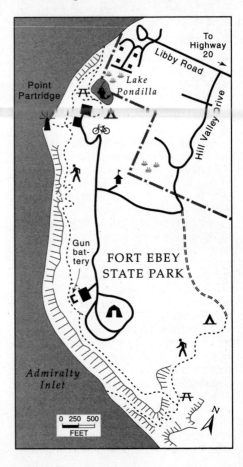

*A steep trail leads down to Partridge Point from Fort Ebey State Park.*

Striped Peak, west of Port Angeles, and at Cape Flattery. Only the first two were completed at the time that U.S. air superiority in the eastern Pacific and Gulf of Alaska made land-based coastal defense batteries obsolete and construction was halted. Today only concrete platforms mark the gun locations, and the bunker now echoes with the voices and footsteps of youngsters playing hide-and-seek among its spooky, dark, deserted rooms.

In addition to the gun battery, the state park includes campgrounds and a day-use picnic area. Two forested campground loops lie in trees south of the battery site. At the north end of the park, a short trail leads to walk-in campsites for bicyclists in the trees along the shore of Lake Pondilla. The tiny lake, less than 0.25 mile around, holds bass. Bald eagles often roost in snags near the lake.

Several hiking trails traverse the 150-foot-

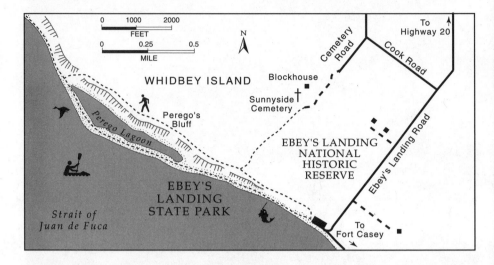

high bluff above the Strait of Juan de Fuca. Two trails from the day-use area drop down gentler slopes to provide beachcombing access to the short stretch of wide sandy beach that lies north of the Point Partridge Lighthouse.

A Department of Natural Resources (DNR) area south of the main park was transferred to the state parks in 1991. Walk-in campsites and a trail down Partridge Point to the beach are a welcome addition to the park as a result of this transfer.

## EBEY'S LANDING
## STATE PARK

**Hours/Season:** Day-use; standard hours; year-round
**Area:** 45.8 acres; 6,120 feet of saltwater shoreline on the Strait of Juan de Fuca
**Facilities:** Vault toilet, interpretive display, 1.5 miles of trail, *no water*
**Attractions:** Hiking, surf fishing, beachcombing, paddling, birdwatching
**Nearby:** Ebey's Landing National Historic Reserve
**Access:** From Highway 20 on Whidbey Island, turn south on Ebey's Landing Road, 0.2 mile west of Coupeville. The park is reached in 3 miles.

Of the several ways to get a state park named for you, the way Colonel Isaac Ebey did it is not among those recom-mended. Ebey, the first white settler on Whidbey Island, homesteaded the rich farmland on the bluff above the park and held several bureaucratic offices in this virgin territory. Thus, when a group of Tlingit Indians sought revenge for the death of a chief at the hands of white men, they looked for a white "chief"—and found him in the person of Ebey. In August of 1857 they surprised him in his home, shot him, and carried his head home as a trophy.

Today the beach section of Isaac Ebey's property now comprises the state park named for him. The park adjoins Ebey's Landing National Historic Reserve, a joint federal and state effort to preserve the nine-teenth-century agricultural character of this historic part of Whidbey Island. It includes Ebey's farmland on the bluff above the beach and a cemetery containing his grave.

Near the parking lot at the beach at Ebey's Landing, interpretive signs tell the story of Isaac Ebey and George Perego, a hermit who lived on the nearby windblown bluff. A 1-mile trail leads from the parking lot inland to Sunnyside Cemetery, which contains Ebey's grave and the James Davis blockhouse, one of the few remaining log forts built during the Puget Sound Indian Wars. The cemetery can also be reached by road.

Another trail follows the lip of Perego's Bluff, with dramatic views out across the Strait of Juan de Fuca, and down the steep face of the bluff to the beach and lagoon below. In about 1.5 miles the path switchbacks down the cleft in the bluff to the cobble beach and returns, on the beach side of Perego Lagoon, to the Ebey's Landing starting point. Beachcombing opportunities abound on the wave-tossed beach along the return trip.

## FORT CASEY
## STATE PARK

**Hours/Season:** Overnight; standard hours; year-round
**Area:** 137.5 acres; 4,000 feet of saltwater shoreline on Admiralty Inlet
**Facilities:** 35 standard campsites, 3 primitive campsites, 63 picnic sites, restrooms, boat launch ramp, 1.25 miles of trail, underwater park
**Attractions:** Camping, picnicking, boating, fishing, scuba diving, hiking, beachcombing, clamming, lighthouse/interpretive center, historic display, interpretive signs
**Access:** From Highway 20 on Whidbey Island, turn south on Engle Road at Coupeville, and reach the park in 3.2 miles. Alternatively, 6 miles south of Coupeville, where the main north–south route changes from Highway 20 to Highway

*The huge guns at Fort Casey are fascinating for all ages.*

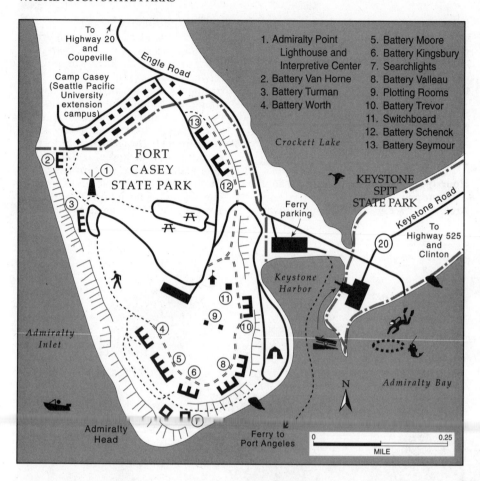

To Highway 20 and Coupeville

Engle Road

Camp Casey (Seattle Pacific University extension campus)

1. Admiralty Point Lighthouse and Interpretive Center
2. Battery Van Horne
3. Battery Turman
4. Battery Worth
5. Battery Moore
6. Battery Kingsbury
7. Searchlights
8. Battery Valleau
9. Plotting Rooms
10. Battery Trevor
11. Switchboard
12. Battery Schenck
13. Battery Seymour

Crockett Lake

FORT CASEY STATE PARK

KEYSTONE SPIT STATE PARK

Keystone Road

Ferry parking

To Highway 525 and Clinton

Keystone Harbor

Admiralty Inlet

Admiralty Bay

Admiralty Head

Ferry to Port Angeles

N

0      0.25
MILE

525, follow Highway 20 west and reach the park in 3.4 miles.

While one wouldn't think an instrument of war could become a major recreational facility, such is the case with several old military forts in the state. Admiralty Head was one of three sites selected in 1896 for the primary defense of Puget Sound. The batteries at forts Casey, Worden, and Flagler were intended to form a "triangle of fire" that would rain death on enemy ships attempting to enter Admiralty Inlet. All are now state parks.

The initial gun and mortar emplacements at Fort Casey were completed in 1899; by 1907 those batteries had been augmented with seven more, completing the armament of the fort. By 1911 fire control systems and searchlight batteries had been added. Although the fort was fully active when the

U.S. entered World War I in 1917, improvements in naval guns, ship's armor, and fire control systems obsoleted these fixed coastal defense forts almost as quickly as they were completed. Most of the guns were removed in 1920 and sent to Europe to be used as artillery pieces mounted on railroad cars. The fort was briefly armed again when some antiaircraft guns were placed here prior to World War II. Because its use as a coastal defense fortification proved impractical, the site was used primarily for the induction and training of troops during both world wars.

The four guns mounted today in batteries Worth and Trevor are not part of the original armament; they were originally at Fort Wint in the Philippines and were brought here for display. All of the old shot rooms and powder magazines and their interconnecting corridors beneath the gun emplacements are open for exploration, but be sure to bring a flashlight—once past the steel outer doors, everything inside is black. Catwalks lead from the gun emplacements to concrete towers that served as fire control stations. Buried in the hillside above the south end of the batteries are concrete-lined rooms from which targets were tracked and their positions plotted to provide data to the gun batteries. Lower on the bluff, below the gun emplacements, another bunker held a 60-inch searchlight that illuminated targets in Admiralty Inlet. U-shaped emplacements on the back side of the hill at the east side of the fort held mortars.

Prior to its use as a fort, Admiralty Head was a lighthouse reservation. The first light, which stood west of the present gun emplacements, shone here in 1861. When the fort was constructed, the building was moved farther back on the bluff; it now serves as the park's interpretive center.

At Fort Casey, modern facilities include hilltop picnic sites in trees above the gun emplacements, and a campground loop on the flat, open beach area below the east side of the bluff. A trail leads from the campground up the bluff to the emplacements, or you can walk along the road. Other footpaths lace the bluff.

The campground sits on earth dredged from adjoining Keystone Harbor, where the ferry to Port Townsend lands. A two-lane boat launch ramp, with a boarding float between lanes, drops into the harbor from the spit on its east side. An artificial reef just offshore in Admiralty Bay forms an underwater park for scuba divers.

Seattle Pacific University uses the old barracks, warehouses, and officers' quarters along the parade ground at the park's entrance as an extension campus.

## KEYSTONE SPIT
## STATE PARK (UNDEVELOPED)

**Area:** 274 acres; 6,810 feet of saltwater shoreline on Admiralty Bay; 7,000 feet of freshwater shoreline on Crockett Lake
**Facilities:** None
**Attractions:** Picnicking, beachcombing, birdwatching, surf fishing, kite flying, windsurfing, scuba diving, interpretation

**Access:** See directions to Fort Casey State Park.

▲ Keystone Spit, a mile-long narrow gravel bar, separates Crockett Lake and Admiralty Bay, immediately adjoining the east side of Fort Casey State Park. In 1896 the land was acquired by the Army Corps of Engineers, who used the western portion of the spit for an engineering camp during the construction of Fort Casey. In order to improve on the primitive fire control methods used at the time the fort was constructed, new observation stations were built in 1908 at the east end of Keystone Spit and at other extreme ends of the fort property to provide a long baseline for triangulating on targets and improving on the accuracy of position plots.

When the fort was surplused, private interests acquired portions of the spit with the intent of turning it into real estate tracts. After the construction of several homes led to a controversy over historical and ecological preservation of the spit, the state Parks Commission acquired all of the undeveloped land in 1988. Today a major portion of the spit, with freshwater shoreline on one side and saltwater on the other, is open for public enjoyment as a place to beachwalk, birdwatch, fish, or fly kites. Crockett Lake, a 250-acre shallow marsh created by the gravel bar, is used by waterfowl as a place to pause or overwinter on their migratory flights. Other marsh-loving birds nest along its edges. Bring binoculars and see how many different species you can spot.

## SOUTH WHIDBEY
## STATE PARK

**Hours/Season:** Overnight; standard hours; weekends and holidays only, November 15 to February 14
**Area:** 85 acres; 4,500 feet of saltwater shoreline on Admiralty Inlet
**Facilities:** 54 standard campsites, 6 primitive campsites, 100-person group camp, 26 picnic sites, picnic shelter, 30-person group day-use area, amphitheater, restrooms, trailer dump station, 3.5 miles of trail
**Attractions:** Camping, picnicking, beachcombing, clamming, crabbing, fishing,

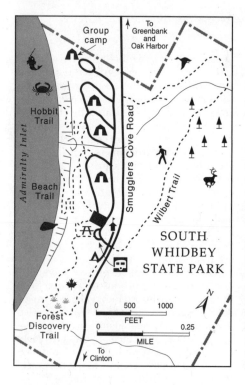

hiking, birdwatching, interpretive programs

**Access:** From the ferry landing at Clinton on Whidbey Island, take Highway 525 north for 9 miles, then turn west on Bush Point Road, which in about 3 miles joins Smugglers Cove Road. Continue north for 1.5 miles to the park entrance.

In most parks bordering on Puget Sound, the beach is the prime attraction, and any inland trails are nice added tidbits, but draw only limited interest. The case is just the opposite at South Whidbey, where the beach, although not to be denigrated, is not as interesting as its trails.

All of the park facilities lie on the west side of Smugglers Cove Road. Picnic sites are on a forested flat near the park entrance. Beyond the day-use parking lot are three campground loops. Trees and dense brush provide campsite seclusion, and wildflowers add color in season. At the end of the campground road, a small loop encircles a group camp. Park rangers conduct weekend interpretive programs during summer months at a campfire circle northwest of the

*A rustic bridge crosses a creek on the route of the Forest Discovery Trail at South Whidbey State Park.*

picnic area; groups may schedule guided interpretive walks.

Two 0.5-mile-long trails to the beach leave the parking lot and campground and wander through a forest of huge, old Douglas fir with a thick undergrowth of salmonberries, blackberries, and a healthy share of nettles. The final stretch of the Beach Trail descends to the shore on a wooden staircase. The Hobbit Trail switchbacks down a drainage (where the namesake of the trail possibly dwelled) to reach the shore northwest of the Beach Trail. The cobble beach lies below a high clay bank with exposed strata of sedimentary rocks.

At the south end of the park, the mile-long Forest Discovery Trail loops along the top of the bluff past alder, cedar, and fir, and Lilliputian forests of ferns, then drops into a ravine. Bridges cross creeks and soggy spots; in spring brilliant yellow skunk cabbage brighten the trail.

The Wilbert Trail, which starts on the east side of the road opposite the park entrance, loops through a forest of 250-year-old western red cedar and Douglas fir. Walk quietly and perhaps see black-tailed deer, raccoons, foxes, rabbits, or squirrels who make the forest home. Look up to tree snags for bald eagles, ospreys, and pileated woodpeckers. This densely forested portion of the park was targeted for logging; however, the hue and cry of environmentalists, and even lawsuits filed on behalf of the trees saved it. (Perhaps the Lorax had a hand in it, too.)

# CAMANO ISLAND STATE PARK

**Hours/Season:** Overnight; standard hours; year-round

**Area:** 134.4 acres; 6,700 feet of saltwater shoreline on Saratoga Passage

**Facilities:** 87 standard campsites, 200-person group camp, 113 picnic sites, kitchen shelter, restrooms, vault toilets, bathhouse, trailer dump station, boat launch ramp, nature trail, 3 miles of hiking trail

**Attractions:** Camping, picnicking, hiking, beachcombing, birdwatching, fishing, clamming, swimming, scuba diving, boating, paddling, nature study

**Access:** At Exit 212 from I-5, 18 miles north of Everett, head west on Highway 532. Turn south on East Camano Drive 3.5 miles after crossing the West Pass bridge onto Camano Island. In 2.5 miles head southwest on Camano Hill Road, which joins West Camano Drive in 4.2 miles. Continue south on West Camano Drive for 3 miles, then turn southwest on Lowell Point Road, and reach the park in 0.6 mile.

You've heard of instant coffee and instant tea. Camano Island State Park could probably be called "instant park." In 1949, after the South Camano Grange successfully lobbied the DNR to make property available for a park, a group of

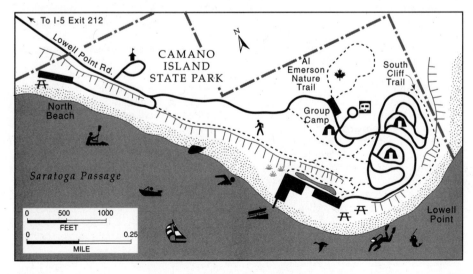

*Launching boats at Camano Island State Park*

900 volunteers turned out and in one day developed the initial park improvements.

The 100-foot-high headland of Lowell Point divides the park. A road snakes down its face to the wide, flat beach at the southwest side of the point where day-use facilities are located. Farther north, near the park boundary, a narrow, grassy plateau between the bluff and the beach holds a second picnic area. The beach along the northern two-thirds of the park is much narrower than that portion west of Lowell Point, and in places it nearly disappears at high tide.

A three-lane concrete boat launch ramp at the north end of the Lowell Point beach tapers gently into Saratoga Passage; however, there are no boarding floats, so wading becomes part of the launching ritual. The broad rocky beach below the driftwood line is one of the best on Saratoga Passage for a lazy day of sunbathing while watching boats cruise the waterway. At a minus tide a few clams may even be found. The wide beach-grass flat between high-tide debris and the bluff has ample room for flying kites, playing ball, tossing Frisbees, or picnicking. A freshwater marsh edged by wild rose that stretches along the base of the bluff behind the parking lot holds surprises such as frogs and salamanders.

Campground loops lie in the woods at the top of the bluff. A group camp here includes an outdoor amphitheater; nature programs may be given by the park staff on request. Here also is the 0.5-mile-long Al Emerson Nature Trail. Numbered stations identify trailside flora and other interesting features such as signs of early logging and forest fires.

South Cliff Trail leaves the campground and skirts the edge of the bluff. Views are south along the narrow finger of Camano Island to its tip at Camano Head, to Gedney Island at the heart of Saratoga Passage, and across the passage to the wooded eastern shore of Whidbey Island. A second trail along the edge of the bluff links the North Beach picnic area with the campground and offers bird's-eye views of boats in Saratoga Passage and across the backbone of Whidbey Island to the horizon-filling Olympics. A spur from this trail weaves through the woods to the group camp.

# MUKILTEO
# STATE PARK

**Hours/Season:** Day-use; standard hours; year-round; floats removed in winter
**Area:** 17.6 acres; 1,495 feet of saltwater shoreline on Admiralty Inlet
**Facilities:** 45 picnic tables, restroom with dressing rooms, boat launch ramp, floats
**Attractions:** Picnicking, boating, fishing, beachcombing, birdwatching, kite flying, scuba diving
**Access:** At Exit 189 from I-5, 6 miles south of Everett, head west on Highway 526 for 3.5 miles to its intersection with Highway 525 (Mukilteo Speedway). Turn north and arrive at the town of Mukilteo and the park in another 2 miles.

Although Mukilteo State Park is primarily a huge, blacktopped parking lot, over a million people visit it annually. What's the attraction? The strip of sandy beach is a nice place for local people to grab a quick picnic; the sandy beach is great for sunbathers, although strong currents and rapid dropoffs make the water unsafe for swimmers; windsurfers (in wet suits to protect themselves from the year-round icy water) take advantage of the winds sweeping along the shores of Possession Sound; and the less venturesome can use the same winds to fly kites.

Finally, double-length parking spaces attest to the fact that one of the main attractions of the park is its boat launch ramp. The four-lane ramp near the lighthouse drops gradually at high-tide levels, then very steeply near the low-tide line. The slope of the ramp, combined with winds and waves that frequently whip the point from the southwest, make it one of the most difficult to use on Puget Sound, but because it is the only one for some distance, it is heavily used. A boarding float along the north side of the ramp lies on the bottom at minus tides.

Two plaques at the park commemorate the location's historical significance as the site of the signing, in 1855, of the Point Elliott Treaty between Territorial Governor Isaac Stevens and the chiefs of the twenty-two Indian tribes living in the area. The chiefs, not understanding the language of the treaty, ceded their lands in exchange for meager reservations and trivial monetary compensation. Unrest over this and other unfair treaties precipitated the Indian Wars of 1855–56.

# WENBERG
# STATE PARK

**Hours/Season:** Overnight; standard hours; year-round
**Area:** 45.9 acres; 1,140 feet of freshwater shoreline on Lake Goodwin
**Facilities:** 65 standard campsites, 10 RV sites, 75 picnic tables, 2 picnic shelters, 150-person group day-use area, children's play equipment, trailer dump station, restrooms, bathhouse, swimming beach, boat launch ramp, 2 swim/water-ski floats, snacks (concession), 0.5 mile of trail
**Attractions:** Camping, picnicking, swim-

*It's great to spend an afternoon waterskiing at Wenberg State Park.*

ming, boating, waterskiing, fishing
**Access:** At Exit 206 from I-5, 7 miles north of Marysville, head west on 172nd Street NE, which at Meridian becomes 172nd Street NW. In 2.4 miles head northwest on Lakewood Road. In 2.7 miles turn south on E Lake Goodwin Road to reach the park in another 1.5 miles.

▲Wenberg State Park packs a lot of fun into a narrow strip of land fronting on Lake Goodwin. A sandy beach faces a roped-off swimming area with a swim float at its deeper outer edge. Another float farther offshore serves as a take-off point for waterskiers. A road leads down along the south side of the park to a two-lane concrete boat launch ramp with a loading dock between the ramps. The 545-acre lake is stocked with rainbow and cutthroat trout, and also contains bass and perch. Early season trout fishing is usually excellent.

The park's uplands hold three campground loops—one a grassy strip with hookup sites, and the other two with standard sites set among brush and maple. Since the park is close to Puget Sound's metropolitan areas, it is extremely popular, and the campground is nearly always full on weekends during summer months.

The day-use area has a large group picnic shelter and a spacious parking lot next to the campground. Short, paved trails lead from here down the wooded hillside to the lake. At the beach a rolling lawn punctuated with stately grand fir, some more than a hundred feet high, holds picnic sites. A concession stand, bathhouse, and a line of picnic tables with fire braziers stretch along a shaded terrace above the lower picnic area.

## ROCKPORT STATE PARK

**Hours/Season:** Overnight; standard hours; closed from mid-November to the end of March
**Area:** 457 acres
**Facilities:** 50 RV sites, 8 walk-in tent sites, 4 adirondack shelters, 3 primitive campsites, 60-person group camp, 33 picnic sites, kitchen shelter, restrooms, trailer dump station, 5 miles of hiking trail

**Attractions:** Camping, picnicking, hiking, birdwatching
**Nearby:** Skagit River Bald Eagle Sanctuary
**Access:** From Exit 230 from I-5, 3 miles north of Mount Vernon, head east on Highway 20. Reach the park in 35.5 miles.

▲Here's one of the grandest chunks of forest primeval to be found in any of Washington's state parks. The preserve, which miraculously was spared the logger's blade, serves as a fitting monument to Scotsman David Douglas, who visited the Pacific Northwest in 1825 on a mission to collect botanical samples for the British Royal Horticultural Society. The gigantic Douglas fir was one of his many discoveries. A plaque near the park entrance describes his achievements.

Impressive, 250-foot-tall specimens of the trees that bear Douglas's name fill the state park, and sunlight barely penetrates the thick forest canopy. Moss-draped cedar and slender stems of maple and alder that arch over trails add to the cathedral-like solemnity. Elderberry and salmonberry ripen on trailside bushes, and even the friendless devil's club bears fiery batons of red berries. Virtually every kind of Northwest fern carpets the forest floor—count how many different ones you see. In July unique Indian pipe blossoms can be found in the moist, rich humus near the base of old firs. The bizarre saprophyte (which has no chlorophyll) is rare, so treat it with care. The park surely is woodpecker nirvana; watch for pileated woodpeckers blissfully attacking enormous tree trunks.

The day-use picnic area is on the right, just inside the park entrance; a group camp lies on a grassy loop east of here. Walk-in sites with adirondack shelters are just a stroll away in the woods north of the picnic area. Campsites with utility hookups are on a loop road on the west side of the park, surrounded by a dense undergrowth.

Trails range around the outer edges of the park and link together, forming a pleasant forest maze. On the south side of Highway 20 between the road and the bank of the Skagit River are two trail loops, Sauk Springs Trail and Skagit View Trail, both gentle and paved for wheelchair access. The latter trail reaches the high bank of the Skagit River, with views of a midriver island. The park lies at the edge of the Skagit River Bald

*Mature bald eagles perch in trees overlooking the Skagit River. (Photo by Bob and Ira Spring)*

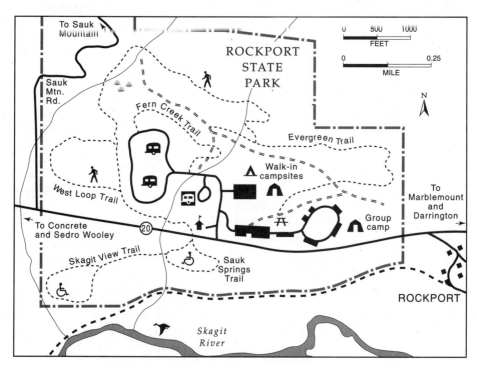

Eagle Sanctuary, and in winter more than 100 eagles at a time may be seen. The huge raptors congregate here to feed on carcasses of spawned-out salmon.

# CASCADE ISLAND STATE PARK

**Hours/Season:** Overnight; standard hours; year-round
**Area:** 17 acres
**Facilities:** 12 primitive campsites, vault toilets, *no water*
**Attractions:** Camping, hiking, picnicking, kayaking
**Access:** From Highway 20 at Marblemount, take the Cascade River Road east for 0.6 mile, then cross the bridge to the south to the South Cascade County Road, and continue east for 1 mile. The park is on the river on the north side of the road.

This primitive campground was originally developed by the DNR in the early 1970s, but the site has deteriorated due to recurring seasonal floods. The park offers access to the Cascade River for kayak float-trips downstream to the Skagit, and beyond to other haul-out points. Short trails wander through the woods adjacent the campground.

# MOUNT PILCHUCK STATE PARK

**Hours/Season:** Day-use; standard hours; year-round
**Area:** 1,893 acres; 6,000 feet of freshwater shoreline on various lakes and streams
**Facilities:** Hiking trails, pit toilets (*unmaintained*), picnic tables, fire lookout with interpretive signs
**Attractions:** Hiking, mountain climbing, scenic views, snowshoeing, ski mountaineering
**Access:** From the northeast side of Granite Falls, take the Mountain Loop Highway north for 10.9 miles to the Verlot Ranger Station. In another 0.9 mile, just beyond the bridge over the Stillaguamish River, turn south on Forest Road 42 (Heather Lake, Mount Pilchuck), and follow it uphill for 6.9 miles to the park.

Although its offerings of a hiking trail and a couple of vault toilets may seem meager compared to those of an upscale, multiactivity park, what Pilchuck offers is spectacular. No other spot in the western Cascades offers such views to any but skilled mountain climbers able to scale high peaks. The summit trail starts at the 3,100-foot level of the mountain, where an ill-fated commercial ski area operated for a

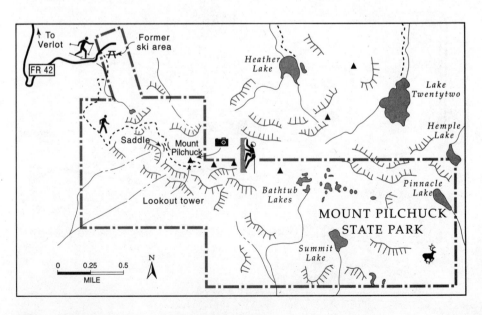

*A ridge leading from the summit of Mount Pilchuck offers grand views.*

few years before lack of a constant snow-pack caused it to be abandoned in the 1970s. Now only a few picnic tables and a pair of battered pit toilets sit beside the parking lot, and the once-groomed slopes are covered with new-growth evergreens. In winter the road is gated at the Heather Lake trailhead, 5.5 miles downhill. The strenuous cross-country ski trip up the road to the old ski area is rewarded on a clear day with views of sharp, blazing-white peaks to the northeast.

The lower section of the trail winds up the boggy drainage of Rotary Creek before swinging west. Small boulders and tree roots that stud the trail make the descent as slow as the ascent. At 4,100 feet the trees give way to rocky slopes and alpine meadows, with enough succulent huckleberries in fall to cause an end to the trip right here. Once out of the trees the faint path, marked by yellow paint, wends across heather-rimmed slabs and boulders. After switch-backing up the sidehill to a 4,700-foot saddle west of the summit, the trail crosses the narrow ridge into alpine timber on the south side of the mountain. Although the ridge-line can be followed to the summit from the saddle, and the way is marked with paint splotches, strenuous boulder scrambling is involved. The regular route is easier and faster, but a little longer.

Although this is not a difficult hike, the elevation gain is over 2,200 feet in about 2.5 miles, and a leisurely round trip will take about 5 hours. You will need route finding experience on the upper portion of the trail in fog or when snow covers the painted markers; novice hikers have become lost or been injured here. The vertical northeast side of the mountain offers challenging routes for experienced mountain climbers.

Those old fire-watchers knew what they were doing when they chose this 5,340-foot summit for a lookout site. Peaks spread in all directions, ranging from nearby White-horse and Three Fingers to the distant masses of Shuksan, Baker, Glacier, and Rainier. To the west the Olympics stretch above Puget Sound. The lookout house offers protection from chilling winds across the summit ridge. Photographic displays inside tell the history of the lookout and identify the major peaks.

**139**

# WALLACE FALLS STATE PARK

**Hours/Season:** Overnight; standard hours; closed Mondays and Tuesdays, October 1 to April 15; camping permitted only in the day-use area

**Area:** 678.2 acres; 6,300 feet of freshwater shoreline on the Wallace River and Wallace Lake

**Facilities:** 6 primitive campsites, picnic tables, restrooms, 2 picnic shelters, 5.5 miles of trail

**Attractions:** Camping, picnicking, hiking, nature study, fishing, berry picking, mountain biking, scenic views

**Access:** At Gold Bar turn north from US 2 onto 1st Street, then in 0.4 mile head west on May Creek Road (Camp Huston, Wallace Falls State Park). In 0.7 mile turn north on Leigh Road, and arrive at the park in another 0.4 mile.

From the highway between Sultan and Gold Bar, Wallace Falls appears as a white ribbon pinned to the forested hillside. The 265-foot-high cataract visible from the highway on the north side of the Skykomish River valley is only one of a series of plunges on the South Fork of the Wallace River that drop nearly 500 feet.

Camping is clearly secondary to the scenery at this state park. Six primitive campsites with picnic tables and fire grates are spread around a wooded loop on the west side of the parking lot. The hiking trail starts from the parking area and splits a short way uphill. The left branch, which follows the bed of an old logging railroad, is a longer but gentler alternative. The right branch, the Woody Trail (named for a state senator active in youth conservation activities), traces a steeper path through second-growth Douglas fir, alder, and cedar above the riverbank. The Woody Trail is open only to foot travel, but mountain bikers may use the railroad grade.

The divergent paths meet again near the bridge over the North Fork of the Wallace River. In short order a picnic shelter and the first view of the falls are reached. This is a good destination for the faint of lung and leg; beyond here the route switchbacks relentlessly upward to two more views of the thundering falls, one of the tallest in the Cascades. The viewpoint at the top of the falls also has an overlook of the Skykomish Valley, framed by uprising peaks. Total distance from the trailhead is 2.5 miles via the Woody Trail and 3.5 via the railroad grade. The trail continues uphill and across a moist flat, where the route can be confused with other tracks trampled through the brush. In 0.5 mile it arrives at an overlook of the smaller upper falls.

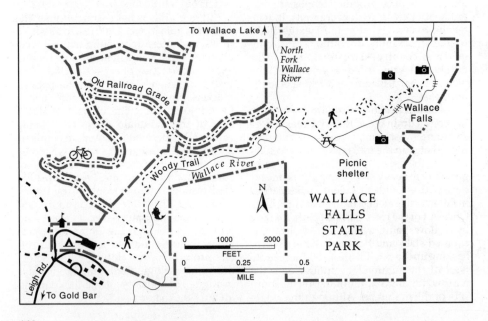

140

The trail indicated on topographic maps continuing from here has not been maintained, and quickly disappears into brushy growth. The DNR has recently transferred a strip of land along the North Fork of the Wallace River to the State Parks Commission, and in the future a trail will be put through to Wallace Lake.

*Trails lead to the thundering cataract of Wallace Falls.*

# REGION 3

- Okanogan
- Methow
- Chelan
- Wenatchee
- Ellensburg
- Upper Yakima River

## CURLEW LAKE
## STATE PARK

**Hours/Season:** Overnight; standard hours; closed from the end of October to the end of March

**Area:** 123 acres; 4,540 feet of freshwater shoreline on Curlew Lake

**Facilities:** 57 standard campsites, 18 RV sites with full hookups, 7 RV sites with water and power only, 5 primitive fly-in sites with tie-downs, 10 picnic sites, fireplaces, restrooms, swimming beach, boat launch ramp, docks, trailer dump station, hiking trail

**Attractions:** Camping, picnicking, fishing, boating, waterskiing, swimming, cross-country skiing, ice fishing, flying

**Access:** Located on the east shore of Curlew Lake off Highway 21, 9.1 miles north of Republic, 12.6 miles south of Curlew.

Campers searching for a respite from the civilized, "golf green" lawns of numerous other state parks in this part of Washington will love Curlew Lake. Rather than pancake-flat campground loops and carbon-copy sites, many of the park campsites that edge the lake are on grassy hummocks and terraces framed by Douglas fir. With some, gear must be carried 30 or 40 feet uphill from the car.

Near the entrance to the main camp area, a two-lane boat launch ramp and adjoining dock provide lake access for boating or

Opposite: *The fish are biting at Curlew Lake.*

fishing. At the day-use area, located farther south along the lakeshore, large ponderosa pines shade picnic tables scattered along a grass slope. Below, a swimming beach has been roped off at a small bay.

Beyond the picnic area a second snug camping area lies at the road end; individual sites are nicely divided by the natural

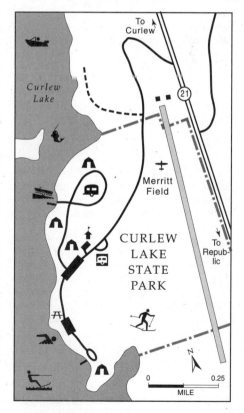

contours of the hillside. This area also has a dock below it on the lake.

Merritt Field (Ferry County Airport), whose north end lies within the park boundary, has five tie-downs for visitors who fly to the park. A trail leads from the airport down the hill, or when possible the park will graciously provide transportation for fly-in visitors with camping gear.

In summer the open, grassy hillsides above the camping area burst with color—blue-purple blossoms of phacelia and lupine, yellow splashes of mule-ears, and white clusters of yarrow. Killdeer skitter through the grass, and at dusk deer emerge. With winter's snow and freezing temperatures, the park attracts ice fishermen and cross-country skiers; restrooms are closed in winter, but the gate is usually left open.

## RANALD MCDONALD'S GRAVE HERITAGE AREA

**Hours/Season:** Day-use
**Area:** 0.1 acre
**Facilities:** None
**Attractions:** Historical marker
**Access:** At Curlew, take the West Kettle River Road west from its intersection with Highway 21. In 9.5 miles turn east, cross the Kettle River, and follow the highway 1.1 miles north to where a single-lane dirt road heads steeply uphill to the east for 500 feet to the cemetery. The site is signed only when approaching from the south.

▲ A simple, tiny country cemetery sits on a bluff overlooking the rich bottomland of the Kettle River. Headstones date back to the 1800s, and many graves are marked only by a plain cross.

The largest stone in the cemetery commemorates Ranald McDonald (1824–1894), the son of a pioneer Scotsman and Princess Raven, daughter of Chinook Indian Chief Comcomly. McDonald was an adventurer who learned Japanese from two sailors at Fort Vancouver, then later deliberately had himself shipwrecked on the shores of Japan, which was closed to all foreigners. Although at that time Western sailors were usually executed, he succeeded in working his way across the country, teaching the English language and promoting more open

and friendly relations between Japan and the U.S.

Other ventures took McDonald to Europe, Australia, and Alaska before he returned to live in a small Washington town near where he is now buried.

## OSOYOOS LAKE VETERANS' MEMORIAL STATE PARK

**Hours/Season:** Overnight; standard hours; weekends and holidays only, from the end of October to the end of March
**Area:** 46 acres; 7,305 feet of freshwater shoreline on Osoyoos Lake
**Facilities:** 80 standard campsites, 6 primitive walk-in sites, 60 picnic sites, kitchen shelter, fireplaces, bathhouse, rest-rooms, groceries and snacks (concession), swimming beach, boat launch ramp, docks, trailer dump station
**Attractions:** Camping, picnicking, swimming, boating, fishing, waterskiing, volleyball, ice skating, sledding, ice fishing, birdwatching
**Access:** On the east side of US 97, immediately north of the Oroville city limits.

▲ As the Okanogan River reaches the international border on its southward journey from the Canadian Rockies, it briefly widens into Osoyoos Lake. Although the bulk of the 14-mile-long lake lies in British Columbia, enough extends into Washington to provide a spacious year-round playground.

Early Indians called the south end of the lake *soyoos*, meaning "the narrows." The story goes that a local Irishman named O'Sullivan added the "O," having little truck with names not beginning in this fashion. The broad flat on the southeast side of the lake was originally used as a campsite by the Okanogan Indians, who also held horse races here. During the mid-1850s the site was used by miners and cattle drivers who followed what was known as the Cariboo Trail north to gold fields on Canada's Fraser River. In later years it served as a fairground for the people of Oroville and finally became the fine state park it is today.

From the park entrance a wide lawn drops down the hillside to the flat, shaded campground loops. The lush grass continues on

*A spirited volleyball game on the shore of Osoyoos Lake*

to the sandy lakeshore, interrupted only by a parking lot between the camping and day-use areas. A bathhouse with a concession stand, a host of picnic sites, and a kitchen shelter serve this area. A roped-off swimming area offers relief from the summer's blazing heat. At the far end of the parking lot, a two-lane boat launch ramp, flanked by a boarding float, drops into the Okanogan River at the point where it exits from the lake.

In this region winters are as cold as summers are hot, and snow and freezing temperatures change the recreational focus of the park from swimming and boating to sledding, ice skating, and ice fishing.

## CONCONULLY STATE PARK

**Hours/Season:** Overnight; standard hours April 1 to September 30; 8:00 A.M. to dusk weekends only, October 1 to March 31
**Area:** 81 acres; 5,400 feet of freshwater shoreline on Conconully Lake
**Facilities:** 65 standard campsites, 10 RV sites with water only, 6 primitive campsites, 80 picnic sites, kitchen shelter, 350-person group day-use area, restrooms, trailer dump station, wading pool, hand-carried boat launch
**Attractions:** Camping, picnicking, fishing, swimming, snowmobiling, boating
**Access:** From US 97/Highway 20 in downtown Okanogan or Omak, follow signs to the park, or continue on 97/20 to Riverside, 5.2 miles north of Omak or 15.9 miles south of Tonasket, turn west onto the Riverside Cutoff Road, signed to Conconully State Park. At a junction in 5.3 miles, head northwest on Highway 215 to reach Conconully in another 10.1 miles. The park is on the west side of the highway just inside the town.

When the Bureau of Reclamation created Conconully Reservoir in the early 1900s as part of an irrigation project, it also provided the local community with a picnic grounds, a baseball field, and a schoolhouse. Even though the property became a state park in 1945, along with several adjoining parcels, it retains the flavor of a community gathering spot.

*Enormous old willows shade picnic tables at Conconully State Park.*

The wide grassy field that spreads around the north end of the reservoir is divided into large spaces by huge venerable willow, fir, and maple trees. Each section provides an ample picnic ground or playfield. The area to the east has designated non-hookup campsites around a loop road. At the opposite end of the park, another loop is equipped with water hookups.

Because it is a reservoir, the level of the lake fluctuates widely. When it is at its fullest, the beachfront is marshy and not particularly suited for swimming; however, tots can frolic in a wading pool at the center of the park near the beach. Rainbow trout, stocked annually, provide fishing opportunities.

Area history is recounted at a sod-roofed cabin and a school bell near the park entrance. The bell is from the old Conconully Schoolhouse, built in 1890, that stood for many years in the heart of what is now the park site. The cabin is a replica of one that was located on a nearby ranch and was used as a courthouse when Okanogan County was first organized in 1888.

A second camping area lies along the lakeshore south of the main park area. Although this campground offers lakeside sites, the dirt-surfaced areas make camping here a bit spartan compared to that in the grassy field of the main area. A dirt ramp for launching cartop boats has been carved from marsh grass that chokes the shore. The gradually sloping shoreline and sandy bottom provide a nice, natural swimming beach. The main park area can be reached by a 0.4-mile-long trail that leads north across a footbridge over the creek that flows between the reservoir and Conconully Lake.

## RUBY TOWNSITE HERITAGE AREA

**Hours/Season:** Day-use
**Area:** 6.4 acres
**Facilities:** Historical marker
**Attractions:** Sightseeing
**Access:** Follow the directions for Conconully State Park. Salmon Creek/Ruby Road heads uphill to the southwest 6.9 miles northwest of the intersection of Riverside Cutoff Road and Highway 215 (3.2 miles southeast of Conconully). Follow this narrow dirt road for 2.8 miles to the historic marker at the old townsite.

▲A narrow, dusty road and a few hidden, weed-shrouded rock foundations are all that remains of what once was the quarter-mile-long main street of the infamous, roistering city of Ruby. The town, born in 1886 following a rich silver strike in the ridges to the west, became one of the major mining camps in the northwest. Miners and speculators pouring into town slaked their thirst with cheap, free-flowing whiskey. The growing population caused Ruby to be named the first county seat.

Fortune was fickle, however, and in 1893, when the price dropped out of the silver market due to the nationwide economic depression, Ruby was abandoned virtually overnight. Now only a historical signboard and plaque mark the site.

## PEARRYGIN LAKE STATE PARK

**Hours/Season:** Overnight; standard hours; closed from mid-November to the end of March
**Area:** 578 acres; 8,200 feet of freshwater shoreline on Pearrygin Lake

**Facilities:** 26 standard campsites, 30 RV sites with full hookups, 27 RV sites with water only, 48-person group camp, 2 primitive walk-in sites, 30 picnic sites, fireplaces, restrooms, swimming beach, bathhouse, vault toilets, trailer dump station, boat launch ramp
**Attractions:** Camping, picnicking, fishing, boating, swimming, waterskiing, cross-country skiing, hiking, snowmobiling
**Access:** From US 20 at the center of Winthrop, head north out of town on Bluff Street, which becomes East Chewuch Road. In 1.6 miles turn east on Bear Creek Road. At a Y-intersection in another 1.8 miles, the paved road makes a sharp turn to the right and reaches the park in 0.5 mile.

▲Some 15,000 years ago, during the last Ice Age, an enormous glacier flowed south from Canada, gouging out the Methow Valley in its course. As it retreated, gravelly till left behind by the melting ice sheet blocked some of the drainages, leaving lakes scattered among the scoured hills. Pearrygin, a spring-fed lake, is a result of this glacial handiwork.

Viewed from the bluff inside the park

*Pearrygin Lake State Park is a green oasis on the shore of the lake.*

entrance, the turquoise lake provides bright contrast to the surrounding hillsides that are parched brown in summer, or in spring painted yellow, blue, and pink with balsam root, sunflowers, lupine, larkspur, and wild rose. In the distance the icy summits of the North Cascades serrate the skyline.

The area itself is an oasis typical of central Washington state parks—a flat, green swath of lawn planted with leafy trees to provide respite from the sun. A sandy beach below the day-use area tapers to a roped-off swimming area. Campground loops flank three sides of the day-use area; many sites back up against the surrounding hillside, while a few edge the brushy lakeshore. Short trails leave the easternmost camp loop to circle around the east shore of the lake or to wander a short distance through the brush toward the park boundary.

A boat launch ramp at the west end of the park provides water access for boating, waterskiing, and fishing. The lake is stocked annually with rainbow trout. Nearby, just outside the park boundary, a small store handles fishing supplies and boat rentals, as well as ice, groceries, and sandwiches.

When winter snow makes swimming, fishing, and waterskiing just a fond memory, cross-country skiers and snowmobilers frequent the park's rolling hills.

## FORT OKANOGAN INTERPRETIVE CENTER

**Hours/Season:** Day-use; 9:00 A.M. to 6:00 P.M., Wednesday through Sunday from June 1 to August 31; open by appointment only from September 1 to May 31
**Area:** 44.7 acres; 1,000 feet of freshwater shoreline on Lake Pateros (Columbia River)
**Facilities:** Interpretive center, restrooms, 3 picnic sites, picnic shelter
**Attractions:** Historical displays, picnicking, viewpoint
**Access:** On Highway 17, 5 miles east of Brewster and 0.3 mile east of the junction of US 97 and Highway 17.

In the early 1800s competition between British, American, and Canadian factions to control the valuable fur trade in the Pacific Northwest led to the establishment of Fort Okanogan as a trading post at the confluence of the Columbia and Okanogan rivers. Although the fort was built in 1811 by American John Jacob Astor, it was sold in 1813 to the Canadian North West Company, which later merged with the British-owned Hudson's Bay Company. It wasn't until the advent of the Oregon Treaty of 1846 that it was once again in American hands.

The Fort Okanogan Interpretive Center details the fascinating story of the fort, the local Indians, and the settlement of the Okanogan area. Dioramas recreate early history; a display of artifacts includes tools, fur traps, and trading items recovered during excavations of the two nearby locations of the fort. Archeologists identified remains of the buildings and walls of the forts before the backwater of Wells Dam began lapping at the sites.

The bluff on which the interpretive center stands provides sweeping vistas of Lake Pateros, the river confluence, and the fort sites. Adjoining the center's parking lot is a small picnic shelter and a few Indian petroglyphs that were moved here prior to the flooding of their original location.

## CHIEF JOSEPH STATE PARK (UNDEVELOPED)

**Hours/Season:** Day-use
**Area:** 297.6 acres; 25,000 feet of freshwater shoreline on Lake Pateros (Columbia River)
**Facilities:** Causeway, primitive boat launch, 4.5 miles of one-lane primitive road
**Attractions:** Hiking, boating, fishing
**Access:** Drive Highway 173 north from Bridgeport. In 4.1 miles, where the highway makes a sharp turn to the west, continue straight ahead on Moe Road. In 0.2 mile, just before Moe Road angles to the northwest, a gated dirt spur road leads east leads across the causeway to the park.

North of Bridgeport, Lake Pateros bends sharply to the south around a broad thumb of land that has been transformed into an island by a narrow channel of water cutting along along its west side. A dirt road crosses a causeway onto the island from the west and links into a network of dirt roads that lace the brush- and tree-covered island. The site is closed to vehicles; day-use walk-in activities are permitted.

## BRIDGEPORT STATE PARK

**Hours/Season:** Overnight; standard hours; closed from the end of October to the end of March
**Area:** 749.7 acres; 7,500 feet of freshwater shoreline on Rufus Woods Lake (Columbia River)
**Facilities:** 10 standard campsites, 20 RV sites, 4 primitive campsites, 75-person group camp, 20 picnic sites, 2 picnic shelters, restrooms, bathhouse, children's play equipment, swimming beach, trailer dump station, boat launch, golf course (concession), restaurant (concession), 0.25-mile hiking trail to a viewpoint
**Attractions:** Picnicking, swimming, boating, fishing, waterskiing, golfing
**Nearby:** Chief Joseph Dam
**Access:** Turn east from Highway 17, 0.4 mile north of Bridgeport, onto a road

signed to the park and reach the park entrance in another 2.4 miles.

Bridgeport State Park sits on the north shore of Rufus Woods Lake, just a short distance upstream from Chief Joseph Dam. The road to the park provides views of the dam—one of the largest in the nation—with its massive powerhouse and row of twenty-seven generator penstocks pouring frothy water into the river below.

The park was nursed out of the surrounding desert, after the completion of the dam in 1955, by the determined labor of Army Corps of Engineers retiree Ralph Van Slyke, who tackled the project with little more than garden tools. Today the sweeping lawns of the park, and the fairways of the adjoining Lakewood Golf Course (on park property and open to the public), prove what irrigation can wrest from a barren landscape.

Cottonwood and aspen shade the green campground loop; scattered outcroppings of rough basalt intrude through the otherwise groomed turf. The day-use area is a broad bowl anchored at both ends by unique tile-roofed stucco picnic shelters, fronted by the swimming beach. A community of marmots that lives near the east side of the

*A family of marmots lives in rocks near the swimming area at Bridgeport State Park.*

swimming area can often be spotted playing in the rocks and quizzically watching park activity.

At the north end of the park, another grassy flat, this one with an amphitheater, is available for group camping. Boats can be launched into the 50-mile-long reservoir via a two-lane concrete ramp, flanked by boarding floats, located a short distance inside the park entrance.

One step from the irrigated oasis of the park, the desert again dominates. Scattered about the parched landscape are fascinating, unusual 30-foot-high basalt "haystack" boulders, which were plucked from the lava flows at the north edge of the Columbia Plateau and deposited here by the massive glacier that flowed over this region some 15,000 years ago. The harsh terrain is habitat for rabbits, coyotes, quail, owls, chukars, partridges, and snakes (including rattlers).

## CROWN POINT
## HERITAGE AREA

**Area:** 13 acres
**Facilities:** Viewpoint vista dome
**Attractions:** Sightseeing
**Nearby:** Grand Coulee Dam
**Access:** From Highway 174, 1.1 miles north of Grand Coulee, turn northeast on a paved road signed to Crown Point Vista and reach the park in 1.4 miles.

Grand Coulee Dam is so stupendous that it is hard to grasp from up close. People who tour the dam may well want to see an overall view of the project. At Crown Point an open concrete pavilion sits atop a high bluff, with an expansive view far below to the imposing concrete spillways and powerhouses of the dam, proclaimed as one of the wonders of the modern world. The adjacent communities of Grand Coulee, Coulee Dam, Electric City, and Elmer City, along with the manmade channel of the Columbia below the dam, complete the scene in the valley beneath. The viewpoint is an excellent spot to watch the spectacular laser light show that is shown on the face of the dam. The 35-minute program runs nightly from Memorial Day through the end of September.

Although the dam, which was completed in 1941, was originally intended as part of the Columbia River Irrigation Project, it played a critical role in supplying electricity for the manufacture of aluminum airplanes in World War II. Today it continues to be a major source of power for the state. No interpretive displays are at the viewpoint; however, a visitor center is located just northwest of the dam on Highway 155, and tours of the dam are conducted year-round.

## BANKS LAKE
## WILDLIFE RECREATION AREA

**Hours/Season:** Overnight; standard hours; year-round
**Area:** 43,799.3 acres; 430,000 feet of freshwater shoreline on Banks Lake
**Facilities:** Primitive camping, 2 boat launch ramps, 5 miles of trail, 10 miles of dirt road; under commercial lease are Grand Coulee Airport, Coulee Playland Resort
**Attractions:** Camping, fishing, flying, boating, waterskiing, hiking, horseback riding, hunting (shotgun only), ice fishing, cross-country skiing, snowshoeing
**Nearby:** Grand Coulee Dam
**Access:** On the east shore of Banks Lake, 0.5 mile south of Electric City on Highway 155.

Surprisingly, Grand Coulee Dam is not located on Grand Coulee, but adjacent to the head of it. It is North and Dry Falls dams, both earthfill dams, that enclose the ends of Upper Grand Coulee, preventing the water from spilling over Dry Falls, thus keeping Dry Falls dry. Banks Lake fills the enormous gash of the canyon—some 27 miles long and 4 miles wide in places. The lake, which serves as an equalizing reservoir used in maintaining a consistent flow of irrigation water for the Columbia Basin Reclamation Project, is filled with water transferred by pumps from Franklin D. Roosevelt Lake.

The State Department of Wildlife and the State Parks and Recreation Commission jointly administer all land adjoining the shoreline of Banks Lake. Bird hunting is permitted in season outside the developed park area. The major developed recreation

*The numerous rock-walled coves on Banks Lake are prime spots for bass fishing.*

areas on the lake are formally part of Steamboat Rock State Park; however, several primitive camping areas and boat launches scattered along the edge of the lake are also administered by the park.

Just south of Electric City, after crossing the bridge over Osborn Bay, a gravel road heads west along the shoreline and in 0.25 mile arrives at a two-lane concrete launch ramp with adjoining parking shaded by a few trees. The site, which has vault toilets and a self-registration station, is used by boaters and fishermen with RVs as a primitive camp spot. Rough dirt roads thread through the adjoining sagebrush-covered desert.

Two other primitive campgrounds can be found on the east side of the lake just north of Castle Rock, 3.2 miles south of Electric City. Both have a self-administered pay station at the head of the dirt roads leading to them, vault toilets, and a spot for hand launching cartop boats. A few campsites have been leveled off near the marshy shoreline, and some picnic tables are scattered under sparse trees.

Another launch ramp is located on the west shore of the lake at the base of Barker Canyon. It's a long haul from civilization by car, but it can be reached by taking Highway 174 northwest out of Grand Coulee for 8.7 miles, then turning south on Barker Canyon Road, which reaches the lakeshore in another 5.3 miles. The ramp, parking, and vault toilet that have been provided here are administered by the Department of Wildlife.

All launch sites on the lake warn of submerged and dangerous obstructions just covered by the waters of the lake. Wind vanes are also found at various sites on the lake; when intermittent high winds sweep the lake, the vanes' flashing yellow lights warn that boaters should immediately seek protection in a safe cove.

For fishermen, the lake is close to heaven, as its many rock-walled coves are home to a large population of both smallmouth and largemouth bass. The lake is stocked annually with kokanee salmon and rainbow trout; it holds walleye, crappie, perch, blue gill, and whitefish as well. Winter ice fishing yields good-sized perch, bass, and kokanee.

**151**

The lake serves as a migratory stopover or nesting grounds for shore and water-birds. Gulls, grebes, and sea ducks that are more normally found along the coast are regularly seen here in fall and winter. Surrounding sage and grasslands host hawks and a regiment of perching birds ranging from shy wrens to bold magpies and ravens.

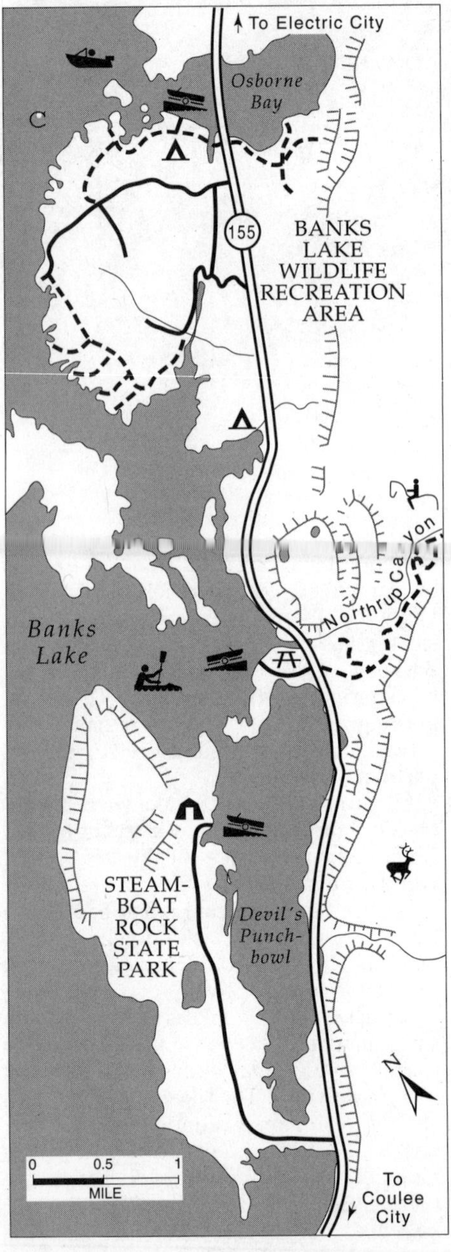

Even for those not interested in fishing, the scenic grandeur of the lake entices. Fingers and arms of the lake, and dozens of small rock islets, are framed by imposing, 700-foot-high basalt cliffs. For more than a century, trails used by Indians, fur traders, and settlers have threaded along the base of the cliffs where roads and highways now run. A major Indian trail followed the eastern shoreline; it later became the American Trail used by military traveling between Camp Chelan and Fort Walla Walla. A route down the west side of the canyon was known as the Okanogan Trail.

# STEAMBOAT ROCK STATE PARK

**Hours/Season:** Overnight; standard hours; year-round; *reservations accepted*

**Area:** 3,523 acres; 50,000 feet of freshwater shoreline on Banks Lake

**Facilities:** 5 standard campsites, 100 RV sites, 30 primitive campsites, 12 boat-in campsites, 53 picnic sites, 200-person group day-use area, restrooms with handicap access, solar vault toilets, children's play equipment, swimming beach, boat launch ramps, boarding docks, 6 mooring buoys, waterski float, 34 miles of hiking trail, snacks (concession)

**Attractions:** Camping, picnicking, swimming, hiking, horseback riding, scuba diving, boating, paddling, fishing, waterskiing, windsurfing, kite flying, sightseeing, nature preserve, cross-country skiing, snowshoeing, ice fishing, hunting in adjacent Department of Wildlife lands (shotgun only)

**Access:** West of Highway 155, 9.3 miles south of Electric City or 26.5 miles north of Coulee City.

The dominating natural feature in the north end of Banks Lake is Steamboat Rock, whose 700-foot-high basalt cliffs once bounded an island in the middle of the ancient Columbia River. With shifts in the course of the river over time, the rock fortress now stands guard over the northwest end of a peninsula in Banks Lake. Although from some views the rock wall seems impregnable, a cleft at the center of its east side breaches the band of cliffs. A short,

*Steamboat Rock overlooks the state park's campground.*

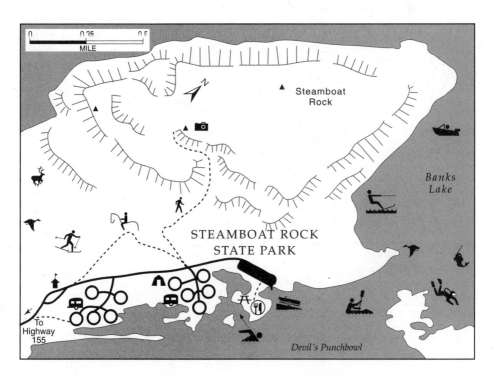

steep trail that starts from the entrance to the northernmost campground area gains 800 feet of elevation in 1 mile before reaching the plateau atop the rock. Once there, rough paths lead around the rim and crisscross its broad, flat, 640-acre summit. No drinking water is available along the route.

The two campground areas and day-use areas that occupy flat, emerald-green lawns edging Banks Lake are protected against the omnipresent wind by rows of tall Lombardy poplar. Campsites are laid out around the perimeter of asphalt access loops, ten sites to a circle. The sandy-shored swimming beach lies in a narrow channel behind a small offshore island. A triangular section of the channel, with the island at its apex, has been roped off to form the swimming area. A two-lane concrete launch ramp, with a dock along one side, is on a small cove to the north.

A second boat launch with adjacent picnic area lies on the west side of Highway 155, 3.4 miles north of the main park entrance road. The two-lane ramp and boarding dock are well protected by the low rock walls of a small cove. A shaded grassy picnic area adjoins the uphill side of the ramp parking lot.

Immediately across the highway from the entrance to the boat launch, a single lane gravel road that climbs up Northrup Canyon is a remnant of a stagecoach and freight wagon road that at one time connected Almira to Bridgeport. Today the road is gated 0.7 mile from the highway. The edge of the flat-topped butte to the north is the Castle Rock Natural Area Preserve. From here several miles of informal hiking and horse trails are open for day-use; the surrounding countryside has deliberately been left in its natural state. In spring and early summer wildflowers are everywhere, tinging the gray-green scablands with hues of yellow, blue, and pink.

# SUN LAKES
# STATE PARK

**Hours/Season:** Overnight; standard hours; year-round

**Area:** 4,023.7 acres; 73,640 feet of freshwater shoreline on Park Lake and numerous smaller lakes

**Facilities:** 175 standard campsites, 18 RV sites, 50-person group camp, 90 picnic sites, 100-person group day-use area, swimming beach, Environmental Learning Center, interpretive center, restrooms, trailer dump station, boat launch ramp, 27.5 miles of road, 15.5 miles of hiking and equestrian trail; concession facilities: golf course, cafe, general store, cabins, laundromat, marina, boat fuel, boat rental, 100 RV sites, riding stable

**Attractions:** Camping, picnicking, boating, fishing, swimming, golf, horseback riding, hiking, paddling, interpretive displays

**Access:** On Highway 17 between Coulee City and Soap Lake. *Sun Lakes State Park,* 5.9 miles south of Coulee City or 16.9 miles north of Soap Lake. *Dry Falls Interpretive Center,* 4 miles south of Coulee City or 18.8 miles north of Soap Lake. *Lake Lenore Caves Historical Area,* 13.9 miles south of Coulee City or 8.9 miles north of Soap Lake.

Sun Lakes State Park, lying in the Lower Grand Coulee, encompasses the northeast end of Park Lake, as well as a jumble of smaller lakes in the chasm below Dry Falls. The park facilities are primarily on Park Lake, where a concessionaire provides extensive resort-type amenities. State park–maintained campgrounds, picnic areas, and swimming beaches are found east and south

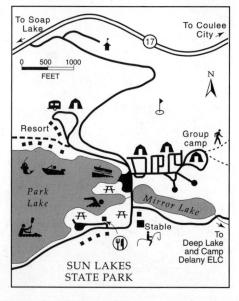

SUN LAKES
STATE PARK

of the resort area. The lakes in the park, which are planted with rainbow trout, offer good fishing in spring and summer.

A narrow paved road heads east up the coulee to a fork. The right fork eventually leads to Deep Lake, a long, narrow plunge-pool at the southeast base of Dry Falls. In another 0.25 mile from the fork a second road to the right leads to Camp Delany, an Environmental Learning Center.

The left fork of this road deteriorates quickly to a one-lane dirt road, rough, rutted, steep, and studded with sharp lava rocks, more suitable for four-wheel-drive vehicles or horses. The route passes Perch Lake and ends at 3 miles in a primitive launch ramp on the shore of Dry Falls Lake. Its convoluted shore and the immense basalt walls that surround it make Dry Falls Lake ideal for canoe or kayak exploration; ducks and turtles often doze on rocks in the lake. Saddle trails that wend through the desert landscape link this area to the main part of the park.

## DRY FALLS INTERPRETIVE CENTER

**Hours:** 10:00 A.M. to 6:00 P.M., Wednesday through Sunday, from mid-May to mid-September. Interpretive talks are scheduled three times daily at 11:00 A.M., 2:00 P.M., and 4:00 P.M. Tours for groups may

be arranged at other times by contacting the park manager at (509)632-5583.

▲ The sheer immensity of the geological forces that sculpted this area of the state almost defies imagination, despite the impressive evidence of their action. Mammoth ice sheets from the Pleistocene epoch, which began about a million years ago, pushed south from Canada and blocked the northbound flow of the ancient Columbia River, forcing it to carve a new channel through the lava-layered plateau to the south.

By the time the glaciers began to retreat, an enormous lake covering large portions of present-day western Montana had built up behind an ice dam. Scientists believe this dam gave way some 16,000 years ago, releasing a vast surge of water, over 300 feet deep, that swept through eastern Washington, almost instantly enlarging the existing river channels. Huge, roaring waterfalls were created that shook the ground and could be heard for miles, but that lasted for only a few weeks. The alternate damming and flooding occurred numerous times over the centuries—some think as many as 40 times—each time sweeping away more of the layered basalt and excavating deep canyons. The coulees that scar the eastern Washington landscape are the remnants of

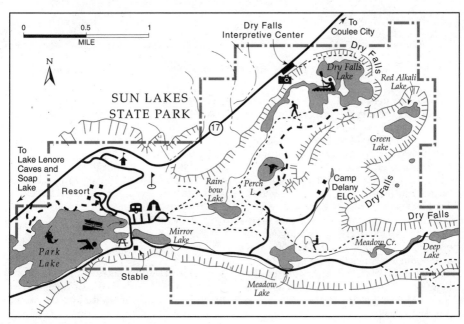

*Dry Falls Lake lies below 400-foot-high basalt cliffs that were carved by a gigantic waterfall.*

the flood channels, and the Grand Coulee, through this area, is the largest and most impressive of them all.

One of the waterfalls in the Grand Coulee began near present-day Soap Lake, but the torrent of water rushing over it rapidly eroded the lip, and by the time the flood subsided, the face of the falls had moved 20 miles upstream to the present site of Dry Falls. Today the dry skeleton of that monstrous falls is a sheer cliff stretching across the coulee, 3.5 miles wide and 400 feet high—some ten times larger than present-day Niagara Falls. The remnants of the plunge pools at its base now form a series of placid lakes at the northeast end of Sun Lakes State Park.

The park maintains an interpretive center at a breathtaking overlook on the northwest rim of Dry Falls. Displays tell of the geological history of the area and of archeological digs that provide evidence of early man's use of the area. For the truly venturesome, a trail leaves the parking lot and works its way down to the base of the cliffs at the northwest corner of Dry Falls Lake, a drop in elevation of nearly 400 feet.

### LAKE LENORE CAVES

A chain of slender lakes leads south from Sun Lakes State Park to Soap Lake, down the floor of the Lower Grand Coulee. Along the eastern rim of Lake Lenore, a glance up at the basalt cliffs reveals a series of caves that pock the walls of the upper layer of lava flow. These caverns were formed naturally when ancient floods plucked loose basalt from the coulee walls. Archaeological evidence shows that prehistoric hunters used these caves for temporary residence during their migrations through the area. Such caves can be found in other places in the Grand Coulee.

Turn off Highway 17 onto a gravel road that ends in a small parking area. From here an asphalt path leads up the talus slope to a stairway breaching the lower band of cliffs. Above, a dirt path leads along the bench between the lava layers for 0.25 mile past several of the caves. Not all are easily accessible. Swifts and swallows nest in the cliffs. Watch in the trailside brush for gray-and-white northern shrikes.

# SUMMER FALLS
# STATE PARK

**Hours/Season:** Day-use; standard hours; year-round
**Area:** 260 acres; 5 miles of freshwater

shoreline on Billy Clapp Lake
**Facilities:** 20 picnic sites, restroom
**Attractions:** Picnicking, fishing, falls viewpoint
**Access:** Turn south off US 2 into Coulee City on 4th Street. In 0.2 mile turn east on Main Street, and in 0.2 mile turn south on McEntee Street, which becomes Pinto Ridge Road as it leaves town. South of Coulee City 8.6 miles, a gravel road leads east down a draw to reach the park in 1.3 more miles.

▲ Summer Falls State Park provides a slight respite of green amid the arid gray coulees of central Washington. The small grassy picnic area on the shores of Billy Clapp Lake sits near the base of a stunning waterfall that pours over the rimrock wall into the lake below. The nearby irrigation canals spill surplus water over the falls only during summer months, thus the name. *Do not swim in the lake here*—whirlpools and undertow make the water treacherous.

The surrounding scrub and a nearby marsh provide habitat for an army of birds, including red-winged blackbirds, Say's phoebes, kingbirds, vireos, warblers, and chats. Red-tailed hawks nest in nearby cliffs.

*Summer Falls drains water from nearby irrigation canals.*

# ALTA LAKE
# STATE PARK

**Hours/Season:** Overnight; standard hours; open for snow activities in winter

**Area:** 180.1 acres; 3,996 feet of freshwater shoreline on Alta Lake

**Facilities:** 149 standard campsites, 31 RV sites (15 with water and power), 11 primitive campsites, 88-person group camp, 20 picnic sites, 2 kitchen shelters, restrooms, trailer dump station, swimming beach, bathhouse, boat launch ramp, dock, 2 miles of hiking trail

**Attractions:** Picnicking, birdwatching, swimming, boating, paddling, fishing, scuba diving, waterskiing, hiking, cross-country skiing, snowmobiling

**Nearby:** Golf course; resort with guided trail rides, boat rental, cabins, store

**Access:** Take Highway 153 west, 0.2 mile south of Pateros. In 1.8 miles an asphalt road, signed for the park, heads south, reaching the entrance in another 2 miles.

The azure jewel of Alta Lake nestles in a side canyon of the Methow Valley. The parched, sagebrush-covered hills give way to rimrock cliffs that line the east side of the lake and steep, pine-edged talus slopes that frame the west. Portions of Okanogan National Forest touch the east and west shores of the lake. At the lake's south end, a meadow marks two small resorts.

Just inside the state park entrance at the north end of the lake is a boat launch, with a lane on each side of a boarding float. The flat sun-baked field north of the boat launch, nominally a random camping area, offers only scattered picnic tables and no shade. The 187-acre lake is planted annually with rainbow trout, and fishing generally is fine, especially early in the season.

The first formal camping area lies on the north side of the road. One loop has sites that have full hookups, while sites along a second loop are for tenting only. A stand of lodgepole and ponderosa pine offers sparse shade, and undergrowth of sumac and serviceberry provides some separation of sites.

Greener campsites are found in the tree-shaded lawn at the west end of the park, just above the beach. Here are a tightly packed hookup loop and a small tenting area at road-end. The broad, green slope above the roped-off swimming beach has picnic shelters, tables, and a bathhouse.

At the northwest corner of the park, a

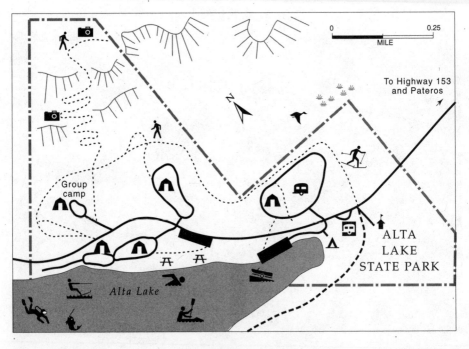

*Views from the hiking trail above Alta Lake extend down to the lake and out to the rolling hills of the Okanogan.*

gated road marks the entry to a group camp set in a meadow bracketed by small pines. The park's hiking trails begin here. One trail follows a wide service road, climbs a gentle ridge, then contours north at the base of the steep sidehill along the west side of the park before returning to the main road near the park entrance. Charred snags along the road stand as sad memorials to a 30-acre fire that burned through here in 1990.

The second trail does not delay in going uphill. After crossing the service road, it heads up the steep talus slope in a relentless succession of switchbacks, occasionally ducking back into the forest cover. After a climb of more than 900 vertical feet in about 0.5 mile, the trail ends at a small forested plateau. Views here are enormous: The deeply carved cleft of the Columbia River lies beyond the forest-topped cliffs to the east; north, the brown, lumpy hills of the Okanogan pile endlessly against the Washington sky; below, boat wakes trace patterns on Alta Lake.

When winter arrives the park is a favorite home base for cross-country skiing and snowmobiling around the surrounding snow-blanketed hillsides.

## ICE CAVES HERITAGE AREA (UNDEVELOPED)

**Hours/Season:** Day-use
**Area:** 160 acres
**Facilities:** None
**Attractions:** Sightseeing
**Access:** Take US 97 north from Chelan, and in 2.8 miles turn north on Apple Acres Road. In another 3.8 miles is a roadside pulloff that marks the park property.

Some years ago, before the days of modern refrigeration, local orchardists dug caves in the talus slopes above the road where water that had collected and frozen during the winter remained as ice until late summer. The caves were used to preserve

**159**

fruit from nearby orchards during the hot fall days that followed the harvest. Refrigerated warehouse storage has long since replaced the caves; entrances are now covered by rockslides, leaving only their memory preserved in the history of this small, obscure park.

## TWENTY-FIVE MILE CREEK STATE PARK

**Hours/Season:** Overnight; standard hours; closed from the end of October to the end of April
**Area:** 235 acres; 1,500 feet of freshwater shoreline on Lake Chelan
**Facilities:** 52 standard campsites, 23 RV sites, 88-person group camp, 6 picnic sites, restrooms, marina with docks and fuel (concession), boat launch ramp, grocery store (concession), volleyball
**Attractions:** Camping, picnicking, boating, wading, swimming, fishing, snowmobiling, cross-country skiing
**Access:** Follow South Lakeshore Drive north from Lake Chelan State Park for 10.3 miles.

Midway along the length of Lake Chelan, South Lakeshore Drive ends its meandering, water's-edge route at Twenty-five Mile Creek. The resort that was located here was one of the oldest in the Chelan Valley, enjoyed by millions of recreationists. In 1975 the State Parks and Recreation Commission, which planned a major expansion of the campground, purchased the resort. Although funding limitations have prevented additions to the campground, all of the old amenities remain and are maintained for the enjoyment of visitors.

Tops on the list is the marina, with its wood-faced piling breakwater protecting a gas float and moorage for about 35 boats. A two-lane launch ramp with a boarding float provides trailered boat access to the lake. Above the ramp a small store carries essential

*Campers along the bank of Twenty-five Mile Creek are treated to the pleasant murmuring of the stream.*

supplies for camping and fishing. The shallow end of the marina basin, inside a footbridge to the breakwater, invites wading and paddling. The bridge provides access to a fishing pier extending from the north side of the breakwater. A small picnic area sits in the shade of trees above the marina.

The campsites are a rustic relief from the landscaped lawns found at many state parks east of the Cascades. Here are gravel pulloffs into dirt or grass sites amid a natural, second-growth forest of cottonwood, ponderosa pine, and birch. Rushing, burbling Twenty-five Mile Creek creates nature's version of "white noise"—a pleasant, continuous background sound that reaches many of the campsites. The creek offers good fishing for rainbow trout.

Because it is surrounded by Wenatchee National Forest, the park is frequently a take-off point for backpacking or hunting treks in the area. Deer, bear, and grouse live in the nearby mountains. In winter the area is popular for snowmobiling and cross-country skiing.

## LAKE CHELAN STATE PARK

**Hours/Season.** Overnight; standard hours; weekends and holidays only, from the end of October to the end of March

**Area:** 127 acres; 6,454 feet of freshwater shoreline on Lake Chelan

**Facilities:** 127 standard campsites, 17 RV sites, 52 picnic sites, picnic shelter, restrooms, trailer dump station, bathhouse, swimming beach, boat launch ramp, docks, waterski floats, children's play equipment, homestead cabin

**Attractions:** Camping, picnicking, boating, sailing, paddling, fishing, swimming, waterskiing, scuba diving, cross-country skiing, snowmobiling, sledding

**Access:** Turn north 1.5 miles southwest of Chelan from US 97A onto a two-lane paved road that follows the south shore of the lake. From the north, the road is signed Lake Chelan State Park, Twenty-five Mile Creek State Park; from the south, the road is signed South Shore Recreation Areas. The park entrance is 6 miles northwest of US 97A.

Ice Age glaciers that carved a deep, 55-mile-long cleft through the Cascades created Lake Chelan. The lake links the ragged peaks of the North Cascades National Park above Stehekin, on its northwestern tip, to the arid plateau east of Chelan, at its southeastern end. Although the ribbonlike lake is scarcely 0.25 mile wide in places, the water plunges to depths of nearly 1,500 feet, while adjoining mountains rise more than 4,000 feet within a couple of horizontal miles. For over half of

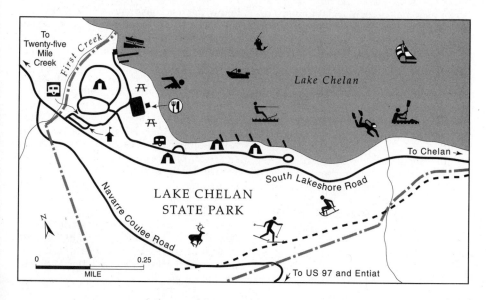

**161**

*The numerous docks at Lake Chelan State Park provide tie-up space for boats.*

its length the shoreline is inaccessible except by boat; the only commercial access to the lake is via the passenger ferry *Lady of the Lake*, which makes regular daylong excursion trips from Chelan to Stehekin and back.

Lake Chelan State Park, scenically situated on the southwest shore of the lake, provides access to this magnificent inland fjord. The park, located 7.5 miles west of the busy tourist town of Chelan, is the largest and most popular public campground in the area. The many water activities the park offers, along with its camping and picnicking attractions, keep it filled throughout the summer. During winter months the park is used for sledding and as a base camp for cross-country skiing and snowmobiling in the area.

Campground hookup sites are tightly packed along the perimeter of the circular grassy picnic area, shaded by black walnut, elm, maple, sycamore, and a few ponderosa pine. The road east from here traverses the hillside above the lake, with tent camp-sites lining both sides of the road. All require short carries of camping gear to sites that are secluded by dense brush; those below the road have views of the lake and easy access to a series of five short docks spotted along the shore. Waterski floats are anchored offshore. Two more campground loops lie at the west end of the park, with sites in a grassy, tree-shaded flat lined by elderberry, wild rose, and snowberry.

Open grassy terraces below the bathhouse/concession stand have picnic tables overlooking the swimming beach. The roped-off perimeter of the sandy beach encloses an offshore swim platform. At the west end of the park shoreline, a single-lane launch ramp drops into the lake next to a 120-foot-long float. A second shorter float is located just to the east.

An old log cabin used by homesteaders is near the day-use parking area. In summer park staff conduct evening campfire programs on the history and wildlife of the region.

# DAROGA
# STATE PARK

**Hours/Season:** Overnight; standard hours; closed from the end of October to the end of March; *group camp open by reservation only*

**Area:** 90 acres; 1.5 miles of freshwater shoreline on Lake Entiat (Columbia River)

**Facilities:** 25 RV sites, 17 walk-in primitive campsites, 100-person group campsite, 33 picnic sites, 2 picnic shelters, 75-person group day-use area, restrooms, vault toilets, trailer dump station, marine pumpout station, bathhouse, swimming beach, boat launch ramps, docks, basketball/tennis courts, baseball/soccer field, volleyball area, 2.1 miles of paved trail

**Attractions:** Camping, picnicking, boating, fishing, waterskiing, sailing, windsurfing, swimming, hiking, birdwatching, tennis, basketball, volleyball, baseball, soccer, bicycling

**Access:** On the east side of the Columbia River, on US 97, 21.1 miles north of Wenatchee

The manicured, emerald lawns of Daroga State Park stand in sharp contrast to the surrounding rolling brown hills of the Columbia Basin. The park was not added to the state park's system until 1990, so for a short time it will have the distinction of being one of the undiscovered gems in the central Washington parks ... until the word gets out.

The physical layout of the park is unique: An incursion of private land and a small lagoon break it into three distinct sections. A slender tree-lined causeway separates the lagoon from Lake Entiat (the Columbia River); only the outer shore of the lagoon lies within the park boundary. Midway, on a widened section of the causeway, is a primitive walk-in campground, ideal for bicyclists or other campers unburdened with heavy loads of gear. The park provides carts to lessen the work of hauling gear to camp. A small dock in a tiny cove at the river's edge permits boaters to take advantage of this isolated site, yet keep their craft close at hand.

To the south, the group camp is a grassy pocket on the shore, virtually isolated from the main section of the park, except for a narrow lakeshore trail along the causeway that links it to the remainder of the park.

The main portion of the park lies to the north, where a wide grass bowl has been laid out with tennis, soccer, basketball, volleyball, and baseball areas. Beyond these, a grassy picnic area stretching along the riverbank includes a bathhouse set above a swimming beach. Trees are newly planted and small, but in years to come will provide welcome shade to the area. The lawn sweeps north, enclosing a huge parking lot for boat trailers just above a two-lane boat launch ramp with a boarding float between. A second long float nearby provides limited short-term moorage.

The extreme end of the park is capped by a campground loop on a small bluff above the river. Cottonwood and poplar stands form a windbreak along the riverside. Signs warn against kite flying, despite tempting

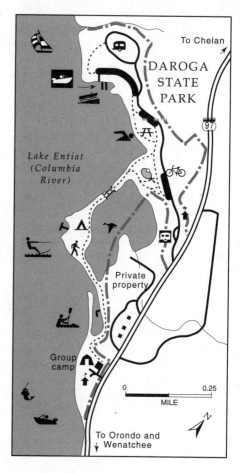

*At Daroga State Park, a slender causeway on Lake Entiat holds some walk-in campsites.*

winds, because major high voltage transmission lines pass directly over the campsite as they span the river and head west.

## LINCOLN ROCK STATE PARK

**Hours/Season:** Overnight; standard hours; year-round
**Area:** 80 acres; 2,300 feet of freshwater shoreline on Lake Entiat (Columbia River)
**Facilities:** 27 standard campsites, 67 RV campsites, 80 picnic sites, 3 picnic shelters, 2 75-person group day-use areas, bathhouse, restrooms, swimming beach, boat launch ramp, moorage, trailer dump station, amphitheater, children's play equipment, tennis courts, paddleball/handball/basketball court, baseball/soccer field, sand volleyball courts
**Attractions:** Camping, picnicking, boating, fishing, sailing, waterskiing, windsurfing, swimming, tennis, basketball, soccer, softball, horseshoes, cross-country skiing, volleyball

**Access:** On the east side of the Columbia River, on US 2, 0.8 mile north of Wenatchee.

⚓ Rocky Reach Dam blocks the flow of the Columbia River north of Wenatchee, creating the placid, 31-mile-long thread of Lake Entiat. On the east shore of the lake, just above the dam, Lincoln Rock State Park utilizes the lake's quiet water for recreational activities ranging from a swimming beach to broad, open reaches for water-skiers and jet-skiers.

The park's namesake, Lincoln Rock, is a basalt cliff on the opposite shore where a nature-sculpted rock resembles the profile of Abraham Lincoln. The profile is best seen from the road along the west side of the lake. The Rocky Reach Dam Interpretive Center, on the west shore, can only be reached by traveling up- or downriver to the nearest bridge crossing at Chelan or Wenatchee.

The park is typical of those in this part of the state, where a green tree-shaded lawn is

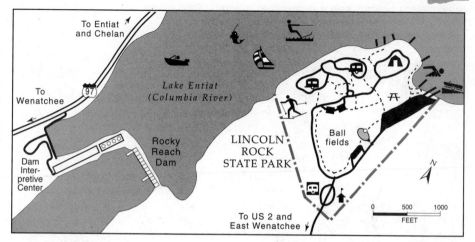

To Entiat
and Chelan

To
Wenatchee
(97)

Lake Entiat
(Columbia River)

Rocky
Reach
Dam

Dam
Inter-
pretive
Center

LINCOLN
ROCK
STATE PARK

Ball
fields

To US 2 and
East Wenatchee

0     500    1000
FEET

N

a welcome respite from the parched brown scabland broken only by irrigated swatches of apple orchards. Unique to this park, however, is the attractive wide border of white river rock used to edge the trails and parking lots.

True to its water orientation, Lincoln provides extensive aquatic facilities. Two single-lane launch ramps each have boarding floats alongside, and another nearby float is available for overnight moorage. Five more small moorage floats have been placed along the shoreline below the lower camping loop. A swimming beach with a shallower wading area occupies an indentation in the northern shoreline at the edge of the picnic area.

Large trees offer shade and wind protection for the day-use area and lower campground loop. Two newer camping loops on a slight bluff above the river on the west side of the park have more expansive views of the lake and dam, but the trees here are also younger and have a few years to go before they provide protection from either sun or wind. An amphitheater at the junction of the campground loops is used for evening interpretive programs.

## WENATCHEE CONFLUENCE STATE PARK

**Hours/Season:** Overnight; standard hours; year-round
**Area:** 197 acres; 13,175 feet of freshwater shoreline on the Wenatchee and Columbia rivers

**Facilities:** 8 standard campsites, 51 RV sites, 75 picnic sites, picnic shelter, restrooms, trailer dump station, swimming beach, bathhouse, boat launch ramps, tennis courts, basketball courts, multiuse playfield, children's play equipment, volleyball court, 2 miles of paved trail, nature trail

**Attractions:** Camping, picnicking, hiking, boating, paddling, sailing, fishing, waterskiing, windsurfing, swimming, tennis, basketball, baseball, volleyball, soccer, bicycling, birdwatching, interpretive walks

**Access:** *From US 2/US 97 west of Wenatchee,* head northeast on US 97 A (signed to Chelan, State Patrol, Highway 28, US 2 E, US 97 N). In 0.3 mile take the exit marked Olds Station, State Patrol, Washington Apple Visitors Center. *From US 97A north of Wenatchee,* take the Olds Station Exit. Both of these exits will lead to Euclid Avenue. Follow this road south for 0.8 mile, where it turns west and becomes Olds Station Road. Reach the park entrance in 0.3 mile.

Confluence: a flowing together. Wenatchee Confluence State Park is located at the flowing together (or junction) of the Wenatchee and the Columbia rivers. The new park, dedicated in the spring of 1991, nicely fulfills the desires of campers wanting an outdoor experience in a comfortable urban setting that provides a variety of

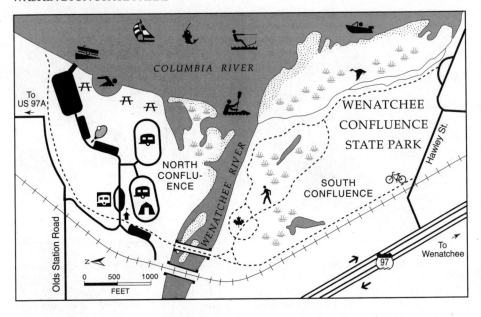

*Wenatchee Confluence State Park offers fine boating on both the Wenatchee and Columbia rivers.*

amenities—a rustic hotel that's not too primitive.

Park campsites are located on loops amid a flat grassy field, with future shade promised by a scattering of fledgling trees. An assortment of sports fields, as well as picnic areas, makes the park popular for local church gatherings, company picnics, and youth group outings. A semicircle of concrete steps on the bank of the Columbia lead down to a roped-off swimming and wading area, protected from the river currents by its cupped design. A nearby boat launch ramp and boarding float ease river access for both trailered and cartop boats.

Despite the civilized nature of the main park area, known as the North Confluence, a second segment on the south side of the Wenatchee River (the South Confluence), retains a more nature-oriented role. A bicycle/pedestrian path crosses a bridge over the Wenatchee River at the west side of the park; a kiosk here describes the character and inhabitants of the marshland. Footpaths lead through the heart of this area and along the riverbank. Residents include eagles, osprey, hawks, great blue heron, a variety of ducks, mink, muskrats, raccoon, and beaver—all only a wingtip from downtown Wenatchee. Sections of the trail close in the winter when eagles and other birds are roosting.

# SQUILCHUCK
# STATE PARK

**Hours/Season:** *Open to groups by reservation only except for skiing;* closed from the end of September to mid-April, except for the ski area, which is open from December 1 to March 1
**Area:** 287.2 acres
**Facilities:** 168-person group camp, 100-person group day-use area, fire circle, 200-person ski lodge, ski tows, winter concession area, 14 miles of trail
**Attractions:** Group camping, picnicking, hiking, skiing, cross-country skiing
**Access:** Take Mission Street south through Wenatchee. At the city limits the street becomes Squilchuck Road, and in 7 miles arrives at the park entrance.

⊥ The bone-dry coulees south of Wenatchee begin to green as the road climbs into the Wenatchee Mountains near Mission Ridge. By the time Squilchuck State Park is reached, surrounding hillsides are covered by a cool coat of evergreen forest. Due to limited state park funds, during summer months this one-time campground becomes a reservation-only group camp. This is a mixed blessing—unfortunate for the casual camper, but a treasure for the family or youth group that, for a nominal fee, can secure private use of this forest retreat.

In winter, also because of state funding problems, the park ski area is operated by Wenatchee Valley College. The ski area lies 0.25 mile beyond the park entrance; a day lodge sits on a knob opposite a broad, groomed slope that is lighted and served by a rope tow. The slopes are open Friday through Monday during the winter.

The road beyond the lodge leads to the campground loop, which has twenty sites and a restroom with showers (tenting only, no trailer hookups). The lodge can also be reserved, winter or summer, for a fee. For group reservation information call (206)664-6373.

Because none of the recreation facilities typical of developed state parks are provided, the area offers a real wilderness experience. You can hike the fire trails along the forested ridges above the campground while enjoying the sounds and scents of the

forest. In winter some of the trails are marked for cross-country skiing.

# PESHASTIN PINNACLES
# STATE PARK

**Hours/Season:** Day-use; standard hours; closed December and January
**Area:** 35 acres
**Facilities:** 5 picnic tables, vault toilets
**Attractions:** Rock climbing, hiking, picnicking
**Access:** On US 2/US 97 8.3 miles east of Leavenworth and 10.7 miles west of Wenatchee, turn north on North Dryden Road to the park entrance in 0.8 mile.

⊥ For years these unique near-vertical sandstone outcroppings rising abruptly from a small ridge above an apple orchard were a popular informal rock-climbing area. The low elevation and dry climate made the pinnacles accessible most of the year, even when other rock-climbing areas in the state were either buried in snow or drenched by rain.

Unfortunately, the owners of the property had to make the area off limits to the public to save the adjoining orchards from climbers who were not always considerate, and to avoid potential financial liability for injuries in this litigious society. Responding to requests from the state's climbing community and outdoor clubs, the State Parks and Recreation Commission came to the rescue. In 1991 it purchased the property encompassing the pinnacles and reopened it as one of two new state parks in the area.

Facilities are meager but adequate for the purpose—just a large parking lot, vault toilets, a kiosk with a map of the area, and a few picnic tables on a bare grass flat. For safety purposes, the park has replaced old rappel and belay anchors with new solidly placed ones, but beyond that the climbing routes are unchanged. Unfortunately, the pinnacles have suffered wear; cracks in the soft sandstone have flaked away from too many years of piton placement, and indiscriminate and excessive use of expansion bolts has marred or fractured friable rock faces. The classic eye-catching pinnacle

**167**

*A rock climber inches up Martian Slab at Peshastin Pinnacles State Park.*

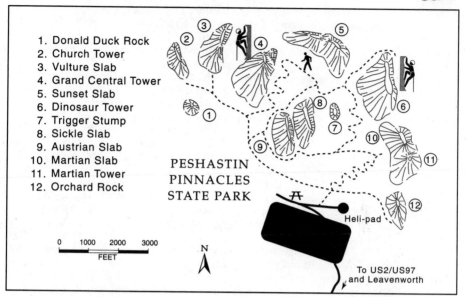

1. Donald Duck Rock
2. Church Tower
3. Vulture Slab
4. Grand Central Tower
5. Sunset Slab
6. Dinosaur Tower
7. Trigger Stump
8. Sickle Slab
9. Austrian Slab
10. Martian Slab
11. Martian Tower
12. Orchard Rock

PESHASTIN
PINNACLES
STATE PARK

Heli-pad

0   1000   2000   3000
FEET

N

To US2/US97
and Leavenworth

"Trigger Finger" exists now only in memory and old photos; it snapped off at the "knuckle" in 1978.

The pinnacles remain an excellent practice spot, however, challenging a wide spectrum of skill levels. Less experienced climbers can gain confidence on Donald Duck Rock or stem a crack to the top of Orchard Rock and experience a vertical rappel. Intermediate-to-difficult routes exist on Martian Slab and Sunset Slab. The west faces of Grand Central Tower and Austrian Slab offer routes rated 5.8 and above. Enjoy the thrill of climbing here safely, but avoid placing new unnecessary "iron" and help preserve the rock for the generations of climbers to follow.

Nonclimbing visitors may enjoy picnicking and watching with binoculars as climbers dangle from spider webs or creep lizardlike up rock faces.

# LAKE WENATCHEE
# STATE PARK

**Hours/Season:** Overnight; standard hours; year-round; camping only in the day-use area from the end of October to mid-April; *permit required in winter in the Sno-park lot*

**Area:** 488.5 acres; 12,623 feet of freshwater shoreline on Lake Wenatchee

**Facilities:** 197 standard campsites, 80-person group camp, 60 picnic sites, 3 picnic shelters, 100-person group day-use area; children's play equipment, restrooms, trailer dump stations, swimming beach, bathhouse, amphitheater, boat launch ramp, boat dock, riding stable (concession), 3.5 miles of equestrian trail, 7.7 miles of hiking and skiing trail, snacks and groceries (concession)

**Attractions:** Camping, picnicking, boating, paddling, fishing, swimming, hiking, horseback riding, cross-country skiing, snowshoeing, snowmobiling, sledding, waterskiing, windsurfing, sailing, scuba diving

**Access:** From US 2, 20.5 miles east of Stevens Pass or 16 miles northwest of Leavenworth, turn north on Highway 207 N (signed to Lake Wenatchee State Park, Nason Creek Campground, Fish Lake, Plain) to reach the main park entrance in 3.7 miles. The north campground is 1.1 miles farther north on Highway 207.

The first state park east of Stevens Pass marks the transition from the dense rain-drenched woodlands of western Washington to the more open Douglas fir and ponderosa pine forests of the drier east side of the Cascades. Lake Wenatchee stretches for more than 5 miles, filling the valley floor between the steep forested sides of the massive Chiwawa and Nason ridges. Wenatchee Ridge rises above the far end of the lake, and beyond are glimpses of the Glacier Peak Wilderness.

The park is located on the southeast corner of the lake, spanning its outlet at the Wenatchee River. At the heart of the day-use area, a gravel beach tapers gently into the tranquil water. Just beyond, a tiny tree-studded island is mirrored on the surface of the lake. A swimming area is marked off by buoys. Picnic tables are scattered along the forested perimeter of the beach; here also a bathhouse and concession stand to cater to the needs of park visitors.

A single-lane boat launch ramp, with an adjoining dock and float, is found around the corner from the beach at the Wenatchee River headwater. From boat or bank, anglers can fish the lake for rainbow, dolly varden, and kokanee salmon. Canoes or rafts can be launched here for float trips down the placid upper reaches of the river, with chances of spotting osprey nests and riverside wildlife.

The woods above the beach contain a group camp and an amphitheater where, on weekend evenings during the summer, park rangers present interpretive programs on the local geology, history, and wildlife. A few trails thread through this section of the woods, offering sample views of the native flora and a dash of color from lupine and other wildflowers in season.

Campground loops amid Douglas fir and ponderosa pine fill the south portion of this section of the park. Signs remind campers that this is bear country; food and coolers cannot be left out and garbage must be put in bear-proof dumpsters. Mosquitos are another park pest, and in recent years concerns over environmental safety and personal health have ended a control pro-

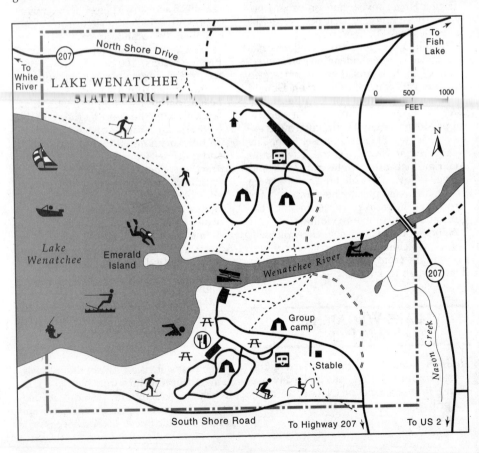

*Kayakers prepare to launch on the Wenatchee River.*

gram using pesticides—be forewarned and bring your own protection.

A stable located just inside the entrance offers horseback rides that begin in the park and continue onto adjoining National Forest land. Day rides of 2, 5, and 10 miles are available, subject to demand, during the summer; wrangler-led overnight pack trips for camping, fishing, or hunting can be scheduled in summer and fall.

A second segment of the park is located on the lakeshore on the north side of the Wenatchee River. The entrance to this section of the park is a mile north of the main park entrance. Here two campground loops are ringed by sites in a pine and fir forest, with thimbleberry and snowbrush prominent in the ground cover. Trails lace the woods surrounding the campground and follow the shoreline of the river and the lake to the park boundaries.

When winter dumps up to 4 feet of snow on the area, the park is a mecca for snowmobilers and cross-country skiers. Over 30 miles of groomed trails are available in the park and on adjoining private and national forest land. Snowmobiles are prohibited on some of the trails.

# WANAPUM RECREATION AREA

**Hours/Season:** Overnight; standard hours; year-round
**Area:** 462 acres; 5,700 feet of freshwater shoreline on Wanapum Reservoir (Columbia River)
**Facilities:** 50 RV sites, 47 picnic sites, restrooms, boat launch ramp, swimming beach, bathhouse
**Attractions:** Camping, picnicking, boating, waterskiing, swimming, fishing
**Access:** Drive 3 miles south of Vantage on Huntzinger Road.

Although Ginkgo Petrified Forest has hosted curious visitors since 1935, no camping facilities were provided in early

**171**

years. Wanapum Recreation Area, which was created after the reservoir behind Wanapum Dam came into being, now fills that need. Green lawns have been wrenched from a grudging desert, and only a persistent watering prevents their regression into sagebrush. Two campground loops have swatches of grass at each site, with a hardy variety of olive trees providing some shade; parched sagebrush marks the outer perimeter of each site. Trails lead from the lower camping loop to the brushy lakeshore.

The day-use area and the boat launch bracket the camping loops at the water's edge. To the north, below a spacious parking lot, two lanes of a launch ramp share a boarding float. South, on another island of green lawn, the picnic area and bathhouse look down on a roped-off swimming beach. Trails through the sagebrush link all of the sites. The popular park is crowded on weekends during the summer.

*A visitor inspects petrified wood at the interpretive center at Ginkgo Petrified Forest State Park.*

# GINKGO PETRIFIED FOREST STATE PARK

**Hours/Season:** Day-use; standard hours; year-round; *interpretive center*, 10:00 A.M. to 6:00 P.M. May 16 to September 15, open to groups by advanced appointment at other times

**Area:** 7,007.9 acres; 8,260 feet of freshwater shoreline on Wanapum Reservoir (Columbia River)

**Facilities:** 10 picnic sites, restrooms, interpretive center, 3 miles of hiking trail, 1-mile interpretive trail

**Attractions:** Picnicking, hiking, sightseeing, interpretive information

**Access:** From I-90 take Exit 136 (Vantage, Huntzinger Road) to Vantage. North of Vantage 0.2 mile, turn west on Ginkgo Avenue, and in 0.4 mile reach the Ginkgo Petrified Forest Interpretive Center. To reach the interpretive trail, drive northeast from Vantage 2.3 miles to the parking lot at the trailhead.

What on earth is a ginkgo, you ask? Well, it's a tree that in its living form is currently found only as cultivated specimens— a "living fossil," unchanged for more than a million years, and the sole survivor of a group of plants that were abundant during the Triassic period, 160 to 230 million years ago. This park is one of the few places on earth where the petrified wood of the ginkgo tree has been found, proving its ancient lineage.

Over 200 species of trees, including Douglas fir, spruce, walnut, and elm, as well as the very rare ginkgo, once grew in the area's lush, moist forest—hard to imagine today when scanning the park's parched desert landscape. Lava that later flowed across eastern Washington decimated these forests, and log-littered lake bottoms were sealed under thick layers of volcanic basalt. Over time the organic material of the logs was replaced by silica-base minerals that faithfully duplicated the structure of the original wood. Floods that followed the Ice Age wore away the basalt layers in places, exposing the fossilized stone logs. This petrified forest was discovered in the 1930s. The initial park facilities were developed by the Depression-era CCC.

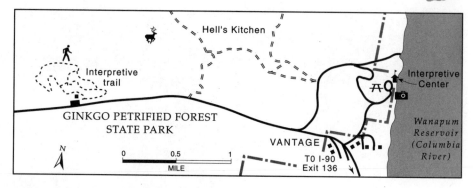

The park interpretive center sits on a promontory just north of Vantage, at the rim of cliffs that bound the Columbia River. The ground outside the center is scattered with examples of fossilized logs. Inside, displays explain how the logs were formed and how the original tree species are identified, and show dozens of samples of cut and polished wood. Other displays cover the various minerals found in the state and the history of geological activity in the region. A short slide program tells of the ginkgo tree and its original habitat. An outside deck equipped with telescopes offers expansive views of the Columbia.

Farther west 2 miles, an interpretive trail loops through the desert past a score of sites where fossils have been uncovered. Unfortunately, the logs are enclosed in cages to preserve them from destructive humans. Beyond the interpretive trail, a 2.5-mile-long hiking trail wanders across the barren sage-covered desert. The hot, dry trail's main appeal is the blush of color from wildflowers in spring and early summer; there's also the possibility of sighting rattlesnakes, lizards, deer, coyote, or a variety of birds that inhabit the area.

## OLMSTEAD PLACE HERITAGE AREA

**Hours/Season:** Day-use; standard hours; tours conducted by appointment only from Labor Day to Memorial Day
**Area:** 217.8 acres
**Facilities:** 12 picnic sites, display sheds, homestead cabin, Olmstead residence, farm buildings, Seaton cabin, 0.5-mile interpretive trail
**Attractions:** Tours of grounds and buildings, annual Threshing Bee Event in mid-September, occasional "old-time" summer events

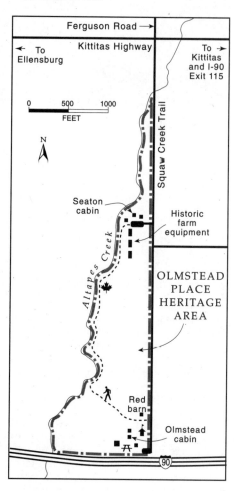

*The original Olmstead cabin has been restored and furnished with articles from the 1870s.*

**Access:** Take Exit 115 (Kittitas) north from I-90. From the north side of Kittitas, turn west on Kittitas Highway. In 3.8 miles, at an intersection signed Ferguson Road to the north, and Squaw Creek Trail to the south, turn south, and in 1 mile reach the park. The Seaton cabin is found here; the red barn and Olmstead cabin are 0.2 mile farther south.

Olmstead Place, in addition to being a historical museum, is a functioning 200-acre farm that still produces wheat, oats, and hay, and has dairy cattle and chickens. This has been an active farm since it was homesteaded in 1875 by Samuel Bedient Olmstead. Olmstead's original cozy log cabin, considered quite comfortable for its day, still stands at the south end of the park. It has been restored and furnished with the Olmstead's belongings and articles typical of the period gleaned from other farms of similar age in the area. During summer months the park provides interpretive talks on the farm and local history at the cabin. Olmstead's later residence, which is adja-

cent, is also open for tours on summer weekends. Visitors can make use of picnic tables that are scattered around the lawn by the cabin.

Behind the house to the west are chicken coops and a fenced field containing a wagon shed, granary, milkhouse, and dairy barn. A large red barn north of the house was built in 1908 to store hay. A number of farm implements of varying vintages are displayed outside the barn.

Altapes Creek meanders along the western boundary of the property, and a 0.5-mile-long, self-guided nature trail follows the creek bank from the red barn to the Seaton Schoolhouse. A brochure available from the park describes sights along the way, such as red osier dogwood (a strong flexible wood used by the Indians for bows and baskets) and trees felled by beavers for food and creating dams.

North of the Olmstead residences, near the bank of the creek, is the Seaton Schoolhouse. This single-room log cabin, built in the 1870s, was moved from another location and reconstructed here on the Olmstead property in 1980. In 1876 the cabin became home to the Terry family. Both Mr. and Mrs. Terry were graduates of a teacher's college, and they used part of the single-room cabin as a small private school for valley children. The interior of the cabin has furniture typical of the period. One corner is fitted out as a schoolroom, with benches, a desk, and a few books.

Several sheds near the schoolhouse contain collections of old farm implements and machinery acquired over the years by a local historical society. A pair of covered wagon replicas are used for scheduled wagon train rides in the valley.

# HELEN MCCABE
## STATE PARK (UNDEVELOPED)

**Hours/Season:** Day-use
**Area:** 64 acres; 2,640 feet of freshwater shoreline on Wilson Creek, including a 7.4-acre, unnamed pond
**Facilities:** Vault toilet
**Attractions:** Fishing
**Access:** Take Exit 110 (Yakima, US 82 E, US 97 S) south from I-90, 1 mile east of Ellensburg. In 3.3 miles take Exit 3 (Highway 821 S, Thrall Road), and head west on Thrall Road for 0.7 mile to its intersection with Canyon Road. The park lies to the south and east of this intersection. Alternatively, take Canyon Road from Ellensburg for 5.8 miles to reach this same intersection.

This property is one of the first acquired as a part of a plan for future recreational development along the Yakima Canyon Recreational and Scenic Highway, which runs south from here through the picturesque canyon to Yakima. Funding for the planned development of the park has never been approved, so it is currently managed in cooperation with the Department of Game and the Kittitas County Field and Stream Club. Its only facilities are a dirt parking lot and a vault toilet near the pond that comprises the heart of the park.

The tree-edged pond has a rough footpath around its perimeter; frequent breaks in the shoreline foliage permit access for fishing. The lake and Wilson Creek contain rainbow trout.

# LAKE EASTON
## STATE PARK

**Hours/Season:** Overnight; standard hours; camping only in the day-use area from mid-November to the end of March, depending on snow
**Area:** 196.1 acres; 24,000 feet of freshwater shoreline on Lake Easton (Reservoir) and 2,000 feet on the Yakima River
**Facilities:** 90 standard campsites, 45 RV sites, 50-person group camp, 40 picnic sites, restrooms, showers, children's play equipment, swimming beach (*unguarded*), boat launch ramp, dock, trailer dump station, 37 miles of cross-country ski trail on state park and adjacent private and U.S. Forest Service land
**Attractions:** Camping, picnicking, fishing, boating, hiking, swimming, paddling, mushrooming, snowshoeing, snowmobiling, cross-country skiing, bicycling
**Access:** From I-90 take Exit 70 (Lake Easton State Park, Easton, Sparks Road) 16 miles east of Snoqualmie Pass and 1 mile west of Easton and follow signs to the park. Park at the boat launch area in winter (this is a designated Sno-park; *permit required*).

Because it is a U.S. Bureau of Reclamation reservoir, and not naturally formed, Lake Easton is subject to manipulation by man. During summer months water of the 237-acre lake laps at the thick vegetation along the shore, leaving only a thread of a beach in a few spots; in winter the water is drawn down, totally changing the nature of the shoreline.

Except for hiking and skiing trails, all of the state park facilities are found in a narrow 2-mile-long strip along the north shore of the lake. The state park is immediately adjacent to the I-90 freeway, and some sections, such as the northwest camping area, are subjected to the steady drone of freeway traffic.

At the east end of the park, two standard camping loops access sites in a stand of fir and pine. From here a road heads west above the lakeshore past a couple of small picnic sites on a wide cove. Short paths connect these sites to a private RV resort at the north park boundary. Near the west end, individual spur roads reach the boat

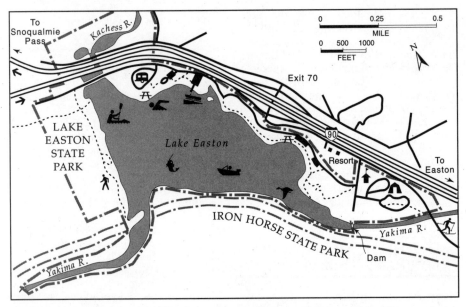

launch, day-use area, and campground loop. A small sandy beach at the heart of the day-use area fronts a roped-off swimming beach. The last spur road leads to a campground loop with hookup sites. The sites here are more jammed together than those in the standard campground loops, but about half of them have glimpses of the lake through the trees. Since day-use area parking is limited, an overflow lot has been provided west of the campground loop.

Trails along the north shore of the beach lead past open spots on the bank where land-bound anglers can compete with boat-

*The old highway that borders Lake Easton State Park is now an ideal spot to bicycle.*

based ones to lure trout. Rainbow trout are planted here annually, and cutthroat and eastern brook trout also number among the catches.

A foot trail leaves the west end of the park road and follows the heavily wooded west shoreline, occasionally closing with the lake to permit fishing access. Another trail heads west through the woods, eventually ending near the park boundary. A variety of birds such as jays, woodpeckers, and owls inhabit the timber. The lake is a migratory stopover for waterfowl.

The park is open year-round; when winter dumps its load of snow visitors use it as a base for snowmobiling and cross-country skiing. Over 37 miles of trails are accessible for winter use in the park and on nearby private and forest service lands.

# IRON HORSE STATE PARK (SNOQUALMIE PASS TO THE COLUMBIA RIVER)

**Hours/Season:** Day-use; year-round; *use permit required in some sections; parking permit required in designated Sno-parks*
**Area:** 1,598 acres
**Facilities:** 84 miles of trail, 16 trestles, 5 tunnels, vault toilets, *no water*
**Attractions:** Hiking, bicycling, horseback riding, wagon trains, cross-country skiing, dog sledding; *motorized vehicles prohibited*
**Accesses:**
  **Exit 54 (Hyak, Gold Creek) from I-90.** At the south side of the freeway, head east on the road to the Department of Transportation Hyak Maintenance Division. In 0.4 mile turn south on Forest Road 22191 signed to the Keechelus Lake boat launch. The trail can be accessed at the boat launch or at a U.S. Forest Service parking lot with space for 200 cars 0.4 mile west of the launch (parking, vault toilets). This is a designated Sno-park.
  **Exit 62 (Stampede Pass, Lake Kachess) from I-90.** Head southwest on Forest Road 54 for 1.1 miles to a Y-intersection with Forest Road 5480 to Lost Lake. Continue on Forest Road 54 for 0.2 mile to intersect the trail at a parking area

next to an AT&T regeneration station. Forest Road 5480 runs west, parallel to the trail, and intersects it again in 1.5 miles at the south end of Lake Keechelus. A designated Sno-park is at a Y in the road 1 mile from the freeway exit.
  **Exit 71 (Easton) from I-90.** Head south on Cabin Creek Road to reach the trail in 0.3 mile (parking, vault toilet).
  **Although not official accesses,** the trail can be reached from Exit 74 (West Nelson Siding Road), or from I-90.
  **Exit 80 (Roslyn, Salmon La Sac) from I-90.** At a T-intersection 0.1 mile south of the freeway, head west on Scale House Road to intersect the trail in 0.8 mile. Limited parking is just beyond the trail.
  **Exit 84 (Cle Elum, South Cle Elum) from eastbound I-90.** In 1 mile turn south on Rossetti Street and cross the river to South Cle Elum. Follow 4th Street to Madison Avenue, turn west, and in two blocks turn south on 6th Street. In one block turn west on N Milwaukee Avenue to reach the trailhead at 7th Street. The old railroad station is next to the trail (parking, vault toilet). This parking area is cleared in winter.
  **Exit 85 (Cle Elum) from I-90.** Follow Highway 970 west into Cle Elum. At a Y-intersection on the west end of town, take the south fork, signed to South Cle Elum, then follow the directions under Exit 84, above.
  **Exit 101 (Thorp Highway, Thorp) from I-90.** Thorp Highway crosses the trail 0.3 mile north of the off-ramp. Just beyond, turn west on West Depot Road, and in 0.3 mile reach a signed parking area. Alternatively, just before the trail crosses the highway, turn east on East Depot Road and reach Gladmar County Park in 1.2 miles (vault toilets). The trail can be reached with a short scramble to a trestle near the park entrance.
  **Exit 109 (Canyon Road, Ellensburg) from I-90.** Follow Canyon Road, which becomes Main Street, north to 8th Avenue, where it becomes A Street. There is a short break in the trail as it crosses the campus of Central Washington University. To access the section of trail that heads west, continue north on A Street to 14th, and park at Kiwanis Park at this intersection. The trailhead is on the north side of 14th. To access the

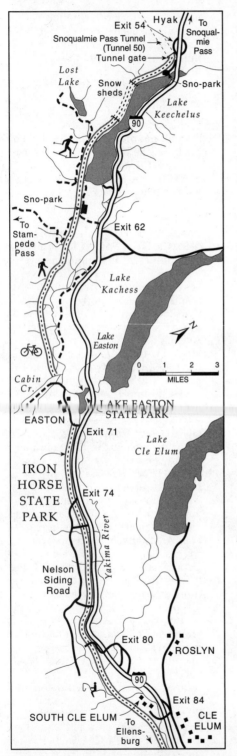

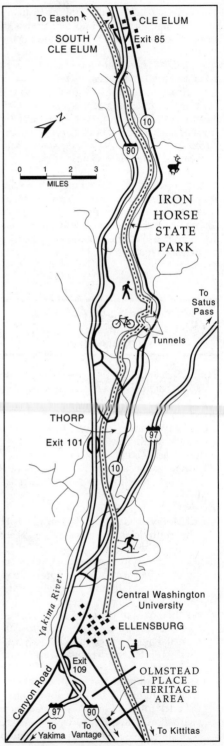

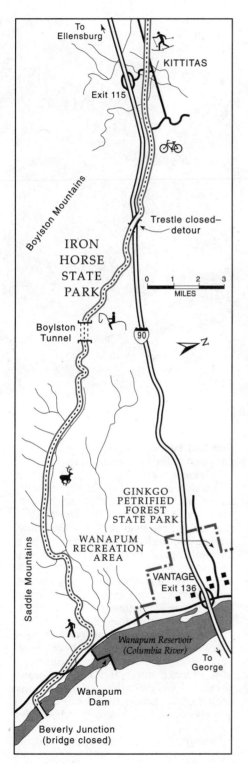

section of trail that heads east, turn east on 8th Street and continue through the campus. At 8th and Euclid Way, stay on 8th for two blocks, then turn north on Maple Street to intersect the trail in one block.

**Exit 115 (Kittitas) from I-90.** In 0.7 mile intersect the trail at the old railroad station on the south side of Kittitas.

**Beverly Junction.** Take Exit 136 (Vantage, Huntzinger Road) from I-90, and 7.3 miles south on Huntzinger Road, intersect the trail. Another short spur leads to the trail in 0.2 mile.

A state park 102 miles long and a measly 100 feet wide must rank as one of the most unusual in the state—if not in the country. Its unique dimensions make it ideal for some unique recreation: In addition to the to-be-expected hiking, mountain bike riding, and cross-country skiing, the trail is used for equestrian trail rides, old-time wagon train treks, and horse-drawn sledge rides. Every January dogsled competitions are staged at the Easton trailhead.

Four accesses that are plowed in winter provide parking for snowshoers and cross-country skiers (snowmobiles are prohibited). The groomed trail that leaves the Crystal Springs Sno-park (Exit 62) offers level, easy skiing along the edge of Lake Keechelus, although it is necessary to remove skis in the snow sheds.

The park had its beginning in 1909 when the Chicago, Milwaukee, St. Paul, and Pacific Railroad laid tracks for its iron horses across Snoqualmie Pass. After 70 years of service, the railroad was forced into bankruptcy by competition and changing modes of transportation. In 1981 the state acquired much of the old railroad right-of-way extending from Rattlesnake Lake, near North Bend, across Snoqualmie Pass, and east to the Idaho border; additional sections of the right-of-way have been purchased from other owners since that time. The segment between Rattlesnake Lake and the Columbia River is now Iron Horse State Park.

The old iron tracks have been removed, and throughout much of its length the trail is a 20-foot-wide gravel path with a maximum 2 percent grade. In some places the few deteriorating railroad ties that remain protrude through the surface. Park devel-

**179**

*The view up Cold Creek from near Lake Keechelus*

opment has been slow (as one would expect for a holding with such strange dimensions), and only a few access points have facilities—and those are minimal, such as parking and vault toilets. Camping is not permitted, and motorized vehicles are prohibited throughout its length.

A few short segments of the right-of-way remain in private hands, and some adjoining landowners have leases for sections of the trail, valid until 1994; the leaseholders require prior notification before the sections of trail they are leasing are used. There are also undecked trestles and other hazards at some points. As a result, use of some sections of the park requires an access permit issued in advance from the state parks area responsible for the section to be used.

The park is described in two parts: Region 5 covers the 18-mile-long section that begins at Rattlesnake Lake near North Bend and runs east to the Snoqualmie summit; this region describes the 88-mile-long section that begins at Snoqualmie Pass and runs east to the Columbia River.

This eastern portion of the park starts at Hyak, at the east end of the old 2.3-mile-long tunnel, Tunnel 50, that runs beneath Snoqualmie Pass. When first constructed, the railroad ran over the pass; the tunnel was put through about 1916. Tunnel 50 is currently closed to the public until engineering studies are conducted and it is made safe for use. Drainage is poor in the tunnel; in places more than a foot of water accumulates during the summer, and in winter icicles dangle from the ceiling. Clouds of moisture belch from the black entrance hole, much like smoke from the mouth of a dragon. A metal gate barricades the western end of the tunnel; the eastern end has heavy wooden doors that may be ajar, but water on the grade usually makes this entrance impassable, and public access is prohibited because the tunnel is unsafe.

From the east end of the Hyak tunnel, the

trail proceeds around the south shore of Lake Keechelus. To the north are spectacular views of the ragged peaks along the Pacific Crest at the head of Gold Creek. The trail contours the forested hillside above the Yakima River, passes through a short tunnel, and is soon paralleled by a companion, the active Burlington Northern track from Stampede Pass. After rounding the thickly forested south shore of Lake Easton, both rights-of-way run arrow-straight along the south side of I-90 until they separate just east of Cle Elum. There is presently a gap in the park from Cabin Creek east to Easton, where the right-of-way still remains in private hands.

At Cle Elum the trail passes the boarded-up ghost of the powerhouse that once provided the electric current to overhead power lines that enabled the engines to pull their loads over the summit. Electric engines were preferred over coal-fired engines for the summit section because they were cheaper and more efficient to operate, and smoke in the long tunnels would be hazardous to train crews and passengers. East from Cle Elum, the roadbed follows the south bank of the Yakima River, descending through the thick riparian woodlands below steep bluffs cut by the river valley. A few miles west of Thorp, the track skirts the foot of a sheer cliff, and the river's undulations are shortcut by a pair of short tunnels through the adjoining hillsides.

From here east to Ellensburg, the landscape flattens, and trestles bridge several roads, creeks, and finally the Yakima River as the trail cuts through open farmland. Until all of the trestles have been decked they are off limits to the public. The campus of Central Washington University interrupts the route briefly in Ellensburg, but from the east side of the campus, the track runs straight and true through farm and field from Ellensburg to Kittitas.

From the relic railroad station at Kittitas, the trail and a parallel road leave the lush farmlands and head into the encroaching gray sagebrush of the central Washington steppes. There is a short detour to the east at its intersection with I-90, where the trestle over the freeway is unsafe to cross and is barricaded.

Once south of the freeway, the track slowly climbs the parched scrub of the Boylston Mountains and passes through 1,980-foot-long Boylston Tunnel. This unique tunnel has walls near the middle that are natural rock, rather than the concrete used in other tunnels. The dark roof serves as lair for owls and bats; occasionally rattlesnakes slither into the cool of the tunnel to escape the outside heat.

East from Boylston the roadbed ignores the contours of the land and runs straight through a seemingly endless series of land cuts and fills. The underlying layers of basalt that are exposed in the cuts offer insights into local geology. This less-used section of trail offers an excellent chance of seeing deer, coyote, hawks, jackrabbits, snakes (including rattlers), and other dryland inhabitants. The track winds down the east end of the Saddle Mountains and then runs below the steep wall of the Columbia Gorge, which sweeps up to a series of spectacular basalt towers.

The army is attempting to acquire large portions of the property south of Boylston for an addition to the Yakima Firing Center Military Reservation. If the army is successful, the impact of such action on public use of the trail is presently unknown. The state park ends as it meets the Columbia River at the barricaded Beverly Junction Bridge. Railroad right-of-way continuing east of the river is owned by the State Department of Natural Resources.

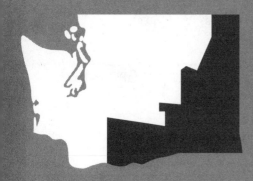

# REGION 4

- *Colville*
- *Spokane*
- *The Palouse*
- *Snake River*
- *Scablands*
- *Columbia River*

## CRAWFORD STATE PARK (GARDNER CAVE)

**Hours/Season:** Day-use; Wednesday through Sunday from May 1 to September 15; access to the cave is by guided tour only; tours conducted Wednesday through Saturday at 10:00 A.M., noon, 2:00 P.M., and 4:00 P.M. when the park is open
**Area:** 48.6 acres
**Facilities:** 12 picnic sites, picnic shelter, restrooms with handicap access, interpretive trail, cave
**Attractions:** Guided cave tours, picnicking
**Access:** From Highway 31 0.3 mile north of Metaline, turn west on Boundary Road (Boundary Dam, Crawford State Park). Follow the road north for 12.1 miles to reach the park entrance.

Although it is tucked away in the far northeast corner of the state, and not along the route to anywhere, Crawford State Park and Gardner Cave are well worth a special trip. This unique park holds the longest (second longest, according to some figures) limestone cave in the state of Washington. Ranger-guided tours explore the upper 494 feet of the 1,055-foot-long cave; a gate bars access to a narrow passage leading to three rooms at the lower end of the cave that are not open to the public.

The cave is said to have been discovered around 1899 by Ed Gardner, a bootlegger who had stills in the area. Legend has it that Gardner lost the cave in a poker game with William Crawford, a Metaline merchant, who gave the property to the state parks in 1921. Early visitors to the park were not sensitive to the delicate nature of the forma-

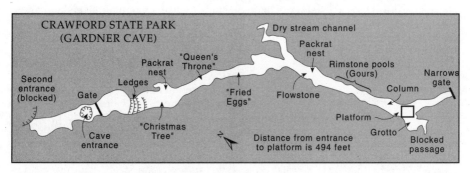

Opposite: *A ranger leads a tour of Gardner Cave.*

tions, and the cave has unfortunately been vandalized. Fine stalactite pipes along the ceiling, which rang like chimes when hit, were broken off by blows from picks, stones, and rifle butts. Initials and dates carved in the limestone indicate that graffiti was as much a problem in the 1920s as it is today.

In the 1950s the State Parks Commission installed wooden ladders, planking, and a crude lighting system and opened the caves to formal public tours. Increased visitation led to the discovery that the oil on human skin stopped the growth of the calcite formations. The 90,000-year-old formations, which grow only in the winter, at a rate of $\frac{1}{2}$ inch every 100 years, were being killed by the touch of visitors. To minimize physical contact with the delicate formations and prevent further deterioration of the cave, in 1977 the park put in the present steel walkways, staircases, and platforms.

Guided tours leave hourly from the parking and picnic area. Since the temperature inside the cave is 41 degrees year-round, a sweater or jacket is advisable. Once inside, the imagination takes hold, and a flowstone formation transforms itself into a Christmas tree, decorated with a walrus, bumblebee, mountain goat, and alligator. Other formations bear names such as the Wedding Cake, Queen's Throne, and Fried Eggs. When the ranger briefly turns off the lights at the lower platform, you can actually hear the cave grow as the calcite-laden water drips from the ceiling into the rimstone pools bordering the walkway.

# CRYSTAL FALLS STATE PARK

**Hours/Season:** Day-use; standard hours; year-round
**Area:** 156 acres
**Facilities:** None
**Attractions:** Scenic views, hiking
**Access:** On Highway 20, 14 miles east of Colville.

A roadside pulloff on the south side of Highway 20 offers pine-framed views down to the Little Pend Oreille River as it drops about 80 feet in a series of white-foamed terraces that form Crystal Falls.

Future plans call for short hiking trails through the forested park property north of the highway and day-use facilities.

# MOUNT SPOKANE STATE PARK

**Hours/Season:** Overnight from May 30 through September 30, day-use the remainder of the year; standard hours
**Area:** 13,820.8 acres
**Facilities:** 12 standard campsites, 85 picnic sites, 2 picnic shelters, 90-person group camp, 2 horse feeding stations, restrooms, vault toilets, 3 cabins, Vista House, 2 rope tows, 20.3 miles of cross-country ski trail, 2 ski lodges, 32 ski runs, 5 ski lifts (concession), 50 miles of hiking and equestrian trail, 77.6 miles of road
**Attractions:** Camping, picnicking, scenic views, horseback riding, hiking, huckleberry picking, downhill skiing, cross-country skiing, snowmobiling
**Access:** Take US 2 north from Spokane, and in 4.5 miles turn east on Highway 206 (Mount Spokane State Park). The park entrance is reached in another 15.5 miles. Ski areas are 5 miles beyond the entrance; the mountaintop is 7.5 miles beyond the entrance. To reach the paved west end of the Day–Mount Spokane Road, drive US 2 to the marked intersection 5.5 miles north of Spokane. Follow the road as it weaves its way northeast to reach the park boundary in 13.5 miles.

If the views from the top were all that Mount Spokane State Park had to offer, that would be enough. However, as a bonus the park contains miles of summer trails for hikers, mountain bikers, and equestrians, as well as snow trails for cross-country skiers and snowmobilers and slopes for alpine skiers.

Inside the park entrance the road climbs through timber for some 1,500 feet to an intersection midway up the mountain in 3 miles. Here the left branch heads to the summit, while the center branch leads to the ski area. On the right is a large Sno-park area for cross-country skiers and snowmobilers. From the Sno-park intersection to the summit, the steep, winding road is nerve-wrackingly narrow, with no guard rail protection on its outer edge—no place for wide RVs or those over 18 feet long. At Bald Knob, 1.2 miles above the parking lot, a grassy picnic area presents scenic views to the west. An adjacent campground loop has a dozen campsites, water, and restrooms.

The 5,881-foot summit of Mount Spokane is reached 7.5 miles from the entrance. The mountaintop offers explosive views north into Canada, northeast to the lofty summits of the Selkirks, east over azure lakes of the Idaho panhandle to the distant rugged peaks of Montana's Bitterroot Range, south to the Spokane plain, and west to the rolling plateau of the Columbia Basin. Crowning the summit is Vista House, which was once used as a fire lookout. The sturdy, weath-

ered rock structure is typical of 1930s CCC construction. The upper station of one of the area's ski lifts and a forest of radio and microwave antennas also share the mountaintop.

In summer the park's trail system accommodates both hikers and horse riders; a horse unloading dock has been provided 0.25 mile inside the park entrance. Several marked trailheads leave the road between the entrance and the Sno-park lot. At a sharp turn 1.9 miles from the entrance, the lower end of the unpaved Mount Kit Carson Loop Road leads to the northwest. Picnic areas are found along the lower end of this road loop, at Deep Creek, and also at the trailheads at Burping Brook, Smith Gap, and Deer Creek.

Another dirt road, the Day–Mount Spo-

*Vista House, at the top of Mount Spokane, offers impressive views of Canada, Idaho, and eastern Washington.*

kane Road, joins the Mount Kit Carson Loop Road 1.6 miles west of its lower end, offering access to the park from the west side of the mountain. Both the Mount Kit Carson Loop Road and the Day–Mount Spokane Road are open within the park only during summer months.

At the hairpin turn at Cook's Cabin, 0.7

mile below the summit, a dirt road, which is the upper end of the Mount Kit Carson Loop Road, heads northwest and in 0.3 mile reaches a picnicking, group camp, and horse camping area. Trails from this road lead to the Mount Spokane summit, to Mount Kit Carson, to Day Mountain, and down to Smith Gap on the lower end of the

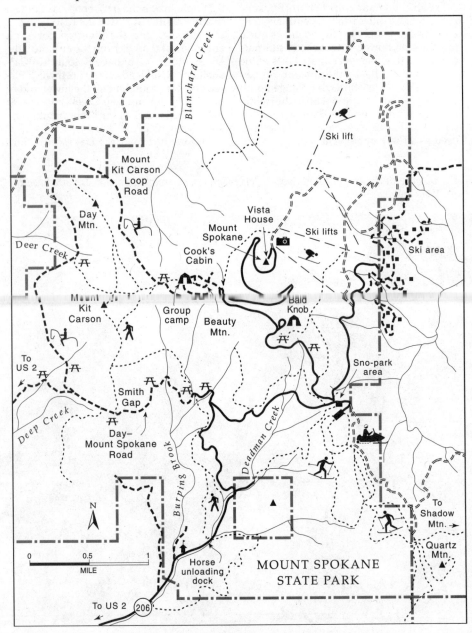

loop road. These trails run through a forest of ponderosa pine broken by open mountain meadows, decorated with bear grass and laced with bushes bearing succulent huckleberries in season.

The park attracts even more visitors in the winter than in the summer, as it is the premier ski area of the Inland Empire. Five chair lifts carry skiers from the two day-lodges to the summit and the lower ridgeline to the north, feeding downhill ski runs ranging from beginner to expert. A private development of condominiums and a restaurant lies just outside the park below the lifts.

The park also caters to the current explosion of interest in cross-country skiing with a day-lodge and over 30 miles of groomed trails originating on the hillside above the Sno-park lot. Trails, ranging from easy to extremely difficult, cut through the wooded hills to the west of the lodge, with the more challenging ones looping around Shadow Mountain. Snow-covered service roads are open for use by snowmobilers.

# RIVERSIDE
# STATE PARK

**Hours/Season:** Bowl and Pitcher area overnight; day-use for the remainder of the park; standard hours; year-round

**Area:** 7,655 acres; 104,750 feet of freshwater shoreline on the Spokane and Little Spokane rivers

**Facilities:** 101 standard campsites, 101 picnic sites, 248-person group camp, 3 kitchen shelters, 100-person and 2 30-person group day-use areas, comfort stations, vault toilets, interpretive center, suspension bridge, 600-acre ORV area, boat launch ramp, canoe put-in and take-out sites, horse rentals (concession), 36.7 miles of hiking and equestrian trail, 47.3 miles of road

**Attractions:** Camping, picnicking, boating, paddling, fishing, hiking, orienteering, horseback riding, historic sites, Indian petroglyphs, motorcycle and ORV riding, snowmobiling, bicycling

**Accesses:** Most access directions start from Division Street (US 2/395), the main north–south arterial through Spokane.

**Bowl and Pitcher Area.** Take Francis Avenue (Highway 291) west from Division Street (US 2/395) to its intersection with Nine Mile Road. In 0.9 mile turn southwest on Rifle Club Road, then in 0.4 mile turn south on A. L. White Parkway. Reach the park entrance in another 1.7 miles.

**Equestrian and Hiking Area.** Take Indiana Avenue west from Division Street to its intersection with Northwest Boulevard, and follow the latter northwest to Cochran Street. Turn south on Cochran, which becomes Meenach Drive, crosses the T. J. Meenach Bridge, and then becomes Fort George Wright Drive. At the intersection with Government Way, turn northeast, and in 1.5 miles turn north on A. L. White Parkway to reach the park in 0.1 mile.

**ORV Area.** *From the south,* from the intersection with the A. L. White Parkway at the entrance to the equestrian and hiking area, continue west on Trails Road 1.8 miles to Old Trails Road. Here turn north, and in 4.5 miles arrive at the ORV unloading site. *From the north,* instead of turning on Rifle Club Road to the Bowl and Pitcher area, continue northwest on Nine Mile Road for 2 miles, then turn west on Seven Mile Road, and in 1.2 miles turn south on Inland Road. The ORV unloading site is reached in 0.5 mile.

**Deep Creek Canyon.** Just east of the Inland Road (north) entrance to the ORV area, turn north on State Park Drive. This dirt road follows the west rim of Deep Creek Canyon, and in 1.1 miles intersects a paved section of State Park Drive that runs along the west side of the river between Seven Mile Road and Carlson Road. State Park Drive, which is a part of the Centennial Trail, may be closed to vehicle traffic at some future date. The trail up Deep Creek leaves State Park Drive (Centennial Trail) 0.5 mile to the northwest. The trail can also be reached by heading west across the Nine Mile Bridge onto Charles Road, then southwest on Carlson Road. In 0.3 mile take State Park Drive (Centennial Trail) south and reach the trail to Deep Creek in 0.8 mile.

**Spokane House Interpretive Center.** On

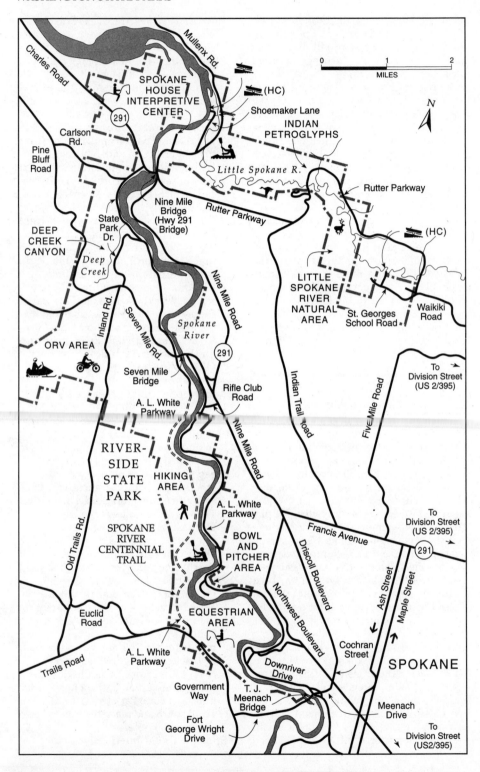

Nine Mile Road, instead of turning onto Rifle Club Road to the Bowl and Pitcher area, continue northwest on Nine Mile Road. In 5.4 miles, at the Nine Mile Bridge, this road becomes Mullenx Road. The entrance to the interpretive center is 0.5 mile north of the bridge.

**Little Spokane River Natural Area and Indian Petroglyphs.** *East trailhead and canoe put-in site,* from Highway 395 take Hastings Road west 1.6 miles to Mill Road. Here turn south, and in 0.6 mile, west on Waikiki Road. In 1.3 miles, where Waikiki turns north, continue west on St. Georges School Road for 0.3 mile to the trailhead, or 0.6 mile to the put-in site. *Middle trailhead and petroglyphs,* as Waikiki Road crosses the Little Spokane River, it becomes Rutter Parkway. In 3.1 miles, on the north side of the river, are the petroglyphs and the start of the trail to the west along the north side of the river. In 0.2 mile, on the south side of the river, is the head of another trail that heads east along the south side of the river. *West trailhead, boat launch, and canoe take-out site,* the west end of Rutter Parkway intersects Nine Mile Road at the Nine Mile Bridge. Turn north off Mullenx Road onto Shoe-

maker Lane 0.8 mile to the north. In 0.4 mile reach the take-out site, and 0.1 mile farther the boat launch ramp. The west trailhead is just northeast of Shoemaker Lane on the east side of the Little Spokane River.

▲ Riverside State Park follows the convoluted course of the Spokane River as it meanders for over 9 miles along Spokane's west side. It includes numerous separate parcels of land, some of which lie inland, that make the park layout confusing to grasp, but at the same time give it a remarkable diversity.

The campsites, most of the picnic sites, and the administrative headquarters are located in the Bowl and Pitcher area. This peninsula, surrounded by a large loop of the Spokane River, is named for a group of unique basalt monoliths along the riverbank on the north side of the peninsula. The road from the north into this section of the park skirts along the top of a sheer bank that drops nearly 200 feet to the river's edge. This steep bank continues to a rock promontory inside the park, accessible by paths from a parking lot. Here are views down into the river gorge with its rapids, to the Bowl and Pitcher formations, and up-

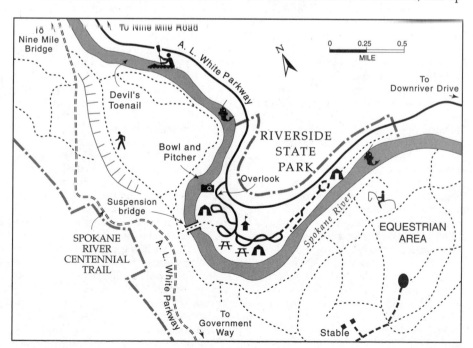

stream to a suspension bridge across the turbulent river.

The road then descends to a bluff that forms the heart of the peninsula. Situated here among ponderosa and jack pine are a campground loop and picnic areas, with sparse grass ground cover worn to dirt in most places by many years of use. Sturdy rustic stone restrooms are of CCC-vintage construction. At the south side of the peninsula, the road drops down to a strip of campsites along a road near river's edge. Here the brushy riverbank is accessible in places, but swimming is prohibited due to dangerous undercurrents. Short trails lace the riverbank and the heart of the peninsula. A path leading from the picnic area to the suspension bridge provides access to the west side of the river.

As the name of the rapids called the "Devil's Toenail" implies, this section of the river is a challenge for kayakers; although the rapids are not exceptionally difficult, the huge volume of water makes this a run only for those with advanced skills. The state park prohibits putting in boats at the park to discourage unskilled boaters with inadequate equipment from running the rapids.

The west bank of the river between Seven Mile Bridge and Spokane Falls Community College is a spider's web of jogging, hiking, and equestrian trails through scrub grass and occasional stands of ponderosa pine. One popular hike begins at the suspension bridge and follows the west side of the river through the scenic Bowl and Pitcher area for 2.5 miles. Hikers can return via the same route or follow spurs up to A. L. White Parkway or to inland horse trails. The Centennial Trail follows now-closed sections of State Park Drive and A. L. White Parkway along the bluff above the west side of the river. Other paths and service roads throughout this section of the park are too numerous to detail; the accompanying maps show the major ones.

Just off the parkway, a park concessionaire manages a stable where guided horseback trips leave hourly for a 5-mile ride. At the north end of the park, an equestrian trail system with 10- and 25-mile loops is available to riders with their own mounts.

A section of the state park dedicated to ORVs lies at the head of the Deep Creek drainage, where steep banks bound a 600-acre open, dry bowl. A moonscape of sandy hillocks within the bowl is scarred by the tracks of motorcycles. Trails for ORVs thread the few wooded sections within the area. Any type of ORV, such as dirt bikes, 3- and 4-wheelers, 4X4s, or snowmobiles, may use this area, provided that licensing, spark arrestor, and muffler regulations are met. A large parking lot with a loading ramp for ORVs has been provided. Restrooms, a picnic shelter, and a few picnic tables are nearby.

Deep Creek and Coulee Creek meet in a narrow 200-foot-deep gorge that threads 0.5 mile north to the Spokane River. An overlook beside the upper dirt portion of State Park Drive gives views deep into the bed of the gorge. The trail up the canyon passes fossil beds with imprints of a 7 million-year-old forest that once grew in the area.

The Spokane House Interpretive Center, on the bank of the Little Spokane River, is located on the site of a fur trading post that was the first permanent white settlement in eastern Washington. The post was established by explorer David Thompson in 1810, but because it proved too far from the main artery of trade, the Columbia River, it was relocated to Kettle Falls in 1826. The interpretive center tells the story of the Spokane House and its rivalry with competing fur companies, and displays artifacts from archaeological digs conducted here. A diorama portrays activities at Spokane House about 1819.

Dirt roads into the woods west from Spokane House lead to primitive picnic sites along the riverbank. Keep an eye out for osprey in tree snags nearby.

For more than 7 miles above its junction with the Spokane River, the Little Spokane River has been designated as the Little Spokane River Natural Area, with ownership of the adjoining property divided between the state parks and Spokane County. The freshwater marshes along the serpentine path of the river teem with songbirds, woodpeckers, ducks, and grebes, and a blue heron rookery is in cottonwood trees along the shore. The river may be closed during the heron's nesting season. Woodlands along and above the riverbank are home to beaver, muskrat, porcupines, raccoons, coyotes, marmots, deer, and black bear.

Visitors may enjoy the natural attractions

*River rapids and unusual basalt rock formations mark the Bowl and Pitcher area of Riverside State Park.*

of the area either on foot or by water. From the parking lot off St. Georges School Road, a short path leads to the upriver canoe or kayak put-in site. From here drift or paddle quietly along the undulations of the river to see what creatures or sights may lie around the next bend. Near the mouth of the Little Spokane, 7.3 miles downstream and just beyond the Highway 291 bridge, is a second parking lot and canoe take-out site.

At a trailhead a short distance east of the put-in site, a footpath heads into the pine forest south of the river and quickly snakes 500 feet up the steep ridgeline in a series of switchbacks before joining an overgrown service road that traverses the wooded, brushy hillside west for 0.5 mile to the park boundary. A companion section of trail leaves the Rutter Parkway just south of the Little Spokane River and heads east through a broad wild-grass field for 0.5 mile before heading up the nearby bluff and wandering through open stands of pine for another 0.75 mile to a service road near the park boundary. Note that some references indicate this section of trail connects with the section from the west, but there is nearly a mile of steep sidehill with only scrambled game trails across private property between the two park boundary signs.

A second trail follows closely along the north bank of the river between the Rutter Parkway bridge and the Highway 291 bridge, a distance of about 2 miles. Because this trail stays close to the marshy riverbank, mosquitos can be a problem during the summer.

Just above the parking lot at the middle trailhead, off Rutter Parkway, a rock face contains the Indian Painted Rocks, colored traces of petroglyphs. Painted symbols of this type are found throughout the West, but their origin and meaning has been lost over time. Some think they record hunting successes, tribal meetings, or religious experiences, but no one knows for sure.

On Shoemaker Lane, a short distance beyond the canoe take-out site on the Little Spokane, is a single-lane boat launch ramp with an adjoining boarding float that provides access to the Spokane River. A short trail from the parking lot leads to the site of the original Pacific Fur Company trading post, a competitor of the Spokane House trading post.

## SPOKANE RIVER CENTENNIAL TRAIL

**Hours/Season:** Day-use; standard hours; year-round
**Area:** 373.9 acres; 18 miles of freshwater shoreline on the Spokane River
**Facilities:** Trail, 2 footbridges, benches
**Attractions:** Hiking, jogging, bicycling
**Access:** The 39-mile-long trail runs east from Riverfront Park in downtown Spokane to the Idaho border, and west from Riverfront Park to Carlson Road, just west of the Nine Mile Bridge.

The Spokane River Centennial Trail is named in honor of the Washington State Centennial, which occurred in 1989. As of 1993, the trail has been completed from the Idaho border to near the Nine Mile Bridge west of the city, although some sections are only road-shoulder bicycle lanes not suitable for hiking. An extension is planned from Nine Mile Bridge to the Spokane House Interpretive Center. Only those sections that exist at this time are described below. The trail is described in two sections: going east from downtown Riverfront Park to the Idaho border, and headed west from the park to Riverside State Park.

The eastern portion of the trail starts in the heart of Spokane near the Opera House in Riverfront Park. From here the paved path, heavily used by walkers, joggers, and bicyclists, heads east, crossing the Kardong Burlington Northern Bridge over the Spokane River, named for Don Kardong, a local runner who initiated an annual race here, purported to be the second largest foot race in the country. Originally a railroad bridge, this structure has been redecked and reconstructed with viewing platforms, tables, and benches on its north side and painted in multihued pastels.

From the bridge the trail passes the Gonzaga University campus, then swings north along the river through Mission Park. From here both jogging and bicycle paths follow the river side of Upriver Drive for nearly 5 miles. Although they merge in places, the jogging path generally follows close to the riverbank, while the bicycle path stays near the shoulder of the road. You can rest at any of the path-side benches along the way.

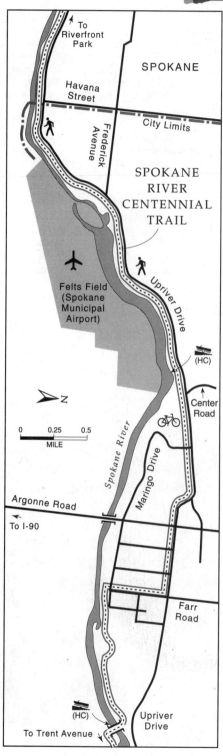

Just west of Center Road, where a tiny roadside park has river access for launching hand-carried boats, the foot portion of the trail ends. Bicyclists may continue along the shoulder of the road. If cyclists turn south from Upriver Road onto Farr Road, then east onto Maringo Drive, they will arrive at another 1-mile-long trail segment leading east to a newly constructed bridge over the Spokane River. Hand-carried boats can be launched at a river access point just west of the south end of the bridge.

The trail then follows the south bank of the river, and at Trent Avenue crosses under this major arterial and a railroad bridge, then skirts the edge of the Walk in the Wild Zoo, where there is parking and trail access. As the route continues east along the river, it again picks up the Burlington Northern right-of-way; parking and access points are at Sullivan Road and the west end of Mission Avenue in the Greenacres district. In another 2 miles, at Barker Road, the trail ducks under the Barker Road bridge, where parking and access are available.

The next convenient access point with parking is at the Harvard Road bridge, on the opposite side of the river from Harvard Park. East from here it follows the riverbank then swings close to I-90 just west of the state Visitor Information Center at the Idaho border. The trail continues west for a short way, ducks under the freeway at the bridge over the Spokane River, then joins a companion Idaho state trail that continues east from this point.

Hiking west from the start point at Riverfront Park, the trail follows a city bicycle route across the Post Street Bridge, then along Ide Avenue, Ohio Avenue, Summit Boulevard, and Pettet Drive to Meenach Drive. It crosses the T. J. Meenach Bridge and follows the river to the boundary of Riverside Park. Here it picks up paved trails through the Riverside Equestrian Area, then follows the west side of the A. L. White Parkway north to Seven Mile Bridge. State Park Drive between Seven Mile Bridge and Carlson Road, just west of the Nine Mile Bridge, is scheduled to be added to the trail.

*The easy grade and smooth surface of the Centennial Trail make it ideal for bicycling.*

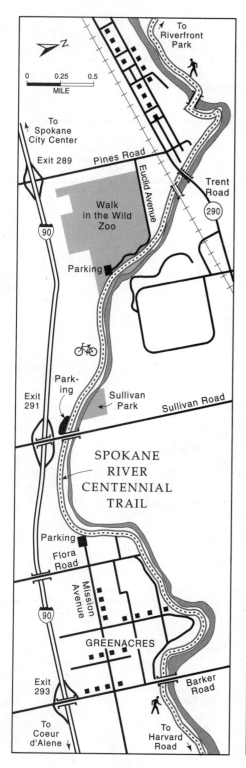

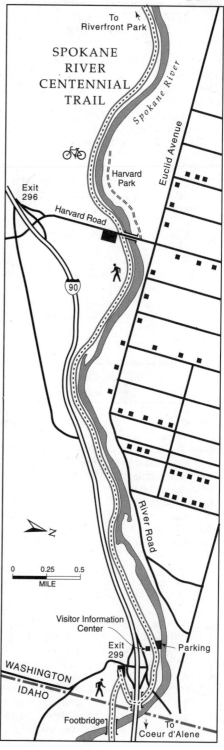

## SPOKANE PLAINS BATTLEFIELD HERITAGE AREA

**Hours/Season:** Day-use; standard hours; year-round
**Area:** 1 acre
**Facilities:** Rock pyramid with commemorative plaque
**Attractions:** Historic site
**Access:** Take US 2 west from Spokane for 9 miles. The monument is on the north side of the highway on Dover Road, west of the entrance to Fairchild Air Force Base and just east of a nearby railroad underpass.

▲ At this road wayside, a stone pyramid bears a plaque commemorating the battle of Spokane Plains, which was fought near here on September 5, 1858. It was here that U.S. troops under the command of Colonel George Wright defeated a combined force of Coeur d'Alene, Palouse, and Spokane Indian tribes.

## LAKE COLVILLE SHORELANDS (UNDEVELOPED)

**Hours/Season:** Day-use; standard hours; year-round
**Area:** 4,422 feet of freshwater shoreline on Lake Colville (Sprague Lake)
**Facilities:** None, *fee for parking*
**Attractions:** Nature studies, fishing
**Access:** Take Exit 245 (Highway 23, Harrington, Sprague) from I-90, and at the east side of Sprague take the truck route through town signed To Sprague Lake. Take Danekas Road southwest from Sprague for 6.4 miles, where a dirt road on the north side of the road provides access to the shorelands.

▲ Near the southwest corner of Lake Colville, a large thumb of land protrudes north into the lake. All of the shoreline of this peninsula, as well as the small cove on its east side, is state park property; however, all of the uplands are privately owned. The Sprague Lake Recreation Association maintains an access point with parking and a single-lane boat launch ramp at the south-west side of the peninsula. There are daily parking fees for use of this access. Anglers can find perch, rainbow trout, largemouth bass, catfish, and crappie in the lake, and the latter are also caught by ice fishing during the winter.

## STEPTOE BATTLEFIELD HERITAGE AREA

**Hours/Season:** Day-use; standard hours; year-round
**Area:** 3.9 acres
**Facilities:** Parking, water, interpretive marker
**Attractions:** Historic site
**Access:** From US 195, 32 miles south of Spokane, take the Rosalia Exit. On the southeast side of Rosalia, turn south from 7th Street (County Road 42 to Latah) to reach the monument.

▲ This granite obelisk marks the site of Steptoe Battlefield, where a combined force of Spokane, Palouse, and Coeur d'Alene Indians decisively defeated U.S. troops commanded by Colonel E. J. Steptoe. After a daylong running battle drove them to defensive positions on a hill near Rosalia, Steptoe's troops conceded their rout and buried their howitzers, muffled their horses' hooves, and retreated under cover of darkness to Fort Walla Walla. The Indian success was short-lived, however, as it brought even more army forces to the Washington Territory and led to a ruthless, full-scale campaign to supress them.

## STEPTOE BUTTE STATE PARK

**Hours/Season:** Day-use; standard hours; year-round
**Area:** 150.4 acres
**Facilities:** 7 picnic sites, 4 stoves, vault toilets, *no water*
**Attractions:** Picnicking, birdwatching, scenic views, hang-gliding
**Access:** From US 195, 6.5 miles north of Colfax, turn north on Hume Road, signed to Steptoe Butte and Oakesdale. At a Y-

*Green wheat fields and purple hills spread for miles below Steptoe Butte.*

intersection in 1.3 miles, continue northeast, and in another 4 miles an inconspicuous sign points to the northwest and a paved road to the park. *Alternatively,* from Highway 27 just south of Oakesdale, turn southwest on a road signed to the park and reach the entrance road in 7.3 miles.

⚠ The promontory of Steptoe Butte towers 1,000 feet over the nearby rolling wheatland, and the summit commands views more than 50 miles to the north to Mica Peak, 100 miles east to Idaho's Bitterroot Range, 75 miles south to Oregon's Blue Mountains, and endless miles west across the Columbia plateau. Around the compass, acre upon acre of grain fields paint the fertile Palouse soil. The butte itself is the tip of a granite peak that was high enough to escape immersion in the lava flows that engulfed the area between 10 and 30 million years ago, and the post–Ice Age blanket of wind-blown soil (loess) that created the surrounding Palouse hills.

The butte is the prototype of such a geological formation, known by scientists worldwide as a steptoe. The 1,101-foot-high butte was used as a reconnaissance point by the troops of Colonel E. J. Steptoe. In May of 1858 his troops were defeated nearby in an engagement with bands of Indians. It is ironic that a defeat led to the colonel's name being forever identified with a unique geological formation (Custer should have been so lucky).

The entrance road heads arrow-straight through wheat fields to the foot of the butte where the park's only amenities, a small picnic area and vault toilets, are found. From here the road winds around the butte three times on its 3.4-mile ascent to the summit. An interpretive sign placed on top amid microwave antennae describes the geological forces that formed the butte and the surrounding countryside. The unobstructed height of the butte and the constant breezes that blow across the summit make this a favorite take-off point for hanggliding enthusiasts. Hawks, too, take advantage of the updrafts around the butte for long, soaring flights.

The mountain was once the site of a hotel and observation point, which burned in 1911 and was not rebuilt. Part of the old foundation is still in evidence.

# CHIEF TIMOTHY STATE PARK

**Hours/Season:** Overnight; standard hours; year-round; *Alpowai Interpretive Center,* Wednesday through Sunday 1:00 P.M. to 5:00 P.M. June through August

**Area:** 282 acres; 11,500 feet of freshwater shoreline on Lower Granite Lake (Snake River)

**Facilities:** 33 standard campsites, 33 RV sites, 24 picnic sites, 8 sun shelters, children's play equipment, trailer dump station, restrooms with handicap access, showers, bathhouse, swimming beach, concession stand, 4 boat launch ramps, day-use float, 5 mooring floats, 8 mooring buoys, Alpowai Interpretive Center

**Attractions:** Camping, picnicking, hiking, swimming, waterskiing, fishing, boating, sightseeing, historical interpretation

**Access:** From US 12, 8.3 miles west of Clarkston, turn north on Silcott Road and cross a bridge to reach the park, located on an island in Lower Granite Lake.

⚠ The steep basalt cliffs and sharply folded strata that form the Snake River canyon create a scenic backdrop for Chief Timothy State Park. The island on which the park is located was once a hill above the pioneer community of Silcott. A ferry ran from here to the opposite bank of the river. The island was created in 1975 when the waters of the Snake River behind the newly built Lower Granite Dam flooded the area. The park lies along the south shore of the island, which hugs the south shoreline of the lake, forming a protected channel for the water-oriented activities at the park.

Day-use areas with large tree-shaded lawns, picnic tables, fire braziers, and sunshading shelters bound both sides of the entrance road. The area to the east emphasizes boating, with four launch ramps paired to boarding floats, a day-use mooring float, and ample parking for vehicles and boat trailers. To the west, the park is people oriented, with a roped-off swim area below a sandy beach, a bathhouse and concession stand, and children's play area.

A long string of campsites with hookups stretches through the grass strip above the beach east of the day-use area; tent camping is available still farther to the east. A

*Sun, shade, and water all are plentiful at Chief Timothy State Park.*

second and newer vehicle camping area lies uphill from the lower one. Five mooring floats and eight mooring buoys are distributed along the water's edge below the campground strip, providing boating campers convenient access to their craft.

The Alpowai Interpretive Center, on the mainland near the park entrance, is a squat stone building buttressed with banks of basalt boulders. Windows look out over the Snake River canyon. Displays at the center describe the geological formation of the landscape, the history of the Nez Perce Indians who inhabited the village of Alpowai at the site, and the story of the pioneer community of Silcott, which was located here between the 1880s and the 1920s. Showcased are artifacts from the archaeological excavations at Silcott prior to the flooding by waters behind the dam. Other displays tell of the Lewis and Clark Expedition, which passed through the area.

## FIELDS SPRING STATE PARK

**Hours/Season:** Overnight; standard hours; camping in the day-use area only from the end of September to the end of March

**Area:** 455.9 acres

**Facilities:** 20 standard campsites, 4 primitive campsites, 14 picnic sites, 2 picnic shelters/warming huts, kitchen shelter, restrooms with handicap access, trailer dump station, children's play equipment, 2 Environmental Learning Centers, 6.5 miles of hiking and cross-country skiing trail, lighted sledding run and tubing hill

**Attractions:** Camping, picnicking, hiking, backpacking, fishing, baseball, cross-country skiing, sledding, baseball, snowmobiling

**Access:** On the east side of Highway 129,

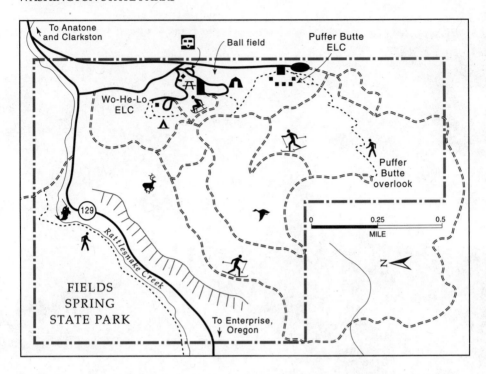

3.9 miles south of Anatone and 28.4 miles south of Clarkston.

The monotony of the flat wheatland plateau south of Clarkston changes abruptly at Rattlesnake Summit, just south of Fields Spring State Park, with the sudden rise of hillsides covered by ponderosa pine, western larch, Douglas fir, and grand fir. This forest encloses much of the park and characterizes the environment found there. In spring and summer, trails through the forest, interspersed with meadows of waist-high wild grass, are ablaze with wildflowers. Bright red skyrocket, Jessica's stickseed, huckleberry, yarrow, and paintbrush all add color to hikes in the area. Nearly fifty species of birds, including hawks, grouse, pheasants, woodpeckers, jays, chickadees, warblers, and finches, are also commonly seen in the park, while four-legged forest dwellers include deer, elk, black bear, and porcupine.

The central day-use area is modest in size, but is supplemented by a grassy baseball diamond a short distance away on the east edge of the park. The campsites surrounding a loop just south of the day-use area have gravel pullouts, tables, fireplaces, and a snug tent space, with each site surrounded by trees and dense brush.

The park has two Environmental Learning Centers: Puffer Butte, on the southeast side of the park, and Wo-He-Lo on the northeast, both of which may be reserved for group use. Rangers will provide interpretive programs and guided walks on request for groups using the centers.

The best and most scenic hike in the park leads up through the forest to the top of Puffer Butte. Trailheads may be found at the day-use area and near both ELCs. The paths all require a steady 1-mile-long climb to reach the summit. A longer but gentler service road from south of the Puffer Butte ELC reaches the summit in 1.5 miles.

Atop the butte the forest gives way to a broad grass-covered ridgeline dropping away to the south. Catch a glimpse of the Snake River, deep within the gorge to the east along the Washington–Idaho border, and the distant snow-covered peaks of Lost River Range farther south in Idaho. Directly south, the 3,000-foot-deep Grand Ronde River Canyon carves into the landscape just north of the Oregon border. To the southwest the smoke-hued summits of the Blue Mountains dominate the view. Several other forested service roads in the park provide longer hikes, but none can match the Puffer Butte view.

Fields Spring is also a popular winter playground. A lighted slope near the Wo-He-Lo ELC has sledding and tubing runs, and two of the picnic shelters are heated to serve as warming huts. In winter most of the service roads become well-marked cross-country ski trails, with routes for every level of skier.

# CAMP WILLIAM T. WOOTEN STATE PARK

**Hours/Season:** *Group use only, by reservation;* year-round

**Area:** 40 acres; 4,100 feet of freshwater shoreline on the Tucannon River

**Facilities:** Environmental Learning Center, 17 cabins, mess hall, chapel, archery range, campfire circle, corral, 1.25-mile interpretive trail, indoor swimming pool, manmade lake, multipurpose field and tennis/basketball courts

**Attractions:** Hiking, swimming, paddling, horseback riding, fishing, field sports, nature study

**Access:** Tucannon Road, a paved two-lane road signed to Camp Wooten, intersects US 12 from the southeast 13.7 miles north of Dayton. Follow this road south for 28.9 miles, then take a spur heading a short distance east through the U.S. Forest Service Tucannon Campground to Camp Wooten. Other secondary roads shown on road maps that appear to offer shorter routes are all partly gravel, narrow, steep, and winding washboards, and are not recommended for large vehicles or low-slung cars.

Camp Wooten is not your "drop-in" state park; the entire facility is an Environmental Learning Center, restricted to group use, by prior reservation. The park, which is a favorite spot for youth or church groups, or even large family reunions, has housing and recreational facilities, but the group must provide its own food, play equipment, medical support, camp supervision, lifeguards, and recreational and ed-

*A nature class fascinates youngsters in the Camp Wooten ELC.*

ucational programs. Cabins are scattered in groups around the perimeter of the park. Some of the buildings are remnants of Camp Tucannon, a 1930s CCC camp.

The camp is in the Blue Mountains of the Umatilla National Forest, not far from the Wenaha-Tucannon Wilderness area. As it nears the park, the Tucannon River valley narrows, and its high, dry, sagebrush-clad sidehills take on a green mantle of ponderosa pine and Douglas fir. The park is tucked between the Tucannon River on the west and a steep, forested ridge to the east. Because a nearby hatchery stocks the river, the trout fishing is excellent.

At the south end of the park, Donnie Lake, a small, shallow, manmade lake, has canoes for paddling. A short tree identification trail loops through the forest to the northeast. At the east side of the lake, a 1.5-mile nature trail climbs quickly uphill through the forest before breaking out on a high grass-covered knob with views down to the lake and camp, and beyond to the Tucannon River valley.

## LEWIS AND CLARK TRAIL STATE PARK

**Hours/Season:** Overnight; standard hours; camping in the day-use area only, from September 30 to March 31

**Area:** 37 acres; 1,333 feet of freshwater shoreline on the Touchet River

**Facilities:** 30 standard campsites, 4 primitive sites, 100-person group camp, 50 picnic sites, 2 kitchen shelters, 50- and 100-person group day-use areas, restrooms, trailer dump station, 1-mile interpretive trail, 0.75-mile birdwatching trail, interpretive kiosk

**Attractions:** Camping, picnicking, hiking,

*A cyclist pauses in the pine-shaded picnic area of Lewis and Clark Trail State Park.*

fishing, birdwatching, sledding
**Access:** The park straddles US 12, 3.7 miles east of Waitsburg or 4.4 miles west of Dayton.

▲ If you're in the vicinity, stop at Lewis and Clark State Park for a lush respite from the surrounding rolling, amber wheatlands. The park marks the site of a stop by Lewis and Clark in May of 1806 on their return from the Pacific Ocean to St. Louis. Although their journal remarks that the area reminded them of the plains of Missouri, it provided them with precious little forage, and the party of 33 had to make do that evening with a meal of a single duck. Just after the Civil War the Bateman family settled here, retaining ownership until the Depression; the property was sold to the State Parks Commission in 1933.

The day-use area on the south side of US 12 has a grass baseball field and a wide lawn punctuated with skyscraping ponderosa pine. The Batemans wisely resisted cutting the stand of pine, although the trees were a tempting source of lumber for building homes. The nearby communities shared the family's devotion to the site, known as Shilo, and in a common effort helped develop the park, hauling over 10,000 stones from the river to construct the unique restroom that still stands today.

The camping area north of the highway lies along the bank of the Touchet River. The rich, moist river bottom supports vegetation so heavy it is an impenetrable tangle except where trails have been carved through it. A group camp lies just inside and east of the entrance. The remainder of the area is a double loop of tent camping sites. A nature trail starts at the restrooms and roams west through the campground loops, circles back along the north perimeter of the park near the river, and returns to its origin from the east side of the park. Numbered stops along the trail correspond to information in a park brochure that identifies the plants and tells of their use by the Indians for food, fuel, and medicine.

In summer the cool shallows of the Touchet River entice adults and kids alike to wade and wallow. The river is planted with rainbow trout and also provides good fishing for German brown trout and steelhead. Kids delight in catching crawfish found lurking under rocks.

## CENTRAL FERRY STATE PARK

**Hours/Season:** Overnight; standard hours; year-round
**Area:** 185 acres; 6,500 feet of freshwater shoreline on Lake Bryan (Snake River)
**Facilities:** 60 RV sites, 2 primitive campsites, 48 picnic sites, 7 picnic shelters, campfire circle, restrooms with handicap access, trailer dump station, bathhouse, swimming beach, 4 boat launch ramps, 3 docks, 2 water-ski docks, marine pumpout station
**Attractions:** Camping, picnicking, hiking, birdwatching, boating, swimming, fishing, waterskiing
**Access:** On the west side of Highway 127, 17.3 miles south of Dusty or 10.4 miles north of Dodge.

▲ In the late 1960s and early 1970s, four dams were built on the Snake River: Ice Harbor, Lower Monumental, Little Goose, and Lower Granite. These dams, which included locks for boats, formed a series of slack-water lakes the entire length of the river to the Idaho border, making it navigable to Clarkston and Lewiston, even for good-sized barges.

The backwaters of Little Goose Dam formed Lake Bryan and created the present shoreline of Central Ferry State Park. With its marine use in mind, the park's designers enhanced the park by dredging two small boat basins to provide safe, protected moorages for visitors. This protection is sometimes warranted, as winds with velocities up to 35 mph can come up suddenly along the river gorge, making the open water rough and dangerous.

In very early times, as its name suggests, a ferry that operated at this point in the Snake River linked Whitman and Garfield counties, but a bridge has long since replaced the ferry.

At the west end of the park, a four-lane launch ramp with a pair of boarding floats leads down to the larger of the boat basins, which is protected at the entrance by a pair of overlapping berms. This basin also contains another 100-foot-long float and marine sanitation facilities. A large lawn holding a few trees spreads from the boat basin to the adjacent camping area. Here

203

campsites line six circular loops. Individual sites are shaded by trees, and most have short sections of fence and brush providing some privacy for the gravel tent pads. A low embankment leads down to the rocky beach below the camping area.

A roped-off swimming beach fronts a day-use area with a tree-shaded lawn, bathhouse, campfire circle, and several beachside picnic shelters. A second small oval boat basin with two floats indents the shore between the camping and day-use areas. A tiny peninsula protecting the basin's outer edge holds a single picnic shelter and table that offer a bit of solitude.

---

## LYONS FERRY STATE PARK

**Hours/Season:** Overnight; standard hours; closed from the end of September to the end of March
**Area:** 1,199.4 acres; 43,250 feet of freshwater shoreline on Lake Herbert G. West (Palouse River)
**Facilities:** 50 standard campsites, 2 primitive sites, 21 picnic sites, 6 picnic shelters, bathhouse, swimming beach, restrooms, trailer dump station, 2 boat launch ramps, 2 mooring buoys, historical display
**Attractions:** Camping, picnicking, hiking, boating, swimming, waterskiing, fishing
**Access:** On Highway 261, 7.2 miles northwest of Starbuck or 14.2 miles southeast of the junction of Highway 261 and Highway 260.

The confluence of the Palouse and Snake rivers was on a route through the area that was used by Indians long before the arrival of the first white man. Near here a professor from Washington State University discovered a rock shelter containing prehistoric fire-charred human bones. These remains, named the "Marmes Man," were carbon-dated at 10,000 years old, far older than any other documented remains in the Western Hemisphere.

The construction of the Lower Monumental Dam across the Snake flooded the Marmes Rock Shelter and the original site of a sacred Palouse Indian burial ground, forever changing the landscape and creating the lengthy shoreline enjoyed by to-

day's visitors to Lyons Ferry State Park.

The park is most popular as a water-oriented day-use area. A long rock breakwater reaches out to a tiny island in the river, then curves and continues parallel to the shore, creating a big, quiet basin fronting the day-use area. A lawn with picnic tables adjoins the two-lane launch ramp at the south end of the area, and a larger grass picnic area lies above the roped-off swimming beach to the north.

The quaint old open-deck Lyons Ferry, now serving as a fishing dock, is tethered to shore at the north end of the basin. Attached to it is a replica of the cable-and-pulley arrangement that permitted the ferry to use the river current to power its crossings. Captain John Mullan constructed one of the first wagon roads through the region in the 1850s. Between 1949 and 1968 a wooden ferry was the primary means of crossing the Snake River just downstream from here.

North of the breakwater, a dirt road ends in a primitive cartop boat launch. Here also

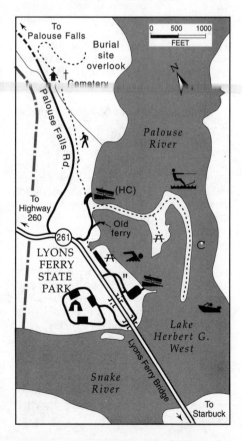

204

*The beach and boats add up to fun at Lyons Ferry State Park.*

is the trailhead for a 0.75-mile gravel trail to the overlook, which has interpretive plaques describing the flooding of the area by the dam, the Marmes Rock Shelter, the Indians and their burial site, and the spectacular Joso railway bridge nearby.

The campground lies on the opposite side of Highway 261. In contrast to the verdant lawns of the day-use area, the campsites consist of rather spartan gravel pulloffs and pads, elbow-to-elbow in places, with minimal shade.

## PALOUSE FALLS
## STATE PARK

**Hours/Season:** Overnight; standard hours; day-use only, from the end of September to the end of March
**Area:** 83 acres; 8,750 feet of freshwater shoreline on the Palouse River
**Facilities:** 10 primitive campsites, 10 picnic sites, picnic shelter, hiking trails, vault toilets, observation shelter, historical display

**Attractions:** Camping, picnicking, hiking, scenic views
**Access:** From Highway 261, 13.5 miles west of Starbuck or 14.4 miles southeast of the junction of Highway 261 and Highway 260, take Palouse Falls Road to the east, reaching the park in 2.2 miles.

At the heart of a rock-rimmed amphitheater, the Palouse River takes a precipitous, 198-foot plunge into a deep green pool, creating one of the most spectacular natural sights in the state. When the sun strikes spray at the base of the falls, a rainbow can often be seen. The falls itself is breathtaking, but its beauty is enhanced by the surrounding rock formations. Just above the lip of the falls, a serrated rib of basalt spires mimics the turrets of a medieval castle, with defenses manned by stalwart seagulls.

From the falls the river continues down the narrow gorge that it has carved over time, enroute to the Snake River. The walls of the river channel are sheer columnar basalt, layered in 100-foot-thick lava flows, separated by narrow shelves clad in dried

**205**

*Palouse Falls is one of the most spectacular sights in the state.*

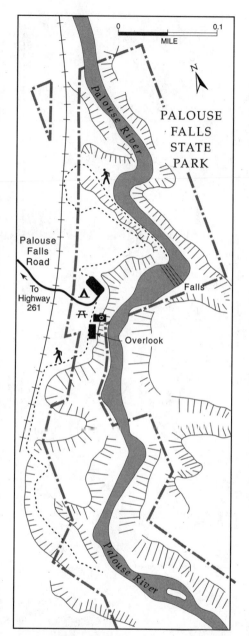

**PALOUSE FALLS STATE PARK**

Palouse Falls Road

To Highway 261

Overlook

Falls

lot follows the gorge, descends abruptly down a wall to the railroad track, then heads to the river's edge, which it follows to the top of the falls. A second beaten-out trail heads south from the parking lot, where again a short, steep descent to the railroad tracks is required. Several hundred yards south on the tracks, a steep path leads to a shelf between the lava layers. This shelf can be followed south for about 0.5 mile to a wide bench, or the trek can be abandoned if one is nervous about traversing its narrower spots. None of the impromptu trails in the park are maintained, and they are not casual undertakings.

Above the parking lot, tent camping is permitted on a small tree-shaded lawn with picnic tables and fire braziers. A companion picnic area with tables and a shelter lies on the opposite side of the road. Uphill from the picnic area, an overlook perches at the canyon rim, with views to the falls.

## SCABLANDS NATURE CORRIDOR (PASCO/FISH LAKE TRAIL)

**Hours/Season:** Day-use; standard hours; year-round
**Area:** 1,575 acres; 134 miles long
**Facilities:** None
**Attractions:** Hiking, horseback riding, bicycling, nature and wildlife observation
**Access:** No formal access points have been developed. The southwest end of the trail can be reached by taking Pasco–Kahlotus Road east from US 12 at Pasco. In 3.7 miles turn south on Martindale Road, which becomes Mehlenbacker Farm Road in 1.4 miles, and crosses the trail at grade level in another 0.8 mile. Other side roads from the Pasco–Kahlotus Road that cross the trail at grade level are Levey Road, Page Road from Murphy Road, Votaw Road from McClenny Road, and McCoy Canyon Road. Other grade-level accesses are at Kahlotus, Sperry, Washtucna, Gray Road at Hooper Junction, Ankeny, Benge, Calloway Road from Ritzville–Benge Road, McCall, Lamont, Martin Road 7 miles east of Sprague, Amber 11 miles southwest of Cheney, Cheney Plaza Road 0.8 mile south of Cheney, and the northeast end of the trail at Myers Park Road

grass and brush. Several of these shelves show faint trails—definitely not paths for one troubled with vertigo! A steep trail that once led from the park down a narrow rock cleft to the base of the falls has been closed because of danger from rockfall (and rattlesnakes).

A dirt road/trail north from the parking

from Cheney–Spokane Road, 3.2 miles northeast of Cheney.

⊥ The Scablands Nature Corridor traces the original roadbed of the Spokane, Portland, and Seattle Railroad, which was built in 1908. State parks acquired the land in 1991 when it was abandoned by the Burlington Northern Railroad. The 134-mile-long route is steeped in history, both geological and human.

Lava flows originating near the Washington–Idaho border 100 million years past covered central Washington with layer upon layer of basalt. This area was then covered by immense continental glaciers, beginning a million years ago, during the Pleistocene epoch, and continuing until about 16,000 years ago. Massive floods that followed the final retreat of these ice sheets ate into the basalt base and gouged out the present washes, gullies, and canyons that are known as the channeled scablands.

When pioneers sought routes through this country, the easiest ones followed the paths of the ancient floods. In the late 1850s, Captain John Mullan laid out a wagon road joining the Missouri River drainage with the Columbia River; 40 years later the first railroads followed much of this original Mullan Road. The imprints of the geological forces that formed the area are still readily visible along the route of the old railbed, and many of the towns and structures along the way have changed little since the early 1900s.

From the southwest end of the trail near Pasco, the route follows the northwest side of the Snake River upstream to Lower Monumental Dam. Several side roads from the Pasco–Kahlotus Road run down canyons to the Snake River, some passing beneath the tall trestles of the old railroad, and others crossing at grade level, offering access to the trail. Near the dam the trail leaves the Snake, swings north through a 0.5-mile-long tunnel, cuts along the middle of the west wall of steep-faced Devils Canyon, and passes through another 2,000-foot-long tunnel just south of Kahlotus before reaching that small town.

From Kahlotus the route heads northeast along the shore of Lake Kahlotus, then down along the floor of the wide, shallow Washtucna Coulee to arrive at the town of Washtucna. After crossing a trestle over the

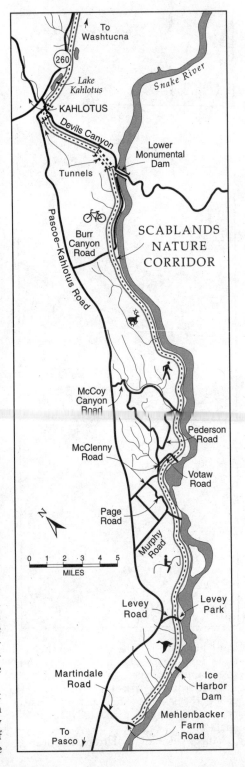

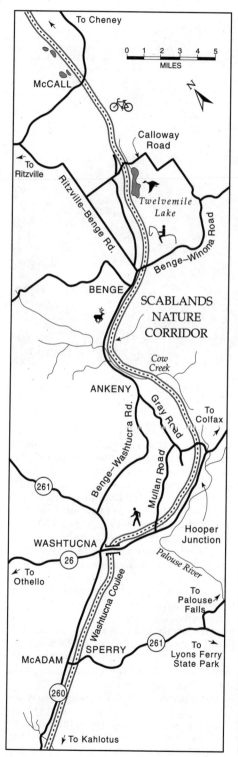

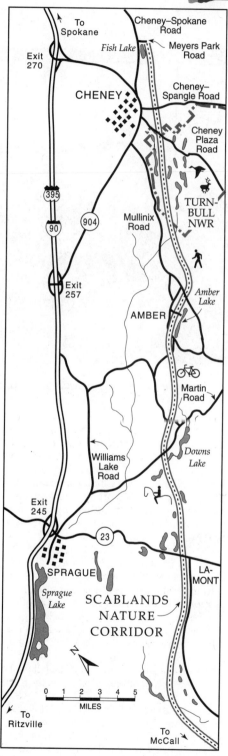

*The trestle over Burr Canyon, which was built in 1908, is listed as a state and national historic landmark.*

active Union Pacific line, the trail follows the general route of the Mullan Trail north up the canyon drainage of Cow Creek, once again crossing the Union Pacific line on a long, high trestle that extends from one rim of the canyon to the other. The trail then climbs out of the deep coulees and reaches the eastern Washington plateau at the town of Benge.

Desolation is the byword for the next 23 miles, as the trail winds through endless dry washes with little trace of human habitation until it arrives at the community of Lamont. The next access point is in another 6 miles, near Downs Lake, east of Sprague, where the roadbed crosses an immense mile-long fill across the coulee just west of Martin Road. In the next 7 miles, the trail passes through a moonscape of basalt post-piles before reaching Amber Lake, the next access point.

Finally, there is a respite from the arid, barren landscape as the trail reaches the forested Turnbull National Wildlife Refuge with its many small lakes, ponds, and sloughs. Leaving the trail within the refuge is prohibited, so binoculars and telephoto camera lenses are advised for those who come to birdwatch. The varied habitat houses a startling array and abundance of birds. Open lakes attract migratory waterfowl such as blue wing and cinnamon teals, ruddy ducks, and whistling swans. The only breeding populations of trumpeter swans in Washington are found here. Marsh birds include Virginia rails, coots, grebes, snipes, and red-winged blackbirds. Land birds in the dry, ponderosa pine forest include hairy woodpeckers, mountain chickadee, red crossbills, and pygmy nuthatches, while ruffed grouse and passarines such as red-eyed vireos and American redstarts may be spotted in aspen groves. Look also for squirrels, chipmunks, badgers, weasels, coyotes, and white-tailed deer.

North from Turnbull the trail passes within 0.5 mile of Cheney as it cuts beneath Cheney–Spangle Road, then continues another 4 miles to its northeast terminus at the north end of Fish Lake.

## POTHOLES STATE PARK

**Hours/Season:** Overnight; standard hours; year-round

**Area:** 640 acres; 6,000 feet of freshwater shoreline on Potholes Reservoir

**Facilities:** 66 standard campsites, 60 RV sites, 2 primitive campsites, 28 picnic sites, children's play equipment, restrooms, vault toilets, trailer dump station, boat launch ramp

**Attractions:** Camping, picnicking, hiking, boating, paddling, fishing, waterskiing, ice fishing

**Nearby:** Potholes Wildlife Recreation Area, Columbia National Wildlife Recreation Area, Goose Lake Wildlife Recreation Area

**Access:** From the west, at Exit 164 (Dodson Road) from I-90, head south on Dodson Road for 10.1 miles, then turn east on Frenchman Hill Road, signed to Potholes State Park, to reach the park in 11 miles. From the east, at Exit 179 (Highway 17, Othello, Moses Lake, Ephrata) from I-90, head southeast on Highway 17 for 9.3 miles, then turn west on O'Sullivan Dam Road, and reach the park in another 11.9 miles.

When O'Sullivan Dam was completed in 1949, raising the water table south of Moses Lake, sand-filled depressions that had been carved by Ice Age glaciers filled with water and created an enormous lake (28,200-acre Potholes Reservoir) and a network of interconnecting shallow ponds and marshes that covers thousands of acres of scabland. The tops of old sand dunes protrude from the water of the reservoir, creating a maze of over a hundred islands at its north end, and making this a paddler's paradise.

Potholes State Park is located on the southwest shore of the reservoir. Its day-use and RV camping areas form an oasis of green amid the surrounding drab desert landscape. Tall rows of Lombardy poplar interspersed with shorter evergreens protect the sites from high winds that occasionally whip the area. Tent campers must be a hardier lot, however, as these sites, rimming two loops on the north end of the park, consist of only a meager gravel pad, table, and fire

pit nestled into the surrounding sagebrush and sand.

The major park recreation involves boating, paddling, fishing, and waterskiing on the reservoir. To support these activities, the park has a paved two-lane boat launch, a separate dirt cartop launch ramp, and two huge lots for parking cars and boat trailers. Although the day-use area fronts on the reservoir, no defined swimming beach is roped off.

The open water, marshes, and willow thickets of the potholes provide nesting areas and migratory stopovers for thousands of waterfowl and other birds, ranging from big heavy-bodied white pelicans, to graceful black-crowned night herons, and delicate little American avocets. Yellow-headed and red-winged blackbirds add splashes of color to cattails. Quiet boaters and fishermen may see muskrats and beavers, while campers enjoy the evening serenade of coyotes. The lakes, which are planted with rainbow trout, also hold largemouth and smallmouth bass, perch, crappie, and walleye.

## MOSES LAKE STATE PARK

**Hours/Season:** Day-use; standard hours, from April 1 to the end of September; weekends and holidays only, from October 1 to March 31

**Area:** 78 acres; 862 feet of freshwater shoreline on Moses Lake

**Facilities:** 72 picnic sites, picnic shelter, restrooms, bathhouse, snacks (concession), swimming beach, boat launch ramp, dock, swimming/waterski floats

**Attractions:** Picnicking, boating, sailing, paddling, swimming, fishing, waterskiing, scuba diving, ice skating, ice fishing

**Access:** Take Exit 175 (Moses Lake State Park) from I-90, and turn north onto Westlake Road. Continue to the park entrance in 0.2 mile.

Moses Lake State Park resembles a typical urban park, with picnic sites scattered throughout a rolling, tree-shaded lawn, a couple of large picnic shelters for family or community group gatherings, and in summer a concession stand pushing sandwiches, ice cream, and cool drinks. Because the park lies on the west shore of Moses Lake, it also provides water-oriented facilities: a bathhouse and roped-off swimming beach, and a two-lane boat launch ramp with a boarding float.

The park is immediately north of the westbound lanes of I-90, so it's an alluring place to stop for a stretch and picnic lunch to break the tedious drive across the endless central Washington plateau. In winter the shallow shoreline waters freeze over, and the swimming area becomes a community ice skating rink.

The numerous, narrow arms of the 6,815-acre lake offer water recreation to everyone's taste. Fishing is the big attraction, but the cool lake also offers a summer respite to swimmers, waterskiers, and boaters who just enjoy a day on the water.

## SACAJAWEA STATE PARK

**Hours/Season:** Day-use, standard hours; year-round
**Area:** 283.7 acres; 9,100 feet of freshwater shoreline on the Snake and Columbia rivers
**Facilities:** Picnic tables, 2 kitchen shelters, 200-person group day-use area, children's play equipment, restrooms, snacks (concession), swimming beach, 3 mooring floats, boat launch ramp, floats, 4 mooring buoys, interpretive center
**Attractions:** Picnicking, boating, fishing, swimming, waterskiing, birdwatching, interpretive displays
**Nearby:** McNary National Wildlife Refuge
**Access:** From US 12, 4.4 miles southeast of Pasco and just west of the bridge across the Snake River, turn southwest on Tank Farm Road. At a Y-intersection in 1 mile, bear east and reach the park entrance in another 0.9 mile.

Nearly every grade-schooler can identify Sacajawea as the Shoshoni Indian woman who accompanied Lewis and Clark on their westward trek from Missouri to the Pacific Ocean and served as their interpreter. Sacajawea State Park and its interpretive center are named after this brave woman. The park is located at one of the party's campsites, at the confluence of two major rivers, the Snake and Columbia. It was here, in 1805, that Lewis and Clark first sighted the mighty river that provided their final access to the ocean.

During pioneer times this site lay on the route used by hunters and trappers seeking their fortune in the Northwest. The park property includes the former site of Ainsworth, a rough-and-tumble railroad town that sprang to life during the construction of the Northern Pacific Railroad bridge across the Snake in the 1880s.

Huge, old trees throughout the flat lawn of the park testify to its age; the initial parcels were deeded to the state in 1931. A swimming beach is roped off along the Columbia River side of the park. The Snake shoreline supports the boating-oriented facilities. Here are three docks with 40-foot-long mooring floats running parallel to the riverbank. A small oval basin indenting the park upriver from them encloses a two-lane launch ramp and boarding floats. Four mooring buoys have been set in the Snake just outside the launch basin entrance.

The Sacajawea Interpretive Center sits at the heart of the park. One of the center's rooms tells of the competing claims to the Northwest that prompted Thomas Jefferson to send the Lewis and Clark Expedition west to establish an American claim to the region, and traces their route to the Pacific and back with montages of photos, maps, and journal reproductions. Videos about the expedition are shown twice daily. A second room houses arrowheads, mortars, pestles, awls, bowls, and other artifacts used by the Indians of the Columbia Basin plateau. Display boards describe facets of the Indian culture, and tell how the tools and implements were made and used.

## CROW BUTTE STATE PARK

**Hours/Season:** Overnight; standard hours; boat launch ramp open year-round, remainder of the park open weekends and holidays only, from the end of October to March 1
**Area:** 1,311.7 acres; 33,910 feet of freshwater shoreline on Lake Umatilla (Columbia River)

*White pelicans, which nest in the vicinity, can often be seen at Crow Butte State Park. (Photo by Bob and Ira Spring)*

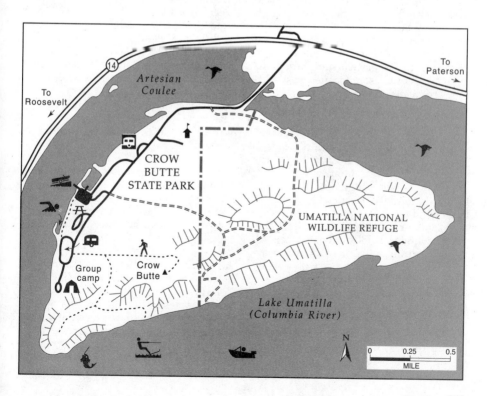

**Facilities:** 50 RV sites, 60-person group camp, 20 picnic sites, 3 picnic shelters, restrooms, trailer dump station, bathhouse, swimming beach, boat launch ramp, boat basin, 2 mooring buoys, 2.25 miles of trail

**Attractions:** Camping, picnicking, hiking, boating, swimming, fishing, waterskiing, birdwatching

**Nearby:** Umatilla National Wildlife Refuge

**Access:** The park is reached by a bridge to an island in Lake Umatilla (Columbia River) on the south side of Highway 14, 12.4 miles west of Paterson or 21.6 miles east of Roosevelt.

Folks in eastern Washington who are surrounded by the tough green-brown rolling hills of the Columbia plateau like their park getaways soft and shady. Crow Butte State Park meets their expectations nicely, with its neatly groomed grassy crescent on the shore of Lake Umatilla. Yet nature is only a stroll from the campground.

A small boat basin, protected to the north by a breakwater, provides boating amenities for the park. The tree-rimmed lawn at the day-use area holds picnic shelters and a bathhouse. Below, a shallow roped-off swimming beach is partially enclosed by the finger of a breakwater. Shade trees and wind-break fences shield campsites from the elements. The group camp, west of the main park areas, is an isolated oasis surrounded by desert sagebrush.

On the east side of the campground, a wide sandy trail enters the desert. (*Be careful venturing off the trail: Signs warn of rattlesnakes.*) In 0.25 mile the east fork heads to the top of 671-foot-high Crow Butte. The west fork climbs to another Y; the east branch leads over a ridge and down a gully to the dune-edged river, while the right branch continues west to a viewpoint of the river and campground. On a clear day Mount Hood is visible in the distance. Although the trail may seem a tedium of gray-green sagebrush, a sharp eye will spot tiny colorful wildflowers, cactus, grasshoppers, beetles, deer, and other desert inhabitants (but hopefully, no rattlesnakes).

Crow Butte is the top of a hill that became an island when the reservoir backed up behind John Day Dam, flooding this stretch of the Columbia River and creating 76-mile-long Lake Umatilla. The island is

reached via a bridge on a causeway across Artesian Coulee. The east end of the island is a portion of the Umatilla National Wildlife Refuge, which extends east on both sides of the river for over 15 miles.

Huge numbers of waterfowl wintered on islands in this stretch of the Columbia before the John Day Dam was built. The wildlife refuge was established to mitigate the loss of islands drowned by the construction of the dam. With the irrigation the dam brought, the birds now have a larger food source from newly created wheat fields, and they now flock here in even greater numbers than before. White pelicans and long-billed curlews nest in the region. From fall through spring this is also a hotel to hundreds of thousands of transient ducks and Canada geese as they wend their way north or south with the seasons.

## YAKIMA SPORTSMAN STATE PARK

**Hours/Season:** Overnight; standard hours; year-round

**Area:** 251 acres; 17,675 feet of freshwater shoreline on the Yakima River

**Facilities:** 28 standard campsites, 36 RV sites, 2 primitive campsites, 120 picnic sites, kitchen shelter, 200-person group day-use area, children's play equipment, restrooms, trailer dump station

**Attractions:** Camping, picnicking, hiking, fishing, birdwatching

**Access:** From I-82/US 97/US 12 on the east side of Yakima, take Exit 34 (Highway 24 E, Moxee, Nob Hill Boulevard)(Yakima State Park, Fairgrounds, Yakima Community College). Head east on Highway 24 for 0.8 mile, then turn north on Keys Road. The park entrance is on the west side of the road in 1 mile, at Gun Club Road.

Yakima Sportsman State Park is a green swale with ponds and a trickling creek along the east side of the Yakima River. The park was named for the Yakima Sportsmans Association, which created it in 1940 as a site to promote game management and the preservation and protection of natural resources. Because the ponds and small lakes within the park are stocked, fishing is limited to youngsters under 15 years old. The Yakima River, which has great fishing for all ages, is known for its catches of large trout.

A pond, which in summer flaunts brilliant pink water lilies, lies in the heart of the broad grassy expanse of the park's day-use area. Shade for picnic tables is provided by a remarkable variety of beautiful, mature deciduous trees, including elm, ash, willow, maple, and catalpa. The north side of the park is framed by more ponds—home not only for fish, but also both domestic and wild ducks and geese. Blue Slough Creek flows through a profusion of brush along the south and west sides of the day-use area. A bridge across the creek leads to the campground area on the south side of the park.

A scramble through the brush west of the campground leads to the dike that edges the Yakima River. The dike can also be reached from the day-use area at a few spots where trees have fallen and bridged Blue Slough Creek. The dike permits river-bank fishing access to the Yakima. A slow and quiet walk along the service road that tops the dike should lead to the spotting of swallows, hawks, owls, red-winged black-birds, or other of the 130 species of birds that have been identified in the area.

*The enlisted men's barracks at Fort Simcoe was originally built in the 1850s.*

## FORT SIMCOE STATE PARK

**Hours/Season:** Day-use; standard hours, from April 1 through September 30; weekends and holidays only, October 1 through March 31

**Area:** 200 acres

**Facilities:** 52 picnic sites, 8 fire braziers, picnic shelter, children's play equipment, restrooms, 10 historic buildings, interpretive center, interpretive displays, 0.5 mile of hiking trail

**Attractions:** Picnicking, hiking, historical interpretation

**Access:** From US 97 at Toppenish, take Highway 220 (White Swan, Fort Simcoe) west for 27.5 miles to arrive at the park.

Fort Simcoe State Park is not for the casual drive-by visitor; the road dead-ends at the park after a 27-mile drive through the hop and grape fields of the Yakama Indian Reservation west of Toppenish. However, for those interested in military or state history, the fort is well worth the drive. Here the abundant cold spring waters of Mool Mool (bubbling waters) nourished a surrounding forest and lush grassland that stood in stark contrast to the otherwise parched countryside. The area had long been used as a campsite by Yakama Indian tribes, and in 1855, when Indian hostilities mandated an advanced military post in Washington Territory, it was selected as the site for a new fort.

In the summer of 1856, during the renewed Indian wars, troops from the fort engaged bands of Spokane, Coeur d'Alene, and Palouse Indians, but the cessation of hostilities and a change in military command led to the abandonment of the fort in 1859. It was turned over to the Bureau of Indian Affairs, and until 1923 served as Indian Agency headquarters. The agency-run school at the fort taught reservation Indians reading and writing and trained them in trades such as carpentry, blacksmithing, and farming.

Today the broad grassy parade field of the fort has been restored, and replicas of the blockhouses that protected its corners have been reconstructed. One of the barracks that housed enlisted men was also rebuilt, and the prim white clapboard homes for the field-grade officers and commanding officer have been restored to their original condition and decorated with period furnishings. The remainder of the fort buildings, including other barracks, junior officer's quarters, warehouses, servants' buildings, laundry, and hospital are now remembered only by concrete markers.

The old Indian Agency commissary has been converted into an interpretive center where displays tell the story of the Indians and history of the fort. Modern park amenities consist of picnic tables, a picnic shelter, and restrooms in a tree-shaded lawn next to the huge parking lot at the entrance to the park.

## BROOKS MEMORIAL STATE PARK

**Hours/Season:** Overnight; standard hours; year-round
**Area:** 700.8 acres

*The ELC facilities at Brooks Memorial State Park include teepees for some campers.*

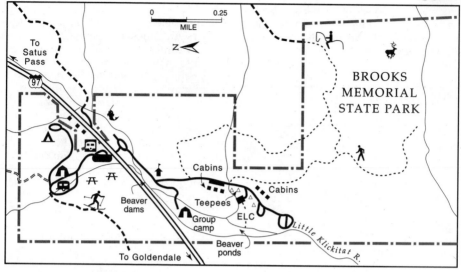

**Facilities:** 22 standard campsites, 23 RV sites, 2 primitive campsites, 50-person group camp, 40 picnic sites, 2 picnic shelters, children's play equipment, restrooms with handicap access, trailer dump station, 3 miles of hiking trail; Environmental Learning Center with dining hall and kitchen, restrooms, 7 cabins, 4 teepees, sports field, and campfire circle

**Attractions:** Camping, picnicking, fishing, hiking, cross-country skiing, snowshoeing, snowmobiling (nearby), nature talks on request, horseback riding (nearby)

**Access:** The park straddles US 97, 141.4 miles north of Goldendale or 2.5 miles south of Satus Pass.

Satus Pass marks the transition between the barren hills at the south side of the Yakima valley and the lodgepole pine forest of the Simcoe Mountains. Brooks Memorial State Park lies in the forested region just south of the 3,149-foot pass. The park, with its group camp and Environmental Learning Center, in addition to the usual picnicking and camping, is heavily oriented toward group recreation.

The picnic area and individual campsites are on the northwest side of US 97. A tree-shaded lawn with a picnic shelter and tables lies just inside the park entrance, and campsites are just beyond. Standard sites have tables and fire braziers on open ground in a stand of ponderosa pine; hookup sites are paved diagonal strips in a swatch of lawn.

Most of the park's area lies southeast of the highway; here are found a group camp and the ELC. The latter has a main lodge and two groups of cabins and teepees. An outdoor amphitheater and grassy playfield are nearby. The full facilities of the ELC make it ideal for scout troops, church camps, and family reunions, while the dry climate of eastern Washington virtually guarantees good weather for a summer gathering.

Trails lead from the ELC to two different environmental experiences. A short trail enters the brush below the playfield and soon reaches the Little Klickitat River, where a series of beaver dams form pools in the trickling stream. Trailside mud and dust reveal tracks of beaver and deer. A gated road near the ELC entrance heads out to a forest-rimmed meadow located on a long extension of the park that projects to the southeast. Ponderosa pine, Douglas fir, white pine, and Oregon oak dominate the forest, and seasonal wildflowers such as lady's slipper, balsalm root, and lupine add color to the open forest floor. Forest inhabitants include deer, raccoons, porcupines, wild turkeys, black bear, coyotes, and bobcats, and raptors such as owls, hawks, and eagles.

Cold, snowy winters and open timber

make the park ideal for cross-country skiing and snowshoeing. Limited park facilities are available during the winter to support these activities.

## GOLDENDALE OBSERVATORY STATE PARK

**Hours/Season:** April 1 to September 30, Wednesday through Sunday, 2:00 P.M. to 5:00 P.M. and 8:00 P.M. to midnight; October 1 to March 31, Saturday 1:00 P.M. to 5:00 P.M., 7:00 P.M. to 9:00 P.M., and Sunday 1:00 P.M. to 5:00 P.M.; other hours by appointment
**Area:** 5 acres
**Facilities:** Lecture room, small science library, photographic darkroom, observatories with 24.5-inch reflecting telescope and 8- inch Celestron telescope, 6 portable telescopes with camera accessories available to the public, astronomical displays, restrooms
**Attractions:** Observing through telescopes, interpretive lectures, scientific displays
**Access:** At the flashing light on Highway 142 at the center of Goldendale, turn north on N Columbus Avenue. At a Y-intersection in 1.1 miles, follow the road signed to the park uphill to the right, and reach the observatory in 0.9 mile.

An astronomical observatory is without a doubt unique among all state parks. The dry cloudless nights typical of the Klickitat Valley and minimal light pollution from the small community of Goldendale combine to provide optimal viewing conditions.

The observatory didn't start out as a state park. It began with four astronomers—M. W. McConnell, O. W. VanderVelden, John Marshall, and Don Conner—who built the large telescope for Clark College in Vancouver, Washington, and selected this hilltop for its location. The city of Goldendale constructed the facilities to house the telescope, aided by a federal grant. The observatory, which was dedicated in 1973, became a state park in 1980.

The main telescope, a 24.5-inch Cassegrain reflector, is the largest of its kind in the nation that is available for public use. In addition to the main telescope, an 8-inch Celestron telescope and six portable telescopes with camera attachments (you provide the camera) are available. Tours and very informative lectures are provided to the general public, and the observatory facilities may be reserved by qualified amateur astronomers for their observing needs.

The observatory building and exhibits are open to the public in the afternoons of scheduled visiting days. The short trip to the wooded hilltop north of Goldendale offers spectacular views of Mount Adams and Mount Hood. Near sunset the public lectures begin with a view of the rim of the sun through the Celestron, followed by an entertaining, informative talk that is geared to making stargazing understandable for the uninitiated and keeping even young visitors interested. When the sky has darkened, visitors are admitted to the main telescope to view whatever is most interesting or prominent in the evening sky. Smaller telescopes outside the building offer more variety. With the observatory dome open, the evening air is quite chilly; warm clothing is advised.

## MARYHILL STATE PARK

**Hours/Season:** Overnight; standard hours; year-round
**Area:** 98.4 acres; 4,700 feet of freshwater shoreline on the Columbia River
**Facilities:** 50 RV sites, 3 primitive campsites, 50 picnic sites, 2 picnic shelters, restrooms, showers, trailer dump station, bathhouse, swimming beach, boat launch ramp
**Attractions:** Camping, picnicking, hiking, boating, sailing, kayaking, fishing, swimming, waterskiing, windsurfing
**Nearby:** Maryhill Museum and the Stonehenge Memorial, John Day Dam
**Access:** On the east side of US 97, just north of the bridge across the Columbia River, 1.6 miles south of the junction of Highway 14 and US 97 (12.9 miles south of Goldendale).

The Sam Hill Bridge, just east of Maryhill State Park, links the major highways that run along the Washington and Oregon sides of the Columbia River. This location, and its proximity to both the Maryhill Museum and the Stonehenge Memorial, makes the park an ideal stopover for visitors. In addition, the park's river access attracts swimmers, boaters, fishermen, waterskiers, and windsurfers.

Trees provide shade and windbreak to the flat green lawns of the camping loops and the day-use area. Below a bathhouse/concession stand, two rock breakwaters frame a gravel swimming beach, protecting it from river currents. The breakwaters also serve as fishing piers for casting a line well out into the river. East of the swimming beach, two launch ramp lanes flank a wooden boarding float.

The lawns serve as space for rigging sailboards. Windsurfing is prohibited in the vicinity of the swimming area, so you should launch from the beach downstream from it. The heavy winds, strong current,

and rough water usually present here demand expert boardsailing skills.

The state park is 5 miles east of Maryhill Museum, a mansion built in the 1920s by railroad entrepreneur Sam Hill. The museum contains a fascinatingly eclectic collection, ranging from Rodin sculptures to nineteenth-century Russian icons, Native American artifacts, and chess sets. Another of Hill's creations, Stonehenge, lies on a bluff midway between the park and museum. It is a full-sized replica (in concrete) of England's prehistoric monument.

# HORSETHIEF LAKE STATE PARK

**Hours/Season:** Overnight; standard hours; closed from the end of October to the end of March

**Area:** 338 acres; 7,500 feet of freshwater

*Many of the campsites at Maryhill State Park face on the Columbia River.*

shoreline on Horsethief Lake and the Columbia River

**Facilities:** 12 standard campsites, 2 primitive campsites, 35 picnic sites, restrooms, trailer dump station, 2 boat launch ramps, 2 miles of hiking trail

**Attractions:** Camping, picnicking, hiking, rock climbing, boating, paddling, fishing, birdwatching, windsurfing, Indian petroglyphs

**Nearby:** The Dalles Dam

**Access:** On the south side Highway 14, 1.5 miles east of the junction of Highway 14 and US 197, or 7.9 miles west of Wishram.

▲ When the railroad was built along the Columbia River, in numerous spots causeways were laid over low, marshy areas. With the building of dams and raising of the water level, many of these marshes flooded and became backwater lakes, enclosed by the causeway. The largest of these is 90-acre Horsethief Lake, just above The Dalles Dam.

Although history does not record the identity of the horsethief who gave the lake its name, other history of the area is well known. This section of river was a gathering site for canoe Indians from the ocean and lower Columbia and nomadic plateau Indians, who met here to fish, barter, and socialize. A permanent settlement was at Wakemap, the present location of Horsethief Lake State Park. When Lewis and Clark stopped here they described it as a great emporium, where neighboring nations assembled. Today a small Indian cemetery lies just inside the park entrance, and a trail along the south edge of the park leads to Indian petroglyphs engraved on rock—some of the oldest known in the Northwest.

Most of the park lies along the west shore of the lake, where irrigation creates emerald lawns, in stark contrast to surrounding parched desert landscape. A line of tall Lombardy poplar provides shade and windbreak to the semicircular picnic area; several more rows of poplar divide it into sections. The camping area is unshaded, however.

Two separate launch ramps provide boat access to both Horsethief Lake and the Columbia River. The lake is planted with rainbow trout, and because it is joined to the river by a culvert, expect to find most of the same fish here that are found in the river proper. Winds that whip up the river are deflected somewhat from the lake, making it a slightly more protected spot for novice windsurfers to practice the tricks of boardsailing, although winds are erratic, due to its nearness to land.

Horsethief Butte, a 500-foot-high basalt mesa, rises dramatically above the lake. A hiking trail leaves from the highway, 1.25 miles east of the park entrance. Some limited parking can be found along the road or at a road-marker wayside. The short trail leads straight to the mesa, then climbs some 200 feet up a cleft to the top. Rock climbers use the area for bouldering and short, roped climbs.

## DOUG'S BEACH STATE PARK

**Hours/Season:** Day-use; standard hours; no facilities from the first of November to end of March

**Area:** 31 acres; 240 feet of freshwater shoreline on the Columbia River

**Facilities:** Sani-cans during the summer months, *no water*

**Attractions:** Windsurfing, kayaking, sunbathing, fishing

**Access:** On the south side of Highway 14, 4.8 miles west of the junction of Highway 14 and US 197 or 2.4 miles east of Lyle.

▲ This section of the Columbia River gorge has some of the most exciting windsurfing available in the world. Steady, strong, 30-mph winds are channeled by the basalt cliffs bordering the river, and westerlies that oppose the direction of the river current raise challenging whitecaps along its course. Large swells, chop, and boat traffic in the river make this an area to be used only by expert windsurfers.

When the wind is up (which is nearly all the time) and weather is good, the shoulders of the highway for more than 0.25 mile are lined with roof-racked vehicles, and the beach and river are a sea of gaudy chartreuse, pink, teal, and purple, as sailboards guided by lycra-clad bodies scamper deftly back and forth across the river. A summer weekend with good winds will find hundreds of sailboards on the river, like flocks

*A sunny day with good winds brings hordes of windsurfers to Doug's Beach.*

of multicolored mayflies.

As a park, Doug's Beach is little more than a river access point. There is no parking except for the shoulders of the highway; use care parking and crossing the road, because traffic is heavy. In summer sani-cans that serve the hordes of surfers are the sole facilities. A swatch of sandy beach grass beside the river serves as a board assembly point, impromptu picnic site, and rest and recreation area for sailors and their retinue. The sightseeing can be as fun as the activity.

The park is also a put-in point for kayakers who experience the same hazards as windsurfers—as well as similar thrills. Gear must be carried some 100 feet from car to launch site.

# REGION 5

- Kitsap Peninsula
- East Shore of Hood Canal
- Puget Sound Basin
- Snoqualmie River
- Green River

## TWANOH STATE PARK

**Hours/Season:** Overnight; standard hours in summer; limited day-use year-round (campground closed from the end of September to mid-April)

**Area:** 182 acres; 3,167 feet of saltwater shoreline on Hood Canal

**Facilities:** 38 standard campsites, 9 RV sites, 13 primitive walk-in sites, 100-person group camp, 111 picnic sites, fireplaces, 2 kitchen shelters, 150-person group day-use area, wading pool, swimming beach, bathhouses, restrooms, showers, concession stand, tennis court, horseshoe pits, dock with float, boat launch ramp, 7 mooring buoys, marine pumpout station, 2 miles of hiking trail

**Attractions:** Camping, picnicking, boating, swimming, hiking, waterskiing, fishing

**Access:** *By land,* take Highway 304 southwest out of Bremerton to its junction with Highway 3. Continue west on Highway 3 for 9 miles to Belfair. Just west of Belfair follow Highway 106 southwest for 7.5 miles to the park. *By boat,* the park is on the southeast shore of Hood Canal, 6 miles east of Union.

▲ Twanoh State Park straddles Highway ⊥ 106 midway along the 10-mile-long "Great Bend" of Hood Canal. The campground and hiking trails are found south of the road in the heavily forested portion of the park, while the beach and day-use facilities lie on the north side.

A two-lane concrete launch ramp and a large parking lot for cars and boat trailers occupy the west end of the beach. To the east, across Twanoh Creek, the main day-use area fills a lawn where huge old fir and cedar trees shade picnic tables, fire braziers, and kitchen shelters. A tennis court and horseshoe pits are nearby. At the east end of the day-use area, a dock with floats that extends into Hood Canal is used both for fishing and boat access to the park; mooring buoys have been placed offshore from the float for visiting boaters.

When summer sun warms the water to an inviting level, bathers flock to the park's broad sand and gravel beach. The swimming area has floats offshore. For small fry, a shallow wading pond lies in the gravel of the upper beach. Nearby bathhouses and a concession stand are open during summer months.

The camping area has a trailer hookup loop around a small tree-shaded flat and a smaller tent-camping loop farther up the narrowing gulch that holds Twanoh Creek. The sturdy rustic restrooms here, as well as most of the buildings in the day-use area, were constructed between 1936 and 1937

Opposite: *The day-use area at Twanoh State Park overlooks Hood Canal.*

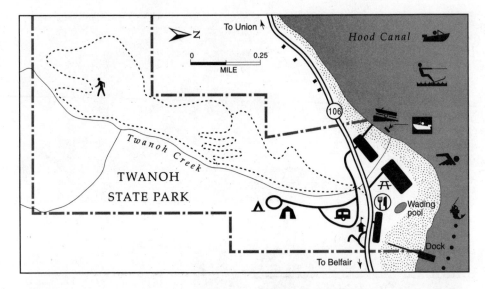

by the Depression-era CCC. A display in the picnic area describes the park activities of the CCC.

The park extends far inland up the green gully of Twanoh Creek. Several miles of trails lace this wooded section; one leg of a trail loop follows the creek bank uphill, cutting through typical moist-forest growth of devil's club, moss, and wispy ferns. Near the park's southern boundary, the trail switchbacks upward to an open huckleberry-covered hilltop, skirts the western edge of the park, and then drops down a ridge through second-growth cedar to rejoin its start point. Halfway through the loop, a shortcut switchbacks steeply from hilltop to creekbed through fir and hemlock forest. The park was logged in the 1890s; observant hikers may spot springboard notches in old cedar stumps.

## BELFAIR STATE PARK

**Hours/Season:** Overnight; standard hours; year-round
**Area:** 62.5 acres; 1,300 feet of saltwater shoreline on Hood Canal
**Facilities:** 137 standard campsites, 47 RV sites with hookups, 205 picnic tables, restrooms, showers, bathhouse, trailer dump station, horseshoe pit, children's play area, swimming beach on a manmade enclosed saltwater basin, *campsite reservation required in summer*
**Attractions:** Camping, picnicking, beachcombing, crabbing, scuba diving, fishing
**Access:** Follow Highway 304 southwest out of town to its junction with Highway 3, then continue west 9 miles on Highway 3 to Belfair. Take Highway 300 west, then south, for 3 miles to reach the park.

When Skokomish Indians of long ago chose this spot near the tip of the "hook" of Hood Canal as a campsite, they were undoubtedly drawn here by the shallow, clam-filled tideflat. Although today the clams and oysters are victims of pollution, and the shores are lined with homes, the site is still a magnet for people eager to enjoy the placid water and pleasant camping it offers.

Since the park's "beach" becomes a mudflat at the slightest hint of a low tide, a unique swimming area has been created: a gravel-rimmed pool, large enough for several dozen paddlers, that is separated from the canal by a rock dike. A tide-gate controls the water level.

The tough, windblown beach grass along the shore gives way to a manicured meadow. Three camping loops, two of which have trailer hookups, lie along the west side of the park. The newest of these sits in a grassy flat broken up with planted ever-

224

*An old rowboat rests against driftwood on the beach at Belfair State Park.*

green and deciduous trees. A more secluded RV hookup loop and tent camping area lie on the west side of Little Mission Creek, surrounded by a stand of Douglas fir, red cedar, and alder, with a scattering of native rhododendrons.

The park and offshore waters are home or way station for squadrons of ducks, geese, and an occasional great blue heron. Crabs that are caught may be eaten, but pollution makes clams and oysters from the mudflat unsafe as food.

## SCENIC BEACH
## STATE PARK

**Hours/Season:** Overnight; standard hours; weekends and holidays only, from the end of September to the end of March
**Area:** 88.2 acres; 1,487 feet of saltwater shoreline on Hood Canal
**Facilities:** 52 standard campsites, 50-person group camp, 75 picnic sites, kitch-

en shelter, fireplaces, restrooms, showers, horseshoe pits, fire rings, volleyball courts
**Attractions:** Camping, picnicking, boating, paddling, fishing, oysters, scuba diving, beachcombing, hiking
**Access:** From the ferry terminal in Bremerton, take Washington Street north to 6th. Head west on 6th, which eventually becomes Kitsap Way, and shortly intersects Highway 3. Take Highway 3 north for 4.6 miles to the Newberry Hill Road/Silverdale exit. Head west on Newberry Hill Road, which joins Seabeck Highway NW in 3 miles. Follow this highway southwest to 0.2 mile beyond Seabeck, then turn west on Miami Beach Road NW. At a Y-intersection in 0.5 mile, turn west on Scenic Beach Road to reach the park entrance.

A Maytime profusion of pink native rhododendron blossoms makes Scenic Beach a favorite spring destination. At other times of the year, the picturesque setting

*Catamarans leave from the shore at Scenic Beach State Park.*

on Hood Canal, with sweeping views across the water to the vast glacier-carved valleys of the Dosewallips and Duckabush rivers and up to snowy Olympic peaks, provides ample reason to visit the park.

The scenic site earned early favor as a private resort. Following the death of the resort owner, Joe Emel, Sr., the land was purchased by the state for a park. The Emel home is currently used as a community center.

Douglas fir, western red cedar, and western hemlock soar skyward in stands of dense forest that rim the roads and campsites. These conifers, along with maple and alder, host an array of birds. Pileated woodpeckers, Steller's jays, juncos, towhees, and wrens are but a few that may be spotted. A short trail connecting the campground loops to the beach leads through the lush growth of salal, rhododendron, Oregon grape, and

huckleberry that screens the campsites.

The park's day-use area, set in open timber, has picnic sites, play equipment, volleyball court, horseshoe pits and a bathhouse. Below a short, steep bank, the cobble beach drops gently into Hood Canal. Above the beach on the west side of the park, the lawns and orchard adjoining the Emel homestead have been converted to another picnic and play area.

## KITSAP MEMORIAL STATE PARK

**Hours/Season:** Overnight; standard hours; year-round

**Area:** 57.6 acres; 1,797 feet of saltwater shoreline on Hood Canal

**Facilities:** 51 standard campsites, 30-

person group camp, adirondack shelters, 51 picnic sites, 2 kitchen shelters, 2 75-person group day-use areas, fireplaces, meeting hall, restrooms, showers, ball field, swimming beach, children's playground, horseshoe pits, volleyball courts, trailer dump station, 1 mile of trail, 2 mooring buoys

**Attractions:** Camping, picnicking, hiking, baseball, volleyball, fishing, boating, paddling, swimming, scuba diving, oysters

**Access:** *By land,* from the ferry terminal in Kingston, take Highway 104 west to Port Gamble, then Highway 3 south to the park; distance from Kingston is 11.5 miles. From the Winslow ferry terminal, take Highway 305 north to its intersection with Highway 3 west of Poulsbo, then Highway 3 north to the park; the distance from Winslow is 16.2 miles. *By boat,* the park is on the east shore of Hood Canal, 3 miles south of the floating bridge. The nearest boat launch ramp is at Salisbury Point County Park.

Meadowlike playfields and a saltwater beach combine to make Kitsap Memorial one of the most popular day-use parks in the Bremerton/Poulsbo area.

A large grassy field with a ball diamond and space for volleyball nets forms the heart of the park. Half the park campsites are tightly packed along one edge of this meadow; the remainder lie on a wooded loop to the north. Evergreen-shaded picnic shelters and tables are scattered on the bluff above the beach, with views out to Hood Canal.

A short hiking trail that circles the group camp on the south side of the park leads through second-growth timber. Holes bored high in tree trunks bear evidence of bug-hungry flickers and pileated woodpeckers; listen for their noisy drilling.

A short path drops from the picnic area down the low bluff to the water. The beach, merely a thin strip of sand at high tide, is mostly barnacle-encrusted rock and cobble when exposed at lower water. While the rocky beach makes for difficult clamming, the tidelands may reward explorers with close encounters with marine life such as starfish, tiny crabs, chitons, limpets, and an occasional oyster. Look, but don't disturb inedible forms; oysters are fair game for

gourmets if current regulations permit.

Two mooring buoys offshore are exposed to wind and tidal currents in the canal, which can sometimes cause a bumpy stay for boaters.

---

# OLD MAN HOUSE STATE PARK

---

**Hours/Season:** Day-use; standard hours; year-round

**Area:** 1 acre; 210 feet of saltwater shoreline on Port Madison

**Facilities:** 2 picnic sites, vault toilet, interpretive display

**Attractions:** Picnicking, clamming, historical display

**Access:** *From the ferry terminal in Kingston,* follow Highway 104 northwest for 2.5 miles, then turn south on Hansville Road NE, which becomes Miller Bay Road, and in 5.7 miles reach Suquamish. Continue south on Suquamish Way for 0.2 mile, then turn south on S Division Street, then southeast on NE McKinstry Street to its intersection with NE Angeline Avenue S at the park. *From the ferry terminal in Winslow,* follow Highway 305 northwest 6.8 miles; just past the Agate Passage bridge, turn north on Suquamish Way. Continue another 1.2 miles to S Division Street, and follow the above directions.

This sandy stretch of shoreline at the entrance to Agate Passage was once the site of one of the largest Northwest Indian longhouses ever built. Archeological digs indicate that the structure, which was occupied by multiple families from the Suquamish tribe, stretched from 500 to 900 feet long. Federal Indian agents burned the longhouse in the late 1800s, hoping that eradicating the native's custom of communal living would force them to adopt the white man's lifestyle.

This was believed to have been the birthplace of Chief Sealth, for whom the city of Seattle was named. His grave is just a few blocks away, in Memorial Cemetery in the town of Suquamish.

An informational display at the park tells the story of the longhouse. The display itself incorporates posts, beams, and a short section of cedar roofing typical of Indian construction techniques.

The small park consists of tree-studded grass terraces that flow down to a broad sandy beach, with views of Port Madison and into Agate Passage. Hand-carried boats can be launched here; the park is sometimes used as an entry point for scuba divers. Only experienced divers should attempt to explore the channel, due to the swift tidal currents.

## CHIEF SEATTLE'S GRAVE HERITAGE AREA

**Hours/Season:** Day-use; standard hours; year-round
**Facilities:** None
**Attractions:** Historic site
**Access:** From Highway 305, just west of the Agate Passage bridge, turn north on Suquamish Way, and in 1.2 miles reach the town of Suquamish. At the south side of town, head uphill for 1.5 blocks to Memorial Cemetery where the gravesite is located.

In one corner of this old cemetery is the grave site of the Duwamish and Suquamish Indian chief Sealth, for whom the city of Seattle is named. Four huge cedar posts topped with carved logs resembling Indian canoes surround the gravestone. These symbolize the traditional native method of burial, where the body was placed in a canoe secured high in a tree.

## ILLAHEE STATE PARK

**Hours/Season:** Overnight; standard hours; year-round
**Area:** 74.5 acres; 1,785 feet of saltwater shoreline on Port Orchard
**Facilities:** 25 standard campsites, 8 primitive campsites, 40-person primitive group camp, 88 picnic sites, fireplaces, 3 kitchen shelters, 50- and 75-person group day-use areas, restrooms, showers, trailer

dump station, horseshoe pits, ballfield, dock with floats, boat launch ramp, 5 mooring buoys, hiking trails
**Attractions:** Camping, picnicking, boating, paddling, beachcombing, clamming, crabbing, waterskiing, hiking, fishing, swimming, scuba diving, historical display
**Access:** *By land,* from the ferry terminal in Bremerton take Washington Street north to 6th (Highway 304). Go west three blocks and head north on Highway 303, cross the Warren Avenue bridge, and reach the park in 1.5 miles. *By boat,* the park is located on the east side of Kitsap Peninsula on the south end of Port Orchard Narrows.

Although it sits in the backyard of Bremerton, Illahee State Park packs enough recreational goodies into its limited acreage that it can absorb the crowd from the nearby city and still have room for visiting folks. A steep, 250-foot-high bluff divides the park into two distinct areas: a wooded upland with camping and picnicking, and the beach with water and shore activities. Near the park entrance, kids enjoy clambering on two historic naval guns taken from World War I ships. A steep road takes several hairpin turns down the bluff between the two areas; for the strong-of-foot, a companion trail switchbacks through cedar, fir, and maple to lead from the upland to the beach.

The tideland below the bluff becomes a wide, gently sloping sandy beach at low tide. A boat launch ramp dips down to the water at the north end of the beach parking, although the steep, zigzag road down the bluff doesn't encourage the hauling of large boat trailers. A dock with four floats, protected from northerly wind and waves by a concrete breakwater, is a popular fishing and sunbathing spot, as well as a park access point for boaters. Five mooring buoys offshore provide dock overflow capacity, and certainly a bit more solitude than the floats.

Port Orchard from here north through Agate Passage is a favorite hangout for scuba divers. An enormous amount of marine life lives on the dock pilings and rocky walls of the channel. Divers must exercise care, due to the heavy boat traffic.

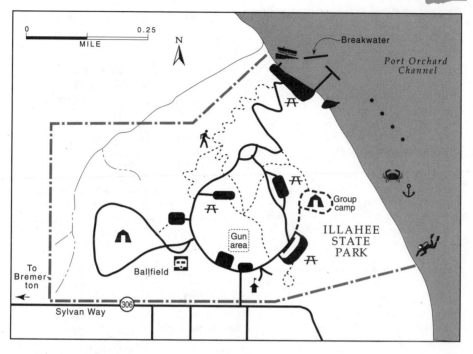

*A sailboat lolls on a mooring buoy at Illahee State Park.*

# FAY-BAINBRIDGE STATE PARK

**Hours/Season:** Overnight; standard hours; year-round

**Area:** 16.8 acres; 1,420 feet of saltwater shoreline on Puget Sound

**Facilities:** 26 standard campsites, 10 RV sites with water only, 80 picnic tables, 3 kitchen shelters, 50-person group day-use area, fireplaces, beach fire rings, restrooms, showers, boat launch ramp, 2 mooring buoys, children's play equipment, trailer dump station

**Attractions:** Camping, picnicking, boating, paddling, scuba diving, fishing, beachcombing, clamming, hiking, historical display

**Access:** *By land,* from the ferry terminal at Winslow, head northwest on Highway 304 for 4.2 miles, then turn east on Day Road, and in 1.2 miles north on Sunrise Drive. The park lies 1.4 miles to the north. *By boat,* the park is immediately south of Point Monroe at the northeast tip of Bainbridge Island. Nearest boat launch ramps are at Shilshole Bay in Seattle and Suquamish.

A swath of sandy beach, cooling salt-air breezes, and pleasant campground make Fay-Bainbridge State Park a hit with visitors. This is the only park on the island that has camping, so it is usually crowded in the summer. The park's hyphenated name commemorates both the original property owner, Dr. Temple S. Fay, and the park location, Bainbridge Island.

The large brass bell near the park entrance was purchased in San Francisco in 1883 by the citizens of the community of

*The windswept beach at Fay-Bainbridge State Park is just a walk-across-the-water from metropolitan Seattle.*

Port Madison, and was to be placed in the school belfry to ring out on important events. Plans went awry, however, and over time the bell was moved to a number of sites on the island, for various purposes. Eventually the much-traveled bell found its final home here at the state park.

The grassy, tree-shaded uplands of the park, reserved for picnicking and tent camping, are not usually as crowded as the more popular beach strip. At the beach, campsites cram one side of the beach road, elbow-to-elbow. Fire rings, horseshoe pits, volleyball posts, and a children's play area are scattered along the sandy beachfront. In summer a concession stand just outside the north park boundary supplies fast food and cool drinks for those who neglected to bring their own.

A surfaced launch ramp at the north end of the park provides access to the sound for trailered boats. Two mooring buoys offshore, unprotected from the wind and waves of the sound, offer a bouncy stay for visiting boaters. Paddlers who put in at the park can roam north around Point Monroe and into the shallow tideflat created by the long, hooking sandspit.

## FORT WARD
## STATE PARK

**Hours/Season:** Day-use; standard hours; year-round
**Area:** 137.1 acres; 4,300 feet of saltwater shoreline on Rich Passage
**Facilities:** 16 picnic tables, boat launch ramp, 2 mooring buoys, vault toilets, hiking trails, 2 bird blinds, underwater park
**Attractions:** Picnicking, beachcombing, hiking, clamming, crabbing, boating, fishing, scuba diving, birdwatching, bicycling, historic Coast Artillery battery emplacements
**Access:** From the ferry terminal at Winslow, turn west on Winslow Way, north on Erickson Avenue, then west on Wyatt Way, and follow it to the west end of Eagle Harbor. From here turn south on Bucklin Hill Road NE and bear right at a Y-intersection onto Blakely Avenue NE. Continue south and east for 2.2 miles, then turn south on Country Club Road,

and in 0.2 mile south on Fort Ward Hill Road NE to reach the upper park entrance in 0.8 mile. To reach the beach entrance to the park, leave Blakely Avenue NE 1.4 miles south of the Y-intersection on West Blakely Road NE, then head southeast on Pleasant Beach Drive NE, which dead-ends at the park.

▲ Fort Ward and Manchester, its companion site across Rich Passage, are vestiges of a coastal defense system from the early 1900s designed to protect the Bremerton Naval Shipyard in the advent of war. The fort's armament consisted of an 8-inch gun battery, a 5-inch gun battery, and two 3-inch gun batteries. The guns were all removed in the 1920s, and the post was transferred to the navy in 1930 for use as a radio school, radio intercept station, and recreation site. During World War II, the site controlled submarine nets that stretched

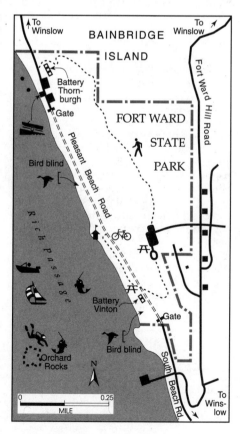

across Rich Passage. After being deactivated, a portion of the old fort was acquired for a state park. The only evidence of the park's military legacy are the mouldering remains of the two 3-inch batteries. Many of the old buildings from the fort are now on private property and are used as residences.

In the upland portion of the park, off Fort Ward Hill Road, wooded picnic sites surround a parking lot. Trails drop from here to the shore. The paved path at the south end of the parking area leads down to the road, emerging near Battery Vinton on the south side of the park. From the north end of the parking area, a dirt trail wends along the park boundary through a greenwood of ferns, ivy, maple, and firs, before descending a small ridge to reach the beach road near Battery Thornburgh, at the north end of the park. *Do not wander off the trail, as there is poison oak in the undergrowth.*

Although the beach road runs through the park, it is open only to foot traffic and bicycles; parking is available at the north beach entrance to the park. Picnic sites are found near the south and north ends of the beach. Elsewhere along the road, short tracks penetrate the dense cover of brush, nettles, and Scotch broom, leading to bird blinds overlooking the beach. Watch for ducks, geese, coots, cormorants, and other waterfowl.

A paved launch ramp is located at the north end of the park beach; offshore from it are two mooring buoys. Because the buoys are exposed to wind, tide, and the wakes of passing boats and ferries, they tend to be bouncy moorages. The area offshore is designated as an underwater park. Scuba divers explore the steep walls along Rich Passage and the undersea crannies of Orchard Rocks, just to the south. It is a long swim from shore to Orchard Rocks, so boat transportation is recommended. Dive with care, as boat traffic is heavy in the area and the current is strong.

---

# MANCHESTER
# STATE PARK

---

**Hours/Season:** Overnight; standard hours; weekends and holidays only, from the end of September to the end of March

**Area:** 111.2 acres; 3,400 feet of saltwater shoreline on Rich Passage

**Facilities:** 50 standard campsites, picnic tables, 2 picnic shelters, 150-person group day-use area, fireplaces, restrooms, showers, trailer dump station, nature trail, volleyball court, horseshoe pit, hiking trails, historic Coast Artillery mine control and gun battery structures

**Attractions:** Camping, picnicking, hiking, fishing, swimming, scuba diving, boating, historical displays

**Access:** *From the ferry terminal at Bremerton,* take Washington Street north to 6th (Highway 304). Follow Highway 304 west until it joins Highway 3 southwest of the city, then continue on Highway 3 to its junction with Highway 16. Follow Highway 16 and then Highway 160 to Port Orchard. Turn onto Bay Avenue, which becomes N Bay Street, then Beach Drive E. Turn north on E Hilldale Road 5.2 miles from Port Orchard, and reach the park in 0.3 mile. *From the ferry landing at Southworth,* head west on Highway 160, and in 3.7 miles turn north on SE Colchester Drive. In 1.7 miles, at the community of Manchester, continue north on Beach Drive E to reach E Hilldale in another 0.8 mile.

▲ Manchester, along with Fort Ward, was a 1900s Coast Artillery fortification intended to protect the entrance to Rich Passage and the Bremerton Naval Shipyard. Manchester was to serve as a control center for remotely firing "torpedos" (as underwater mines were called in those days) when observers spotted enemy ships in the vicinity. The torpedos were to be placed in the passage only in the event of imminent hostilities; such a threat never occurred, and eventually the defense system became obsolete and was abandoned.

Today the park's most unique attraction is a large brick structure just above the beach that once served as a warehouse for storing the torpedos until they were deployed, but now it has been converted to an enormous picnic shelter that can be reserved for group use. A smaller, gutted concrete building nearby served as the "mining casemate," or fire control center, where cables leading to the underwater torpedos were connected to electrical firing triggers. On

*A park visitor inspects the torpedo warehouse at Manchester State Park.*

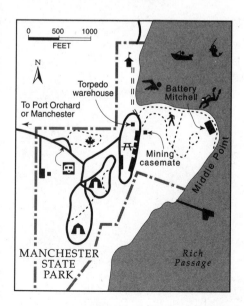

the northmost point of the park is Battery Mitchell, a large concrete gun emplacement, built to mount two 3-inch guns that were to prevent small boats from disarming the minefield. The guns were never installed.

The park sits on a small, shallow cove, which warms enough for wading in summer months. Scuba divers put in here to explore underwater rocks off the point. The wide lawn between the torpedo warehouse and the beach hosts several sunny picnic spots.

Trails lead along the beach to the gun battery site and circle the hillside above. Walk quietly, and perhaps spot deer, fox, and squirrels that make the park home. Stay on the trails, however, to *avoid the park's poison oak and stinging nettles*. A short nature trail that loops through the woods opposite the park entry-station describes local trees and plants.

233

Two campground loops are located upland, near the park entrance. Heavy undergrowth and timber provide reasonable seclusion to the sites that rim the loops.

high tide; at lower tide levels, the mudflat below might offer up a few clams. Boats launched here have ready access to Blake Island, lying just a mile to the northeast.

## HARPER STATE PARK

**Hours/Season:** Day-use; standard hours; year-round
**Area:** 3 acres; 777 feet of saltwater shoreline on Puget Sound
**Facilities:** Boat launch ramp
**Attractions:** Boating, fishing
**Access:** From the ferry landing at Southworth, head west on Highway 160. Reach the park in 1.2 miles, at the intersection of Highway 160 and Olympiad Road.

This park consists of a short stretch of beach and an unimproved gravel boat launch ramp. The ramp is only usable at

## BLAKE ISLAND STATE PARK

**Hours/Season:** Overnight; standard hours; year-round
**Area:** 475.5 acres; 17,307 feet of saltwater shoreline on Puget Sound
**Facilities:** 54 campsites, adirondack shelter, 75-person group camp, 54 picnic sites, 3 picnic shelters, 50-person group day-use area, restrooms, showers, pit toilets, 2 porta-potty dump stations, marine pump-out station, moorage with 12 floats, 21 mooring buoys, underwater reef, 2 volleyball courts, nature trail, 12 miles of hiking trail, (concession) restaurant with Northwest Indian dances

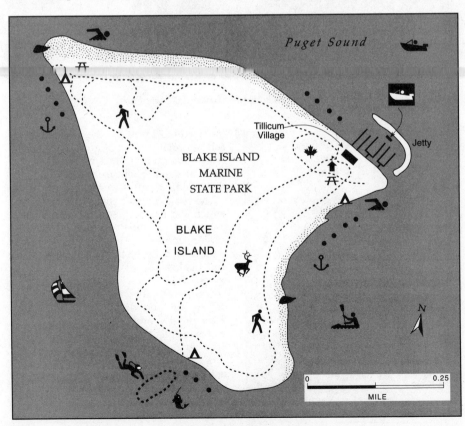

*Blake Island's boat basin is usually jam-packed on summer weekends.*

**Attractions:** Camping, picnicking, boating, paddling, fishing, beachcombing, clamming, birdwatching, hiking, scuba diving, swimming, Indian dances

**Access:** *Boat access only.* Blake Island lies off the east side of the Kitsap Peninsula, south of Bainbridge Island. For private boats, nearest launch facilities are Don Armeni launch ramp in Seattle, or at Manchester or Des Moines. It can be reached from the Seattle waterfront via a Tillicum Tours boat ( *fee*).

▲ This boat-in state park is not restricted to those people fortunate enough to have a boat of their own—transportation to the island is also available via a regularly scheduled commercial tour boat from the Seattle waterfront. The tour boat ride normally

includes a traditional Northwest Indian salmon dinner and authentic native dances in a longhouse. Contact the management of Tillicum Tours regarding cost and availability of space if wanting only the ride and not planning to partake of the dinner, or if wanting to stay on the island and catch a later boat.

Blake Island is by far the most popular of all of the state's marine parks. It is but an hour or so from Puget Sound's most populous cities, it has a well-protected moorage, and the island has a wide spectrum of recreational activities. At night the island offers spectacular views of the brilliantly lit skyline of Seattle and nearby communities, glow-worm ferries, and overhead beads of light from the airport's jet traffic. The distant city lights fail to dull the expanses of stars sparkling brightly in the evening sky.

During the early 1900s, the entire island was the private estate of William Pitt Trimble, a Seattle lawyer. The foundations of the home, some now-wild plants from the extensive garden, and a few other meager remnants of the estate can still be seen.

The pier and floats in the moorage basin on the island's northeast tip is the heart of activity. The pier and the first float inside the rock jetty are reserved for tour boats and park management, and one side of the next float is saved for loading and unloading only. Summer weekends find the floats jam-packed; boaters should respect the demand for float space, and take up only the minimum they need. Space is on a first-come, first-served basis.

Above the basin are the Indian longhouse and a broad lawn with picnic shelters, fire rings, and ample room for ball games and Frisbee tossing. A group of designated tent-camping spots, separated mostly by Scotch broom, line a road to the east. The beach below these sites is shallow and sandy—one of the best on the island for clamming, wading, sunbathing, or perhaps even building a sand castle.

For boaters wishing to avoid the crowd in the moorage basin, mooring buoys are set outside the jetty on both sides of the point, off the northwest tip of the island and along the middle of the south shoreline. These last two locations also have tenting sites on shore. Anchoring is a viable alternative at any of these locations.

Hiking trails on the island are mostly old service roads that are wide and reasonably flat. The least strenuous is a short nature trail just behind the longhouse; signs along this trail point out traces of early logging activities, identify various plants, and tell how local Indians used those plants.

The longest trail traces the perimeter of the island on the bluffs above the beach, dropping down to the beach at the campgrounds on the sandy northwest tip and the south shore. At lower tide levels, visitors can walk the rocky beach. Other trail segments wander through the timbered core of the island. On any of the trails expect encounters with deer, chipmunks, and squirrels. Due to overpopulation, the deer are quite small and tend to mooch from humans; don't feed them—it only makes them more dependent on humans for survival.

A buoy-marked artificial reef lying off the south side of the island provides excellent fishing from boats for lingcod and rockfish. Experienced scuba divers familiar with diving in strong tidal currents can explore the reef. Check current local regulations regarding spearfishing before taking any fish in this manner.

# SALTWATER STATE PARK

**Hours/Season:** Overnight; standard hours; year-round

**Area:** 87.4 acres; 1,445 feet of saltwater shoreline on East Passage

**Facilities:** 50 standard campsites, 2 primitive sites, 40-person group camp, 128 picnic tables, 3 picnic shelters, kitchen shelter, 4 day-use group areas (30-person, 50-person, 100-person), children's play equipment, restrooms, outside scuba rinse shower, vault toilets, trailer dump station, 3 mooring buoys, artificial reef, concession stand

**Attractions:** Camping, picnicking, scuba diving, swimming, fishing, beachcombing, hiking, boating, paddling

**Access:** *By land*, take Exit 149 (Highway 516, Kent–Des Moines) west from I-5. At the first traffic light, turn south on Pacific Highway S, and in 0.8 mile, turn west on S 240th Street. After 1.2 miles turn south on Marine View Drive (Highway 509), and in 0.8 mile, where Marine View Drive turns southeast, continue straight ahead on 8th Place S to reach the park in two blocks. *By boat*, the park lies 2 miles south of the Des Moines Marina, the nearest launch site.

McSorley's Gulch may not be immediately recognized by its name, but most Puget Sound park-goers are quite familiar with the state park that surrounds this deep, forested ravine. Over three-quarters of a million people visit Saltwater every year, making it the most-used state park on Puget Sound. On sunny summer weekends, cars queue at the entrance, one allowed to enter only when another departs. Most of the park activity centers on the beach, so hikers

*Scuba divers prepare to explore the sunken barge that forms an underwater reef at Saltwater State Park.*

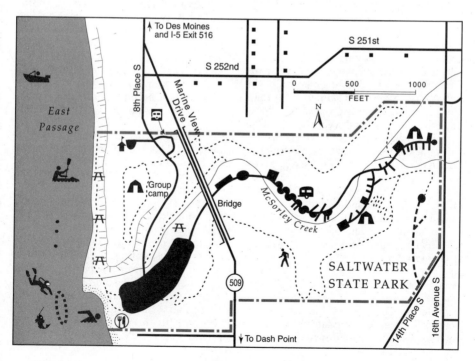

who seek out remote, shaded trails are usually still able to find some degree of solitude, even on busy weekends. On brisk winter days, visitors may find they are sharing the entire park with only a few other stalwart souls.

McSorley Creek trickles down the gulch to the shore. A road wends up the narrow gully past trailer camping spots to branch into two sets of tent camping sites, many fronting on the creek. The steep, wooded hillsides mask the noise of traffic on the bridge 200 feet above, giving the campground an unexpected degree of seclusion. A group camp sits high on the bluff at the northwest end of the park.

Just east of the park's concession stand, a 2-mile loop trail climbs a wooded ridge to the rim of the gulch. Bigleaf maple, Douglas fir, hemlock, and cedar form a green canopy, and bright spatterings of wildflowers paint the trailside. The path continues high on the hill around the perimeter of the park, cuts through the tent camping area, then finally returns to the lower picnic meadow. A midway spur trail also connects to the tent camping area.

Picnic tables are scattered to the north along the grassy beach strip backed by a steep clay bluff. More picnic areas, including group shelters, are available in a meadow above the beach along the edge of McSorley Creek. Alcoholic beverages are prohibited in the day-use areas.

In 1992 a project began that will clean up the creek and surrounding vegetation in order to restore runs of salmon, cutthroat, and steelhead. Such a program has been underway for several years in the Des Moines Creek watershed to the north.

The rock riprap bulkhead protecting the northern segment of the beach gives way at McSorley Creek to a tapering, sand-bottomed swimming beach, one of the best on all of Puget Sound. Little marine life remains on the heavily used beach; however, a sunken barge and old tires placed 50 feet offshore near the south edge of the park form an underwater reef that harbors marine life such as plumose anemone, nudibranchs, starfish, a plethora of fish, and even an occasional octopus. The site is a favorite for scuba divers. Mooring buoys north of the reef accommodate visiting boaters. Kayaks put in here can range north to

Des Moines, south to Redondo and Dash Point, or shoot straight across East Passage to Maury Island, 5 miles away.

# DASH POINT STATE PARK

**Hours/Season:** Overnight; standard hours; year-round

**Area:** 397.6 acres; 3,301 feet of saltwater shoreline on East Passage

**Facilities:** 110 standard campsites, 28 RV sites with hookups, 80-person group camp, 71 picnic sites, picnic shelters, restrooms, outside rinse shower, trailer dump station, 7.4 miles of hiking trail

**Attractions:** Camping, picnicking, beachcombing, fishing, swimming, scuba diving, marine life study, hiking, boating, paddling

**Access:** *From I-5 headed south,* take Exit 143 (Federal Way, S 320th Street) and turn west on SW 320th Street. In 3.2 miles turn north on 47th Avenue SW. After three blocks head west on SW Dash Point Road (Highway 509) and follow it to the park entrance in 0.75 mile. *From I-5 headed north,* take Exit 137 (Fife, Milton) and head north on 54th Avenue E (Valley Avenue), which becomes Taylor Way in 3.2 miles. Continue on Taylor Way to its intersection with 11th Street in 2.3 miles, then turn northeast on 11th Street. In 0.5 mile turn northwest on Marine View Drive (Highway 509), which becomes East Side Drive. Follow this road for 4 miles to the park.

The beach at Dash Point was a favorite with local beachcombers and fishermen long before 1958, when it and the first sections of forested upland were acquired for a state park. Key to the park's popularity is the gradual slope of the sandy beach, which at a minus tide bares out more than 2,000 feet, exposing some intertidal life for easy exploration. Check out a piece of seaweed for tiny mollusks and insects clinging to it. Gathering clams from the beach is unsafe due to pollution. The summer sun warms the shallow water, making it inviting for wading and swimming.

The park divides naturally into three distinct areas: the beach, a grassy, tree-shaded

flat atop the bluff, and the forested campground south of the highway. Picnic sites are near the beach and scattered about the flat on top of the bluff. A group camp is separated from the upper picnic area by a slight ravine. Campsites for individuals are located in the south section of the park, around heavily wooded loop roads. One long loop is equipped with trailer hookups; a second is divided into quadrants of tenting sites.

A network of trails links all of the picnic areas and campsites to the beach. South of the campground, more than 6 miles of additional hiking trails meander through the dense forest of maple, fir, and alder, leading nowhere special, but providing some intimate glimpses of squirrels, birds, deer, and other woodland critters.

## WEST HYLEBOS WETLANDS STATE PARK

**Hours/Season:** Day-use; standard hours; year-round
**Area:** 58.4 acres
**Facilities:** 1-mile self-guided nature walk

**Attractions:** Hiking, birdwatching, nature observing
**Access:** From I-5, take Exit 142B (Highway 161S, Puyallup) 1.6 miles south of Federal Way, and head west on S 348th Street to Pacific Highway S, 0.6 mile. Continue west on S 348th for 0.5 mile, and watch for 4th Avenue S, an obscure single-lane road to the south. Turn left onto 4th, and in 2 blocks turn east at a sign into a small parking lot.

This small, natural enclave on the southern outskirts of Federal Way contains one of the most thorough and enjoyable courses in botany, biology, and ecology to be found in the state. West Hylebos Wetlands State Park was acquired in small parcels from local residents with the aid of community groups. The creation of the park and the 1-mile nature trail that it holds has been the ongoing project of Francis and Ilene Marckx, whose home adjoins the state park.

The nature trail leaves the parking lot and loops through a forest and bog at the headwaters of Hylebos Creek, most of it on a wood plank pathway. Numerous small green signs along the route identify the

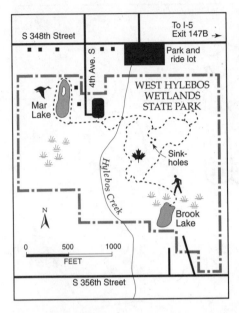

profusion of trees, shrubs, herbaceous plants, ferns, and mosses. In another section on the west side of the park are not only native flora, but "living fossils"—trees such as coast redwood, ginkgo, and giant sequoia that have recently been planted here as examples of the forests that covered the region some 30 million years ago.

Large signs provide explanations of geological features: a pair of sink holes, a foot or so in diameter at the surface, but over 20 feet deep (their source being either underground springs or the vestige of an ancient lake bed); glacial erratics; drumlins; and the sticky black sediments carried by the ice sheet that covered the area more than 12,000 years ago. Other trail signs relate to biology, telling of such things as the butterflies that visit the region, Douglas squirrels' stripping of cedar bark for nesting materials, and the life cycle of bark beetles and their interaction with the trees.

*The boardwalk detours around a tree at West Hylebos Wetlands.*

Also described is the ecological impact of development in the Federal Way area. After heavy rains, water that can no longer be absorbed by the concrete and asphalt that come with population growth rushes through in ever-deepening streams, causing periodic, massive flooding.

A series of twenty-four numbered posts along the trail are keyed to descriptions in Stephen Whitney's book *Nature Walks In and Around Seattle*. Copies of this section of the book may be available for loan at the start of the walk.

## KOPACHUCK STATE PARK

**Hours/Season:** Overnight; standard hours; year-round

**Area:** 103 acres; 3,500 feet of saltwater shoreline on Carr Inlet

**Facilities:** 41 standard campsites, 15- and 35-person group camps, 79 picnic sites, 4 kitchen shelters, 3 restrooms, trailer dump station, 2 mooring buoys, underwater marine park, 1 mile of trail

**Attractions:** Camping, picnicking, clamming, waterskiing, fishing, scuba diving, beachcombing, birdwatching, swimming, boating, paddling

**Access:** *By land,* from Highway 16, 3.3 miles north of the Tacoma Narrows Bridge, take the exit marked Gig Harbor City Center, Kopachuck State Park. Head southwest on Wollochet Drive NW, and in 0.5 mile bear west on Hunt Street NW, then in 1 block turn north on 46th Avenue NW. Continue north for 1 mile, and turn west on Rosedale Street NW. In 2.5 miles turn south on Ray Nash Drive NW, and in 0.7 mile continue straight ahead on Kopachuck Drive NW, to reach the park in another 1.7 miles. *By boat,* the park is located on the east shore of Carr Inlet, 2 miles north of Fox Island and just north of Horsehead Bay. The nearest launch ramp is at Horsehead Bay.

Kopachuck State Park derives its name from two words in the Chinook trade jargon of the Northwest Indians, "kopa" meaning "at," and "chuck" meaning "water." This was certainly an apt description, as the Puyallup and Nisqually tribes used the shoreside site for seasonal fishing and clamming.

The park has a blunt nose-shaped beach that curves outward into Carr Inlet. The south end is covered with cobbles and driftwood, while the north end, nearest the heart of the park, is gently sloping sand. This shallow sandy beach bares well out into the inlet at low tide, exposing an extensive foreshore for clamming and beachcombing. Shallow water also means warmer water, and in summer this is a favorite spot for saltwater swimming.

An old barge that was sunk offshore to create a reeflike shelter for fish and marine invertebrates is designated an underwater marine park. Scuba divers regularly explore this relatively easy dive site. Two mooring buoys bob offshore for visiting boaters' use.

Picnic sites are sprinkled along the wooded hillside above the beach, as well as just above the shoreline. Trails to the beach lead down through the picnic area from either end of the parking lot. Campsites lie in the upper wooded flat near the park entrance. Although heavy forest growth blocks all views of the water and the Olympic Mountains, the greenery provides some campsite privacy. Short, easy trails from the campground loop wend through salal, false Solomon's seal, and sword fern to the picnic area and beach.

## CUTTS ISLAND MARINE STATE PARK

**Hours/Season:** Day-use; year-round

**Area:** 5.5 acres, 2,100 feet of saltwater shoreline on Carr Inlet

**Facilities:** 10 mooring buoys, pit toilet, underwater marine park, *no water*

**Attractions:** Beachcombing, clamming, fishing, swimming, scuba diving, boating, paddling

**Access:** *Boat access only.* Cutts Island lies 0.2 mile west of Kopachuck State Park and is a subsidiary of that park. Nearest launch ramps are at Horsehead Bay and Wauna; hand-carried boats can be launched from the beach at Kopachuck.

Cutts Island is a secluded "boaters-only" outpost of Kopachuck State Park. At low tide a sandbar nearly links it to nearby Raft Island. It is an easy paddle from the park, but use care in a heavily loaded boat or if the wind or tide are strong.

The island has a checkered history of names. In 1792 it was named Crow Island by Peter Puget of the Vancouver Expedition. The Wilkes Expedition of 1841 dubbed it Scotts Island after the expedition's quartermaster. Early settlers called it Deadman's Island, reflecting the native tribes' use of the island to inter their dead in canoes

*Cutts Island is only a short paddle away from Kopachuck State Park.*

placed in trees. The source of its current name is a mystery.

At high tide the island has virtually no beach, and the barren clay cliffs at its north end rise 40 feet from the water's edge to a tuft of trees above, giving the island a unique "Mohawk haircut" appearance. Lower tide levels expose a cobble and boulder beach to the south and portions of the sandy bar to the north. Clams can be found here, but digging is pretty strenuous in the cobble areas. Ten mooring buoys are located around the island, and the only onshore amenity is a pit toilet. No campsites are available, and fires are prohibited on the island.

# PENROSE POINT
# STATE PARK

**Hours/Season:** Overnight; standard hours; weekends and holidays only, from the end of September to mid-April
**Area:** 152.1 acres; 11,751 feet of saltwater shoreline on Carr Inlet
**Facilities:** 83 standard campsites, 50-person group camp with shelter, 90 picnic sites, 2 kitchen shelters, restrooms, RV dump station, floats, 8 mooring buoys, 2.5 miles of hiking trail, nature trail
**Attractions:** Camping, picnicking, fishing, clamming, swimming, beachcombing, boating, paddling, hiking
**Access:** *By land,* from Highway 16, 2.5 miles north of Gig Harbor, take the Highway 302 exit, marked to Purdy and Key Peninsula. Follow the Key Peninsula Highway south for 17.5 miles (3.5 miles south of Home), then turn east on Cornwall Road. In 0.3 mile, at Lakebay, turn south on Delano Road, and in 1 mile, at its junction with 158th Avenue, turn north to reach the park in 0.2 mile. *By boat,* the park is located on the west shore of Carr Inlet at Mayo Cove, 2 miles north of McNeil Island. The nearest launch ramps are at Mayo Cove and Von Geldern Cove.

Whether you arrive by land or water, this beautiful park on the south shore of tiny Mayo Cove will appeal to you. Penrose Point State Park provides a nice balance of wheel vs. rudder facilities, and its long, slender peninsular end gives it far more shoreline than land-based parks usually enjoy.

Camping is located along a maze of timbered circles at the west side of the park above the dock area. The park entrance road T's above the beach; the west arm goes to parking above the dock; the east arm leads to the group camp and day-use areas. A large, open lawn with picnic tables along the perimeter was once a swamp that was

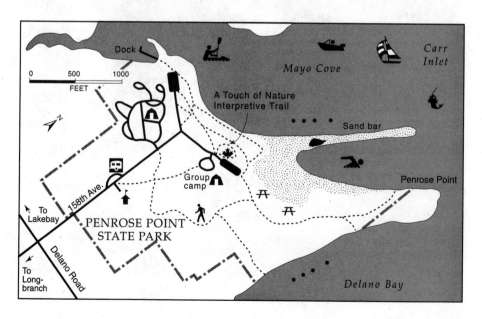

243

*Huge old cedar, fir, and maple trees shade the campsites at Penrose Point.*

filled and groomed to its present meadowy state through the group effort of surrounding communities.

Several short trails lace the timbered strip above the Mayo Cove beach. A 0.25-mile-long nature loop that leaves the day-use parking lot introduces walkers to bigleaf maple, evergreen huckleberry, sword fern, western hemlock, Douglas fir, madrona, Pacific yew, western red cedar, and red alder, as well as a variety of birds, insects, and other small forest critters. A longer trail, with several indistinct side spurs, heads through the woods to the beach on the east side of the point; still another heads uphill from the day-use area, eventually splitting into forks to the park maintenance buildings, the campground, and the group camp.

At the west end of the park, near the head of the cove, a flat finger of land protects a small basin with a dock and a 90-foot float. Boaters need to enter the cove cautiously at low tide, as the entrance becomes choked between this protecting finger and a sandspit protruding from the north.

Mooring buoys are also provided off the north and east sides of Penrose Point. Those to the north seem far offshore, but the reason becomes readily apparent at low tide, when a long cobble spit emerges from the water to form a shallow, horseshoe-shaped cove below the day-use area. The drying spit offers hardscrabble clamming at low tide.

# EAGLE ISLAND
# MARINE STATE PARK

Hours/Season: Day-use; year-round
Area: 10 acres; 2,600 feet of saltwater shoreline on Balch Passage
Facilities: 3 mooring buoys, *no water, no toilets*
Attractions: Fishing, clamming, beachcombing, boating
Access: *Boat access only.* Eagle Island lies in Balch Passage between Anderson and McNeil islands. Nearest launch ramps are at Steilacoom and Drayton Passage.

▲ This miniscule island was named not for the bird, but for Harry Eagle, one of the party members of the Wilkes Expedition.

No one notes whether Harry was as small in stature as his namesake island.

The park has no shoreside facilities. Sporadic tags of toilet tissue attest, unfortunately, to the lack of formal sanitary facilities (and the boorishness of some visitors). Inland, the island has a primitive trail through thick brush and madrona; short spurs lead to the beach. *Be wary of poison oak,* which abounds. The narrow beach is mostly gravel, with the exception of a pleasant point of sand on the south end of the island near Anderson Island—a nice spot for sunbathing or clamming.

Three mooring buoys are set off the south side of the island in 15 feet of water. Take care to avoid a submerged reef off the west side of the island that is marked by a navigation buoy at its north end.

# HALEY PROPERTY
# (UNDEVELOPED)

Area: 177.9 acres; 2,900 feet of freshwater shoreline on a lake; 1,980 feet of saltwater shoreline on Case Inlet
Facilities: None
Access: *By land,* take Highway 302 southwest from Purdy to Key Center, and continue south from Key Center on the Key Peninsula Highway for 3.5 miles to Jackson Lake Road. Head southwest on Jackson Lake Road for 0.5 mile, then turn west and follow a gravel road for 1.1 miles to a Y-intersection. Here turn sharply to the northwest and reach the park property in 0.2 mile. *By boat,* the property is on Case Inlet north of Herron Island and due east of Dougall Point on Hartstene Island. Nearest launch ramps are at Vaughn Bay, Grapeview, or Robert F. Kennedy Recreation Area.

▲ This property, acquired from the Haley of Brown and Haley candy fame, is scheduled for development by the State Parks Commission in the near future. Initial development plans anticipate road access, a day-use parking area, and a trail to the beach area. The property includes steep, forested hillsides inland that surround a small manmade lake created by damming a creek that runs through the north side of the property. A flat, bare strip of land separates the lake from the shore of Case Inlet. At low tide clams can be harvested on a wide, gently sloping gravel beach that fronts the property on Case Inlet.

## STRETCH POINT STATE PARK

**Hours/Season:** Day-use; year-round
**Area:** 4.2 acres; 610 feet of saltwater shoreline on Case Inlet
**Facilities:** 5 mooring buoys, *no water, no toilets*
**Attractions:** Picnicking, boating, beachcombing, fishing, clamming
**Access:** *Boat access only.* On the northeast point of Stretch Island on the west side of Case Inlet. Nearest launch ramps are at Fair Harbor and Vaughn.

⚓ Although Stretch Island itself is accessible by a bridge from the mainland, private property blocks any upland approach to the state park located at its northeast tip. For those who can reach the park via water, mooring buoys have been placed along the perimeter; the beach drops off so steeply that they seem only a step away from shore.

The beach is gloriously smooth sand, with possibilities for clams at low tide. There is no garbage pickup, so please be considerate of the visitors following you—keep it clean and pack out garbage.

## JARRELL COVE MARINE STATE PARK

**Hours/Season:** Overnight; standard hours; year-round
**Area:** 42.6 acres; 3,506 feet of saltwater shoreline on Pickering Passage
**Facilities:** 20 standard campsites, 17 picnic sites, 2 picnic shelters, restrooms, 2 docks with floats, 14 mooring buoys, marine pumpout station
**Attractions:** Camping, picnicking, fishing, clamming, boating, paddling, hiking, birdwatching
**Access:** *By land,* from Highway 3, 7 miles north of Shelton, take Pickering Road southeast to Hartstene Island. After crossing the bridge onto the island, turn north

on North Island Drive, and in 3.5 miles, at Wingert Road, bear north on a dirt road to reach the park in another 0.8 mile. *By boat,* the park is at Jarrell Cove on the north side of Hartstene Island, 2 miles southwest of Dougall Point. Nearest launch ramps are at the Hartstene Island bridge, Fair Harbor, and Robert F. Kennedy Recreation Area.

⚓ Although accessible by land, Jarrell Cove is considered by the state to be a marine park. Because of the remoteness of the island by road, boaters are the predominant visitors. The park's natural attractions are best accessed from the water, and most of its facilities are boater-oriented.

The passage into this narrow inlet is squeezed between a private marina on the west and a park dock and float on the east. Exercise caution if using this as it rests on the mud at extreme minus tides. The remainder of the cove is filled with park mooring buoys; all have at least 10 feet of water below at lowest tide levels. Another longer dock with a float is placed at the southwest tip of the park, filling most of the entrance to a smaller branch cove.

This side cove to the east is a must for exploration by dinghy, kayak, or canoe. At high tide trees, brush, and vines press right

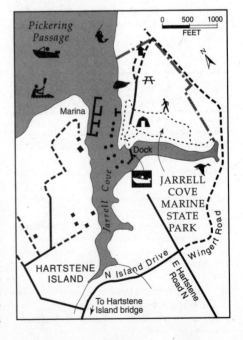

*Boaters leave the docks at Jarrell Cove. The commercial marina on the opposite side of the cove is in the distance.*

to water's edge along many tiny fingers and coves, giving the place an Everglades feeling. Best retreat with the water as the tide goes out, for this enchanting little passage soon transforms to a gooey mudflat. Look sharp while in this waterway for residents of a heron rookery in the vicinity.

Short trails from the camp area push through the brush on the bank above the finger cove. Water access from them is limited, and the beach is steep, slick, and muddy at low tide.

Campsites are laid out along a short trail just above the entrance dock for boaters choosing to sleep ashore. The main camping area in the center of the park is a large, open meadow with few well-defined campsites; just pick a convenient chunk of grass and that becomes your turf.

## HARTSTENE ISLAND
## STATE PARK

**Hours/Season:** Day-use; standard hours; year-round
**Area:** 310 acres; 3,100 feet of saltwater shore-

line on Case Inlet
**Facilities:** Hiking trail
**Attractions:** Hiking, clamming, beach-combing
**Access:** From the Hartstene Island bridge, drive north on North Island Drive for 3.2 miles to the intersection with East Hartstene Island Road North. Here turn south, and in 1 mile turn east on East Yates Road. Follow this single-lane gravel road for 1 mile, and at a Y-intersection turn right to reach the trailhead parking in 0.3 mile.

The Department of Natural Resources transferred this land to the state parks system in 1990. With the exception of a small section of old-growth Douglas fir on the southeast corner of the property, most of the uplands were recently clearcut; however, alder and second-growth fir are starting to erase signs of the logging.

From the parking area a graveled trail leads across a flat for 0.25 mile to the head of a canyonlike drainage. Here the trail drops steeply down the 100-foot-high forested bank, with steeper sections aided by log stairsteps. A few rustic benches are

247

provided along the way for rest stops on the uphill drag.

The trail breaks out onto the gravel beach on the east side of Hartstene Island between McMicken Island and the point north of it. The gently sloping beach has clams that may be harvested at low tide. An additional 3,100 feet of DNR tidelands run south from the state park boundary; at minus tides these muddy tideflats can be walked to a drying sandbar off the east side of McMicken Island for land access to that marine state park.

## McMicken Island Marine State Park

**Hours/Season:** Day-use; year-round
**Area:** 11.5 acres; 1,661 feet of saltwater shoreline on Case Inlet
**Facilities:** 5 mooring buoys, *no water*
**Attractions:** Picnicking, fishing, boating, paddling, clamming, beachcombing, hiking, swimming
**Access:** *By land,* at low tide walk the beach south 1 mile from Hartstene Island State Park and cross on a sandbar. *By boat,* McMicken Island is on Case Inlet off the east side of Hartstene Island. Nearest launch ramps are at Robert F. Kennedy Recreation Area, Fair Harbor, and Johnson Point.

This small island is an excellent place to get off the boat and stretch your legs with a short hike around its perimeter. Unimproved trails lead through brush and second-growth forest (*and also poison oak— be careful!*). On the south end of the island, a fenced-in area with a cabin and sheds is private property, on a lifetime lease to the person who sold the island to the state.

The beaches along the north, east, and south sides of the island are cobble with boulders below vertical rocky banks. To the west a sandspit emerges at low tide to link McMicken to Hartstene Island. McMicken can be reached by land at extreme minus tides by walking the public tidelands from the beach-access trail at Hartstene Island State Park. When exposed, the sandy beach affords good clamming, and the shallow waters are warm enough for wading or swimming.

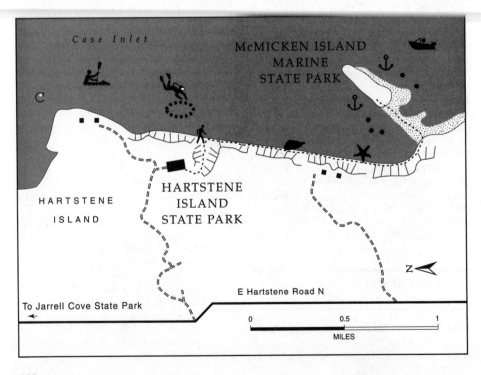

*Driftwood decorates the beach at McMicken Island State Park.*

Mooring buoys lie on both the north and south sides of the island; nearby is ample additional room to anchor in good-holding ground. Boaters should remember the drying spit and avoid passing west of the island, even at high tide.

## HOPE ISLAND MARINE STATE PARK (UNDEVELOPED)

**Hours/Season:** Day-use; year-round
**Area:** 109 acres; 8,450 feet of saltwater shoreline on Squaxin Passage
**Facilities:** None
**Attractions:** Picnicking, hiking, beachcombing
**Access:** *Boat access only.* Hope Island lies at the confluence of Totten Inlet, Hammers-

ley Inlet, and Pickering Passage. Nearest launch ramps are at Arcadia and Boston Harbor.

⚓ This last remaining undeveloped island in south Puget Sound was purchased by the State Parks and Recreation Commission in August of 1990. The heavily forested island, which had been owned by a Tacoma family for 80 years, was first sold by their estate to a developer, who planned to divide it into housing lots. Just in time the state managed to acquire funding and bought the entire island for a little over $3 million.

Plans are still under review by the Parks Commission, but they envision restricting the park to low-intensity use. Use of the island is not encouraged at this time. Those who do go ashore should take all trash with them when they leave; fires are not permitted.

# SAINT EDWARD STATE PARK

**Hours/Season:** Day-use; standard hours; year-round

**Area:** 316 acres; 3,000 feet of freshwater shoreline on Lake Washington

**Facilities:** 25 picnic sites, 25-, 50-, 75-, and 100-person day-use group areas, over 7 miles of hiking trail, 1 mile of equestrian trail, athletic field, indoor swimming pool, tennis courts, handball courts, gymnasium

**Attractions:** Picnicking, hiking, soccer, fishing, tennis, handball, swimming, racquetball, softball, birdwatching, orienteering, horseback riding

**Access:** *From the north,* 2 miles west of Bothell, take 68th Avenue NE south from Bothell Way NE (Highway 522). Sixty-eighth becomes Juanita Drive NE, and the park entrance is 1.5 miles south of Bothell Way. *From the south,* take Market Street (which becomes 98th Avenue NE), north out of Kirkland to its junction with NE Juanita Drive. Head west on NE Juanita Drive, which becomes Juanita Drive NE as it turns north. The park entrance is reached 3.5 miles from the 98th Avenue intersection.

These quiet wooded grounds on a bluff above the northeast shore of Lake Washington were operated by the Seattle Archdiocese as a Catholic seminary from 1931 to 1977. When it was sold to the state for recreational use, instead of the usual primitive land of many new parks, the state received fully developed property that included an athletic field, tennis and handball courts, indoor swimming pool, gymnasium, and fully appointed seminary building. Today the seminary building is used for park administrative offices, but the remainder of the grounds and the pool are open for public use.

The entrance road from Juanita Drive NE is not conspicuously marked; the only signs here are for the Saint Thomas Center, which was retained by the diocese, and some substance abuse recovery centers that lease space at Saint Thomas. The park is only identified farther down the entry road. A lighted footpath near the entrance road leads from Juanita Drive to the pool area. The athletic facilities, picnic sites, pool, and seminary complex are all located amid

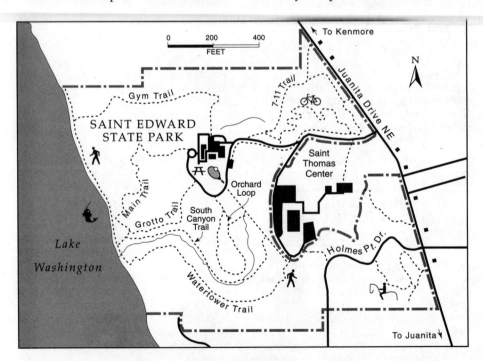

close-clipped lawns on a flat bluff. Below it a forested 275-foot-high hillside drops steeply down to the lake.

Several trails lead down the hillside, all eventually joining at a small grassy terrace above a boulder bulkhead and a sandy pocket beach. Cool your feet by wading; swimming is not advised, as the shoreline drops away steeply about 30 feet out.

The northernmost trail, 0.6 mile in length, is appropriately named Gym Trail. It starts at the gymnasium parking lot and heads north through alder, cedar, and occasional Douglas fir to the rim of a deep ravine along the north side of the park. The trail drops quickly down the south side of the ravine through ground cover of maidenhair and sword fern and a profusion of devil's club. On reaching the low bank of the lake, the trail runs north along the shore a short distance to the park boundary, and south to the small beach mentioned above. There is precious little lake access, however, as the trees run right down to the water's edge.

Main Trail (0.6 mile) leaves the west side of the seminary building as a service road, weaving gently down a broad ridge to the lakeshore. A much steeper Grotto Trail (0.3 mile) begins at the southwest corner of the grounds and drops precipitously down the side of another ravine to join the Main Trail near the water.

A deep ravine hooks uphill south of the seminary. South Canyon Trail (0.6 mile) follows the floor of the ravine, while Watertower Trail (1.1 miles) climbs steeply up the backbone of the ridge to the south of the ravine before swinging back to the southeast side of the seminary complex. For a gentler walk, take the Orchard Loop Trail (0.6 mile) as it wanders around a small knoll south of the seminary.

The 7-11 Trail leaves the playfield and runs to the northeast corner of the park to emerge across Juanita Drive from a small grocery store. One can almost visualize it being pounded out by furtive seminarians sneaking out in the evening for forbidden snacks. A 3-mile-long multipurpose trail designed to accommodate mountain bikes is also on this wooded flat at the northeast corner of the park.

Horseback riding is permitted in the southeast corner of the park, south of Holmes Point Drive.

# BRIDLE TRAILS
# STATE PARK

**Hours/Season:** Day-use; standard hours; year-round

**Area:** 481.5 acres

**Facilities:** 30 picnic tables, stoves, water, restroom, horse show arena with grandstand and 2 warm-up rings, snack stand (concession operated during shows), small schooling ring, 28 miles of trail

**Attractions:** Horseback riding, horse shows, picnicking, jogging, walking, birdwatching, orienteering

**Access:** The park, which is immediately west of Highway 405 at the Bellevue/Kirkland city limits, is bounded on the west by 116th Avenue NE, on the north by NE 60th Street, and on the east by 132nd Avenue NE. The arena and grandstands are on the west side of the park off 116th Avenue NE at NE 53rd Street.

Twenty years ago Bridle Trails State Park was a remote enclave in the hinterlands of Bellevue devoted to the use of riders from the nearby numerous stables, farms, and ranches. Like a camel, suburbia got its nose in the tent, and now it has nearly taken over; the equestrian facilities have been pushed out until only a handful still exist. What stables remain struggle against rising taxes, developers' bulldozers, and annoyed neighbors—many of whose original motive for moving there was their quest for country atmosphere.

While the park remains a magnet for equestrians, and about as many people ride the trails today as did years ago, some must come from farther afield, guiding their mounts along road shoulders or on the 2-mile-long bridle path that comes up from Marymoor County Park in Redmond; many even tote their horses in trailers to use the trails or compete in shows held at the park.

The arena and grandstands on the west side of the park are used by horse clubs who hold both English and western riding shows here virtually every weekend from spring through fall. Competitions, which are usually practice-type "schooling shows," include events such as hunt seat and stock seat equitation, western trail, barrel racing, dressage, jumping, and in-hand showing.

There is no charge to spectators.

At one time a stable on the north side of the park had horses for rent, but it has closed, and there is now no place nearby where they are available. If using the park, remember that nearby stables are private; do not go onto the property.

One does not have to ride a horse, however, to enjoy the state park; hikers frequent the trails, and it is used for orienteering competitions. Trails are so numerous that it is possible to spend several hours in the park and not see a rider at all. Walkers should remember that horses have the right-of-way. When approached by a rider, move to the side of the trail and stand quietly. Dogs must be on a leash and under control. Horses must be ridden in a manner that does not endanger the life and limb of any person, and must not be left unattended.

None of the mazelike trails are marked, and their meandering routes are confusing. The only wide-open trail in the park is an arrow-straight service road under a power transmission line that splits the middle of the park. The remainder of the trails wind in profusion through the forest. The trails more popular with riders are reasonably wide and well maintained, with occasional muddy spots in marshy areas or during the wet winter months. Narrower paths and a web of interconnecting footpaths are also taken by venturesome equestrians, but are more often used by hikers. Do not stray off the trails; a few years ago a horse and rider broke through rotted timbers covering an old well and the mount was killed.

Whether on foot or horseback, if one leaves the main paths getting lost is an almost-certainty, although staying lost is

*The arena at Bridle Trails State Park hosts small "schooling shows" on summer weekends.*

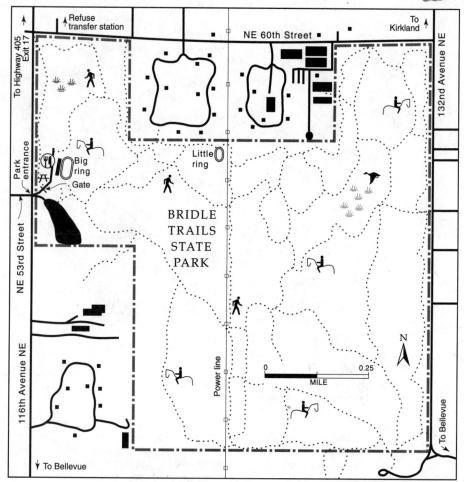

highly improbable. Aids to orientation are brief glimpses of surrounding roads from trails that are near the outer edge of the park, the drone of traffic on I-405 to the west, and the crash and clatter of a refuse transfer station at the northwest edge of the park. However, in the thick woods at the center of the east half of the park, clues to your location disappear. A map of the park created by the Sammamish Orienteering Club is an asset.

The park is an example of the lowland forest that once covered the Puget Sound region. In some sections huge, decaying stumps testify to past logging. The most common trees are western hemlock, Douglas fir, and some western red cedar. A few small groves hold moss-clad bigleaf maple, and in places tall stands of thin fir are packed tightly together like toothpicks in a box. An impenetrable growth of alder, vine maple, and devil's club surrounds a sizable marsh in the heart of the east section of the park and a smaller one in the northwest corner. Coyotes, squirrels, and numerous small rodents, as well as a wide variety of forest birds, live in the park.

## LAKE SAMMAMISH STATE PARK

**Hours/Season:** Day-use; standard hours; group camp overnight; year-round
**Area:** 509.7 acres; 6,858 feet of freshwater shoreline on Lake Sammamish
**Facilities:** Day-use area with 475 picnic ta-

*Little can surpass a hot summer's day at Lake Sammamish State Park.*

bles, 5 kitchen shelters, 100- and 300-person group day-use areas, restrooms, vault toilets (in group camp), swimming beach, bathhouses with showers, snacks (concession), trailer dump station, children's play equipment, sports field, jogging trail, horseshoe pits, boat launch ramps, docks, 200-person youth group camp

**Attractions:** Picnicking, swimming, boating, sailing, paddling, waterskiing, windsurfing, fishing, birdwatching, softball, soccer, jogging, orienteering

**Access:** At Issaquah, take Exit 15 (Lake Sammamish State Park, Renton, Highway 900) from I-90, cross north over the highway on Renton/Issaquah Road, then turn west on SE 56th Street to reach the park in 0.4 mile. The launch ramps and group camp are in the north section of the park, which can be reached by turning east on SE 56th Street, and in 1.2 miles drive northwest on E Lake Sammamish Parkway SE for 1 mile to the park entrances.

⚓ Lake Sammamish State Park, a water playground that boasts one of the largest freshwater beaches in the greater Seattle

area, becomes a summertime magnet for crowds bent on boating, waterskiing, windsurfing, swimming, or sunbathing—or for watching those who do. With more than 1.5 million visitors each year, escape from the masses would seem impossible, yet surprisingly enough, just a few feet away from the frenetic beach and picnic areas are quiet paths through woods and shrubs to secluded shorefronts or to wide, untrammeled meadows. Over half of the park's acreage is preserved as natural area where more than a hundred species of birds, as well as coyote, fox, raccoon, opossum, deer, weasel, beaver, muskrat, and porcupine exist only a Frisbee-toss from the sunburned throngs.

The heart of the park (aside from a huge parking lot) is the wide grass picnic area, shaded by large old poplar, maple, willow, and birch. Here a snack stand, bathhouse, several picnic shelters, children's play equipment, volleyball nets, and horseshoe pits complement the usual collection of picnic tables and fire braziers. To the west is the wide sandy beach with roped-off swimming areas, a swimming float, and farther offshore a waterski float. Two group picnic areas with large kitchen shelters are placed at the south end of the day-use area, adjoined by a softball diamond and soccer fields just inside the park entrance. The group picnic areas may be reserved, although they are in such demand that they are usually fully booked for the summer as soon as reservations are opened in January. Three other picnic shelters in the park are on a first-come, first-served basis.

A wide, marshy natural area separates the beach from the boat and group camps. A wooden bridge at the north corner of the parking lot crosses placid Issaquah Creek and leads to the center of a trail on the perimeter of the natural area. The east leg shortly arrives at a large, open field of pasture grass and thistles, while the wooded west leg parallels the creek and eventually arrives at a shaded grass thumb at the beach where the creek meets the lake. A narrow spur leads northeast from this trail through blackberry brambles and a canopy of dense brush to a tiny pocket cove amid encircling marshland.

The entrance to the boat launch area is on the north side of the park, some 2 miles beyond the main park entrance. Due to the volume of traffic here, four ramps are reserved for launching, the remaining five ramps designated for pick-up, and a separate area is provided for tying the boat down to the trailer to avoid any dallying at the ramps.

Across the road from the launch area is the Hans Jensen Youth Group Camp, named for the man who donated much of the park property. A gravel road leads past a grassy parking area and up the heart of a narrow meadow that is flanked by dense woods. Picnicking/tent-camping sites adjoin the road; at road's end are a picnic shelter and campfire circle. The group camp, which is available to youth groups only, requires advance reservations.

## SQUAK MOUNTAIN STATE PARK

**Hours/Season:** Day-use; standard hours; year-round
**Area:** 613 acres
**Facilities:** Natural area, trails, *no water*
**Attractions:** Hiking, nature study, bird-watching
**Access:** The park lies south of the Issaquah

city limits, east of SE Renton–Issaquah Road (Highway 900), and north of SE May Valley Road. It is not possible to reach the park boundary by car; trails from Issaquah lead to the park. To find them, take Newport Way NW west from Highway 900, and in 1.5 miles turn southeast onto Mountain Park Boulevard SW, which winds steeply uphill. In 0.9 mile, turn left on Mountainside Drive SW. At a hairpin turn in 0.4 mile, an unmarked trail leaves the end of a paved pulloff that has parking for five or six cars. Another access, also unmarked, leaves the end of Sierra Court SW in the Forest Rim residential area farther uphill, but there is no parking here. Yet another access trail leaves Highway 900 1.7 miles south from the Newport Way NW junction. Here a gated dirt road on the west side of the highway leads uphill to the park boundary. There is limited parking along the roadside.

▲ The residential development of Issaquah has crept its way up the steep north side of Squak Mountain in a perpetual quest for the grandest and highest home with the most far-reaching views. At the uppermost limit of the city, these intrusions bump up against the boundary of Squak Mountain State Park. The 600-acre section of land, encompassing the upper portions of the mountain, was donated to the State Parks Commission with the provision that it would forever remain in its natural state. Only the very top of the mountain, where a small piece of King County property is festooned with communications antennas, is excluded from the park. In the future the northwest corner of the park may have parking and sanitation facilities.

Roads once laced the upper reaches of the mountain, but these are now mostly overgrown. The lack of any signs or trail maintenance, and the confusion of paths taking off willy-nilly into the brush, make the park an orienteering challenge not to be taken lightly by casual visitors. If nature excites you, the park can fulfill your desires, but don't come here for scenic views—they are completely masked by the dense forest growth.

The best access to the park is the one from Mountainside Drive. It joins the other two routes just northwest of the park boundary and enters the park as the North Ridge Road Trail. Moss-encrusted maple, cedar, and a few Douglas fir make up the forest here. In about 0.25 mile this wide path forks, with the western leg shortly leaving the park property. In a few hundred feet, at another fork, a rather inconspicuous trail leads uphill to the south, while the more beaten path heads east along the hillside.

To reach the Squak Mountain summit, take the south fork; although it is covered by ferns in places, it is still readily followed. After another 200 feet of elevation gain, it joins an overgrown road, sometimes called the Lower Summit Road Trail, that comes in from west of the park boundary. Another 0.25 mile uphill is another fork in a grove of alder at the head of a creek drainage. Here it is better to stay on the leg that contours to the east, which shortly turns uphill for the final 150-foot climb to the mountaintop. The other leg to the west soon reaches a ridgeline—and yet another fork, the uphill leg of which has been called the Bullitt Fireplace Road. It climbs steeply up a ridgetop, then drops down again in its route toward the mountaintop. The trail

quickly becomes very obscure, and only the sight of antennas makes it possible to confidently reach the summit.

From the lowest fork, the trail that heads east, the East Side Road Trail, traverses the hillside between 1,325 and 1,350 feet of elevation, most of the time through dense brush that gives way to stands of alder along creek drainages. Four stream drainages are crossed as the trail progresses along the steep sidehill along the north side of the mountain, then turns south and starts to drop gently down the mountain's ever-steepening west flank, becoming progressively more primitive. Only once does the thick forest-cover part enough to permit views of the Issaquah Creek valley and Tiger Mountain rising above.

# OLALLIE STATE PARK

**Hours/Season:** Day-use; standard hours; year-round
**Area:** 521.1 acres (including Twin Falls

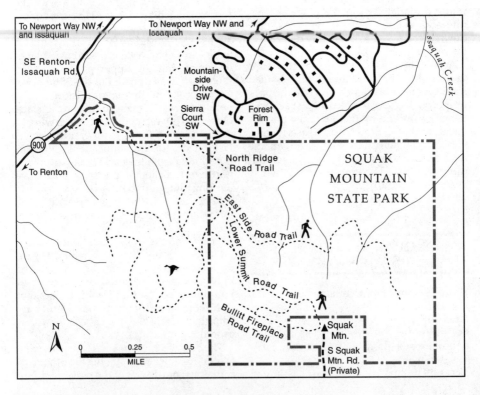

256

Natural Area); 21,588 feet of freshwater shoreline on the South Fork of the Snoqualmie River

**Facilities:** Vault toilets, hiking trails, viewpoints

**Attractions:** Hiking, fishing, interpretive signs, views of Twin Falls

**Access:** *To reach the west trailhead to Twin Falls,* take Exit 34 (Edgewick Road) from I-90, 4.5 miles east of North Bend. Turn south on 468th Avenue SE, and in 0.6 mile, just before the bridge over the South Fork of the Snoqualmie River, turn east on SE 159th Street, reaching the Twin Falls parking lot in 0.3 mile. *For the east trailhead to Twin Falls,* take Exit 38 (Fire Training Center) from I-90. The exit from the eastbound lanes is 7.3 miles east of North Bend, and the exit from the westbound lanes is 2 miles farther east; the old Snoqualmie Pass Highway runs along the south side of the river, connecting the two ends of the exit. At the eastbound exit, just south of the bridge over the Snoqualmie River, turn west on a gravel road into the Twin Falls parking area. From the westbound exit, follow the old Snoqualmie Pass Highway west 1.9 miles to the Twin Falls parking area. Olallie State Park lies just north of the old Snoqualmie Pass Highway, 0.7 mile east of the Twin Falls parking area.

Olallie State Park spans a 3.5-mile-long segment of the Snoqualmie River. The historic Snoqualmie Pass Wagon Road, which was completed in 1869, once passed through here, and traces of logs from its corduroy roadbed can be found within the park. The section of present-day road between the east and west ends of Exit 38 is a portion of the now-becoming-historic Sunset Highway (old Snoqualmie Pass Highway). The park lies north of the old highway, between the two ends of this exit.

The east end of the road through the park ends just below Weeks Falls, where there is a power plant built to balance power needs with the ecological requirements of the river's fish. Upstream from the falls, an adjustable weir diverts water into the power generators only when the amount of water is adequate to assure that the remaining river flow will support the needs of fish inhabiting the river. Screens have been installed at the turbine intakes to further re-

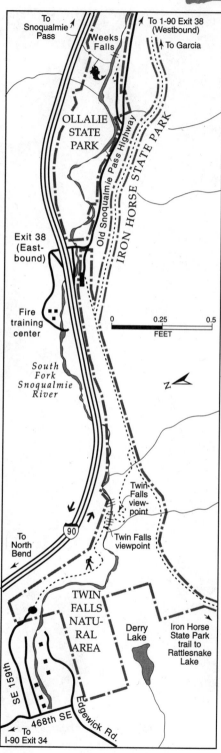

257

*The lower falls at Twin Falls Natural Area roars over a 150-foot-high cliff.*

duce fish mortality. Anglers can take advantage of access trails to try their luck at luring the river's rainbow and cutthroat trout.

## TWIN FALLS NATURAL AREA

▲ At Twin Falls the South Fork of the Snoqualmie River drops more than 300 feet through a rocky gorge in a series of glistening cascades. Newly developed trails provide breathtaking viewpoints of the falls. From the east end of the park, the path starts on a barricaded access road that gives way to a trail in 0.7 mile. Total distance to the falls is 1.6 miles, with an elevation loss of 500 feet, which must be regained on the return hike from the falls. From the west, the trail distance to the falls is 1.3 miles, with an elevation gain of 230 feet.

From a viewing platform at the upper falls, look directly into the throat of a narrow gorge that boils with a series of 20- to 50-foot cataracts. From here a wooden stairway leads down to a bridge just above the lower falls and further views of the upper cascades. A short length of trail and stairs on the north bank lead down to an eagle's aerie platform with a view of the river as it roars over a sheer 150-foot cliff at the lower fall and drapes adjoining rock walls with wispy veils of water.

---

# IRON HORSE STATE PARK (SNOQUALMIE SUMMIT TO RATTLESNAKE LAKE)

---

**Hours/Season:** Day-use; standard hours; year-round; *use permit required*
**Area:** 448 acres
**Facilities:** 18.1 miles of trail, 3 trestles
**Attractions:** Hiking, mountain biking, horseback riding, wagon-train riding, cross-country skiing, snowshoeing; *motorized vehicles prohibited*
**Accesses:**

**Annette Lake Access.** Take Exit 47 (Tinkham Road, Denny Creek, Asahel Curtis) from I-90. After crossing the South Fork of the Snoqualmie River, head east for 0.7 mile to the Annette Lake trailhead. Take the trail uphill, crossing under power transmission lines, and in 1 mile intersect Iron Horse Trail.

**McClellan Butte Access.** Take Exit 42 (Tinkham Road, West Entrance) from I-90, and park at the gaging station just south of the South Fork of the Snoqualmie River. Follow the McClellan Butte trail uphill. The trail crosses under a power line right-of-way and intersects Iron Horse Trail in 0.7 mile.

**Garcia Access.** Take Exit 38 (Fire Training Center) from I-90. The eastbound end of this exit is 7.3 miles east of North Bend, and the westbound end is 9.3 miles east of North Bend; the old Snoqualmie Pass Highway runs along the south side of the river between the two ends. Near the east end of this exit, turn south onto Forest Road 9020. Follow this rough, very steep dirt road east for 1 mile to the intersection with the trail at the old Garcia stop. Parking is limited.

**Olallie Access.** Take Exit 38 from I-90 as described for the Garcia Access. At the western end of Exit 38, just south of the bridge over the South Fork of the Snoqualmie River, turn west on a gravel road into the Twin Falls Natural Area parking lot. Hike or bike the service road headed uphill and west to intersect the Iron Horse Trail in 0.2 mile.

**Rattlesnake Lake.** Take Exit 32 (436th Avenue SE) from I-90, 4.5 miles east of North Bend, and head south for 2.5 miles on 436th SE, which becomes Cedar Falls Road SE. Just north of Rattlesnake Lake, a gravel road heading east toward the Cedar River Watershed crosses the old railroad bed. An extension of the railbed southwest from here to the west end of Rattlesnake Lake that runs through the watershed property is posted with NO TRESPASSING signs.

▲ This is a continuation of the ribbonlike state park that was formerly the roadbed of the Chicago, Milwaukee, St. Paul, and Pacific Railroad. The eastern portion of Iron Horse State Park was described in Region 3, along with its history.

Only at the Garcia and Rattlesnake Lake accesses can this western segment of the

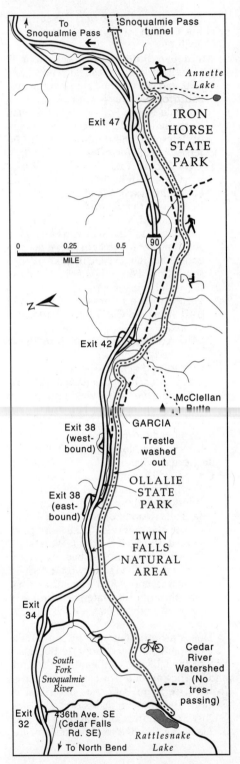

park be reached directly by roads; the other accesses must be reached via short trails. The upper end begins at the west entrance to the 2.3-mile-long Snoqualmie Pass tunnel. The tunnel entrance is gated, and up to a foot of water stands in places along the old railbed. Blasts of moist, frigid air roll from the tunnel mouth, even on the warmest of days. Drainage problems are being evaluated and the tunnel may be opened if it is repaired.

West from the tunnel, the trail traverses an open hillside with spectacular views to peaks north of the pass: Snoqualmie, Guye, Denny, the Tooth, Hemlock, Bryant, Chair, and Roosevelt. Across the valley the avalanche-swept slopes of Granite Mountain turn brilliant colors with fall frosts. To the west the view down Snoqualmie Valley is terminated by the serrated ridge leading south from the snag tooth of McClellan Butte.

The trail heads into the woods along Humpback Creek near the Annette Lake access. Here a collapsing snowshed west of the creek is bypassed by a dirt road along its outer edge. Trees again block views until the airy trestle over Hansen Creek, where there are more views of the Snoqualmie Valley and Bandera Mountain and Mount Defiance to the north side of the valley. Slopes west of the Hansen Creek trestle are prone to avalanche, so cross-country skiers coming up from McClellan Butte should not venture beyond here.

The next access is another 5 miles west at the McClellan Butte Trail. From here the Iron Horse Trail loops below steep cliffs, with more views north to the steep forested ridges west from Mount Defiance. In another mile the trail crosses one of its two road accesses: the forest road at the old Garcia station. To the west one more high trestle crosses the expanse of Mine Creek, then there is a break in the trail at the Hall Creek trestle, where the center of the span was washed away by floods caused by extensive clearcutting on the upstream slopes. Two miles to the west, the trail can be accessed from a spur trail uphill from the Twin Falls parking lot. A large gravel pit scars the face of the hillside to the north. After passing a power substation above Twin Falls, the trail swings southwest from the Snoqualmie River past an abandoned gravel pit at the old Ragnar Station, then

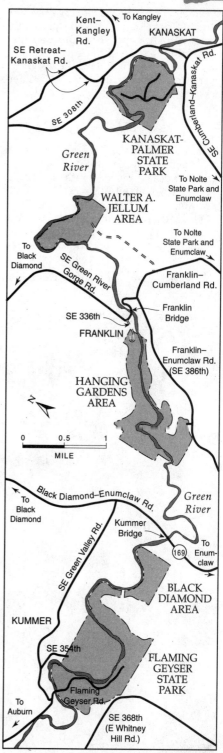

descends gradually through the thickly forested hillside above Boxley Creek to Rattlesnake Lake.

# GREEN RIVER GORGE CONSERVATION AREA (UNDEVELOPED)

**Area:** 1,968 acres (includes developed state parks, described below); 14 miles of freshwater shoreline on the Green River
**Facilities:** See the following descriptions of developed state parks
**Activities:** Paddling, rafting, tube floating, fishing, camping, picnicking, hiking, birdwatching, nature study
**Access:** See the following descriptions of developed state parks and undeveloped areas

The Green River Gorge is an exquisite "hanging garden" with miniature waterfalls wisping down vertical walls, rock grottos draped in ferns and moss, frothing whitewater rapids, and cold, crystal pools. The river slices through layers of sandstone and shale—300 feet deep in places—for 14 twisting miles. Historically, the Green River area was exploited for its coal, clay, and cinnabar (from which mercury is derived). As the mineral resources were depleted, the gorge was recognized anew for its natural beauty and recreation potential. In 1969 the state legislature established the Green River Gorge Conservation Area and directed the State Parks and Recreation Commission to protect the unique natural and geological features of the area.

The Parks Commission set about acquiring property, developmental rights, timber-cutting rights, and trail easements in the area. Between 1969 and 1986 it obtained over 35 parcels of land. Today developed state parks are Flaming Geyser, Nolte (which does not lie on the Green River, but is nearby), and Kanaskat-Palmer, although only the latter has camping facilities. Undeveloped state property includes the Black Diamond Area, the Hanging Gardens Recreation Area, and the Walter A. Jellum Area.

The commission would like to acquire the sections of property along the rim of the gorge that connect these holdings, but some

261

of this rim property has already been residentially developed. In some places the best that can be hoped for is future acquisition and protection of the gorge walls, so that at least from river level the visual appearance of a serene, unblemished wilderness will be protected.

### BLACK DIAMOND AREA

**Area:** 163.5 acres; 8,544 feet of freshwater shoreline on the Green River
**Access:** Located on the south side of the Green River about 1,000 feet west of the Kummer (Highway 169) Bridge, the Black Diamond Area continues along the rim of the gorge to connect with the east side of Flaming Geyser State Park. *There is pres-*

*ently no land access to this property without trespassing across private property.*

### HANGING GARDENS AREA

**Area:** 369 acres; 20,200 feet of freshwater shoreline on the Green River
**Access:** *On the south side of the Green River,* from Highway 169, 1.5 miles south of the Kummer Bridge, turn northeast on SE 386th Street (Franklin–Enumclaw Road). In 2.4 miles an obscure cable-gated logging road heads northwest into the park property. *On the north side of the Green River,* take the SE Green River Gorge Road (Lawson Street) east from the center of Black Diamond, and in 4.3 miles, just west of the Franklin Bridge, SE 336th

*The Hanging Gardens Area of the Green River Gorge is a rock grotto draped with ferns and moss.*

Street heads west for a few hundred feet to a gate at the park boundary.

⚓ At the south access point, park at the gated road-end and hike north along the road. In a short distance, this route heads northwest along the fence of the Black Diamond watershed, and then continues northwest atop a densely wooded ridgeline leading toward the river. At the lip of the gorge, the trail drops steeply down the ridge and descends to a sandy beach at a sharp bend in the river. The vertical, fern-draped wall of the hanging gardens soars upward on the opposite side of the river.

From the north access point, the gated road heads southwest past the site of the onetime coal mining town of Franklin. At a switchback in 0.5 mile, this road crosses the roadbed of the Franklin–Black Diamond Railroad, long since nothing but a memory. Follow the level railroad grade, now a poorly maintained trail, as it continues west; some scrambling is required where a creek

has washed out a trestle. In about a mile the trail improves as it intersects an access road to the Black Diamond watershed pump station.

For an alternate route, at the railroad grade continue uphill and west on the old road that leads to the gated mouth of the 1,300-foot-deep Franklin #2 coal mine shaft. From here a trail traverses west to the overgrown Franklin Cemetery adjacent to the Black Diamond watershed road. A few hundred feet west, the watershed road switchbacks some 400 feet down the north side of the gorge to the river's edge, where a suspension bridge supports a water pipeline that crosses the river. Here are views of river rapids and possibly kayakers daring this section of the river. Back atop the rim of the gorge, the railroad grade/road continues west for another 0.5 mile before reaching the boundary of the park property.

## WALTER A. JELLUM AREA

**Area:** 331.9 acres; 20,040 feet of fresh-water shoreline on the Green River

**Access:** Follow directions for the south side access to Hanging Gardens, and continue northeast another 1.6 miles on the Franklin–Enumclaw Road to its junc-

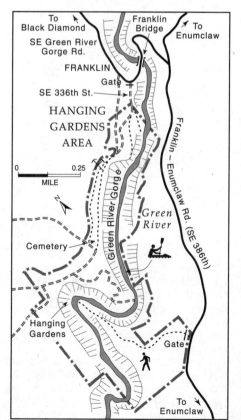

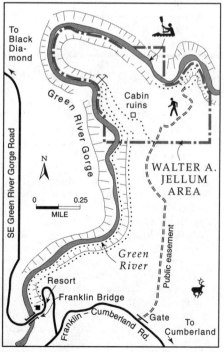

tion with the Franklin–Cumberland Road, just south of the Franklin Bridge. Head east on the Franklin–Cumberland Road for 0.4 mile to where a gated logging road leads northwest through a clearcut to the Jellum Area. A public easement permits hiking the road.

▲ The Jellum Area of the Green River gorge ⊥ includes all of a broad thumb of property that pokes northwest into a wide bend of the river. Walk the logging road from the access point described above for 0.9 mile to a Y-intersection just inside the park boundary. The left leg of this Y leads to the ruins of a cabin on a sharp point over the river, where a footpath swings down to the collapsed entrance to an old cinnabar mine. One wonders if the grizzled miner who tried to eke out his livelihood here was aware of the natural treasures that surrounded him.

The right fork of the Y leads another 0.5 mile to the top of a small northerly protrusion that the river wraps around. Two steep scramble trails drop over the edge of the rim on either side of this nub of a ridge to reach a boulder-hopping path along the riverbank between them.

## KANASKAT-PALMER STATE PARK

**Hours/Season:** Overnight; standard hours; year-round
**Area:** 296.8 acres; 12,900 feet of freshwater shoreline on the Green River
**Facilities:** 31 standard campsites, 19 RV sites, 4 primitive campsites, 65 picnic sites, 80-person group camp, 100-person group day-use area, kitchen shelter, 4 picnic shelters, restrooms, trailer dump station, 3 miles of hiking trail, boat launch (hand carry)
**Attractions:** Camping, picnicking, hiking, rafting, paddling, fishing, nature study
**Access:** *From the north,* take Highway 169 south from Renton, and at 1.7 miles south of Maple Valley turn east on SE Kent–Kangley Road. At an intersection in 3.5 miles, turn south on SE Retreat–Kanaskat Road, which joins SE Cumberland–Kanaskat Road in another 3.2 miles. Head south 1.9 miles to the park entrance. *From*

*the south,* at the flashing yellow light 2.8 miles north of Enumclaw, turn east from Highway 169 onto SE 400th Street, which becomes SE 400th Way in 0.4 mile, joins SE 392nd Street in another 0.7 mile, and then T's into Veazie–Cumberland Road in 0.8 mile more. Alternatively, from Highway 410, 0.6 mile east of Enumclaw, turn north onto 284th Avenue SE (Farman Road N), which becomes Veazie–Cumberland Road. Follow this road north (at Cumberland it becomes SE Cumberland–Kanaskat Road). The park entrance is 2.5 miles north of Cumberland.

▲ Just as it begins its tortuous descent ⊥ through the gorge, the Green River sweeps around a small, low plateau. Kanaskat-Palmer State Park sits on this plateau, surrounded on three sides by the river. Its location makes the park the prime spot for those planning to run the river, as well as for those who come to fish, play in its pools, or enjoy the surrounding lush forest.

In the center of the park, two campground loops have sites rimmed by trees and undergrowth; an isolated group camp is secluded in trees near the northeast side of the park. Along the park's western edge, the day-use areas have ample space for games and gamboling. Trails lead to the riverbank and follow along its edge, providing access for fishing. Trout catches are good in the summer, but it is in winter, when steelhead run, that fishing begins in earnest and hardy anglers flock to the river. A steelhead-rearing pond is directly across the river from the park.

Three boat put-in/take-out sites are provided in the park. *Everyone attempting to run the river should have proper equipment and knowledge of whitewater techniques, and should familiarize themselves with river conditions.* Between the upstream and middle launch sites, the rafting is Class II+, requiring intermediate skills. At the middle launch site, where the river takes a right-angle turn and heads due south, it becomes Class IV and demands expert skill in handling the boiling rapids, powerful waves, and dangerous rocks.

Although seasonal changes will affect the river conditions, the water level is largely controlled upstream at Howard Hansen Dam. River-runners can call the Army Corps of Engineers office number listed in

*Kids explore the rocks and pools of the Green River at Kanaskat-Palmer State Park.*

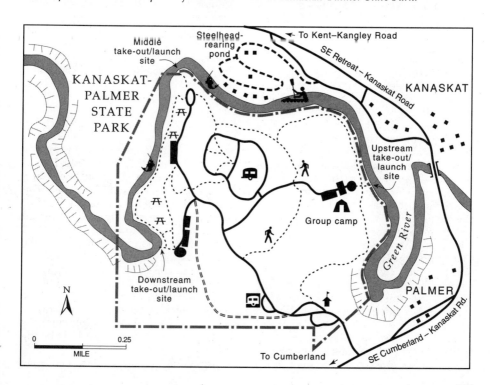

Appendix A for information on the current water level. The river is at its most difficult from late fall to mid-June, but even in summer rafters and kayakers must exercise care. When the river is high enough, experienced boaters equipped with the proper gear can run the river for 14 miles from here through the gorge to Flaming Geyser State Park.

# NOLTE
# STATE PARK

**Hours/Season:** Day-use; standard hours; closed from the end of October to mid-April
**Area:** 117.2 acres; 7,174 feet of freshwater shoreline on Deep Lake
**Facilities:** 60 picnic sites, 3 picnic shelters, 2 50-person group day-use areas, swimming beach, fishing docks, boat launch ramp (hand-carry), horseshoe pits, interpretive trail, 2 miles of hiking trail
**Attractions:** Picnicking, fishing (*gasoline motors prohibited*), swimming, paddling, hiking, jogging, birdwatching
**Access:** See directions to Kanaskat-Palmer State Park. Nolte is 3.8 miles south of Kanaskat-Palmer on the Veazie–Cumberland Road.

Deep Lake has been a favorite family retreat since the early 1900s, when the Nolte family developed and operated a private resort along its shore. With the death of Miss Minnie Nolte in 1972, the property was willed to the state for use as a park so future generations could continue to enjoy the scenic getaway.

The parking area adjoins an expansive lawn that tapers down to the sandy swimming beach. Concrete pads with picnic tables and barbecues are scattered in the grass above the beach. Two large picnic shelters may be reserved for groups.

In spite of its rather modest 39 acres, at some points the lake is over 100 feet deep, thus its name. Two fishing docks that extend into the lake near the picnic area give youngsters a chance to catch catfish, perch, and crappie, while experienced anglers can try for more-elusive trout. A road spur and short trail 0.2 mile north of the main entrance permit easy launching of cartop boats; cars, however, must be parked in the main

lot. Gas motors are prohibited on the lake.

A wide, 1.4-mile-long trail circles the lake, with frequent spurs down to fishing spots along the shoreline. A bridge crosses Deep Creek, which feeds the lake. Perhaps you may spot some of the local deer or small creatures such as weasels, squirrels, and skunks. Migratory waterfowl drop by for a brief stay in spring and fall. A short interpretive trail loops though the woods on the southeast side of the park.

# FLAMING GEYSER
# STATE PARK

**Hours/Season:** Day-use; standard hours; year-round
**Area:** 666.9 acres; 34,345 feet of freshwater shoreline on the Green River
**Facilities:** 172 picnic tables, 6 picnic shelters, 2 restrooms, 150- and 300-person group day-use area, 4 miles of hiking trail, salmon-rearing ponds, boat launch ramp (hand-carry)
**Attractions:** Picnicking, hiking, fishing, rafting, paddling, tube floating, interpretive salmon- and steelhead-rearing display, birdwatching
**Access:** From Highway 169, 1.4 miles south of Black Diamond, turn west on SE Green Valley Road. In 2.7 miles turn south on Flaming Geyser Road (228th Place SE), and cross the bridge over the Green River to reach the park entrance.

Although "flaming geyser" conjures up the image of a fire-breathing natural dragon, the park's namesake is presently less dramatic. In 1911 miners drilled a coal test-hole at the edge of Christy Creek, and in a coal seam over 1,000 feet down hit pockets of methane gas and salty water. For many years fire from the ignited gas roared as much as 25 feet into the air, and up to 20 gallons of water a minute flowed from the hole. Today the gas is largely depleted, the flame is a modest 6 to 10 inches high, and the water flow is reduced to a dribble. A few yards farther up the creek, Bubbling Geyser, which resulted from exploratory drilling for methane gas exploration, is marked only by a small pool of bubbling gray mud.

The flaming geyser is now merely an

266

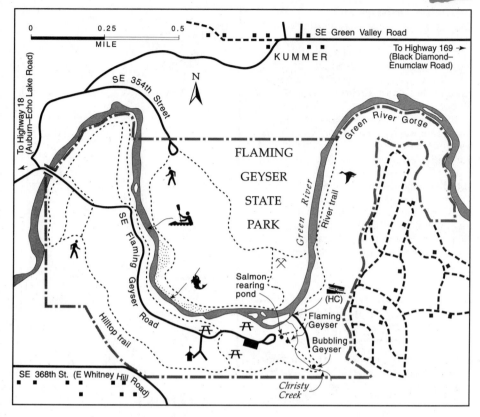

interesting attraction in the lovely park that sits at the end of the Green River gorge. The heart of the park, on the south side of the river, is a mowed meadow shaded by cottonwood, yellow cedar, and huge, stately 100-foot-high maples. Picnic sites and shelters border the meadow, with adjoining horseshoe pits, poles for volleyball nets, swingsets, play structures, and ample open space for ball games. The picnic shelters can be reserved for groups.

Several trails weave through the park. The longest, 1.4 miles, follows the wooded hilltop above the heart of the park. Another trail heads east from Christy Creek below the steep banks of the gorge, touching the river in several points. At a Y-intersection just beyond the creek, a short spur heads north to an opening along the river's edge. The other leg of the Y swings away from the river briefly, then in 0.5 mile returns to the river at the site of a former ford across this shallow portion of the river. The trail then continues along a wooded riverbank for

another 0.5 mile, to where the river swings east into the narrowing throat of the gorge. A short way beyond this point, scramble passage can be made only during periods of low water.

Because there are four distinct types of habitat in the park—riverbank, meadow, marsh, and woodland—the trail is heaven for birdwatchers; in the forest look for the parrot-bright red, yellow, and black flash of the western tanager. Large rectangular holes in conifers are evidence of pileated woodpeckers. Other park residents include deer, raccoon, black bear, beaver, and otter.

The Green River is relatively placid at this end of the gorge and becomes even calmer as it continues west through farmland. During the low water levels of summer, this section of the river is popular for floating on small inflatables, inner tubes, and air mattresses. When water is higher, however, even this part of the river requires some skill, as well as proper safety equipment. The state park is the take-out point

**267**

for whitewater boaters who have bested the more tumultuous sections higher in the gorge.

Most of the flat, broad thumb of land on the north side of the river is also park property. It's a nice spot for picnicking or sunbathing, but has no restrooms, tables, or other facilities. To drive to it, turn south on SE 354th Street 0.4 mile east of the bridge toward the main part of the park. A 1.5-mile trail loop leaves the road-end parking lot; the south leg heads downhill past an orchard and across the flat, wooded peninsula to reach the river's edge at its west tip. The trail continues along the riverbank past sandy beaches and shallow pools before turning north at the east side of the peninsula. Here the remnants of an early coal mine mark the start of the trail segment that returns inland to the parking lot.

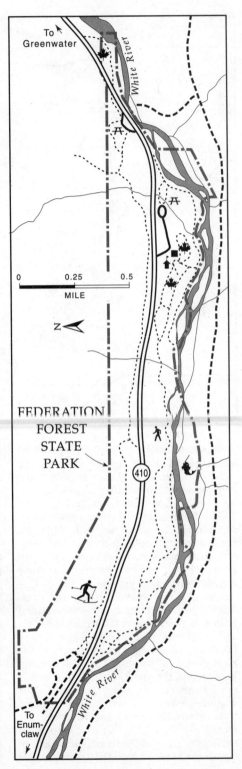

## FEDERATION FOREST STATE PARK

**Hours/Season:** Day-use; standard hours; year-round; *interpretive center*, Wednesday through Sunday 10:00 A.M. to 5:00 P.M. from April 16 through October 31; by appointment at other times

**Area:** 618.9 acres; 19,800 feet of freshwater shoreline on the White River

**Facilities:** 47 picnic sites, 2 kitchen shelters, restrooms, vault toilets, interpretive center and displays, 1.5 miles of interpretive trail, 9.5 miles of hiking trail

**Attractions:** Picnicking, hiking, fishing, interpretive center, cross-country skiing, guided nature walks (by appointment)

**Access:** 15.8 miles southeast of Enumclaw on Highway 410.

While many of Washington's state parks have recreation as a focus, Federation Forest is a showcase for ecosystems, with humans present only as guests. The park includes the Catherine Montgomery Interpretive Center, which holds displays designed to acquaint visitors with the plant and animal life in the seven different biotic zones found in the state. Adjoining five of the displays are windows with views of small outdoor plots that are living dioramas of plants of that zone. Other display panels describe the geological evolution of the White River valley and the history of the Naches Trail—one of the first pioneer trails from eastern Washington to Puget Sound. Vestiges of that trail run through the park.

The park, which lies at the boundary between the Coast Forest and Mountain Forest zones, contains a diversity of flora and fauna. Visitors can observe the various ecosystems found in these two zones and their respective flora from the nearly 10 miles of trail and three nature trail loops that thread through the park. Guidebooks are available; a separate pamphlet has a checklist of some ninety-four different birds that visitors might see.

Just west of the interpretive center, a kiosk marks the start of the two Fred Cleator interpretive trails. West Trail, 0.9 mile long, and East Trail, 0.4 mile long, together wind through five different major forest communities. River Trail, a 0.75-mile branch of East Trail, parallels the bank of the White River, following a portion of the old Naches Trail. Gape upward at virgin trees that our pioneer forefathers saw in 1853 on their brutal trek across the Cascades. A second kiosk, located adjacent to the highway 0.6 mile east of the main park entrance, marks the start of a shorter nature trail that describes the devastating effect of a major windstorm that occurred in the winter of 1983. The park's level trails are popular cross-country skiing routes in the winter.

A short road spur leads east from the interpretive center parking lot to a loop of tree-shaded picnic tables. From here a long, elevated boardwalk crosses a creek and marsh to emerge from the trees at another picnic area where tables and fire braziers line the edge of a grassy plateau that overlooks the braided riverbed. A third picnic area is located at a pulloff loop north of the highway, about 0.5 mile east of the main park entrance.

*Immense trees overwhelm the sky at Federation Forest State Park.*

# APPENDICES

## A. ADDRESSES AND TELEPHONE NUMBERS

State Parks, Headquarters: 7150 Cleanwater Lane, Box 42650, Olympia, WA 98504-2650; (206) 753-2027

State Parks, Southwest Region: 11838 Tilley Road S, Olympia, WA 98512; (206) 753-7143

State Parks, Northwest Region: 220 Walnut Street, Box 487, Burlington, WA 98233; (206) 755-9231

State Parks, Eastern Region: 2201 N Duncan Drive, Wenatchee, WA 98801-1007; (509) 662-0420

State Parks, Puget Sound Region: 1602 29th SE, Auburn, WA 98002; (206) 931-3907

---

Alta Lake State Park: 40 Star Route, Pateros 98846; (509) 923-2473

Anderson Lake State Park: contact Fort Worden State Park

Banks Lake Wildlife Recreation Area: contact Steamboat Rock State Park

Battle Ground Lake State Park: 18002 NE 249th Street, Battle Ground 98604; (206) 687-4621

Bay View State Park: 1093 Bay View–Edison Road, Mount Vernon 98273; (206) 757-0227

Beacon Rock State Park: MP 34.83 L, State Road 14, Skamania 98648; (509) 427-8265

Belfair State Park: NE 410 Beck Road, Belfair, 98528; (206) 275-0668

Birch Bay State Park: 5105 Helwig Road, Blaine 98230; (206) 371-2800

Blake Island State Park: Box 277, Manchester 98353; (206) 731-0770

Blind Island Marine State Park: contact Lime Kiln Point State Park

Bogachiel State Park: HC 80, Box 500, Forks 98331; (206) 374-6356

Bridgeport State Park: Box 846, Bridgeport 98813; (509) 686-7231

Bridle Trails State Park: contact Lake Sammamish State Park

Brooks Memorial State Park: 2465 Highway 97, Goldendale 98620; (509) 773-5382

Bywater Bay State Park (Wolfe Property): contact Fort Flagler State Park

Camano Island State Park: 2269 Lowell Point Road, Stanwood 98292; (206) 387-3031

Camp William T. Wooten State Park: Route 1, Box 33, Pomeroy 99347; (509) 843-3708

Central Ferry State Park: Route 3, Box 99, Pomeroy 99347; (509) 549-3551

Chief Joseph State Park: contact Alta Lake State Park

Chief Timothy State Park: Highway 12, Clarkston 99403; (509) 758-9580

Clark Island Marine State Park: contact Lime Kiln Point State Park

Conconully State Park: Box 95, Conconully 98819; (509) 826-7408

Crawford State Park (Gardner Cave): General Delivery, Metaline Falls 99153; (509) 446-4065

Crow Butte State Park: Box 217, Paterson 99345; (509) 875-2644

Crown Point Heritage Area: contact Steamboat Rock State Park

Crystal Falls State Park: contact Mount Spokane State Park

Curlew Lake State Park: 974 Curlew Lake State Park Road, Republic 99166; (509) 775-3592

Cutts Island Marine State Park: contact Kopachuck State Park

Daroga State Park: HCR, Box 38A, Orondo 98843; (509) 664-6380

Dash Point State Park: 5700 SW Dash Point Road, Federal Way 98003; (206) 593-2206

Deception Pass State Park: 5175 N State Highway 20, Oak Harbor 98277; (206) 675-2417

Doe Island Marine State Park: contact Lime Kiln Point State Park

Dosewallips State Park: Box K, Brinnon 98320 (206) 796-4415

Doug's Beach State Park: contact Maryhill State Park

Eagle Island Marine State Park: contact Jarrell Cove Marine State Park

Ebey's Landing State Park: contact Fort Casey State Park

Elbow Lake State Park (Undeveloped): contact Millersylvania State Park

Fay-Bainbridge State Park: 15446 Sunrise Drive NE, Bainbridge Island 98110; (206) 842-3931

Federation Forest State Park: 49201 Enumclaw–Chinook Pass Road, Enumclaw 98022; (206) 663-2207

Fields Spring State Park: Box 37, Anatone 99401; (509) 256-3332

Flaming Geyser State Park: 23700 SE Flaming Geyser Road, Auburn 98002; (206) 931-3930

Fort Canby State Park: Box 488, Ilwaco 98624; (206) 642-3078. *Lewis & Clark Interpretive Center*: (206) 642-3029

Fort Casey State Park: 1280 S Fort Casey Road, Coupeville 98239; (206) 678-4519

Fort Columbia State Park: Box 236, Chinook 98614; (206) 777-8221. American Youth Hostel: Fort Columbia State Park, Box 224, Chinook 98614; (206) 777-8755

Fort Ebey State Park: 395 N Fort Ebey Road, Coupeville 98239; (206) 678-4636

Fort Flagler State Park: Nordland 98358; (206) 385-1259

Fort Okanogan Interpretive Center: contact Alta Lake State Park

Fort Simcoe State Park: 5150 Fort Simcoe Road, White Swan 98952; (509) 874-2372

Fort Ward State Park: 2241 Pleasant Beach Drive NE, Bainbridge Island 98110; (206) 842-4041

Fort Worden State Park: Box 574, Port Townsend 98368; (206) 385-4730. *Port Townsend Marine Science Center:* (206) 385-5582

Ginkgo Petrified Forest State Park: Vantage 98950; (509) 856-2700

Goldendale Observatory State Park: 1602 Observatory Drive, Goldendale 98620; (509) 773-3141

Grayland Beach State Park: contact Twin Harbors State Park

Green River Gorge Conservation Area (Undeveloped): contact Flaming Geyser State Park

Griffiths-Priday State Park: contact Ocean City State Park

Helen McCabe State Park: contact Ginkgo Petrified Forest State Park

Hood Canal State Park Tidelands: contact Dosewallips State Park

Hoodsport Trail State Park: contact Lake Cushman State Park

Hope Island Marine State Park (Undeveloped): contact Jarrell Cove Marine State Park

Horsethief Lake State Park: Box 734, Dallesport 98617; (509) 767-1159

Ike Kinswa State Park: 873 Harmony Road, Silver Creek 98585; (206) 983-3402

Illahee State Park: 3540 Bahia Vista, Bremerton 98310; (206) 478-6460

Iron Horse State Park (Rattlesnake Lake to Columbia River), Ellensburg to Columbia River: contact Ginkgo Petrified Forest State Park; Rattlesnake Lake to Ellensburg: contact Lake Easton State Park

James Island Marine State Park: contact Lime Kiln Point State Park

Jarrell Cove Marine State Park: E 391 Wingert Road, Shelton 98584; (206) 426-9226

John R. Jackson House State Park: contact Lewis and Clark State Park

Jones Island Marine State Park: contact Lime Kiln Point State Park

Joseph Whidbey State Park: contact Fort Ebey State Park

Kanaskat-Palmer State Park: 32101 Kanaskat–Cumberland Road, Ravensdale 98051; (206) 886-0148

Keystone Spit State Park (Undeveloped): contact Fort Casey State Park

Kitsap Memorial State Park: 202 NE Park Street, Poulsbo 98370; (206) 779-3205

Kopachuck State Park: 11101 56th Street NW, Gig Harbor 98335; (206) 265-3606

Lake Chelan State Park: Route 1, Box 90, Chelan 98816; (509) 687-3710

Lake Cushman State Park: N 7211 Lake Cushman Road, Hoodsport 98548; (206) 877-5491

Lake Easton State Park: Box 26, Easton 98925; (509) 656-2230

Lake Sammamish State Park: 20606 SE 56th Street, Issaquah 98027; (206) 455-7010

Lake Sylvia State Park: Box 701, Montesano 98563; (206) 249-3621

Lake Wenatchee State Park: 21588A Highway 207, Leavenworth 98826; (509) 763-3101

Larrabee State Park: 245 Chuckanut Drive, Bellingham 98226; (206) 676-2093

Leadbetter Point State Park: contact Fort Canby State Park

Lewis and Clark Campsite Heritage Area: contact Fort Canby State Park

Lewis and Clark State Park: 4583 Jackson Highway, Winlock 98596; (206) 864-2643

Lewis and Clark Trail State Park: Route 1, Box 90, Dayton 99328; (509) 337-6457

Lime Kiln Point State Park: 6158 Lighthouse Road, Friday Harbor 98250; (206) 378-2044

Lincoln Rock State Park: Route 3, Box 3137, East Wenatchee 98802-9566; (509) 663-9603

Long Beach Seashore Conservation Area: contact Fort Canby State Park

Loomis Lake State Park: contact Fort Canby State Park

Lyons Ferry State Park: Box 157, Starbuck 99359; (509) 646-3252

McMicken Island Marine State Park: contact Jarrell Cove Marine State Park

Manchester State Park: Box 36, Manchester 98353; (206) 871-4065

Maryhill State Park: 50 Highway 97, Goldendale 98620; (509) 773-5007

Matia Island Marine State Park: contact Lime Kiln Point State Park

Matilda N. Jackson State Park: contact Lewis and Clark State Park

Millersylvania Memorial State Park: 12245 Tilley Road S, Olympia 98502; (206) 753-1519

Moran State Park: Star Route 22, Eastsound 98245; (206) 376-2326

Moses Lake State Park: Star Route, Box 5, Moses Lake 98837; (509) 765-5852

Mount Pilchuck State Park: contact Wenburg State Park

Mount Spokane State Park: N 26107 Mount Spokane Park Drive, Mead 99021; (509) 456-4169

Mukilteo State Park: contact Wenberg State Park

Mystery Bay Marine State Park: contact Fort Flagler State Park

Nolte State Park: 36921 Veazie–Cumberland Road, Enumclaw 98022; (206) 825-4646

North Beach Seashore Conservation Area: contact Ocean City State Park. *Ocean Shores Environmental Interpretive Center:* (206) 289-4617 .

Ocean City State Park: Route 4, Box 2900, Hoquiam 98550; (206) 289-3553

Olallie State Park: contact Lake Sammamish State Park

Old Fort Townsend State Park: 1370 Old Fort Townsend Road, Port Townsend 98368; (206) 385-3595

Old Man House State Park: contact Fay-Bainbridge State Park

Olmstead Place Heritage Area: Route 5, Box 2580, Ellensburg 98926; (509) 925-1943

Osoyoos Lake Veterans' Memorial State Park: Route 1, Box 102A, Oroville 98844; (509) 476-3321

Pacific Beach State Park: Box 267, Pacific Beach 98571; (206) 276-4297

Pacific Pines State Park: contact Fort Canby State Park

Palouse Falls State Park: contact Central Ferry State Park

Paradise Point State Park: 33914 NW Paradise Point Road, Ridgefield 98642; (206) 263-2350

Patos Island Marine State Park: contact Lime Kiln Point State Park

Peace Arch State Park: Box 87, Blaine 98230; (206) 332-8221

Pearrygin Lake State Park: Route 1, Box 300, Winthrop 98862; (509) 996-2370

Penrose Point State Park: 321 158th KPS, Lakebay 98439; (206) 884-2514

Peshastin Pinnacles State Park: contact Wenatchee Confluence State Park

Pleasant Harbor State Park: contact Dosewallips State Park

Posey Island Marine State Park: contact Lime Kiln Point State Park

Potholes State Park: 670 O'Sullivan Dam Road, Othello 99344; (509) 765-7271

Potlatch State Park: N 21010 Highway 101, Shelton 98584; (206) 877-5361

Rainbow Falls State Park: 4008 State Highway 6, Chehalis 98532; (206) 291-3767

Reed Island Marine State Park: contact Battle Ground State Park

Riverside State Park: 4427 N Aubrey L. White Parkway, Spokane 98205; (509) 456-3964

Rockport State Park: 5051 Highway 20, Concrete 98237; (206) 853-8461

Rothschild House Heritage Site: contact Fort Worden State Park

Sacajawea State Park: 2503 Sacajawea Park Road, Pasco 99301; (509) 545-2361

Saddlebag Island Marine State Park: contact Lime Kiln Point State Park

Saint Edward State Park: Box 602, Kenmore 98028; (206) 823-2992

Saltwater State Park: 25205 8th Place S, Des Moines 98198; (206) 764-4128

Scablands Nature Corridor (Pasco/Fish Lake Trail): contact Region 4 Headquarters

Scenic Beach State Park: Box 7, Seabeck 98380; (206) 830-5079

Schafer State Park: Route 1, Box 87, Elma 98541; (206) 482-3852

Seaquest State Park: Box 3030 Spirit Lake Highway, Castle Rock 98611; (206) 274-8633

Sequim Bay State Park: 1872 Highway 101 E, Sequim 98392; (206) 683-4235

Shinilam Lake State Park: contact Fort Canby State Park

South Beach Seashore Conservation Area: contact Twin Harbors State Park

South Whidbey State Park: 4128 S Smugglers Cove Road, Freeland 98249; (206) 321-4559

Spencer Spit State Park: Route 2, Box 3600, Lopez 98261; (206) 468-2251

Spokane River Centennial Trail: contact Riverside State Park

Squilchuck State Park: contact Wenatchee Confluence State Park; (509) 844-3044

Squak Mountain State Park: contact Lake Sammamish State Park

Steamboat Rock State Park: Box 370, Electric City 99123-0352; (509) 633-1304.

Steptoe Butte State Park: contact Central Ferry State Park

Stretch Point State Park: contact Jarrell Cove Marine State Park

Stuart Island Marine State Park: contact Lime Kiln Point State Park

Sucia Island Marine State Park: contact Lime Kiln Point State Park

Summer Falls State Park: contact Sun Lakes State Park

Sun Lakes State Park: HCR 1, Box 136, Coulee City 99115; (509) 632-5583

Tolmie State Park: 6227 Johnson Point Road
  NE, Olympia 98506; (206) 753-1519
Triton Cove State Park: contact Dosewallips
  State Park
Turn Island Marine State Park: contact Lime
  Kiln Point State Park
Twanoh State Park: E 12190 Highway 106,
  Union 98592; (206) 275-2222
Twenty-five Mile Creek State Park: Route 1,
  Box 142A, Chelan 98816; (509) 687-3710
Twin Falls Natural Area: contact Lake Sam-
  mamish State Park
Twin Harbors State Park: Westport 98595;
  (206) 268-9717
Wallace Falls State Park: Box 106, Gold Bar
  98251; (206) 793-0420
Wanapum Recreation Area: contact Ginkgo
  Petrified Forest State Park
Wenatchee Confluence State Park: 333 Olds
  Station Road, Wenatchee 98801-5938;
  (509) 664-6373
Wenberg State Park: 15430 E Lake Goodwin
  Road, Stanwood 98292; (206) 652-7417
West Hylebos Wetlands State Park: contact
  Dash Point State Park
Westhaven State Park: contact Twin Harbors
  State Park
Westport Light State Park: contact Twin Har-
  bors State Park
Yakima Sportsmans State Park: 904 Keys
  Road, Yakima 98901 (509) 575-2774

**Other useful phone numbers:**

*Washington State Ferries:*
Information: 1-800-542-0810 or
  1-800-542-7052
Seattle terminal: (206) 464-6400
Anacortes terminal: (206) 293-2188
Lopez terminal: (206) 468-2252
Orcas terminal: (206) 376-2134
Friday Harbor terminal: (206) 378-4777

Army Corps of Engineers (for information on
  the water level of the Green River): (206)
  764-6702

Red Tide Hotline: 1-800-562-5632

Whale Hotline (to report whale sightings):
  1-800-562-8832

U.S. Coast Guard (for marine and air emergency): 1-800-592-9911

**Radio contacts:**

*Marine V.H.F.:*
Coast Guard distress and hailing: Channel 16
Coast Guard liaison: Channel 22A
Marine Operator, Bellingham: Channels 28
  and 85
Marine Operator, Victoria, B.C.: Channel 27

# B. QUICK REFERENCE TO FACILITIES AND RECREATION

The table on the following ten pages provides a quick overall reference to the facilities and activities found in the state parks.

Letter codes in the columns refer to specific features of the facility or activity in that
column. For example, in the *Camping* column, the letter *S* refers to standard campsites (which have no power, water, or sewer
hookups), *P* to primitive sites, and *RV* to
recreation vehicle sites (which have hookups), although some may not include all
three types of hookups).

*Swimming beaches* are noted where specific swimming areas have been designated.
Many of these provide roped-off areas,
floats, and lifeguards. However (as noted
in the front matter), due to present financial
difficulties, many of the state parks may not
currently have lifeguards on duty, and may
have removed the ropes and floats because

of concerns over swimmer safety on unguarded beaches. Swimming is at your
own risk.

While *boating* or *paddling* are possible in
virtually any park that fronts on a body of
water, these activities are noted where they
are particularly popular.

A number of water-oriented parks with
launch ramps have floats to aid in boarding
boats. The *moorage* column includes only
those parks where overnight tie-ups are
permitted on floats.

*Water sports* includes water skiing, jet skiing, wind surfing, and surfboarding.

*Field sports* covers a broad range of activities such as volleyball, baseball, soccer,
tennis, horseshoes, and golf.

*Nature study* includes parks that have nature trails, or in which tidepools or bird or
animal watching are a particular attraction.

## PARK AND PAGE NUMBER (* = UNDEVELOPED) — REGION 1

| Park | Interpretive displays (Nature, Historical, Museum) | Nature study | Winter sports | ORV | Bicycling | Equestrian trails (Beach) | Rock climbing | Walking/Hiking | Field sports | Water sports | Beachcombing | Shellfish | Artificial reef | Scuba Diving | Fishing (Shore, Boat, Pier) | Boat launch (Ramp, Hand Carry) | Moorage (Floats, Buoys) | Boating, Paddling | Swimming Beach | Waterfront (Salt, Fresh) | Handicap facilities | Dump station (RV, Boat) | ELC | Group day-use (# persons) | Group camp (# persons) | Picnicking | Camping (Standard, RV, Primitive) |
|---|---|---|---|---|---|---|---|---|---|---|---|---|---|---|---|---|---|---|---|---|---|---|---|---|---|---|---|
| Bogachiel State Park 25 | | | | | | | | • | | | | | | | S | | | P | | F | • | RV | | | | • | S,P / RV |
| Hoko River State Park* 25 | | | | | | | | • | | | • | • | | | S | | | | | S,F | | | | | | | |
| Sequim Bay State Park 26 | | • | | | | | | • | • | | | • | | • | B,P | R | F,B | B,P | | S | • | RV | • | | | • | S,P / RV |
| Anderson Lake State Park 27 | | | | | | | | • | | | | | | | S,B | R | | | | F | | | | | | • | |
| Old Fort Townsend State Park 28 | H,N | • | | | | | | • | | | | • | | | S,B | | B | B | | S | • | RV | | 100 | 75 | • | S,P |
| Rothschild House Heritage Area 29 | H | | | | | | | | | | | | | | | | | | | | | | | | | | |
| Fort Worden State Park and Conference Center 30 | H,N | • | | | • | | | • | • | | • | • | • | • | S,B | R | F,B | B | | S | • | RV | | 100 | | • | P, / RV |
| Fort Flagler State Park 33 | H | • | | | • | | | • | | • | • | • | • | • | S,B,P | R | F,B | B | | S | • | RV | • | 100 | 40,80 | • | S,P / RV |
| Mystery Bay State Marine Park 35 | | | | | | | | | | | | • | | • | | R | F,B | B | | S | | B | | | | • | |
| Bywater Bay State Park (Wolfe Property) 36 | | | | | | | | | | | • | • | | | | | | B | | S | | | | | | | P |
| Hood Canal State Park Tidelands* 37 | | | | | | | | | | | • | • | | • | | | | | | S | | | | | | | |
| Dosewallips State Park 38 | | | | | | | | • | | | | | | | S,B | | | | | S,F | • | RV | | | 135 | • | S,P / RV |
| Pleasant Harbor State Park 40 | | • | | | | | | | | | | | | | S | | F | B | | S | | | | | | | |
| Triton Cove State Park 41 | | | | | | | | | | | | | | • | | R | F | B | | S | | | | | | | RV |
| Hoodsport Trail State Park 41 | | | | | | | | • | | | | | | | | | | | | | | | | | | • | |
| Lake Cushman State Park 42 | | | | | | | | • | | • | | | | | B | R | B | B | • | F | • | RV | | | 60 | • | S,P / RV |
| Potlatch State Park 44 | | • | | | | | | • | | | | • | | • | B | | B | B,P | | S | • | | | | | • | S,P / RV |
| Tolmie State Park 45 | H,N | | | | | | | • | | | • | • | • | • | B | | | B,P | | S | • | | | | | • | |
| Schafer State Park 47 | | | | | | | | • | | | | | | | S | | | P | | F | | | | | 100, 200 | • | S,P / RV |

Facilities and activities by park. Parks are listed as rows (with page numbers); facilities/activities as columns. A bullet (•) indicates the activity is available. Letter codes follow the column headers: Camping (S=Standard, RV, P=Primitive); Dump station (RV, Boat); Waterfront (S=Salt, F=Fresh); Boating (B, P); Boat launch (R=Ramp); Fishing (S=Shore, B=Boat, P=Pier); Equestrian (B=Beach); Interpretive displays (N=Nature, H=Historical, M=Museum).

| Park and page number (* = undeveloped) | Camping (Std, RV, Prim) | Picnicking | Group camp (# persons) | Group day-use (# persons) | ELC | Dump station (RV, Boat) | Handicap facilities | Waterfront (Salt, Fresh) | Swimming Beach | Boating, Paddling | Moorage (Floats, Buoys) | Boat launch (Ramp, Hand Carry) | Fishing (Shore, Boat, Pier) | Scuba Diving | Artificial reef | Shellfish | Beachcombing | Water sports | Field sports | Walking/Hiking | Rock climbing | Equestrian trails (Beach) | Bicycling | ORV | Winter sports | Nature study | Interpretive displays (N, H, M) |
|---|---|---|---|---|---|---|---|---|---|---|---|---|---|---|---|---|---|---|---|---|---|---|---|---|---|---|---|
| Lake Sylvia State Park 48 | S,P | • | 120 | 200 | | RV | | F | • | B,P | | R | S,B | | | | | | | • | | | | | | | |
| North Beach Seashore Conservation Area 50 | S, RV | • | | | | | • | S | | P | | | S | | | • | • | • | | • | | B | | | | • | |
| Pacific Beach State Park 53 | | • | | | | RV | • | S | | P | | | S | | | • | • | | | | | | | | | • | |
| Griffiths-Priday State Park 53 | S,P, RV | • | | 200 | | | • | S,F | | P | | | S | | | • | • | | | • | | B | | | | • | |
| Ocean City State Park 53 | | • | 40 | | | RV | • | S,F | | P | | | S | • | | • | • | • | | • | | B | | | | • | |
| Ocean Shores Environmental Interpretive Center 55 | | | | | | | | | | | | | | | | | | | | | | | | | | | H,N |
| South Beach Seashore Conservation Area 55 | | • | | | | | • | S | | P | | | S | | | • | • | • | | • | | B | | | | • | |
| Westhaven State Park 56 | | • | | | | | | S | | P | | | S | • | | • | • | • | | • | | B | | | | | |
| Westport Light State Park 58 | | • | | | | | | S | | | | | S | • | | • | • | • | | • | | B | | | | | |
| Twin Harbors State Park 58 | S,P, RV | • | 84 | 100 | | | • | S | | | | | S | | | • | • | | | • | | B | | | | • | N |
| Grayland Beach State Park 60 | P, RV | • | | | | | | S | | | | | S | | | • | • | | | • | | B | | | | • | N |
| Long Beach Seashore Conservation Area 62 | | • | | | | | | S | | P | | | S | | | • | • | | | • | | B | | | | • | |
| Leadbetter Point State Park 65 | | • | | | | | | S | | | | | S | | | • | • | | | • | | | | | | • | |
| Skating Lake State Park 66 | | | | | | | | | | | | | | | | | | | • | | | | | | | | |
| Pacific Pines State Park 66 | | • | | | | | • | | | | | | | | | | | | | • | | | | | | • | |
| Loomis Lake State Park 67 | | • | | | | | • | S | | | | | S | | | • | • | | | | | | | | | • | |
| Fort Canby State Park 68 | S,P, RV | • | | | | RV | • | S,F | | B | | R | S | | | • | • | | | • | | | | | | • | H,M |
| Fort Columbia State Park 71 | | • | | | | | | F | | | | | B,S | | | | • | | | • | | | | | | • | H |
| Lewis and Clark Campsite Heritage Area 72 | | • | | | | | | | | | | | | | | | | | | | | | | | | | H |
| Willie Keil's Grave Heritage Area 73 | | | | | | | | | | | | | | | | | | | | | | | | | | | H |

| Park and page number (* = undeveloped) | Interpretive displays (Nature, Historical, Museum) | Nature study | Winter sports | ORV | Bicycling | Equestrian trails (Beach) | Rock climbing | Walking/Hiking | Field sports | Water sports | Beachcombing | Shellfish | Artificial reef | Scuba Diving | Fishing (Shore, Boat, Pier) | Boat launch (Ramp, Hand Carry) | Moorage (Floats, Buoys) | Boating, Paddling | Swimming Beach | Waterfront (Salt, Fresh) | Handicap facilities | Dump station (RV, Boat) | ELC | Group day-use (# persons) | Group camp (# persons) | Picnicking | Camping (Standard, RV, Primitive) |
|---|---|---|---|---|---|---|---|---|---|---|---|---|---|---|---|---|---|---|---|---|---|---|---|---|---|---|---|
| Rainbow Falls State Park 74 | | • | | | | | | • | • | | | | | | S | | | P | | F | | RV | | 150 | 60 | • | S,P |
| Elbow Lake State Park* 75 | | | | | | | | • | | | | | | | B | HC | | B,P | | F | | | | | | • | P |
| Millersylvania Memorial State Park 76 | | • | | | | | | • | • | | | | | | S,B,P | R | | B,P | • | F | • | RV | • | 300 | 20, 40 | • | S,P,RV |
| John R. Jackson House State Park 78 | H | | | | | | | | | | | | | | | | | | | | | | | | | | |
| Matilda N. Jackson State Park 78 | H | | | | | T | | | | | | | | | | | | | | | | | | 100 | | • | |
| Lewis and Clark State Park 79 | N | • | | | | | | • | | | | | | | S | | | | • | F | • | | | | 80, 120 | • | S |
| Ike Kinswa State Park 80 | | | | | • | | | • | | • | | | | | B,S | R | | B,P | | F | | RV | | | | • | S,P,RV |
| Packwood State Park* 82 | | | | | | | | • | | | | | | | S | | | | | F | | | | | | • | S,P,RV |
| Seaquest State Park 82 | N,M | • | | | | | | • | • | | | | | | B | R | | B | | F | • | | | 100 | 50 | • | S,P |
| Paradise Point State Park 83 | | • | | | | | | • | | | | | | | S | R | | B,P | | F | • | RV | | | | • | S,P |
| Battle Ground Lake State Park 84 | | T | | | | T | | • | | | | | | • | B,S | R | | B | • | F | | RV | | 150 | 32, 50 | • | S,P |
| Reed Island Marine State Park 86 | | • | | | | | | • | | • | | | | | B,S | | F | B | | F | | | | | | • | P |
| Beacon Rock State Park 86 | | | | | • | T | • | • | | | | | | | B | R,H | B | B,P | | F | | | | 50 | 200 | • | S,P |
| **REGION 2** | | | | | | | | | | | | | | | | | | | | | | | | | | | |
| Patos Island Marine State Park 91 | | • | | | | | | • | | | • | • | • | • | B | | B | B,P | | S | | | | | | • | P |
| Sucia Island Marine State Park 92 | | • | | | | | | • | | | • | • | | • | B | | F,B | B,P | • | S | | | | | 16, 25 | • | P |
| Matia Island Marine State Park 95 | | • | | | | | | • | | | • | • | | • | B | | F,B | B,P | | S | | | | | | • | P |
| Clark Island Marine State Park 96 | | • | | | | | | • | | | • | • | | • | B | | B | B,P | | S | | | | | | • | P |
| Stuart Island Marine State Park 97 | | • | | | | | | • | | | | • | | | B | | F,B | B,P | | S | | B | | | | • | P |
| Posey Island Marine State Park 99 | | • | | | | | | | | | • | | | • | B | | | P | | S | | | | | | • | P |

| Feature | Jones Island Marine State Park 99 | Doe Island Marine State Park 101 | Moran State Park 101 | Blind Island Marine State Park 105 | Lime Kiln Point State Park 106 | Turn Island Marine State Park 107 | Spencer Spit State Park 108 | James Island Marine State Park 110 | Undeveloped State Park Property in the San Juan Islands* 110 | Peace Arch State Park 112 | Birch Bay State Park 112 | Larrabee State Park 115 | Cone Islands State Park* 118 | Huckleberry Island State Park* 118 | Saddlebag Island Marine State Park 119 | Bay View State Park 120 | Burrows Island State Park* 121 | Deception Pass State Park 121 | Joseph Whidbey State Park 125 |
|---|---|---|---|---|---|---|---|---|---|---|---|---|---|---|---|---|---|---|---|
| Interpretive displays (Nature, Historical, Museum) | | | N,H | | N | | | | | | N,H | N | | | | | | N,H | |
| Nature study | | | • | • | • | • | • | • | | • | | • | | | | | • | • | |
| Winter sports | | | | | | | | | | | | | | | | | | | |
| ORV | | | | | | | | | | | | | | | | | | | |
| Bicycling | | | • | | | | | | | | | • | | | | | | • | |
| Equestrian trails (Beach) | | | | | | | | | | | | | | | | | | | |
| Rock climbing | | | | | | | | | | | | | | | | | | | |
| Walking/Hiking | • | • | • | | • | • | • | • | | | • | • | | | • | | | • | • |
| Field sports | | | | | | | | | | | • | | | | | | | | |
| Water sports | | | | | | | | | | | • | • | | | | | | | |
| Beachcombing | • | • | | | | • | • | | | | • | • | | | | | • | • | • |
| Shellfish | • | | | | | • | • | | | | • | • | | | • | | | | |
| Artificial reef | | | | | | | | | | | | | | | | | | | |
| Scuba Diving | • | • | | • | | • | | • | | • | • | • | • | • | • | | | • | |
| Fishing (Shore, Boat, Pier) | B | B | B,S | B | | B | B | B | | B | S,B | B,S | | | B | S,B | | S,P,B | S |
| Boat launch (Ramp, Hand Carry) | | | R | | | | | | | | R | | | | | | | R | |
| Moorage (Floats, Buoys) | F,B | F | F | B | | B | B | F,B | | F | | | | | F,B | | | | |
| Boating, Paddling | B,P | B,P | P | B,P | | B,P | B,P | B,P | | B,P | B,P | B,P | B,P | | B,P | P | B | B,P | |
| Swimming Beach | | | • | | | | | | | | | | | | | • | | • | |
| Waterfront (Salt, Fresh) | S | S | F | S | S | S | S | S | | S | S,F | S,F | S | S | S | S | S | S,F | S |
| Handicap facilities | | | • | | | | • | | | | • | • | | | | • | | • | |
| Dump station (RV, Boat) | | | RV | | | | RV | | | | RV | RV | | | | | | | |
| ELC | | | • | | | | | | | | | | | | | | • | | |
| Group day-use (# persons) | | | | | | | 50 | | | 300 | | 50, 100 | | | 50 | | | | |
| Group camp (# persons) | | | | | | | 60 | | | | 24, 40 | 40 | | | | 50 | | 60 | |
| Picnicking | • | • | • | • | • | • | • | • | | • | • | • | | | • | • | | • | • |
| Camping (Standard, RV, Primitive) | P | P | S,P | P | | P | S,P | P | | | S,P, RV | S,P, RV | | | P | S,P, RV | | S,P | |

PARK AND PAGE NUMBER (* = UNDEVELOPED)

| Feature | Fort Ebey State Park 126 | Ebey's Landing State Park 128 | Fort Casey State Park 129 | Keystone Spit State Park* 131 | South Whidbey State Park 131 | Camano Island State Park 133 | Mukilteo State Park 135 | Wenberg State Park 135 | Rockport State Park 136 | Cascade Island State Park 138 | Mount Pilchuck State Park 138 | Wallace Falls State Park 140 | Curlew Lake State Park 143 | Ranald McDonald's Grave Heritage Area 144 | Osoyoos Lake Veterans' Memorial State Park 144 | Conconully State Park 145 | Ruby Townsite Heritage Area 146 | Pearrygin Lake State Park 147 | Fort Okanogan Interpretive Center 148 |
|---|---|---|---|---|---|---|---|---|---|---|---|---|---|---|---|---|---|---|---|
| Interpretive displays (Nature, Historical, Museum) | H | H | H,M |  |  | N |  |  |  |  | H | H |  |  | H |  |  | H | M |
| Nature study |  | • |  | • | • | • | • |  | • |  |  | • |  |  |  | • |  |  |  |
| Winter sports |  |  |  |  |  |  |  |  |  |  | • |  | • |  |  | • | • | • |  |
| ORV |  |  |  |  |  |  |  |  |  |  |  |  |  |  |  |  |  |  |  |
| Bicycling | • |  |  |  |  |  |  |  |  |  |  | • |  |  |  |  |  |  |  |
| Equestrian trails (Beach) |  |  |  |  |  |  |  |  |  |  |  |  |  |  |  |  |  |  |  |
| Rock climbing |  |  |  |  |  |  |  |  |  |  | • |  |  |  |  |  |  |  |  |
| Walking/Hiking | • | • | • |  | • | • |  | • | • | • | • | • | • |  |  | • |  | • |  |
| Field sports |  |  |  |  |  |  |  |  |  |  |  |  |  |  |  | • |  |  |  |
| Water sports |  |  |  | • |  |  |  | • |  |  |  |  | • |  |  | • |  | • |  |
| Beachcombing | • | • | • | • | • | • | • |  |  |  |  |  |  |  |  |  |  |  |  |
| Shellfish |  | • |  |  | • | • |  |  |  |  |  |  |  |  |  |  |  |  |  |
| Artificial reef |  | • |  |  |  |  |  |  |  |  |  |  |  |  |  |  |  |  |  |
| Scuba Diving |  | • | • |  | • | • |  |  |  |  |  |  |  |  |  |  |  |  |  |
| Fishing (Shore, Boat, Pier) | S | S | B | S | S | B,S | B | B |  |  |  | S | B |  | B | B |  | B |  |
| Boat launch (Ramp, Hand Carry) |  |  | R |  |  | R | R | R |  |  |  | R | R |  | R | HC |  | R |  |
| Moorage (Floats, Buoys) |  |  |  |  |  | F |  |  |  |  |  | F |  |  | F |  |  |  |  |
| Boating, Paddling |  | P | B |  |  | B,P | B | B | P |  |  |  | B |  | B | B |  | B |  |
| Swimming Beach |  |  |  |  |  |  | • | • |  |  |  |  | • |  | • | • |  | • |  |
| Waterfront (Salt, Fresh) | S,F | S | S | S,F | S | S | S | F |  | F | F | F | F |  | F | F |  | F | F |
| Handicap facilities | • |  |  |  | • | • | • | • | • |  |  | • | • |  | • | • |  | • | • |
| Dump station (RV, Boat) |  |  |  | RV |  | RV |  | RV | RV |  |  |  | RV |  | RV | RV |  | RV |  |
| ELC |  |  |  |  |  |  |  |  |  |  |  |  |  |  |  |  |  |  |  |
| Group day-use (# persons) |  |  |  |  | 30 |  |  | 150 |  |  |  |  |  |  |  | 350 |  |  |  |
| Group camp (# persons) |  |  |  |  | 100 | 200 |  |  | 60 |  |  |  |  |  |  |  |  | 48 |  |
| Picnicking | • |  | • | • | • | • |  | • |  |  | • | • | • |  | • | • |  |  | • |
| Camping (Standard, RV, Primitive) | S,P |  | S,P |  | S,P | S |  | S,R | P,RV | P |  | P | S,P,RV |  | S,P | S,P,RV |  | S,P,RV |  |

**REGION 3**

| Feature | Chief Joseph SP* 148 | Bridgeport SP 149 | Banks Lake WRA 150 | Steamboat Rock SP 152 | Sun Lakes SP 154 | Summer Falls SP 157 | Alta Lake SP 158 | Twenty-five Mile Creek SP 160 | Lake Chelan SP 161 | Daroga SP 163 | Lincoln Rock SP 164 | Wenatchee Confluence SP 165 | Squilchuck SP 167 | Peshastin Pinnacles SP 167 | Lake Wenatchee SP 169 | Wanapum Rec Area 171 | Ginkgo Petrified Forest SP 172 | Olmstead Place Heritage Area 173 | Helen McCabe SP* 175 | Lake Easton SP 175 |
|---|---|---|---|---|---|---|---|---|---|---|---|---|---|---|---|---|---|---|---|---|
| Interpretive displays (Nature, Historical, Museum) | | | | | N,H | | | | | | | N | | | | | N,M | H | | |
| Nature study | | | | • | | | • | | | | • | • | | | | | • | • | | |
| Winter sports | | | • | • | | | • | • | • | | • | | • | | • | | | | | • |
| ORV | | | | | | | | | | | | | | | | | | | | |
| Bicycling | | | | | | | | | | | • | • | | | | | | | | • |
| Equestrian trails (Beach) | | | | T | T | T | | | | | | | | | T | | | | | |
| Rock climbing | | | | | | | | | | | | | | • | | | | | | |
| Walking/Hiking | • | • | • | • | • | | • | | • | | | • | | | | | • | • | | • |
| Field sports | | • | | | • | | | • | | • | • | • | | | | | | | | |
| Water sports | | • | • | • | | | • | | • | • | • | • | | | • | • | | | | |
| Beachcombing | | | | | | | | | | | | | | | | | | | | |
| Shellfish | | | | | | | | | | | | | | | | | | | | |
| Artificial reef | | | | | | | | | | | | | | | | | | | | |
| Scuba Diving | | | | • | | | • | | • | | | | | | • | | | | | |
| Fishing (Shore, Boat, Pier) | B | B | B | B | B,S | S | B | B | B | B | B | B | | | B | B | | | S | B,S |
| Boat launch (Ramp, Hand Carry) | HC | R | R | R | R | | R | R | R | R | R | R | | | R | R | | | | R |
| Moorage (Floats, Buoys) | | | | F,B | | | | F | F | F | F | F | | | F | | | | | F |
| Boating, Paddling | B | B | B | B,P | B,P | | B | B | B,P | B | B | B,P | | | B,P | B | | | | B,P |
| Swimming Beach | | • | | • | • | | • | • | • | • | • | • | | | • | • | | | | • |
| Waterfront (Salt, Fresh) | F | F | F | F | F | F | F | F | F | F | F | F | | | F | F | | | F | F |
| Handicap facilities | | • | | • | • | • | • | • | • | • | • | • | | | • | • | | | | • |
| Dump station (RV, Boat) | RV | | | RV | RV | | | RV | RV | RV | RV | RV | | | RV | | | | | RV |
| ELC | | | | | • | | | | | | | | | | | | | | | |
| Group day-use (# persons) | | | | 200 | 100 | | | | 75 | | 75,75 | | 100 | | 100 | | | | | |
| Group camp (# persons) | | 75 | | | 50 | | 88 | 88 | | 100 | | | 168 | | 80 | | | | | 50 |
| Picnicking | • | • | | • | • | • | • | • | • | • | • | • | • | • | • | • | • | • | | • |
| Camping (Standard, RV, Primitive) | S,P,RV | P | | S,P,RV | S,RV | | S,P,RV | S,RV | S,RV | P,RV | S,RV | S,RV | | | S | RV | | | | S,RV |

Key to park columns:

1. Iron Horse State Park
2. (Snoqualmie Pass to the Columbia River) 177
3. REGION 4
4. Crawford State Park (Gardner Cave) 183
5. Crystal Falls State Park 184
6. Mount Spokane State Park 184
7. Riverside State Park 187
8. Spokane River Centennial Trail 192
9. Spokane Plains Battlefield Heritage Area 196
10. Lake Colville Shorelands* 196
11. Steptoe Battlefield Heritage Area 196
12. Steptoe Butte State Park 196
13. Chief Timothy State Park 198
14. Fields Spring State Park 199
15. Camp William T. Wooten State Park 201
16. Lewis and Clark Trail State Park 202
17. Central Ferry State Park 203
18. Lyons Ferry State Park 204
19. Palouse Falls State Park 205
20. Scablands Nature Corridor* 207

(* = UNDEVELOPED)

| PARK AND PAGE NUMBER (feature) | 1 | 2 | 3 | 4 | 5 | 6 | 7 | 8 | 9 | 10 | 11 | 12 | 13 | 14 | 15 | 16 | 17 | 18 | 19 | 20 |
|---|---|---|---|---|---|---|---|---|---|---|---|---|---|---|---|---|---|---|---|---|
| Interpretive displays (Nature, Historical, Museum) | | | | N | | | H,M | | H | | H | H | H,M | | | H | | H | H | |
| Nature study | | | | ● | | | | | | ● | | ● | | | ● | ● | ● | | | ● |
| Winter sports | ● | | | | | ● | ● | | | | | | | ● | | ● | | | | |
| ORV | | | | | | | ● | | | | | | | | | | | | | |
| Bicycling | ● | | | | | | ● | ● | | | | | | | | | | | | ● |
| Equestrian trails (Beach) | T | | | | | T | T | | | | | | | | T | | | | | T |
| Rock climbing | | | | | | | | | | | | | | | | | | | | |
| Walking/Hiking | ● | | | | | ● | ● | | | | | ● | ● | | ● | ● | ● | ● | ● | |
| Field sports | | | | | | | | | | | | ● | ● | | ● | | | | | |
| Water sports | | | | | | | | | | | | ● | | | | | ● | ● | | |
| Beachcombing | | | | | | | | | | | | | | | | | | | | |
| Shellfish | | | | | | | | | | | | | | | | | | | | |
| Artificial reef | | | | | | | | | | | | | | | | | | | | |
| Scuba Diving | | | | | | | | | | | | | | | | | | | | |
| Fishing (Shore, Boat, Pier) | | | | | | | B,S | | | B,S | | | B | S | S | S | B | B,S | | |
| Boat launch (Ramp, Hand Carry) | | | | | | | R, HC | | | | | | R | | R | R | R | R | | |
| Moorage (Floats, Buoys) | | | | | | | | | | | | | F,B | | | F | B | B | | |
| Boating, Paddling | | | | | | | B, P | | | | | | B | | P | B | B | B | | |
| Swimming Beach | | | | | | | | | | | | | ● | | ● | ● | ● | ● | | |
| Waterfront (Salt, Fresh) | | | | | F | | F | | F | F | | | F | F | F | F | F | F | F | |
| Handicap facilities | | | | ● | | | | | | | | | ● | ● | | ● | | | | |
| Dump station (RV, Boat) | | | | | | | | | | | | | RV | RV | | RV | RV, B | RV | | |
| ELC | | | | | | | | | | | | | | ● | ● | | | | | |
| Group day-use (# persons) | | | | | | | 30,30, 100 | | | | | | | | | 50, 100 | | | | |
| Group camp (# persons) | | | | | | 90 | 248 | | | | | | | | | 100 | | | | |
| Picnicking | | | | ● | ● | ● | ● | | | | | ● | ● | ● | | ● | ● | ● | ● | |
| Camping (Standard, RV, Primitive) | | | | | | S | S | | | | | S, RV | | S,P | | S,P | P, RV | S,P | P | |

| Feature (* = UNDEVELOPED) | Potholes SP 211 | Moses Lake SP 211 | Sacajawea SP 212 | Crow Butte SP 212 | Yakima Sportsmans SP 214 | Fort Simcoe SP 215 | Brooks Memorial SP 216 | Goldendale Observatory SP 218 | Maryhill SP 218 | Horsethief Lake SP 219 | Doug's Beach SP 220 | Twanoh SP 223 | Belfair SP 224 | Scenic Beach SP 225 | Kitsap Memorial SP 226 | Old Man House SP 227 | Chief Seattle's Grave Heritage Area 228 | Illahee SP 228 | Fay-Bainbridge SP 230 |
|---|---|---|---|---|---|---|---|---|---|---|---|---|---|---|---|---|---|---|---|
| Interpretive displays (Nature, Historical, Museum) | | | M | | | M,H | | N | H | H | | | | H | | | | H | H |
| Nature study | | | • | • | • | | • | | | • | | | | | | | | | |
| Winter sports | • | • | | | | | • | | | | | | | | | | | | |
| ORV | | | | | | | | | | | | | | | | | | | |
| Bicycling | | | | | | | | | | | | | | | | | | | |
| Equestrian trails (Beach) | | | | | | T | | | | | | | | | | | | | |
| Rock climbing | | | | | | | | | | • | | | | | | | | | |
| Walking/Hiking | • | | | • | | | • | | • | • | | • | | • | • | | | • | • |
| Field sports | | | | | | | • | | | | | • | • | | • | | | • | |
| Water sports | • | • | • | • | | | | | • | • | • | • | | | | | | • | |
| Beachcombing | | | | | | | | | • | • | | | | | | | | • | • |
| Shellfish | | | | | | | | | | | | • | | • | • | • | | • | • |
| Artificial reef | | | | | | | | | | | | | | | | | | | |
| Scuba Diving | | • | | | | | | | | | | • | | • | • | • | | • | • |
| Fishing (Shore, Boat, Pier) | B | B | B | B | S | | S | | B | B | | B | S | B | B | | | B | B |
| Boat launch (Ramp, Hand Carry) | R, HC | R | R | R | | | | | R | R | | R | | | R | | | R | R |
| Moorage (Floats, Buoys) | | F | F,B | B | | | | | | | P | F,B | | | B | | | F,B | B |
| Boating, Paddling | B,P | B,P | B | B | | | | | B,P | B,P | B | B,P | | B,P | B,P | | | B,P | B,P |
| Swimming Beach | | • | • | • | | | | | • | | | • | • | | • | | | • | |
| Waterfront (Salt, Fresh) | F | F | F | F | F | | F | | F | F | F | S | S | S | S | S | | S | S |
| Handicap facilities | | | • | • | | • | • | | • | | | • | • | | | | | • | • |
| Dump station (RV, Boat) | RV | | RV | RV | | RV | | | RV | RV | | B | RV | | RV | | | RV | RV |
| ELC | | | | | | • | | | | | | | | | | | | | |
| Group day-use (# persons) | | | 200 | | 200 | | | | | | | 150 | | | 75, 75 | | | 50, 75 | 50 |
| Group camp (# persons) | | | | 60 | | | 50 | | | | | 100 | | 50 | 30 | | | 40 | |
| Picnicking | • | • | • | • | • | • | • | | • | • | | • | • | • | • | • | | • | • |
| Camping (Standard, RV, Primitive) | S,P, RV | | | RV | S,P, RV | | S,P, RV | | P, RV | S,P | | S,P, RV | S, RV | S | S | | | S,P | S, RV |

REGION 5 (Twanoh State Park 223 through Fay-Bainbridge State Park 230)

| Feature | Fort Ward 231 | Manchester 232 | Harper 234 | Blake Island 234 | Saltwater 236 | Dash Point 238 | West Hylebos Wetlands 239 | Kopachuck 241 | Cutts Island 241 | Penrose Point 243 | Eagle Island 245 | Haley Property* 245 | Stretch Point 246 | Jarrell Cove 246 | Hartstene Island 247 | McMicken Island 248 | Hope Island* 249 | Saint Edward 250 | Bridle Trails 251 |
|---|---|---|---|---|---|---|---|---|---|---|---|---|---|---|---|---|---|---|---|
| Interpretive displays (Nature, Historical, Museum) | H | H |  | H |  |  | N |  |  |  |  |  |  |  |  |  |  |  |  |
| Nature study | • | • |  | • |  | • | • | • |  | • |  |  |  | • |  |  |  | • | • |
| Winter sports |  |  |  |  |  |  |  |  |  |  |  |  |  |  |  |  |  |  |  |
| ORV |  |  |  |  |  |  |  |  |  |  |  |  |  |  |  |  |  |  |  |
| Bicycling | • |  |  |  |  |  |  |  |  |  |  |  |  |  |  |  |  |  |  |
| Equestrian trails (Beach) |  |  |  |  |  |  |  |  |  |  |  |  |  |  |  |  |  | T | T |
| Rock climbing |  |  |  |  |  |  |  |  |  |  |  |  |  |  |  |  |  |  |  |
| Walking/Hiking | • | • |  | • | • | • | • |  |  | • |  |  |  | • | • | • |  | • | • |
| Field sports |  | • |  | • |  |  |  |  |  |  |  |  |  |  |  |  |  | • |  |
| Water sports |  |  |  |  |  |  |  | • |  |  |  |  |  |  |  |  |  |  |  |
| Beachcombing | • |  |  | • | • | • |  | • | • | • | • | • | • |  |  | • | • | • |  |
| Shellfish | • |  |  |  |  |  |  | • | • | • | • | • | • | • |  | • |  |  |  |
| Artificial reef |  |  |  | • | • |  |  | • | • |  |  |  |  |  |  |  |  |  |  |
| Scuba Diving | • | • |  | • | • | • |  | • |  |  |  |  |  |  |  |  |  | • |  |
| Fishing (Shore, Boat, Pier) | B | S | B | B | B | B |  | B | B | B | B |  | B | B |  | B |  | S |  |
| Boat launch (Ramp, Hand Carry) | R |  | R |  |  |  |  |  |  |  |  |  |  |  |  |  |  |  |  |
| Moorage (Floats, Buoys) | B |  |  | B,F,B | B |  |  | B | B | F,B | B |  | B | F,B |  | B |  |  |  |
| Boating, Paddling | B | B | B | B,P | B,P | B,P |  | B,P | B,P | B,P | B,P |  | B | B,P |  | B |  |  |  |
| Swimming Beach |  | • |  | • | • | • |  | • | • | • |  |  |  |  |  | • |  | • |  |
| Waterfront (Salt, Fresh) | S | S | S | S | S | S |  | S | S | S | S | S,F | S | S | S | S | S | F |  |
| Handicap facilities |  | • |  | • | • |  |  | • |  | • |  |  |  |  |  |  |  | • |  |
| Dump station (RV, Boat) |  | RV |  | B | RV | RV |  | RV |  | RV |  |  |  | B |  |  |  |  |  |
| ELC |  |  |  |  |  |  |  |  |  |  |  |  |  |  |  |  |  |  |  |
| Group day-use (# persons) |  | 150 |  | 50 | 30,50,100 |  |  |  |  |  |  |  |  |  |  | 25,50,75,100 |  |  |  |
| Group camp (# persons) |  |  |  | 75 | 40 | 80 |  | 15,35 |  | 50 |  |  |  |  |  |  |  |  |  |
| Picnicking | • | • |  | • | • | • |  | • |  | • |  |  | • | • |  | • |  | • | • |
| Camping (Standard, RV, Primitive) |  | S |  | P | S,P | S,RV |  | S |  | S |  |  |  | S |  |  |  |  |  |

PARK AND PAGE NUMBER (* = UNDEVELOPED)

| Feature | Lake Sammamish State Park 253 | Squak Mountain State Park* 255 | Olallie State Park 256 | Iron Horse State Park | (Snoqualmie Summit to Rattlesnake Lake) 259 | Green River Gorge Conservation Area 261 | Kanaskat-Palmer State Park 264 | Nolte State Park 266 | Flaming Geyser State Park 266 | Federation Forest State Park 268 |
|---|---|---|---|---|---|---|---|---|---|---|
| Interpretive displays (Nature, Historical, Museum) | | | N | | | H | | | N | N.H.,M |
| Nature study | • | • | • | | | • | • | • | • | • |
| Winter sports | | | | | • | | | | | • |
| ORV | | | | | | | | | | |
| Bicycling | | | | | • | | | | | |
| Equestrian trails (Beach) | | | | | T | T | | | | |
| Rock climbing | | | | | | | | | | |
| Walking/Hiking | • | • | • | | | • | • | • | • | • |
| Field sports | • | | | | | | | • | | |
| Water sports | • | | | | | | | | | |
| Beachcombing | | | | | | | | | | |
| Shellfish | | | | | | | | | | |
| Artificial reef | | | | | | | | | | |
| Scuba Diving | | | | | | | | | | |
| Fishing (Shore, Boat, Pier) | B | | S | | | S | S | S.P.,B | S | S |
| Boat launch (Ramp, Hand Carry) | R | | | | | | HC | HC | HC | |
| Moorage (Floats, Buoys) | | | | | | | | | | |
| Boating, Paddling | B,P | | | | | P | P | P | P | |
| Swimming Beach | • | | | | | | | • | | |
| Waterfront (Salt, Fresh) | F | | F | | | F | F | F | F | F |
| Handicap facilities | • | | | | | | • | • | • | • |
| Dump station (RV, Boat) | FV | | | | | | RV | | | |
| ELC | | | | | | | | | | |
| Group day-use (# persons) | 100, 300 | | | | | | 100 | 50, 50 | 150, 300 | |
| Group camp (# persons) | 200 | | | | | | 80 | | | |
| Picnicking | • | | | | | • | • | • | • | • |
| Camping (Standard, RV, Primitive) | | | | | | | S.P., RV | | | |

PARK AND PAGE NUMBER
(* = UNDEVELOPED)

# INDEX

The MOUNTAINEERS, founded in 1906, is a nonprofit outdoor activity and conservation club, whose mission is "to explore, study, preserve, and enjoy the natural beauty of the outdoors...." Based in Seattle, Washington, the club is now the third-largest such organization in the United States, with 12,000 members and four branches throughout Washington State.

The Mountaineers sponsors both classes and year-round outdoor activities in the Pacific Northwest, which include hiking, mountain climbing, ski-touring, snowshoeing, bicycling, camping, kayaking and canoeing, nature study, sailing, and adventure travel. The club's conservation division supports environmental causes through educational activities, sponsoring legislation, and presenting informational programs. All club activities are led by skilled, experienced volunteers, who are dedicated to promoting safe and responsible enjoyment and preservation of the outdoors.

The Mountaineers Books, an active, nonprofit publishing program of the club, produces guidebooks, instructional texts, historical works, natural history guides, and works on environmental conservation. All books produced by The Mountaineers are aimed at fulfilling the club's mission.

If you would like to participate in these organized outdoor activities or the club's programs, consider a membership in The Mountaineers. For information and an application, write or call The Mountaineers, Club Headquarters, 300 Third Avenue West, Seattle, Washington 98119; (206) 284-6310.

*Send or call for our catalog of more than 200 outdoor books:*
*The Mountaineers Books*
*1011 SW Klickitat Way, Suite 107*
*Seattle, WA 98134*
*1-800-553-4453*

Seattle residents **Marge and Ted Mueller** are avid outdoor enthusiasts who have explored Washington's mountains, forests, deserts, and waterways for more than thirty years. Their first book, *Northwest Ski Trails*, was published in 1968. To research *Washington State Parks*, they logged several thousand miles by land and water, traveling to every corner of the state to visit each of the state parks.

The Muellers are the authors of the popular *Afoot and Afloat* series also published by The Mountaineers.

*Heidi Mueller photo*